Perils of Prosperity

Realities, Risks and Rewards of the Global Knowledge Economy

Revised Edition

John J. Sarno

AuthorHouse™
1663 Liberty Drive
Bloomington, IN 47403
www.authorhouse.com
Phone: 1-800-839-8640

© 2011 by John J. Sarno. All rights reserved.

No part of this book may be reproduced, stored in a retrieval system, or transmitted by any means without the written permission of the author.

First published by AuthorHouse   09/14/2011

ISBN: 978-1-4389-4616-0 (sc)
ISBN: 978-1-4389-4617-7 (hc)
ISBN: 978-1-4670-2847-9 (ebk)

Library of Congress Control Number: 2009900561

Printed in the United States of America

Any people depicted in stock imagery provided by Thinkstock are models, and such images are being used for illustrative purposes only.
Certain stock imagery © Thinkstock.

This book is printed on acid-free paper.

Because of the dynamic nature of the Internet, any web addresses or links contained in this book may have changed since publication and may no longer be valid. The views expressed in this work are solely those of the author and do not necessarily reflect the views of the publisher, and the publisher hereby disclaims any responsibility for them.

Dedication

For Diane Belcuore

The most successful person I know

Table of Contents

Preface xi
Preface to First Edition xxv

1. Drift or Mastery 1
2. The Knowledge Economy 49
3. Work, Social Identity and Autonomy 73
4. Reengineering and the Changing Nature of Work 123
5. The Knowledge Firm 137
6. A Digression on Private Property 149
7. The Protection of Intellectual Property 159
8. The Role of Government 177
9. The Role of Markets 217
10. The Economics of Knowledge 225
11. Deregulation and Decentralization 239
12. On The Nature of Leadership 247
13. Information Ethics 265
14. We the People 275

Epilogue 301
Epilogue to Revised Edition 313
Sources 319
Index 327
About the Author 339

"Share your knowledge. It's a way to achieve immortality."

                                                    Dalai Lama

Preface

Perils of Prosperity was rushed to print in January 2009 to coincide with the swearing in of Barack Obama and the executive MBA class that I was starting that month at the New Jersey Institute of Technology. The class focused on legal and ethical issues in the global economy and I assigned the book and the class graciously worked around the distractions of typographical and cut-and-paste errors. Having now taken responsibility for the editorial shoddiness of the first edition, the nature and purpose of the book remains ambiguous.

As a polemic, its critique of the status quo tends toward gauziness and subjectivity. As advocacy, its argument makes no case but the obvious. As reporting, it relies exclusively on secondary sources. Oddly then, *Perils of Prosperity* succeeds as typical business fare—subjective, obvious and unoriginal—but its dense incomprehension and rambling passages could never advance a consultancy. In short, it can only be viewed as a provocation to a dialogue.

Indeed, the dialogue within the class was exceptional. As one student noted in his evaluation, the class was a "worthwhile learning experience" that didn't "settle for the soft answers, but provoked a deeper level thought on the issues of our day." I believe that new insight and knowledge was created. In the end, however, we never did get around to addressing the question implied in the book's Epilogue.

Observing that America was experiencing a state of mourning or loss, I wrote in Epilogue: "It is likely that America is on the verge of developing new tools that will affect all aspects of life. Economic growth and national purpose are likely not over. In fact, it is likely that new life has already begun." What is that new life? Since I made that observation, Americans seemed to have settled into what some have called a "new normal."

The difficult and sustained recessions and financial panic in the first decade of the new century has left a permanently altered economy and has actually accelerated the forces of modern globalization that began at about 1980. For nearly every job cut in the United States by an American corporation, another was created abroad. From 2000 to 2010, U.S. multinationals cut 2.9 million jobs in America but created 2.4 million overseas. While not every job created outside the United States by a U.S. corporation would have been created domestically, developing countries like China and India offer expanding consumer markets and low wages. For example, by one estimate China earned just four dollars from the production of an iPod that sells for $299 in the U.S. Thus, even during a time of enormous economic challenges, corporate profits have soared. By the end of the decade, American corporations held over two trillion dollars in cash, more than the size of the annual federal budget deficit, about half of which held abroad beyond the reach of the Internal Revenue Service.

In the book, like other observers of wider cultural and ethical trends, I speculated about whether Americans would stoically adapt to the "new normal" by embracing a new ethic focused less on consumption and more on production and investment. Regrettably, I was caught up in a popular myth and terribly naïve. The nearly 15 trillion dollars U.S. economy is based overwhelmingly on consumer consumption, nearly 70 percent. In many ways, this consumption is the sign of a mature economy that has transcended the old rules of scarcity and that has vaulted into the era of abundance and affluence. Indeed, Americans living below the poverty line are far better off than many "middle class" people in Asia and Africa. But part of the "new normal" is really a reprise of the old way of capital's tendency to accumulate into fewer and fewer hands during periods of economic upheaval and financial panic. Thus, as wages fell for the average American corporate profits and capital gains soared.

As economists have observed in years past, the wealthy can purchase only so much luxury goods, certainly not enough to prop up the world's biggest economy. To make up for the loss of purchasing power, Americans and their government relied on massive borrowing to keep the economy going during the "Great Recession" of 2008-2010. This merely continued a thirty year trend. President Obama's $830 billion stimulus program enacted in 2009 increased government borrowing with the intent of priming the pump. When all was said and down, federal government spending reached about a quarter of the entire economy. In addition, the Federal Reserve literally printed money (in reality, created the money electronically) through purchases of Treasury bonds and securities to the tune of $2 trillion, lowering borrowing rates to near zero. By 2011, the federal government's operating deficit was about ten percent of the economy and the cumulative debt amounted to about the size of annual Gross National Product, or close to $14 trillion.

In July, 2011 Senators Olympia Snow and Jim Demint arguing for a constitutional amendment to balance the federal budget observed: "In the real world, if a household brought in $44,000 annually but spent $74,000 by borrowing $30,000 each year to sustain its spending habits, such behavior would be considered reckless and irresponsible." But what would the senators say if that hypothetical American household did exactly that? *Reckless* and *irresponsible?* In 2011, after years of chronic unemployment and stagnating wages for most people, household indebtedness still remained at an all time high. Collectively, Americans borrowed the equivalent of 135 percent of their annual incomes even during the worst economic slowdown in 75 years.

I discussed this debt burden in the context of a restive, undifferentiated nationalism that went beyond the mere suspicion, even hatred, for President Obama after his election. Indeed, in the Epilogue I noted the viciousness of the 2008 presidential campaign and how the new media was making it difficult for the average voter to discern the difference between fact and fiction. But the point is that some of the same developing countries that have been the destination for American corporations have also been purchasing U.S. sovereign debt. So by 2011, China surpassed Japan as the biggest holder of U.S. Treasury securities, exceeding one trillion dollars. In effect, China takes with one hand and gives with the other, thus supporting America's consumption based economy in exchange for manufacturing jobs.

Yet as manufacturing jobs leave the U.S. in droves, America remains the world's top manufacturer by far. The U.S. out-produces China by more than 40%. In 2009 U.S. manufacturers produced nearly $1.7 trillion in goods. America firms produce more and better quality goods with less labor because of capital investments that has increased productivity, or output per hour. In short, low end manufacturing has been ceded to other countries as American firms focus more on high-end products that require skilled labor to produce. But for the eight million less skilled production workers that have been displaced since 1980, higher productivity has meant long periods of welfare, unemployment and lower wages. Even for those Americans that have held on to their jobs, prodigious productivity has oddly left them feeling insecure and vulnerable and perhaps looking to place blame for what is perceived as America's decline.

"When somebody writes the history of our time fifty or one hundred years from now," says Laurence Summers, "it is unlikely to be about the Great Recession of 2008 . . . or about the fiscal problem that America confronted in the second decade of the twenty first century. It will be about how the world adjusted to the movement of the theater of history toward China." Summers, economist, scholar, president of Harvard, and presidential economic advisor, believes with many others that the western influence over all human endeavor that has dominated for the last five hundred years is waning. However, while I accept this shift I do not view this transformation as a clash of civilizations. In contrast, I believe that human nature is nearing an evolutionary turning point.

Since the beginning of human history competition over physical resources defined the struggle for survival, a zero sum game where one person's gain was another's loss. Conflict over resources is as old as recorded history. China and the West remain in competition over the physical resources of the planet—land, water, oil, minerals and jobs. A military confrontation cannot be ruled out. Indeed, some observers on both sides of the Pacific believe a military confrontation is inevitable so both sides prudently plan for the possibility. But the two economies are linked at all micro and macro levels and together form a center of gravity for a global network that encompasses nearly every country in the world. Unlike the Cold War when the center of gravity emanated from the adversarial nature of the relationship between the U.S. and the Soviet Union as an extension of the Second World War, the reality of the two biggest competitors co-existing as compatriots is quite different and poses different and unique challenges. In short, mismanaged economic competition between the U.S. and China could bring on a worldwide economic collapse of unimaginable long term consequences.

As during the Cold War, irrational people on both sides could bring the parties to the brink. But ultimately, competition gave way to cooperation and collaboration. With both sides sharing the same goals, it became possible to develop win-win strategies. Cultural and business exchange created bonds that transcended suspicion and eventually the Politburo realized that the Soviet command-and-control governing structure suppressed individual initiative and ingenuity and undermined the work ethic. Cooperation and collaboration then is the next big step for both West and East, assuming that cultural exchange can alleviate the fear and suspicion that exists on both sides.

For now, the U.S.-China relationship is a win-win for both sides but many Americans view the world as a zero sum game. In a national poll in 2011 about four in ten Americans viewed an economically powerful China as a threat and more than half held the view that America was in a long term economic decline. Government debt has long replaced the Cold War as the most potent political issue and has placed the role of government in the center of our political and social discourse. One of the things I observed in the book was that if the federal budget could somehow be magically balanced it would not only reduce the size and role of government, it would result in the biggest transfer of wealth from the poor to the wealthy in modern human history by triggering a fire sale of America's private and sovereign assets. And who has the available cash to scoop up these assets? The winners would be very same nations that have built up immense cash reserves in sovereign wealth funds by swapping paper for jobs. It wound be one of the great ironies of history if balancing the federal budget resulted in the swift internationalization of American industry, finance and culture. Privatizing America's public assets would be the equivalent of the momentous privatizations of the Chinese or Soviet economies in the remaining days of the twentieth century and would unleash a torrent of wealth and property which could inevitably create an oligarchy that would rival that of America's Gilded Age. Much should trickle down to the average American, or so the thinking goes.

Indeed, by 2010 foreign investment, not including government securities, in the U.S. already exceeded $230 billion. One study suggests that Chinese firms alone increased their investments in the U.S. by 130 percent per year since 2005, investing in everything from greenfield projects, wind turbine plants, steel mills, banks and brokerage firms. Japanese companies employ almost 700,000 Americans with an annual payroll of nearly $50 billion. In 2008, the average job created by foreign investment paid $71,000 per year according to the White House Council on Economic Advisors, about one-third above the U.S. average. Such is the case because many foreign firms will pay a premium to upgrade their technology and capture higher levels of the value chain. Thus, America can succeed in a globalized, privatized economy with a strategy that plays to its strengths, which in my view is based on innovation at all levels of the economy, or what I have dubbed an "innovation ethic." And it's the nurturing of that ethic which forms the core of the book. Corporations and government play a huge role as direct investors and by maintaining an environment that ensures foreign money (and people) continue to come into the country. At the same time, if public resources are to be privatized or deregulated, markets, organizations and people must be competitive enough to avoid a type of wage and debt slavery.

In addition to maintaining a level of excellence to compete globally, corporations face the unprecedented challenge of fulfilling their profit driven missions at a time when the nation is engaged in difficult transition from a labor-intensive to an information-intensive economy. As I have noted, this transition has already dislocated millions of Americans, as inflation-adjusted wages for the average American have stagnated. This fact has had an enormous impact on families, student achievement, physical and mental health, crime rates and lifestyle decisions of all types, including decisions that have a direct and immediate impact on medical treatment, retirement, marriage, divorce rates, childrearing and job mobility.

For the first time since the 1930s, Americans' confidence in both government and business has dropped. For the first time in 50 years, polls show that the majority of Americans have soured on corporate America. A majority of Americans now report that long-term unemployment is either caused, or is made worse by, the outsourcing of jobs abroad. Polls also show that the majority of Americans believe that financial crisis of 2008-2009 was caused by corporate greed. The majority of Americans want limitations on executive compensation and for the first time ever, the majority of Americans believe that trade policies hurt American workers. These opinions are hardening all along the political continuum. Economic nationalism is being advocated on both the right and the left and the gimlet eye is cast toward America's foreign trade partners, particularly China.

According to a 2011 Kaufman Foundation report, tens of thousands of U.S. educated foreign nationals from China and India are returning home, many believing that economic opportunities are better. In 2010, foreign students studying on temporary visas earned six of ten engineering degrees in the U.S. These people have intelligence, skills, and ambition. Indeed, since 1995, immigrants have started more than half of the companies in Silicon Valley. Yet a large segment of the American population says "good riddance" caring little of the great benefits of diversity. And the foreign nationals have left the U.S. apparently without too much concern as long as the financial grass is greener in their home countries.

Implicit with the best and brightest leaving America behind (and America leaving its own citizens behind with inferior education systems) is the observation that democracy may not be indispensible to economic freedom. Indeed, the deconstruction and decentralization of media has blurred the lines between fact and fiction. Information is highly politicized making it difficult to form a democratic consensus on how to solve some of our most important problems. Emotion has trumped objectivity and rational discourse is imperiled. As a result, many Americans have simply dropped out of the democratic process altogether, thus perpetuating the sense of alienation and disconnectedness. Millions don't bother to vote, let alone spend any time engaged in civic or political issues.

At the same time, corporations, labor unions and other groups spend tens of millions of dollars annually to influence legislation. Enabled by the U.S. Supreme Court in *Citizens United v. Federal Elections Commission*, decided in 2010, corporations, unions and advocacy groups can anonymously give unlimited amounts of money to buy access to state and federal governments. Reading the writing on the wall, Americans have tuned out and turned off, more likely identifying with a commercial brand than a political party. The result for many is a transactional, commoditized, public reality governed by 24/7 advertising that permeates all public media. For most Americans the sole purpose of working is to further consumption.

Similarly, I have also argued that the Internet and open-source models would facilitate the emergence of decentralized, innovative social systems. True this is occurring but I simply did not anticipate how corporations and governments would enclose and dominate this new frontier. In the West, the promise of spontaneous innovation and engaged civic participation facilitated by an open Web is quickly giving way to a creation of a vast consumption portal. In other parts of the world, the Web is fast becoming a grotesque spying machine.

As I pointed out, Americans once mocked and ridiculed Russians for waiting on long lines to buy consumer goods. We called them unfree, even slaves. We extolled the virtues of civic engagement and democracy. We pitied the Soviets and the Europeans too, for their dead-end jobs and lack of job mobility and innovation. We believed that democracy formed the foundation of economic freedom, innovation, opportunity and growth. Today, Americans think nothing of waiting on long lines for many hours for a sale or the latest gadget—it is considered an entitlement. In my view, democracy, along with America's industrial base, is withering away, resulting in less innovation not more. In my view, autocratic, command-and-control social systems degrade human capital and stifles ingenuity. Although it appears that economic growth can occur without a robust democracy, as it appears to be occurring in China and elsewhere, innovation and entrepreneurialism is less likely to occur under the control of a monopoly—political or corporate. Indeed, the policy of "indigenous innovation" promoted by China seeks to leverage monopoly power not to spark original innovation but to appropriate and copy it. It is a view of economic growth as genetic engineering, as the intellectual property of the West is appropriated and incorporated into the economic DNA of China in the hopes of eventually creating a new, stronger and more resilient organism. It is economic growth from the top. It is not unlike the monopoly practices of American corporations that engage in antitrust violations or the big technology firms that acquire innovative startups.

In contrast, in a more or less free market the most successful and enduring innovations, the game changing technologies, have not come from monopolists. Most of the big, transformative breakthroughs have come from start-ups founded by individuals motivated by both profit and purpose. This tends to promote organic economic growth from the bottom up. In short, democratic institutions and free markets allow individuals to fulfill their human potential by giving full range to the trial and error of improvisation and risk taking. Thus, it can be argued that in addition to an educated and skilled workforce, an informed, engaged citizenry able to support democratic institutions is just as indispensible to national and individual success in the globalized, knowledge-intensive economy.

Finally, my students are left to consider how one can live a life in a post-modern, post-industrial American which is becoming increasingly less free and still maintain some degree of personal dignity and integrity. It is a question that I cannot presume to answer for another. However, in helping to at least create a framework for individuals to address the question for themselves, we have discussed human history and evolutionary biology and have at least reached a consensus that each person in society is capable of moral agency. My own view is that moral agency is difficult to achieve within most corporations because of the lack of individual autonomy. By in large, most employees are not paid to think or to assume personal responsibility even over their own work product. They are paid simply to perform their jobs efficiently at the pleasure of their superiors. In short, most employees are paid to do what they are told.

"Autonomy" refers to a person's capacity for self-determination—free will—in the context of moral choices. Autonomy is demonstrated by a person who decides on a course of action out of respect for moral duty. That is, an autonomous person acts morally solely for the sake of the greater good, independently of other incentives, like a paycheck or other form of pleasure. Compliance with a moral code creates the essence of human dignity and personhood.

We know that autonomy is not absolute and is usually, to one extent or another, given to another authority, such as by agreeing to follow governing laws. In a corporation, employees cede autonomy and agree to conform to corporate rules in order to be team members.

In class, we have focused on Lawrence Kohlberg's theory of moral development, which postulates a stage theory of moral thinking from childhood to adulthood. In Kohlberg's first stage, the child assumes that powerful authorities hand down a fixed set of rules which he or she must obey. At this stage, the child defers to superior power or prestige. In other words, the child conforms. At this early stage of child development, there is no substantive notion of free will or self-determination. The child's primary concern is receiving rewards and avoiding punishment.

In 2002 Betty Vinson, a mid-level accountant at WorldCom pleaded guilty to securities fraud. Her lawyer was quoted as describing Ms. Vinson as a "victim of unscrupulous higher managers." In other words, Ms. Vinson was only following orders. She had no choice, no capacity to decide. Viewed through the lens of Kohlberg's theory of moral development, Vinson lacked free will and was essentially operating at the moral level of a child.

In contrast, Cynthia Cooper, WorldCom's internal auditor pursued what she called "the rotten accounting." Faced with an angry supervisor who threatened her with discharge, Ms. Cooper reported accounting improprieties to the audit committee of the board. When WorldCom's comptroller was confronted by the committee, he admitted that the accounting could not be justified.

Cooper was able to achieve and maintain a degree of dignity and a sense of personhood within WorldCom's degrading, oppressive environment. Vinson did not.

I have posited that "innovation" is an organizing principle that can serve as a foundation for corporate structures—the belief that a free people who spontaneously organize can create flexible social structures that produce new solutions to solve big complex problems. The innovation myth is inseparable from autonomy and is redefining the pursuit of happiness. I have argued that intrinsic happiness is based on autonomous individuals freely choosing to engage others in sustained and meaningful effort that promotes the greater good. I have called the personal choice to engage others, the "innovation ethic"; the effort itself, "knowledge work"; and the individuals who make the effort, "knowledge workers." These are merely short hand designations that are meant to evoke a spirit, attitude, or general outlook of a time and place.

I have tried to teach my students that in the face of shrinking physical resources, collective knowledge building and innovation are the most important strategic tasks for most firms. Some students just assume that we will innovate out of any problem, whether it's global warming or nuclear proliferation. But unlike production work—knowledge work can't be forced out of people. To create a climate in which employees contribute their creativity and expertise, leaders need to develop collaboration, communication and conflict resolution skills and manage at the highest levels of integrity. Decision-making must be fair and ethical. Trust and commitment must be instilled within the team and across teams to avoid hoarding of ideas. Knowledge workers must be motivated intrinsically from within just as much, perhaps more, than by a paycheck. Innovation is not a passive exercise. It requires discipline, continuous effort and athleticism.

The hard work of management and leadership at all levels is to encourage and nurture an open and sustainable environment where information is freely shared and expectations for performance are transparent. The measure of the leader's success is how well they inspire employees to not only to perform their best, but also to perform at the highest level of trust, sharing and cooperation. Various case studies, whether WorldCom, Enron or BP Petroleum, demonstrate at best profound ethical lapses by leaders and an uninspiring work ethic among the workforce. At worst, the cultures in these organizations perpetuated egregious fraud and criminality.

I have tried to call it straight. Much of corporate work is dehumanizing. Since the corporate form of organization and control and the work that is performed from within these hierarchical structures are inescapable, for many workers autonomy and intrinsic happiness are only remotely attainable. But the principle of innovation and the evidence of technological and scientific advancement that follow are most likely powerful enough to instill the hope necessary to ensure survive and advance progress.

The innovation ethic presupposes working with awareness, passion and a level of engagement that expresses both individuality and an attachment to community. "Innovators" therefore do not need to be original or ingenious and do not need to create or invent something new. However, to be faithful to an innovation ethic, workers need to contribute something of value by working with heart, body and mind on tasks that they are asked to perform or choose to do.

I hypothesize that knowledge workers tend to be intrinsically motivated and tend more to share information than hoard it. I have opined that social media can facilitate productive knowledge work. Finally, I have speculated that knowledge workers within open environments that add value will also instinctively aspire to be ethical leaders and good stewards of collective assets. I also want to be clear that without a free and robust market supported by democratic institutions, the "knowledge economy" may further entrench corporate governing elites. And that too is a peril of prosperity as it becomes ever more difficult for individuals to fulfill their aspirations and act ethically within command-and-control, monopolized social structures.

Consequently, laws must also evolve. The master-servant rules that supported the industrial economy, when physical labor was exchanged for a paycheck, do not lend itself to personal autonomy, free agency and knowledge based work. Likewise, the work-for-hire doctrine tends to disadvantage and demotivate employees. Intellectual property law fosters monopoly which tends to suppress competition and innovation. In short, as "property" becomes less physical and more intellectual and intangible, property law must also evolve to serve the needs of innovators.

In the meantime, I have argued that most corporations suppress innovation and personal integrity through the deliberate de-skilling and modularization of work. Contrary to management propaganda, when performing much of what is called "corporate work," workers are more or less disengaged. Employers accept this disengagement because they are not paying employees to innovative. In fact, during the Great Recession of 2008-2010 employers released most experienced and educated members of the workforce. While this outcome has much to do with age discrimination, it has more to do with computer programs that permit cheaper and less experienced employees to productively perform corporate work.

I have taken the liberty in this second addition of *Perils of Prosperity* to not only correct substandard editing but also to revise and update the original text with new economic data, laws and case law.

John J. Sarno
September 11, 2011

Preface to First Edition

On a perfect Sunday afternoon on the first day of autumn in Princeton, New Jersey I was watching the final ten minutes of a soccer game. The players, twelve and thirteen year old girls, were playing with focused determination. The contest was very competitive. As the end of the match neared, parents cheered and whooped, as the girls bore down for the last few minutes.

It reminded me of a game I had watched years earlier on Mulberry Street in Newark (N.J.), as group of city kids created magic on a basketball court with the same joy and improvisation, using space in unexpected and spontaneous ways, creating something from nothing. I remembered reading somewhere that Great Britain had ruled an empire from the pitch and I imagined these young people, these competitors with their focused intensity and ingenuity, creating the next generation Internet platforms in the not too distant future, perhaps the text speech applications and translation software that would transcend nationality and that would truly connect the world's cultures.

For that brief moment in time, everything seemed perfectly crisp, clear and simple. The girls and boys playing beautifully in joyous competition seemed to encapsulate the perfect mix of teamwork, concentration, spontaneity, collaboration and endurance—the qualities necessary to succeed in a world that is scarcely recognizable from the world that existed forty years ago when I was their age. My reverie lasted quite some time but later in the day I picked up the *Wall Street Journal* and read how the biggest U.S. technology companies, including IBM, Google and Microsoft are increasingly expanding research facilities in China. Electrical engineers are cheaper in China, which produces 700,000 electrical engineering graduates each year, but the companies also say the increasing gravitation of their customers to China is another reason for opening research and development facilities there. "China is a huge laboratory in which we can work," John E. Kelly III, IBM's director of research was quoted as saying.

That laboratory also proved to be a type of spider's web as well, as state-owned firms in China engage in "indigenous innovation." Often in exchange for the lure of vast consumer markets, foreign corporations in China have willingly given up proprietary knowledge, trade secrets and intellectual property. Automobile, aerospace, high-speed rail and green-energy companies and other technology firms have all made the deal to trade intellectual property for market penetration. Some companies like General Electric and Siemens AG have mildly complained and Google has discontinued some operations on the Chinese mainland after a cyber attack on its intellectual property, but many firms are planning long-term for global mergers.

I must admit, even as I have long believed that free markets and trade provide superior mechanisms for allocating resources and creating wealth and opportunity, I felt vaguely bewildered, worried and threatened. I have known these children for a long time, watched them grow up and compete with joy, seen their promise and believed in their potential. They are worthy and deserving of an opportunity for success and I wondered how it got to the point that America's best and most innovative technology companies no longer viewed the United States as their "huge laboratory" for innovation.

I wondered too whether the working lives of these children where already predetermined by immutable technological and evolutionary forces dominated by transnational corporations and government social programs, or whether they would be able to exercise at least a vestige of freedom and dignity in pursuing their dreams.

After years of practicing law, training, teaching and counseling managers and advising businesses, it was at this moment that I decided to write this book.

This book is about the realities, risks and rewards associated with a global environment that is increasingly becoming ruled by information and knowledge, an economy that requires innovation and collaboration to win. Various observers describe today's global economy as one in transition to a *knowledge* economy, as an extension of an *information* society. This transition may require the rewriting of the rules and practices that determined success in the industrial economy but that may no longer apply in an interconnected, globalized economy where intangible resources such as know-how and ingenuity are as critical as machinery and other capital resources.

I have written this book with those children in Newark and Princeton in mind, and mine too, but I am also writing for my executive MBA students and also thinking about the thousands of supervisors and managers at the hundreds of firms for which I have provided management training. I did not set out to write a business book, *per se*, but rather a book that I hope will provoke present and future leaders to understand the social and ethical context of their working lives. Steven Johnson has referred to this context in evolutionary terms as humans take available knowledge, make connections and create new insight. The secret to innovation is connecting the odds and ends, he says. But to my dismay, I have found some the brightest people ill prepared for the challenges of the knowledge-intensive global economy. By in large, it is not the lack of ambition or the willingness to work hard that is the problem—both are in ample supply. What is missing is an integrated and engaged way of thinking and a deeper understanding of how seemingly casual events and discrete choices are interrelated. While all of these executives have enormous amounts of information at their disposal, what many lack is the intuition to find meaning in the jumble of data and to make sense of seemingly disconnected events. Business schools do no teach this. Instead, they teach technique and collaboration, which are important, but they do not teach meaning—meaning in one's work and the social context within which business decisions are made.

Likewise, executives and managers at most firms have been trained in various production methods and have been taught to squeeze as much efficiency out of their people as possible. While many speak of their employees as their most important asset, that can only be true when employees are paid for creating and leveraging knowledge. Since production and efficiency are often incompatible with innovation, most employees are considered more as a liability than as an asset. The typical employer manages employees as if they were risks, rather than as assets. What passes for "knowledge management" is a software platform that standardizes inputs so as to achieve uniform outputs. Little independent thinking is required. As such, "human capital" is probably the most underutilized and least productive resource within the firm.

Moreover, the organizational structures of most firms simply do not enable widespread innovation to occur. As a result, innovation is left to the sole domain of an elite cadre of highly knowledgeable workers. Most other labor is subject to outsourcing. This hierarchy is supported by biological evolutionary dogma and justifies corporate restructuring and outsourcing, as firms seek comparative advantage. As communications technology and new media allow firms to tap into a global knowledge pool for innovative products and applications, what some call "brain circulation," much of the American workforce has in large part been commoditized.

But I am convinced that America and the other advanced economies are quickly nearing their next evolutionary step in a world of increasingly diminishing physical resources. When the Book of Genesis proclaimed that God gave the Earth to mankind so that humans could freely exercise dominion over it, it created the foundation of western economic and social progress—private property—and the natural selection that resulted from competition over resources. For better or for worse, America's civic creed of liberty and property is an enduring affirmation of this biblical command. It is my belief that America is not in decline. It is in transition. And at this crossroads in the early twentieth century, a new global dynamic challenges both liberty and property, and therefore the core of our beliefs, at least in the democratic West.

Much of the strain and anxiety is caused by the big gap between the haves and have-nots. The byproduct of liberty and property has always been inequality, which can be justified on ethical grounds as long as individuals have more or less equal opportunity to compete and the winners do not breed excessive cynicism and apathy by owning too much property and wealth or by being too oppressive and corrupt. At that point, the incentives for productive work reach diminishing returns, thus requiring compulsory labor if the economy is to produce. Thus, to the extent democratic institutions reallocate or transfer property from the haves to the have-nots through government welfare and other social programs, the community's wellbeing is promoted. And as long as welfare payments are below wages, for most people there is an incentive to engage in productive work.

In 2010, 45 percent of all Americans lived in a household were someone received government benefits. Most of these benefits were in the form of social security, Medicare and unemployment payments. Cumulatively, these benefits represented about 9.4 percent of after tax income. In contrast, in France government benefits payments represent nearly one-third of after tax income. That same year, the U.S. posted the highest poverty rate among developed economies. One in seven, or 15 percent of Americans were poor, 45 million in total. When excluding social security, Medicare and healthcare for the poor, welfare spending represented a fraction of the overall economy.

Indeed, policy decisions made since the end of the Cold War has lead to a massive transfer of wealth from labor to capital, from the public domain to the private. Notwithstanding the cries of "socialism" in the United States over national health care and other social programs, it is concentrated property in the form of corporations, investment funds and other institutions that has trumped government. At the same time, in the developing East, particularly in China, growing national wealth has proven compatible with centralized government that more or less manages the economy—a type of crony capitalism. As corporations merge and new transnational institutions form, a new East-West governing model for business and industry is emerging, which can be called, without irony, state capitalism.

American internet providers and social networks from Yahoo! to Twitter have agreed to censor websites and comply with the security apparatus in various countries, including China, in exchange for customers. Privacy and speech rights have been compromised worldwide. In the U.S. digital tracking of personal information is ubiquitous. Thus, global commerce and technology are combining to transform our notions of autonomy and personal dignity. Privacy rights that would have been cherished a generation ago are willingly relinquished in the U.S. and not even recognized in much of the world. Labor rights too are compromised worldwide and child labor is common. Most of the world's workers labor from paycheck to paycheck, although in China, India, Africa and other developing economies, a robust middle class is emerging, thus proving, at least on the surface, the compatibility between autocracy and security.

Rapid internationalization is also driving the emergence of an East-West governing model, as U.S. firms are becoming increasingly more dependent on foreign capital and talent. To some, the inevitable stress caused by this new reality is calling into question their basic assumptions about sovereignty and nationality. Consider the innovator in need of software engineers who turns to programmers in Belarus, Ukraine, Poland, Ireland, Israel or Pakistan, all of whom tap into their own networks to complete the tasks given to them at a fraction of the cost of U.S.-based developers. According to Joseph Sternberg of the *Wall Street Journal*: "We're heading for a day when a Malaysian architect will sketch out a new office tower for London, a Philippine architect will prepare detailed renderings, and a Chinese engineer will assess the structural soundness of the designs. Or a specialist firm in Bangalore will administer health benefits for a Kansas company."

The rapid changes in China, India and other developing economies threaten many in the West in the zero sum competition of physical assets. Some have also argued that a clash of core values—freedom versus authoritarianism—is inevitable. But science has shown that values are malleable. Once thought immutable, scientific breakthroughs have conclusively demonstrated that Western values of liberty, property and democracy have not been imprinted permanently by natural selection. As the genome becomes deciphered and human DNA is revealed, it is beyond doubt that all humankind is basically identical. Nationality, race, religion, class and even gender have been socially constructed by communities to, among other things, legitimize power, allocate resources and mediate conflict. Markets are not biological organisms and democracy is but one way of organizing institutions, although it may be the best way to give free expression to human activity.

No doubt that most Americans would say that they are free and that they live in a democracy, even though they do not bother to cast a vote. Democracy, at least as it may be defined as one man, one vote, is simply not relevant to them. In that regard, many Americans are already quite close to their Chinese counterparts in understanding that state ideology is merely a pretext for maintaining the power of the governing elite. Collectively, the people will tolerate ideology as long as their economic position appears secure. But if they see their economic prospects slipping away and experience greater inequality, ideology is seen for what it is—a social construct that can be changed. At that point of realization, a new governing structure can emerge, as it did during the Great Depression.

For global corporations, national governing ideologies are relative. Profit transcends national loyalty and fidelity to national ideologies are a hinder the goal of market penetration. The rule of law is viewed as relative as well. In *Built to Last*, James Collins and Jerry Porras celebrated Johnson and Johnson Company as an exemplar of corporate ethics. The company "explicitly speaks first of ideals beyond profit," they wrote. In 2008, the world's second-biggest seller of medical products, paid $70 million to settle claims that the company bribed doctors in Europe and paid kickbacks in Iraq to sell products and win contracts. In short, global corporations will almost always play by the rules of the host country.

Paradoxically, as the Internet and other technologies continue to dramatically reduce transaction costs, it calls into question the fundamental purpose of the command-and-control, often corrupt, organization. In the past, the organization was necessary to concentrate power, amass capital, allocate resources, make capital investments and direct labor. In a knowledge intensive economy, however, the ethical imperative is to create and maintain structures that unleash innovation. In contrast, anti-democratic, monopoly structures—state capitalism—will ensure that individuals who are already ill-equipped for adapting during this era of rapid transformation will remain perpetual labor cost, subject to chronic insecurity and dislocation, and in some areas of the world, East or West, to a type of state-supported serfdom.

The Internet has also decentralized labor pools and the ease with which entrepreneurs can engage global talent explains why start-ups initially create so few jobs in the United States. Educated in the Unites States and nurtured by dreams of power and profit, these innovators no longer need American labor to succeed. But calls for government intervention to protect Americans from this type global integration may undermine the innovation and creativity that is the natural consequence of the natural global forces of co-mingling and integration. In any event, restricting the free flow of information and labor is impossible in a networked world. At the same time, American corporations that benefit from American domicile, including intellectual property protection, free trade protocols and legal and military protection abroad, must take care to invest in the health and well being of the domestic community, which means creating jobs in the U.S. as well as abroad.

And herein lays the problem. Many corporations say that they would invest in the U.S. for high value talent, what I have called "value added knowledge work." So in the end, my view is that autonomy equates with innovation, integrity and value. Thus, social structures should permit people to be as free as possible to innovate and to compete and to ensure that they have the autonomy to make the personal decisions that have the biggest impact on the quality of their lives and their families and the live of the community. However, simply being left alone and free to choose a course of action does not mean that the action is a good one. Firms and individuals can be overindulgent and complacent—can waste resources, over consume, become overextended, become unethical, and commit crimes—and in doing so can harm the economy as a whole. Exposure and criticism are warranted, and this book contains a healthy dose of both. For example, consider that the United States has the world's biggest economy—25% of global output, or nearly 15 trillion dollars. Consider too that America houses 25% of the world's prison population. One in four Americans are functionally illiterate. One in seven Americans live in poverty, primarily children and young adults. Finally, consider that a social networking site called Twitter has been breathlessly called the "future of American innovation" by *Time*. The magazine should have called the platform "the future of American jobs" considering that Twitter, a decentralized platform is made possible by smart code writers and programmers that create few standard jobs.

It was President Lincoln that said that the purpose of government is to so for the people what they cannot do for themselves. The former railroad lawyer and Whig and long advocated government spending on roads, canals, bridges and other improvements of national scope and importance. Later, during the war years he grew to recognize that government could be elevated into a living moral force capable of inspiring people toward social and economic justice. During his time in office Lincoln signed the Railroad Act, the Homestead Act and the law that implemented the Freedmen Bureau, widely expanding the range of the national interest and the role of the federal government in actively pursuing that interest. Not too long after, Chancellor Bismarck created the modern welfare state in Germany primarily to ensure the security of the governing elite. Whether in a democracy or an authoritarian state, too much inequality is bad for the system. Unbridled survival of the fittest competition is destructive. Thus, to preserve the governing structure government must play a vital role in ensuring equal opportunity.

For nearly a century, the federal government has also played an important role in fostering innovation, job creation and economic growth. The Sherman Antitrust Act ensures fair market competition. The National Labor Relations Act permits collective bargaining. The Highway Act created a modern transportation system that gave birth to a suburban housing and commercial boom. These are but a few examples. Congress has repeatedly exercised its spending power to make investments in research and development and new technologies and has always been engaged in promoting national infrastructure from canals to bridges, from railroads to highways, from shipping and air flight to space travel, from electrification to the Internet. However, while government spending lays an indispensable foundation for economic growth, it cannot necessarily create the big breakthrough that becomes America's next big success story, nor can it fully recognize the entrepreneur's next game changing idea. Only the market has consistently demonstrated that it can fulfill this vital role. Only focused and ethical leadership can maintain the delicate balance between completion, freedom and individual rights on the one hand

and personal responsibility, collective action and the preservation of the community as a whole on the other. As such, the burden rests squarely on government, business and the American people to rise to the challenge—a very tall order, considering that ethical lapses on all levels and within every major American institution over the last two decades have eroded trust and credibility. Whether in private industry, government, academia or mainstream media, leadership at the top has revealed itself to be corrupt, incompetent or both. A Gallup poll in 2008 revealed a nation in the throes of a crisis in confidence. A majority had lost trust in most every social and political institution. Some have speculated that the concentration of power and the erosion of transparency and accountability have resulted in widespread institutional failure, mostly clearly seen in massive product recalls, fraud and bribery in the private sector and the abject dysfunction of the political system.

And while the American public has every right to complain and to be skeptical of their leaders and to bemoan their lack of accountability, one is left wondering about the responsibility and accountability of the American people. In 2008, 1.7 million reports of child abuse were logged in America. Los Angeles County alone logged 173,000 such reports, an indicator that the most basic measure of personal responsibility in a society, the care and nurturing of future generations, is under strain. It seems pointless for the average American to expect their leaders to conduct themselves with high moral standards and to be accountable when they cannot even fulfill the most basic ethical obligation owed to themselves and their community.

When looking at America, particularly over the last decade or so—the dominance of consumption over production; of celebrity over authenticity; of brand names over national purpose; of cool detachment over passionate engagement; and of the market transaction over nurturing relationships—it does feel like an end point.

It is plausible that this cultural morbidity may be a psychic reaction to profound feelings of physical and emotional insecurity. This same timeframe started with a massive terrorist attack, followed by a state of constant war and economic and financial turmoil, which included enormous job losses and mortgage foreclosures, all of which is reverberates in a perpetual media feedback loop. In response, there has been a complete lack of leadership at all levels. Even after waves of corporate malfeasance, executive compensation skyrocketed. Wall Street bonuses after the taxpayer bailout were the highest on record. Political leadership became dysfunctional, even destructive as America's credit rating was subject to a self-inflicted wound. As the symbols of parental authority and trust lost all credibility, in one long terrible moment it became apparent that the sense of American duty, honor, unselfishness and essential goodness was merely an ugly self deception, a mask for venality, greed and cynicism.

But the end point for one generation is also a point of departure for another.

An underlying assumption in this book is that even though executive leaders cannot control most events within or without the organization they obviously can still make a big difference in outcomes. I have also assumed that power corrupts and that absolute power corrupts absolutely, as the complex demands of the globalized knowledge economy come crashing down on leaders and followers alike.

Some executives believe that analyzing vast amounts of information and having the ability to master complexity are today's paramount skill set. Others believe it's about speed, resiliency and execution. Many extol communication skills, particularly listening. Some merely parrot the words "innovation" and "transparency" because it sounds good. Most stick to the script. Going off script often results in a lawsuit. Some have PR. All have damage control. Still others simply float in stream of corporate buzz. To most it's about the power to crush all competitors and to beat down all threats.

The inconvenient truth is that most shareholders want amoral, ruthless leaders that push the envelope of law and ethics. In the political arena, the First Amendment guarantee of free speech legalizes all manner of conflicts of interest. Unethical conduct is simply the byproduct of the free market, each person on their own to weigh the realities of their situation, the risks associated with their choices and the rewards that are the direct consequence of these choices, whether self serving or altruistic. To the extent I offer any advice to my students, it is to be humble, to be suspicious of power and hierarchy and to tell the truth as much as possible. Whether they believe that my advice will help them and their organizations is left entirely up to their free choice.

Indeed, somehow throughout the feeling of moral decay, economic collapse and financial crisis, Americans remained a generous and giving people. Charitable contributions continued to be made by individuals all along the economic strata and volunteer activity often encouraged by schools, religious groups and civic organizations never ceased. Millions of dollars were donated to tsunami and earthquake victims' abroad and the tide of volunteers that streamed to a devastated New Orleans eventually overwhelmed the resources of the city.

A new environmental ethic took hold on college campuses and a renewed awareness of global ecological issues emerged. Promising medical treatments and therapies were explored and the science of genetics began to open up new ways of understanding humankind and its relationship to the environment.

Therefore, I take care to remind my students of what Charles Darwin really said: *"It is not the strongest of the species that survive, or the most intelligent, but the ones most responsive to change."*

John J. Sarno
January 2009
Somerset County, N.J.

1. Drift or Mastery

Passing through the turn of the century, enormous economic forces combined to create a new American dynamic. The tangible evidence of American power and progress had engulfed the nation as awesome technological achievements of the free market created affluence unknown in human history. Advances in communications and transportation and radical changes in modes of living seemed a breach of continuity, a rupture of history. The *Churchman*, an influential journal declared: "There are a thousand evidences that the present state of things is drawing to a close, and that some new development of social organization is at hand." At the same time, the American economic system appeared to be rushing toward the brink of collapse. The century in question is, of course, of the *nineteenth* century.

In 1893, the United States, as well as the rest of the industrialized world, had been nearly overwhelmed by the most severe economic depression it had ever experienced. Economic and social dislocations were massive: the pressures of urbanization, poverty, immigration, labor and farmer unrest, populist and social agitation, the power of giant corporations, trusts and other combinations, and other forces of global proportions, converged to challenge the existing economic and social order. Back in the United States in the fall of 1893, after a summer in Europe, William James saw something new in America—"force and directness in the people, but a terrible grimness, more ugliness than I ever realized before."

Perhaps just as dramatically, the American identity, based on the ideals of liberty and freedom, was also changing. In 1890, the U.S. Superintendent of the Census reported: "Up to and including 1880 the country had a frontier settlement . . . but at present the unsettled area has been so broken into by isolated bodies of settlement that these can hardly be said to be a frontier line. In the discussion of [the frontier's] extent, its westward movement, it cannot, therefore, any longer have a place in the census report." Thus, the American frontier had officially ended and as it receded, the cities swelled. By 1890, three-fourths of New York City's population of 1.2 million residents lived in tenements. The number of tenements and their impoverished inhabitants had more than doubled in twenty years. With the number of homeless people increasing, displaced New Yorkers were housed on barges in the East River. To Frederick Jackson Turner, the influential historian, the brief official statement made by the Superintendent meant "the first period of American history had closed."

In 1893, Turner wrote: "What the Mediterranean Sea was to the Greeks, breaking the bond of custom, offering new experiences, calling out new institutions and activities, that, and more, the ever retreating frontier has been to the United States directly." In short, the enormous and expanding opportunities provided by the American frontier, to settlers, profiteers and missionaries alike, formed a significant basis for democracy, individualism and optimism. However, as observed by Anders Stephenson in *Manifest Destiny*, "Turner's argument merely underlined in the popular mind that the United States was no longer a society of sturdy pioneers. If American identity was indeed the process of pioneering the frontier and the latter had ceased to exist, what sort of new form might that identity assume?" Industrialism and urbanization would provide the answer.

As noted by Paul Kennedy in *The Rise and Fall of the Great Powers*, with the Civil War over the United States was able to break up the big plantations and exploit rich agricultural land, vast raw materials "and the marvelously convenient evolution of modern technology (railways, the steam engine, mining equipment, to develop such resources." American business expanded globally, enabled by innovations in communications and transportation, creating new markets for manufactured goods and thus vast new opportunities for profit. Mass production and the expansion of foreign markets promised to create a "new economy," one that would be able to finally eliminate, or at least mitigate the infernal boom and bust cycles, securing the perpetual growth of living standards and national wealth. As late as 1879, Great Britain remained the world's leading industrial power accounting for 32 percent of total world industrial production. By 1900, the United States surpassed Great Britain as the number one industrial power in the world with nearly 40 percent of the world's industrial output.

As the old order of improvised and expansive frontier traditions and customs became rapidly replaced by a new centralized, industrial order, it was Walter Lippmann who asked a profound question in 1914. Once you possess the power and means for unleashing and controlling life and work, what ends will be achieved? In his most important work, *Drift and Mastery*, Lippmann observed that the profit motive was a poor incentive for creating a good society. "Private commercialism is an antiquated, feeble, mean, and unimaginative way of dealing with the possibilities of modern industry" he wrote. He added: "modern industry was created by the profiteer, and here it is, the great fact of our lives, blackening our cities, fed with the lives of our children, a tyrant over men and women, turning out enormous stocks of produce, good, bad, and horrible."

Lippmann wrote as an optimist and idealist, a member of a new generation of Americans facing for the first time the problems of a post-frontier America, a modern, newly industrialized America. The promise of the future, he argued, lay neither in the self-serving boosterism of the businessman nor in the class-conscious delusions of the revolutionary, but in replacing, or at least reforming, the profit motive with the fidelity and pride of the craftsman and the sense of service of the salaried professional. In effect, Lippmann was advocating for a national purpose which would emerge from the transformation of industry and a society enabled by new social organizations and technologies. He thought that corporations managed by educated, salaried professionals could help create a more humane industrialism. Mastery of the enormous problems of industrialization, Lippmann argued, was attainable through scientific and rational planning and organization, which could be flexible enough to foster human curiosity, ingenuity and creativity.

Lippmann, a rationalist, was optimistic about man's moral development and like Thomas Jefferson and other Founding Fathers believed that scientific reason was the basis for morality. Unlike the prevailing free market view best exemplified by John Templeton, investor and mutual fund pioneer, who said, "The true idealist preaches not class hatred but universal love; not to redistribute the wealth but to multiply the wealth; not more regulation but more freedom; not security but opportunity. The true idealist is the missionary for freedom and competition," Lippmann offered a more nuanced role for government. Regulation guided by reason could guide corporate decision making to encompass wider societal goals beyond making private profit.

If the frontier had molded a type of rugged individualism, spontaneous ingenuity and can-do attitude, the second great chapter of American history has been defined by an attitude that accepts the concentration of power—economic, financial, industrial and political—as indispensable to achieving economic security and social progress. America's financial markets mobilized the capital reserves from all over the world and placed these enormous resources at the disposal of new firms. "It was the investment in the new and improved processes of production," wrote Alfred Chandler, "not innovation that initially lowered costs and increased productivity ... Investment created the modern industrial enterprise and built the new or reshaped industries in which further, cumulative innovations in product and process would come." It was investment, concluded Chandler, that above all else drove the "second industrial revolution," creating the "modern legal, financial, and educational environment in which modern industrial enterprise operated in the U.S. throughout the twentieth century."

In reality, the twentieth century, often referred to as the "American Century" lurched from crisis to crisis and America was unable, generally speaking, to reconcile the tensions that Lippmann brought to light: the conflicts between expansion and consolidation, tradition and change, emotion and rationality, conformity and autonomy, security and opportunity. To Lippmann, change and adaptation were necessary to master the new realities of industrial capitalism. Industrialization and the concentration of power required by modern, global capitalism could only be reconciled with individual autonomy through the creation of new social structures and institutions, laws, tools, and a restructured relationship between capital and labor.

Idealists like Templeton had faith that a permanent state of prosperity could be achieved through a market that gave free reign to the creativity and ingenuity of the American people. In reality, however, the market, particularly the financial markets, were captive to speculators and cheats. Nevertheless, the near magical belief in the stock market reached its apotheosis in the late twentieth century. In that century's last decade, the gospel of yet another "new economy" promised a magical fusion of communications technology, software predictions and Wall Street wizardry that would finally solve the modern American dilemma of how to make a society both rich and happy. Much of that magic ended in 2001.

By March 2001, $4.6 trillion worth of stock market value evaporated. The dot com bust shook the nation's confidence in the new economy and the attacks on the World Trade Center and the Pentagon shook the nation's sense of physical security. In the immediate aftermath of September 11, 2001, there was an immense outpouring of grief and patriotism. Wal-Mart reported sales of 450,000 flags in just the first three days after the terrorist attacks. Polls later in the month showed that eight in ten Americans were displaying the flag at their homes and workplaces or on their cars or clothes. The media reported many anecdotes of investment bankers, stockbrokers, lawyers and the like who had pledged to give up their lucrative but unsatisfying careers in search of more meaningful and purposeful lives. No doubt some did, but for many more the visceral emotions and desire for meaning and belonging faded as the mundane realities of money making returned. Still, a deep sense of anxiety and insecurity had taken hold with the realization that the world's only remaining superpower, fortress America, was vulnerable to a devastating attack from zealots with box cutters. Perhaps even more unsettling was the realization that U.S., its institutions, ways and customs, were deeply despised by others in the world.

In short order, the U.S. Congress appropriated $1.2 billion for a construction project and the newly formed Department of Homeland Security promptly hired posthole diggers to build a 650-mile security fence along the Mexican border to keep out illegal workers, drug smugglers and others perceived as doing Americans harm. By 2008 a new fence went up every week in Arizona and California, mile after mile of posts, wire, plates and rails, through deserts and rocky hillsides. David Von Drehle, who covered the construction for *Time* observed that the sections of the security fence were "a hodgepodge of designs. The best sections—of tall concrete-filled steel poles deeply rooted, closely spaced and solidly linked at the top—are bluntly functional. The worst—rusting, graffiti-covered, Vietnam-era surplus—are just skeevy walls of welded junk. Whether you think it's a sad necessity or a crude brutality, the fence is not a sight that stirs pride." Moreover, "[e]ven the great Wall of China was not impermeable." While the security fence may keep some Mexicans out, it cannot wall off Mexico from the United States; or, for that matter, separate America economically or psychologically from the rest of the world.

Indeed, the United States has entered the twenty first century with 6.6 billion people in the world, most living in an interconnected global economy producing an astounding $60 trillion of output annually. With the collapse of communism, Americans had taken for granted that their country had won the Cold War and as the world's sole superpower, was omnipotent both economically as well as militarily. Moreover, the American creed of free enterprise had seemingly spread around the world through the World Bank and other international institutions. But the spread of free markets has created wealth not only in America, but around the world as well. Americans, with their unparalleled standard of living, find the gap in average income per person between the United States and other industrialized economies and much of the developing world, especially in Asia, is narrowing fast. Indeed, one hundred and twenty four countries grew their economies at over 4 percent annually from 2000 to 2007, including thirty countries in Africa. For the American worker, no longer playing the only game in town, global free enterprise had dramatically increased competition.

By 2008 America remained the largest economy in the world, producing a quarter of the world's output in goods and services. U.S. exports of goods made up 13.5 percent of U.S. Gross Domestic Product (GDP), the highest percentage since export statistics have been kept. However, for the first time in modern history, the output of developing countries represented about half the world's economy. Collectively, these economies have been growing about seven percent a year since 2002. In 2007, central banks in these countries, particularly Asian ones, added about $1.4 trillion in Western currencies to their reserves, about $800 of it in dollars, according to the Council on Foreign Relations. In turn, foreigners pumped $920 billion into U.S. stocks, bonds and government securities in 2007. Almost 40 percent of this capital, about $361 billion, came from developing economies, including twenty-one percent from China. Considering the United States' trade imbalance requires borrowing at a pace of $2 billion *per day*, massive foreign investment in the United States, including the gobbling up of companies and assets, prevents the type of destabilizing inflation that could sink the U.S. economy and lead to the default of the world's biggest economy. In other words, America's massive trade debt favors both the U.S. economy and the developing economies. Certainly Americans enjoy products made cheaply abroad, but are they willing to pay the price of the internationalization of their jobs, neighborhoods and, perhaps, their country.

In *The Post-American World*, Fareed Zakaria has observed that post-9/11 Americans can now see a new world coming into being, but fear it is being shaped in distant lands and by foreign people. "The underlying reality across the globe is enormous activity," he writes. "The results are clear and stunning . . . Poverty is falling in countries that house 80 percent of the nation's population . . . The global economy has more than doubled in size over the past 15 years . . . Global trade has grown by 133 percent in the same period. The expansion of the global economic pie has been so large, with so many counties participating, that it has become the dominant force of the current era."

Intel Corporation has estimated that 20 percent of the world's population was connected to the Internet in 2007. The company estimates that at the current rate there will be enough cell phones or other hand held devices connected to the Internet that every person on Earth would own such a device within a decade. Software applications for such devices will have quadrupled. Enabled by this next wave of interconnectivity driven by open source platforms, some commentators have speculated that freelance project workers could be retained through an electronic auction where knowledge workers bid on short and long term projects. In short,

American workers could be faced with competing with workers located anywhere in the world with an Internet connection, which is anywhere in the world. In this new era the price of some labor will be bid down like a toaster on eBay.

Moreover, as Thomas Homer-Dixon points out in *The Ingenuity Gap*, nearly every statistic that gauges the degree of connectivity among human beings or the movement of information, people and things shows exponential growth. These global connections have in turn made social and economic systems more complex, thus making traditional social and economic hierarchies unworkable in many cases. As large, command and control corporations begin to decentralize and take greater advantage of communications networks and global labor markets, once secure jobs created and maintained by big organizations have become fragmented around the globe.

Many Americans have not fared particularly well in the global economy. Real hourly wages for most workers have risen only one percent since 1979 to 2006, even as those workers' productivity has increased 60 percent. According to the U.S. Census Bureau, the median American family made $58,407 in 2006. That's $991 less, adjusted for inflation, than the median in 2000. At the same time, corporate profits have skyrocketed, ironically reaffirming classic eighteen-century economic dogma in the "new" economy. As observed by David Ricardo: "There is no way of keeping profits up but by keeping wages down."

According to economists Thomas Piketty and Emanuel Saez, 75 percent of all income gains from 2002 to 2006 went to the top one percent of households making $382,600 per year or more. While some economists suggest that wages are an inaccurate measurement of income because they do not account for the value of employment-based fringe benefits and refundable tax credits, the sustained decline in the number of U.S. taxpayers clearly reflect stagnating overall incomes. In 2008 57 million working Americans paid no federal income taxes according to the Tax Policy Center, an increase of 20 percent since 1984. No doubt, the combined impacts of trade policies, illegal immigration and welfare reform account for the fact that only 62 percent of households paid federal income taxes

1. Drift or Mastery

in 2008. But a sizable percentage of these households have also seen their incomes flatten during the first decade of the twentieth century.

As corporate profits and executive compensation have soared and most of the wealth has concentrated at the top among the top earners, government spending has increased to prop up the purchasing power of the average American working for ever diminishing wages. From 1070 to 2005, the U.S. economy grew by nearly 400 percent, from a $3.5 trillion to a nearly a $14 trillion economy. Due to investments in labor saving technology, per capita GDP nearly doubled but incredibly per capita income stayed flat. While medium income increased by 32 percent during this time, this was primarily because women entered the workforce to bring in extra income. At the same time, after tax income of top earners tripled. In other words, the massive wealth created by increased productivity over the last thirty years or so has gone in large measure to top income earners.

Responding to this mass inequality, federal government spending increased by 221 percent. By 2010, more Americans worked in government jobs than in manufacturing. Almost one in two Americans lived in a household were someone received government benefits, primarily a social security, Medicare or unemployment payment. Still, by 2008 the poverty rate reached 15 percent, or 45 million Americans. With one in seven Americans living at or below the federal poverty level, with the biggest increases in poverty in America's suburbs, nearly 18 million American families experienced food shortages in 2008, more than any time since before the food stamp program was created in 1964.

The fast growing economies, particularly in Asia, may be changing the center of gravity of the world economy. As Fareed Zakaria has pointed out, "the rise of China and India is really just the most obvious manifestation of a rising world. In dozens of big countries, one can see the same set of forces at work—a growing economy, a resurgent society, a vibrant culture, and a rising sense of national pride." Many of these economies are seen as providing a global model for growth and economic sustainability, even though their political structures are autocratic. A 21-member Commission on Growth and Development, headed by Nobel Prize-winning economist Michael Spence, spent two years and $4 million trying to figure out a fundamental economic question: Why do only some countries get rich and the vast majority don't? The panel, funded by the World Bank, the Hewlett Foundation and grants from several nations, studied 13 economies that have grown at least 7 percent a year for at least 25 years since 1950 to determine the factors that underpinned successful economic performance. Among other factors, the Commission found that democracy wasn't essential for growth. Autocratic governments that allow "vigorous debate" internally on economic policies are sufficient, the report said. In short, the Commission had provide cover to American corporations to enter the markets of the developing world and to play by local rules, which in some cases means giving up intellectual property protection.

To boost growth, the Commission urged developing nations to spend heavily on infrastructure and endorsed government subsidies to build local industries. China's "ingenious innovation" strategy has put western firms on notice that in many cases the price of participating in profitable infrastructure projects will be the sharing of proprietary and intellectual property. Critics of this policy contend that these firms are merely trading short term profit for a much smaller market share long term, as Chinese companies eventually gain the competitive edge. Chinese firms say that they are only engaging in the widely accepted practice of reverse engineering. In either case, the reality facing most Americans is that in response to the IP protectionism practices abroad, advanced economies in the West, particularly the United States, have adopted trade policies that have accelerated the disruptive transition from an industrial to an information-intensive economy. In this emerging knowledge-intensive economy, the application of knowledge assets, rather than physical or labor-intensive assets, will make the difference between success and failure, not necessarily big infrastructure projects. By the same token, if American firms are required to give up its intellectual property in the short term, more and better intellectual assets must be created to increase productivity in the future.

Productivity is the essence of a society's survival. It allows a steady increase in the standard of living. Though the United States lost one million manufacturing jobs between 1980 and 1990, manufacturing output remained a steady 14 percent of GDP because fewer workers produced more per hour. Productivity increases the wealth of nations and is an essential ingredient for raising standards of living. It was Adam Smith in *The Wealth of Nations*, who observed that improvements in productivity resulted from employee ingenuity. "A great part of the machines made use of in those manufacturers, in which labor is most subdivided, were originally the invention of common workmen in order to facilitate and quicken their own particular part of that works." As productivity increased, Smith advocated increasing wages "so that it increases the industry of the common people." Further, he wrote, "as wages of labour are the encouragement of industry" higher wages "animates [the workmen] to exert that strength to the utmost. Where wages are high, accordingly, we shall always find workmen more active, diligent and expeditious, then when they are low." Smith pointed to the example of the American colonies as an illustration of how higher wages motivates industry and invention.

However, from 2005 to 2010, median household income actually dropped from $49,477 to $48,223. This does not account for the value of employer-sponsored health care and other non-taxable benefits associated full time employment. But the share of people covered by employment-based health insurance fell to 59.7 percent in 2006 from 64.2 percent in 2000. While fewer working Americans get their health care coverage from an employer-sponsored plan, the costs of health care have escalated dramatically. In 2005, annual health spending in the United States was close to $2 trillion, about 16 percent of GNP, up from 12.3 percent of GNP in 1990—double the amount spent on health care by other developed economies. Since 1970, health care costs have grown on average of 2.5 percentage points faster than GNP, thus putting an enormous financial strain on individuals, employers and the nation as a whole. In short, while the "hidden paycheck" may disguise the true earnings of the American family, the strain of employer-sponsored health care has reached the critical point of unsustainability.

During this same time frame, for the top tenth of one percent of earners income grew by over 22 percent, excluding capital gains. This growing income and wealth gap, the biggest since prior to the stock market crash in 1929, suggests that the capital investments and ensuing productivity gains during the last decade of the twentieth century that benefited the average worker reached a point of diminishing return. In fact, the trend toward lower wages since then is striking. According to Louis Uchitelle, a business writer for the *New York Times*, using a twenty-dollar per hour job as a middle class benchmark, or $41,600 per year for a 40-hour per week job, the proportion of the workforce earning at lease that hourly rate declined from 23 percent in 1979 to 20 percent in 1980, to 18 percent in 1989, and to 16 percent in 2000. In manufacturing, where the twenty-dollar per hour rate was the standard, only 1.9 million hourly workers earn that rate, down nearly 60 percent since 1979.

As Brink Lindsey writes in *The Age of Abundance*:

> In the contemporary knowledge economy, the critical determinant of economic success is a well-developed capacity for abstract thinking, which makes possible long-term planning, large-scale organization, and use of extremely arcane and specialized knowledge. At the low end of the skills continuum, members of the underclass operate within such a narrow time horizon and circles of trust that their lives are plagued by chronic chaos and dysfunction. At the high end, members of the managerial and professional elite amass high levels of human capital in the form of expertise and relationships, which allow them to produce significant economic value and claim commensurate rewards.

Some of these rewards are enormous indeed. According to the Congressional Research Service, the average pay for chief executive officers was more than 180 times the average worker pay in 2005, up from a multiple of 90 in 1994. Total direct compensation of CEOs in 2007 was a median $8.8 million, counting salaries, bonuses and other incentives, as well as the value of restricted stock, stock options and other long-term incentives. At the uppermost extreme, the top-earning hedge fund manager of 2007 made $3.7 *billion* dollars. Even among the rank and file workers, the bulk of pay raises have gone to "top performers." In 2008, Mercer, LLC, a human resources consulting firm, reported that for more than 12 million employees at over one thousand mid-size and large U.S. employers, bonuses and raises had been skewed toward employees that exceeded expectations, as defined by management performance appraisals.

Since corporate customers are worldwide, it does not appear that corporate executives, at least publicly, have much concern with this enormous disparity in earnings, although some shareholders are beginning to seek a voice in evaluating executive performance and evaluating executive compensation packages. Nevertheless, corporate law ensures that these decisions fall within the sole province of the company's board of directors. In *The End of Work*, Jeremy Rifkin taps the profound cynicism that excessive executive compensation breeds: "The business community has long operated under the assumption that gains in productivity brought on by the introduction of new technologies rightfully belong to the stockholders and corporate management in the form of increased dividends and larger salaries and other benefits," he writes. "Workers' claims on productivity advances, in the form of higher wages and reduced hours of work, have generally been regarded as illegitimate and even parasitic. Their contribution to the production process and the success of the company has always been viewed as of a lesser nature than those who provide the capital and take the risk of investing in new machinery."

As the U.S. economy has become more globalized, the gap between the high and low earners in the United States has grown dramatically. Economists have attributed the widening gap primarily to technological and demographic changes that have increased the premium paid to those with advanced skills and education. A rational response to this transformation would be to choose the task of improving the education and skill levels of American workers. But many workers, particularly in big corporations, are already at a disadvantage. While they are expected to work in knowledge-intensive ways, the technology that they are required to use has deconstructed the nature of their work and has de-skilled many jobs, making most employees vulnerable to continued automation and outsourcing. Ironically for most firms, "knowledge management," which is based on reaching high levels of efficiency and standardization is almost completely incompatible with innovation. Since most employees are paid to perform efficiently, innovation is left to the sole province of an elite and highly paid cadre of employees and consultants. For most corporations, innovation means acquiring the intellectual property of smaller firms and making sure that whatever knowledge assets produced by employees are controlled, hoarded and exploited. Current legal rules, based on nineteenth century property law, favor corporate ownership of intellectual property at the expense of employee autonomy and security. As a result of both law and technology, knowledge and knowledge work are becoming increasingly privatized, creating a new social reality and work ethic. However, common law and public policy have not evolved sufficiently to preserve the economic liberty and autonomy of knowledge workers making it difficult to realize the full value of knowledge work.

Instead of creating greater contractual protection for workers and promoting policies that diffuse knowledge for innovation and job creation, government spending has increased to respond to middle-class anxiety about stagnant wages and insecurity about health insurance. Even as Americans express concern over government spending, which resulted in a $1.26 trillion budget deficit in 2010, many oppose cuts. Direct payments to individuals cost $2.4 trillion in 2010, up 79 percent, adjusted for inflation, from a decade earlier. This represents 64.3 percent of all federal outlays that are recorded on the books, the highest percentage in the seventy years the government has been measuring it. The percentage was 46.7 percent in 1990 and 26.2 percent in 1960.

Not surprisingly, in a *Wall Street Journal*/NBC News poll conducted in 2010, only 29 percent of respondents reported that cutting federal spending and the national debt as a top priority. Only 13 percent opposed the Recovery Act enacted the year before which cost nearly $900 billion. Seventy percent do not support cuts in Social Security or Medicare. Americans appear to have widely accepted the role of government spending to maintain purchasing power but as the United States emerges from its first decade of the twenty first century, Americans view their economy in almost entirely negative terms, even as millions around the world have adopted the free enterprise system to lift themselves out of poverty.

Some suggest that this negativity and the widening income and wealth gaps could stoke a nationalistic and/or populist reaction, even as sovereign wealth funds from Asia and the Middle East have propped up near bankrupt financial institutions in the U.S. and Europe. Stagnating wages have soured Americans on free trade which many now believe lowers living standards in the U.S. In 2010, more than half of all Americans believed that free trade policies hurt the U.S., up from 46 percent in

2007 and 32 percent in 1999. In fact, worries about the outsourcing of jobs are one of the few issues that white and blue collar workers seem to share. In the same *Wall Street Journal*/NBC News poll, 83 percent of blue collar workers agreed that outsourcing of manufacturing jobs to foreign countries with lower wages was the main reason for high unemployment and lower wages. Among professionals and managers, the belief was even stronger. Presumably, some of these people were involved in the decision to outsource jobs and when the reasons were candidly discussed. Ninety five percent of the professionals and managers that responded to the poll blamed outsourcing for unemployment and low wages. Whereas the outsourcing of manufacturing jobs has been the dominate factor underlying workers' anxiety about free trade since 1980, the outsourcing of professional jobs is now commonplace.

Moreover, in an April 2008 Gallup poll, 68 percent of respondents said that wealth "should be more evenly distributed" in the U.S., the highest percentage saying so since Gallup started asking the question in 1984. A smaller majority, 51 percent, agreed that "heavy taxes on the rich" were needed. Similarly, a *Financial Times*/Harris Poll conducted in May 2008, found growing worldwide support for raising taxes on the wealthy. The poll found that 8,748 adults in eight countries believed the wealthy should be taxed more.

However, raising taxes on the wealthy may be counterproductive in the long term. According to the economist Kurt Hauser: "Raising taxes encourages taxpayers to shift, hide and underreport income . . . Higher taxes reduce the incentives to work, produce, invest and save, thereby dampening overall economic activity and job creation." Moreover, government policies that try to redistribute wealth merely mask the fundamental nature of the challenges facing most Americans in the twenty first century. To a great extent, America's long-term success will depend on its ability to compete globally with value-added knowledge and the willingness of workers to acquire the skills and abilities to make new technologies happen, as opposed to redistributing resources through tax code manipulations. However, it is clear that new technologies are destabilizing even deconstructing corporations and accelerating the outsourcing of jobs, which would otherwise have remained within the organization. Increasingly the jobs that do remain require more than some knowledge; instead these jobs require *value added* knowledge work. This work can be defined as the cluster of abilities, skills and temperaments that accentuates an organization's strengths. A CEO Project report issued in 2005 illustrates this point. About one hundred chief executive offers from fast-growing firms, primarily manufacturers employing between 100 to 200 employees and booking annual revenue within the $16 to $60 million range. When asked to identify the competitive strengths of their firms, the top four answers reported were: proprietary technology (36 percent), unique approach (31 percent), process innovation (10 percent) and operational excellence (5 percent). In other words, the perceived strengths of the firm were directly connected to the ability to exploit the ingenuity and know how of the talent pool. Similarly, the biggest business opportunities that the CEOs identified were related to new products, processes and improvements; again opportunities driven by innovation.

Interestingly, when asked to rate their existing talent, nine of ten respondents issued a grade of "B" or better. However, when asked to identify their biggest obstacles to growth, 29 percent identified insufficient talent and another 24 percent identified slow product development and marketing problems. Another 16 percent identified lack of capital as a serious impediment to growth. What this data suggests is that business success is based primarily on intangible factors relating to human capital and while most executives will state publicly that their existing talent pool is sufficient, they will nevertheless report that their biggest constraint to growth is attracting and retaining the "right" talent, the type of employee that plays to the firm's strengths in creating and directing proprietary technologies and in developing unique and innovative improvements to processes. In short, these executives are reporting an innovation gap among exiting employees and recognizing that filling this gap is crucial for success.

Such value added knowledge work is critically important but only a relatively small percentage of elite workers perform it. In 2010, with over 15 million workers unemployed, many employers reported trouble filling open positions. Employers report that the pool for specialized jobs, particularly knowledge-intensive jobs, is small. Most organizations are focused on production, efficiency and the elimination of waste. They are not necessarily interested in the know how of the average employee, and the average employee is satisfied by doing just enough to avoid discipline. To the extent that upper management is focused on retaining highly valuable knowledge workers, supervisors lack the skills to create a suitable environment. Knowledge workers tend to be primarily motivated by intrinsic factors, but remain interested in position and compensation. As Homer-Dixon has observed, while idealism and job satisfaction motivate knowledge workers, the opportunity for profit seems to drive innovation the most. Therefore, striking the right balance between external and intrinsic rewards should be an important function of upper management. Managing knowledge workers requires such core values as honesty, fairness, integrity, humility and openness, qualities that are more or less inimical to the production values of efficiency and productivity. However, as organizations are forced to be knowledge intensive to compete, many are taking care to change the corporate culture. As for the knowledge worker, he or she must also be guided by a core set of values. For the knowledge worker, lifestyles and the desire for self-fulfillment resemble a secular creed. As such, a commitment to autonomy, esteem and lifelong learning are essential to their well-being and happiness.

But a crisis is already evident in the American educational system and current economic incentives favor personal debt and consumption over investments in learning and innovation. Moreover, a desire for a better educational system will not ensure success. Citing Economic Policy Institute reports, Louis Uchitelle has noted: "The nation's political leaders—Democrats and Republicans alike—have argued that education and training are the route back to middle class wages for those who have fallen out. But the demand isn't sufficient to absorb all those workers that the leaders would educate. Even now [2008], roughly 15 percent of college-educated workers find themselves in jobs for which they are overqualified." What these reports suggest is that a bachelor's degree by itself may not be the ticket to a middle class lifestyle. Since the aptitudes and abstract reasoning skills necessary for value added knowledge work are not equally dispersed throughout the population, the continuing transition from an industrial to a knowledge economy may result in the long-term suppression of wages for most Americans and perhaps a permanent class of long-term unemployed.

In July 2008, *Time* reported the results of its *Time*/Rockefeller Foundation survey of Americans' attitudes about the economy and their own state of economic well being. An overwhelming 85 percent of Americans thought that the U.S economy was seriously off track, and three out of four believed that the next generation would have more economic struggles. About three in four stated that they were more economically insecure than ten years earlier. Further, almost eight in ten respondents stated that they wanted more government help, specifically by increasing government spending on public-works projects and off setting the costs of day care.

While government policies could be enacted to provide better incentives for livelong learning and re-tooling, democratic institutions can only change when the people want to change, when the will of the people demands it. Scarcely half of American children in the nation's fifty largest cities will leave the public schools with a high school diploma in hand, according to America's Promise Alliance. U.S. law has guaranteed equal educational and employment opportunity regardless of race but these children are disproportionately African Americans. Their homes are disproportionately located in the nation's largest school districts. More than half—53 percent—of African American males drop out of high school compared with 22 percent of white males, unconscionable numbers regardless of race. Millions of American children and young people every year are being deprived of the opportunity to compete in the twenty first century.

At the same time, America's prisons are bursting with the chronically maladjusted, and the permanently unemployable. One of the less recognized toxic byproducts of the deindustrialization of America (as measured by manufacturing jobs not productivity) is the fact that U.S. has the largest incarceration rate in the world. According to the Justice Department's Bureau of Justice Statistics, America's prison population topped 2 million inmates for the first time in history in 2002. The fifty states, the District of Columbia and the federal government held 1,355,748 prisoners (two-thirds of the total incarcerated population), and local municipal and county jails held 665,475 inmates. By 2002, America's jails held 1 in every 142 U.S. residents. Males were incarcerated at the rate of 1,309 inmates per 100,000 U.S. men, while the female incarceration rate was 113 per 100,000 women residents. Of the 1,200,203 state prisoners,

3,055 were younger than 18 years old. In addition, adult jails held 7,248 inmates under 18.

The number of additional jail inmates grows faster than the number of new jail beds. States spent $29.5 billion for prisons in 2001, about a $5.5 billion increase from 1996, after adjusting for inflation. Excluding capital spending, the average cost of operating State prisons in 2001 was $100 per U.S. resident, up from $90 in 1996. Correctional authorities spent $38.2 billion to maintain the nation's state correctional systems in fiscal year 2001, including $29.5 billion specifically for adult correctional facilities. Day-to-day operating expenses totaled $28.4 billion, and capital outlays for land, new building, and renovations, 1.1 billion. The average annual operating cost per State inmate in 2001 was $22,650, or $62.05 per day. Among facilities operated by the Federal Bureau of Prisons, it was $22,632 per inmate, or $62.01 per day. In America, the increase in cost of corrections outpaced the cost of health, education, or conserving natural resources. This investment seems to have no impact on lowering crime rates. Instead, this dramatic incarceration rate may be a manifestation of a shallow economy and deteriorating social structure. Two-thirds of prisoners released annual are rearrested, according to the U.S. Justice Department.

America has incarcerated a substantial part of an entire generation of working age African American men, an indelible badge of shame for any society that purports to advance opportunity for all of its citizens. To fill the gap left by such a big absence of working age men, America has imported millions of undocumented workers from Mexico and Central America, many of whom are functionally illiterate. But having sacrificed so many young men to incarceration, the nation has put at risk every other young person in the country. Of those students who have earned a high school diploma, their prospects may not be that much better than their peers who have left school without a diploma. According to the National Assessment of Educational Progress, 46 percent of twelfth-graders are functioning below the "basic" level of proficiency in science, while only two percent have qualified as "advanced." Between 1992 and 2005, twelfth-grade reading skills dropped dramatically. According to the NAEP report, only 24 percent of twelfth-graders are capable of composing organized, coherent prose in clear language with correct spelling and grammar.

Current immigration patterns and birth rates almost guarantee that the majority of the U.S. population will consist of minorities by 2050, with the biggest increase among Hispanics. Yet, on average, African American and Hispanic high school students continue to lag four years behind their white peers in math and reading. Nationally, only 55 percent of black students graduate on time as compared to 78 percent of their white counterparts. The figure is 47 percent for black males.

It is beyond the scope of this discussion to examine in depth the critical issues of public education in the United States but there are currently 29 million teenagers in America and this segment is growing at twice the rate of the overall population. As mentioned above, the educational status quo is graduating millions students who are ill prepared for the knowledge economy. In fact, a report issued by a group of retired generals and admirals states that 75 percent of young Americans between the ages of 17 and 24 are unable to enlist in the military due to poor education, criminal records, drug use, obesity and other disqualifications. At the same time, one American is turning 50 years of age every 7.5 seconds and millions of current workers will be retiring. The current education system dates back to the Industrial Revolution. At the time, America needed to prepare displaced agricultural workers for factory jobs and to assimilate millions of immigrants. The schoolhouse, like the factory, was organized around mass production standards. This education system was efficient and measurable, and it churned out students who were ready to face the demands of the nation's then *new* industrial economy. But today teaching by rote and following rigid academic agendas is inimical in the emerging knowledge-based economy.

Jobs requiring manual labor and little ingenuity have been outsourced to countries where laborers make less money than their American counterparts. In theory, outsourcing should create new wealth for Americans. American firms outsource to leverage the skills of workers that produce goods and services more efficiently than the firms could otherwise produce, freeing them up to produce goods and services that it could not otherwise afford, such as products embedded with a high degree of knowledge. However, most Americans do not seem well suited to compete in the knowledge economy, where science, technological and cultural literacy may make the critical difference between success and failure. A 2006 National Science Foundation survey found that as many as 25 percent of Americans did not know the earth goes around the sun. According to a study on adult literacy sponsored by the U.S. Department of Labor, upwards of 90 million Americans are so poorly educated that they cannot even write a brief letter explaining an error on a credit card, figure out a bus schedule, or use a calculator to figure out the difference between a sale and a regular price. According to the report, one out of every three adults in the United States is functionally, marginally, or completely illiterate. More than 20 million Americans are unable to read or have less than a fifth-grade ready level. An additional 35 million have less than a ninth-grade reading level. Not surprisingly, half of the people with low literacy rates live in poverty.

Illiteracy rates are actually increasing in America. In 1995, 90 million Americans were functionally illiterate. By 2003, the number jumped to 92 million, or an astounding 48 percent of the adult population. This is partially due to the high dropout rates among Hispanic and African American students, which are nearly double that white students, and the fact that over a third of all immigrants arriving in the United States since 2000 do not have a high school diploma. Even among the students who graduate high school, less than a third are proficient in basic reading and math, according to the Alliance for Excellent Education. These dismal outcomes are at least partially responsible for the widening wage gap in America. As noted, from 2000 to 2006, as GDP, adjusted for inflation, expanded by 8.4 percent per person, wages for the average worker with a high school diploma went down 3 percent. In 2006, the household income earned by the lowest 20 percent of households stood at 3.6 percent of total household income. The top 5 percent earned 100 times that amount. At the bottom of the workforce, the United States has many more unskilled and workers than in any other developed economy. In this regard, America resembles India more than Germany. Although the numbers are much greater due to India's enormous population, unskilled labor in India serves the needs of the middle class as domestic servants. Include landscapers and it is the same in the U.S.

As major parts of the world develop and become richer, Americans are faced with increasing competition from workers in other countries. Maintaining living standards in the United States is becoming harder. In the global economy, only knowledge intensive work is rewarded and the elite workers who create and use value-added knowledge have been able to hang onto a work ethic, nearly artisanal in nature, based on personal expression and fulfillment. After a generation of corporate downsizing, half of all college graduates now believe that self-employment is more secure than a full-time job. According to *Inc.*, seven out of ten high school graduates want to start their own business. Many are willing to defer gratification and work hard to succeed. In so doing, some have already been hardened by the Darwinian struggle of the global economy. Of those who have gotten a foothold in this knowledge-intensive world, they want nothing more than to be left alone by government. Generally speaking, they are struggling for their security and rewards and have little interest in sharing it with people who have either made poor choices or who are simply unlucky. At present, they are not advocates for attempting to bridge the knowledge gap by transferring and/or diverting their hard-earned money into pubic investments. If the slow, stupid or impulsive are left without meaningful work, so be it; or as Michael Kinsley has noted: "The computer revolution has bred a generation of smart loners, many of them rich and some of them complacently Darwinian, convinced that they don't need society-nor should anyone else."

Two decades of polling by the Pew Research Center may give credence to Kinsley's generalization. On question asked annually is whether "government should care for those who can't care for themselves." In 1987, 71 percent of American's agreed; in 2007, only 69 percent agreed. While a significant majority believes that government has a responsibility to those who cannot care for themselves, the acceleration of global forces and their impact on the security of the average American appears to be influencing how much compassion Americans are willing to extend to those who place a demand on social and economic resources. The struggle over scare jobs has strained social bonds and while most people do not want government entitlements reduced or curtailed, it appears that they may be willing to entertain the possibility of goring the millionaire next door.

Andrew Cherlin and Bradford Wilcox have written about a generation that can't move up the economic ladder not only because they are unprepared for the contemporary job market but also because they are disconnected to fundamental social institutions such as marriage and religion. "They're becoming socially disengaged, floating away from the college-educated middle class," they write. They also ask the question whether this social disengagement will leave this cohort vulnerable to political appeals based on fear and anger.

This cohort is known as the Millennial Generation because they have come of age at the dawn of the new millennial. They were born roughly between 1980 and 1995 and are the largest age group in America, numbering approximately 80 million. There are 17 million more millennials than Baby Boomers and 27 more than Generation Xers. This is a generation raised in a "free" society—free speech, free wi fi, free music and movies, free apps, free love and free entertainment of all kinds—set loose into the marketplace, vulnerable to identity crisis and status anxiety. As such, many have become prey to advertisers perpetuate that exploit their sexual inhibitions and profound insecurities. The millennials represent the highest number of single-parent households and are the most under and unemployed group, both of which correlate consistently with higher poverty and crime rates and lower levels of education and health.

From a different angle, Reihan Salam has dubbed the "new" economy, the "dropout" economy. Salam sees the same drift observed by Cherlin and Wilcox among what they called "blue collar" individuals that lack a college degree permeating the "middle class" as less than one third of young people accepted to college actually finish. "People who feel obsolete in today's information economy will be joined by millions more in the emerging post-information economy, in which routine professional work and even some high-end services will be more cheaply performed overseas or by a machine." Yet, Salam believes that social networks will create a freer society more mobile society as the command-and-control structures of work and centralized government disintegrate.

Facebook, the social networking website reported nearly one hundred million active users in 2010. Many, like Reihan Salam have suggested that social networking techniques allow users to adopt new techniques for personal expression enabling them to function effectively within the hyper-globalized interconnected world of the near future. The new social technologies do seem to be accelerating the disintegration of traditional hierarchies with peer-to-peer information sharing, thus over the long run, promoting teamwork, creativity and entrepreneurship. In 2005, an Intel Corporation survey of its employees found that nearly two in ten of its professionals had never met their boss face-to-face. Surveys of other technology firms, such as Cisco Systems, Microsoft and Sun Microsystems, reported even higher percentages. Social networking technologies both decentralize the organization and enable spontaneous combinations and re-combinations of teams.

But as governments in Asia, Eurasia, the Middle East and Africa have shown, social networking platforms do not exist in a vacuum. Applications developed by Western technology firms like Cisco Systems, Blue Coat Systems, and Siemens AG have allowed governments to spy on political dissidents. Thus it is clear that these technologies have no intrinsic moral value as they can be used just as easily for repression as they can be used for liberation. The social networking platforms do not coordinate people's action, they merely provide a tool for such coordination. A moral center is therefore necessary to emanate human activity much the same as spokes enable the wheel to use the natural laws of Momentum to get move forward. And where the human activity is centered on innovation, collaboration and the free exchange of ideas, it is freedom that is at the moral center of all activity. And where human freedom and autonomy form the moral center of human activity, a free market becomes the equivalent of the natural law of Momentum.

As Friedrich Hayek noticed, as Adam Smith had before, free markets did a reasonable good job of coordinating people's actions, even though that coordination was not part of anyone's conscious intent. The market, said Hayek, was a spontaneous order. By spontaneous, Hayek meant unplanned—the market was not designed by a central authority but evolved as the result of human actions. The modern Internet was conceived in the same way. It is not controlled from the top or from the center. Instead, it has evolved from the interaction of a decentralized, heterogeneous group of individuals. The modern Internet was not designed by a social planner, but emerged or evolved spontaneously from a network of interactions among agents with shared or common knowledge, such as a programming language.

Repressive governments conspire with corporations to control the Internet and the social networking platforms that emanate from it similar to how corporations create and manage company intranets. Big telecommunications firms that provide the pipeline to the Internet also seek to manage the Internet from the middle by restricting consumers' access to networks and to charge a fee for faster service or branded content. By doing so these telecom companies seek to impose artificial scarcity on the nonrivalrous nature of information the same way a water utility charges a fee to manage the water supply. But water is a physical resource subject to overconsumption to the determent to the community. So it makes sense to regulate water, a natural resource, for the benefit of the whole community. Information, on the other hand, is not subject to overconsumption. So—called "net neutrality" proponents like Vinton Cerf, considered a "father of the Internet" and co-inventor of the Internet Protocol and Tim Berners-Lee, co-creator of the World Wide Web, and many others have spoken out in favor of the freedom inherent in an open, decentralized Internet to innovate and exchange information.

In many cases, therefore, both governments and corporations, often in combination, seek to restrict access to information and ideas for various ends, whether to suppress dissent, create revenue streams, or protect intellectual property. These restrictions tend toward autocracy and monopoly which undermines the free markets and democratic institutions that are the foundation for innovation. Thus, monopolies and central command authorities built for controlling the industrial economy can be seen as perpetuating the concentration of information, power and wealth that is presently tearing at the fabric of an ordered and productive society and impeding the evolution of new social systems necessary to compete and succeed in the twenty first century knowledge economy.

Both Hayek and Smith viewed free markets and the voluntary human interactions that created and nurtured them in evolutionary terms. Thus, most external attempts to impede or inhibit its natural, spontaneous workings, either by government, cartel or labor unions have the potential to be dangerously anti-evolutionary. Today, matt Ridley has speculated that free trade serves an evolutionary or socializing function. Through the exchange of ideas and technologies human progress "was no longer limited by the size of human brains," he says. Through spontaneous networks "intelligence became collective and cumulative." Ridley suggests that human interaction and trade exchange were the foundational events responsible for the explosion of cultural advancement and economic progress for over 45,000 years. Thus, social networks that deconstruct centrally controlled or monopoly structures and that enable dispersed individuals to combine for project work can be framed as a process of evolutionary pre-destination.

Ridley and other science writers, particularly those with a background in genetics, argue that the predictions of a bleak future throughout human history, such as widespread Malthusian famine, haven't come true because of the innate human characteristics of free trade in goods and ideas. These "rational optimists" believe that human progress is, in essence, genetically predetermined. In that regard, what is now called "genetic anthropology" serves the same basic function as did Social Darwinism in the nineteenth and twentieth centuries which promoted the view that both God and Nature ensured the survival of the fittest through free trade.

Accordingly, the natural forces of free enterprise require a company in Baltimore to enter the world market for widgets at the same or better price as a company in Bangalore. American consumers get cheaper widgets, but American widget companies must employ foreign laborers who work cheap, thus putting American widget-workers out of a job. Ironically, it is advances in the very technology that provided American tech workers with so many high wage jobs at the end of the twentieth century that may be their undoing in the twenty first. Reliable and fast communications technologies and the penetration of the Internet into the developing world have made location irrelevant. For companies like Google, Microsoft, Apple and other technology firms, the primary driver for outsourcing is specialization, which can be succinctly captured in the two words often used by consultant: "core competency". This management creed means that every organization should focus only on its central business and acquire everything else from suppliers. With each firm concentrating on production of a specific item, whether goods or services, a high degree of specialization is achieved, which can lead to significant efficiency gains. Higher productivity means fewer resources are required to produce the same quantity of goods and services and resources that are freed can be used to produce new or other goods and services, or can be invested in research and development activities. This, in a nutshell, is genetic anthropology for business.

It is therefore not surprising that companies, big and small, have outsourced to countries where capable people work for low wages. This reality is most evident among the brand name consumer product companies. John Ermatinger, president of Levi Strauss' U.S. division put it succinctly when explaining why the apparel company was shutting twenty two plants in the United States and Canada from 1997 through 1999: "Our strategic plan in North America is to focus intensely on brand management, marketing and product design as the means to meet the casual clothing wants and needs of consumers. Shifting a significant portion of our manufacturing from the United States and Canada markets to contractors throughout the world will give the company greater flexibility to allocate resources and capital to its brands. These steps are crucial if we are to remain competitive."

There is wide recognition that given the cost advantages and unlimited supply of competent workers, jobs now leaving the United States will not come back. The savings that corporations are achieving through outsourcing reduces consumer prices and raises shareholder profits, but without necessarily creating any jobs at home. Consumers with stagnating wages must rely on debt to bridge the gap. Workers must add additional hours. The restructuring of the pharmaceutical industry illustrates how jobs outsourced aboard will most likely be permanently lost. "There are lots of people in India, China and Eastern Europe who can make products of the same quality as ours but at significantly less cost," said Bristol-Meyers Squibb CEO James Cornelius, in a *Wall Street Journal* interview in 2007. "We don't do any basic research yet in these lower-cost countries, but over the next few years, to be successful you'll have a constant emphasis on looking for that," he added.

Alan Lacy, CEO of Sears, Roebuck and Co. created a controversy, when he stated flat out:

> But I think, beyond that, to me, a very interesting trend right now is the whole non-U.S. opportunity that's available, and . . . if you think about personal intelligence and drive

> being randomly distributed by population—you know, there are four or five times as many smart, driven people in China than there are in the U.S. And there are another four or five, three or four times as many people in India that are smarter or as smart or have more drive. And if technology is now going to basically reduce location as a barrier to competition, then essentially you've got something like whatever that was, seven or nine times, more smart, committed people that are now competing in this marketplace against certain activities. So, I think that the outsourcing potential, particularly of some of the more commodity-like knowledge worker activities, we're just beginning to see the first of that curve. I think that, just given the nature of technology and given the nature of those workforces, and given the fact that we've had a decrease in the supply, prices are going to fall. So we're going to see, I think, this huge incentive to shift some of these more commodity-like, knowledge worker jobs offshore.

Lacy's unvarnished comments drew sharp criticism but the essential truth of his remarks is undeniable. The unremitting demands of the global economy will clearly require solutions to prevent an intractable crisis in the United States. Traditionally, the classic solution to the problem of job loss created by technology has been to promote education and retraining programs. In *The Work of Nations*, Robert Reich has put forth the classic response to maintaining American competitiveness as requiring nutrition programs for school children, stimulating preschool programs, excellent public schools, financial help for college students, public investment in infrastructure, including research facilities, and on-the-job training. He concedes that the tax revenue to pay for these investments would come from high wage earners. He realizes that while there may be a consensus as to what should be done, there appears to be a lack of political will to engage in such a massive transfer of wealth without the threat of an economic crisis. But the crisis has already arrived. It may be hidden by the cheap prices from foreign consumer goods and the cheap money that supports credit debt, but the crisis has arrived just the same. In any event, some prominent economists suggest that since the commoditization of knowledge work and outsourcing are the natural, evolutionary consequence of the current stage of the global economy, the *third* industrial revolution, the real political will calls for doing nothing, or at least very little. If an unlimited supply of workers with similar skills is available at the end of a broadband wire for a tenth of the salary, the law of comparative advantage, to say nothing of natural selection, demands nothing less than to tap this pool of labor.

Wall Street, of course, institutionalizes this natural selection and therefore is a big driving force of outsourcing. While Wall Street executives spend an inordinate amount of their time featherbedding and scheming for their own pecuniary interests, shareholders ultimately benefit at some point. When Hewlett-Packard acquired Electronic Data Systems, the world's second largest technology services firm, in 2008, the worry on Wall Street was not over whether the deal would better posture H-P against IBM in the technology services business. Instead, Wall Street analysts fretted about too many EDS employees being based in the United States when competitors were cutting costs by sending jobs offshore. In response, H-P announced the layoff of 24,000 employees, basically replacing more expensive U.S. employees with oversees employees who will work for less.

In this survival of the fittest market, some economists say Silicon Valley is in danger of losing a sizable piece of its knowledge based industry in much the same way as Detroit lost its dominance to Japan in the automobile industry. In the evolution of the global economy financial services and high value manufacturing stayed in the U.S. but much moved to Japan; low end manufacturing moved to China but China is using "indigenous innovation" and investments in foreign companies to move up the value chain; and more knowledge-intensive work is migrating to India. This is a simplification because in practice the developed and developing economies of the world are colliding and competing at all levels and across all industries. In response to this competition, Silicon Valley is adapting as start-ups broaden beyond software technology to include a growing number of bioscience and clean technology firms. In evolutionary terms, therefore, innovators should simply be left alone to compete and adapt.

Social Darwinian remains strongly influential over decisions on how far government should go in assisting the displaced and unemployed. Peter Singer, who the *New Yorker* once called "the most influential living philosopher," and others advocate a strict utilitarian view of the global economy. Believing that humans are not egalitarian by nature, they point to the collapse of communism worldwide as evidence that socialism has left humankind worse off than if governments would have left people to compete and form natural hierarchies and rankings. For those who choose not to engage in the race for life, government owes very little. "You keep them to a really bare minimum," noted Singer in an interview published by *Reason* in 2000. "It doesn't take much to feed someone that they're getting enough calories and so that they're not seriously hungry or undernourished. It doesn't take much to provide someone with the opportunity to have a warm, dry bed if they are willing to use it. You keep them at a very bare minimum."

Doing the absolute minimum is an appealing choice because it embraces the allure of technology or as Virginia Postrel has said the "symbols of an ideal world disguised as problem solving." Minimal intervention is also justified as being in accord with the laws of nature. Thus, there is no need for any large, centralized, government-imposed approach, to more equitably distribute jobs and other resources. The complex, interconnected networks that make up the global economy are capable of self-organization and adaptation. These financial, scientific and social arrangements make possible a decentralized innovation, where individuals and groups work in parallel, scattered across time zones to solve common problems and create new businesses and the jobs that go with it. Like the collaborative development of software applications and operating systems enabled by peer-to-peer technologies, the current economic transformation should be left to natural forces of innovation and creative destruction, with networks and communities of interest forming and reconfiguring spontaneously to maximize the productive power of global knowledge. As economist Julian Simon has put it: "There is no physical or economic reason why human resourcefulness and enterprise cannot forever continue to respond to impending shortages and existing problems with new expedients that, after an adjustment period, leave us better off than before the problem arose." This is classic liberal economic theory, a paraphrase of Adam Smith, dressed up with new age paraphernalia for the twenty-first century.

But the history of economic growth and upward mobility throughout American history, particularly during the twentieth century, demonstrates a willingness to support free enterprise with financial incentives, low interest rates and outright grants. And during times of economic recession, government has not hesitated to cushion the blow. Since the end of the Second World War there have been ten recessions. On average they lasted seven months and involved a peak monthly unemployment rate of 7.6 percent. The worst recessions were 1973 to 1975, followed by another serious downturn in 1981-1982. Sandwiched between these recessions was stagflation and biting inflation. But after nearly two decades of stagnant productivity and wages, office software and the Internet took hold and workers increased productivity, allowing wages to rise without significant price inflation throughout the nineties. The costs of energy, including oil, actually declined relative to inflation.

The stock market boomed as well. Since 1936 there had been eleven bear markets. On average they lasted twenty months and involved a decline of 34 percent. From 1982 through 1999, the stock market provided extraordinary returns. Low borrowing rates facilitated by the Federal Reserve Bank enabled capital investments that increased productivity. When fully realized, a "Goldilocks" ensued. As non-core jobs were outsourced, American firms freed up even more resources that could have been invested in the core businesses, which could have created the need for more skilled workers. But with few restrictions on how private sector firms decide to allocate their resources, big technology firms acquired the knowhow of smaller firms through mergers. As a result, few new net jobs were created in the U.S. Instead, the new breakthroughs that lead to marketable products such as the iPhone created jobs abroad.

More innovations are on the immediate horizon in the form of stem cell research, genetic therapies, biotechnology, bio-fuels, green technologies and nano technology that hold out the promise of creating jobs in the U.S. But the crisis that faces the United States today is the time lag between job destruction and job creation. In the meantime, Americans are free to make career choices to their best advantage. Ideally, individuals make rational decisions based on signals from the market. For example, as manufacturing jobs have declined, Americans have taken jobs in the service sector, particularly in health care. Indeed, growth in health care has fueled local economies across the country as medical and health care facilities continue to replace factories. Aging baby boomers and national health care reform will most likely continue to create jobs in health care over the long term.

While economic reporting tends to focus on snapshots in time, the America's labor market is not static and most workers will continue to take their cues from the market. In 2006 alone, 55 million U.S. workers quit, were terminated, or were laid off from their jobs. During this same time period, 57 million were hired. Even after the financial meltdown in 2008 and the thousands of layoffs that followed, many who go beyond undergraduate school are still gravitating to finance jobs, primarily for the potential for high salaries. In 1980, finance workers made about ten percent more than comparable jobs in other fields. By 2005, that premium was 50 percent. Less than one-third of MBA graduates are pursuing corporate management jobs, compared with two-thirds in 1970. In short, many of the best and brightest are taking their cues from the market and are still pursuing careers in finance. However rational these career choices are, they may not be the wisest allocation of human resources for society as a whole.

In a 2005 report, Duke University researchers concluded that the United States graduated 137,437 engineers a year with at least a bachelor's degree. India graduates about 112,000 and China, 351,537. Accordingly, the United States issues more such degrees per million residents than either India or China. But the demand for knowledge workers in the U.S. is exceeding supply and the U.S. is already facing a shortage of engineers. Lockheed Martin, the big defense contractor, estimates that starting in 2015, about half of its science and engineering jobs will need to be filled. Meanwhile, interest in engineering as a career is declining among many U.S. students. In a 2007 survey of more than 270,000 college freshmen conducted by the Higher Education Research Institute at UCLA, 7.5 percent said that they intended to major in engineering, the lowest level since the 1970's. National security restrictions preclude the company and other defense contractors from outsourcing many jobs overseas. But there are thousands of U.S. firms that have no such restrictions.

From 1993 to 2006, the U.S. increased the number of science and engineering Ph.D. graduates by 24 percent. But South Korea experienced a 189 percent jump over that same period and China gained more than 1,000 percent. In 2010, the Chinese government issued a ten year national strategy that sets the goal of two million patent applications a year by 2015, up from about 625,000 in 2009. Moreover, foreign corporations are often required to share their intellectual property with Chinese partners as a cost of doing business in the country. Some, like Avit Myhrvold, the CEO of the investment firm Intellectual Ventures, believe that China almost certainly produces more highly educated scientists and engineers that the U.S. does.

China is far outpacing the U.S. in the growth in research and development because its economy a whole is developing rapidly. But to date the U.S. holds the comparative advantage in high value engineering and manufacturing and on the whole invested one-third of the $1.1 trillion dollars in 2007 on R&D. Most of this investment has come from the private sector. Of the $3.5 trillion spent by the federal government in 2010, only 1.6 percent went to non-defense, physical capital, R&D, education and training. But even with all of the private investment, less than 2 percent of the American workforce is employed in traditional R&D. This percentage is actually declining as China and other developing economies quickly move up the value chain.

One cannot blame the many bright, young people pursuing finance careers rather than careers in engineering, science and technology if that is where the money is. Americans are free to choose their careers and the national government has no power to direct individual career choices. Their educations have been quite expensive though. As a result, Americans between the ages of 25 and 34 carry more debt than any other generation. From 2000 to 2006, personal debt increased $2.5 trillion. By 2007, Americans had $951.7 billion in total revolving debt, most of it on credit cards. A year later, consumer debt hit $2.6 trillion. College graduates in particular carry a huge amount of debt relative to their incomes. According to the public policy research institute Demos, college graduates leave school with about $20,000 in student loans. In 2007, credit card debt stood at $4,358 on average, 47 percent higher for young people. So educated, financially strapped young people are seeking careers that pay more in the short term than careers that may actually make more meaningful contributions to America's long-term competitiveness. In the first decade of the twenty first century, finance went into overdrive, creating innovative and risky derivatives that tapped seamlessly into global capital markets. Even after near the near collapse of the financial sector, the industry is still attracting some of the nation's most promising talent. As an indication of how the finance industry is critical to overall economic performance, industry profits accounted for 27 percent of pre-tax profits among all other industrial sectors in 2007, up from 13 percent in 1980. Well over seven million professionals were employed in the finance sector in 2008, more than in manufacturing, transportation, mining and agriculture combined.

The demands of the emerging knowledge-intensive economy are presenting issues of enormous complexity. The tools used to meet the demands of the industrial economy have served Americans relatively well during the post-World War II period. For example, to deal with the difficult transition from a wartime economy to a peacetime economy, Congress passed the Employment Act, which required the Federal Reserve Bank to augment its inflation-fighting policies with policies that would stimulate consumption, giving it wider latitude to inflate the currency. Concerns about the oversupply of manufactured goods were particularly acute after the war. While United States' GNP surged more than fifty percent in real terms during the war, Europe as a whole (excluding the Soviet Union) had fallen by about twenty five percent. The few years after 1945, Japan too was prostrate, an occupied territory and dependent on American aid. The output of American factories and farms caused widespread fear that even America's enormous domestic market might not be able to absorb these goods and therefore maintain employment levels. Thus, the Federal Reserve was permitted to freely pump dollars into the economy to stimulate domestic demand.

Foreign trade also helped America export the excess supply of goods and government spending created tens of thousands of government jobs. But with firms investing profits in labor-saving machinery, factories still poured out more and more goods with the need for fewer workers. Under the constant fear of recession and mass unemployment, in 1973 the Fed was again was enlisted by Congress to do something about rising unemployment. Not able to create manufacturing jobs, the Fed again pumped dollars into the economy to jump start consumer demand, perhaps too much so as the currency inflated dramatically. With Japan and Germany exporting goods that the U.S. consumer could still afford, America's economy moved from one based on production to one based on consumption. Eventually, consumption replaced production as a measure of national prosperity. Seemingly the economic laws of scarcity, which had dominated economic thought for centuries, fell beneath the advance of credit, debt and the abundance of goods produced abroad. Even as the percentage of manufacturing to GNP remained constant, Americans went from being producers to consumers. Service jobs quickly replaced manufacturing jobs. And while service jobs paid less than manufacturing jobs, the Fed's generosity encouraged Americans to borrow and spend freely on cheap foreign imports. By 1980, consumption surpassed production in the value of the goods and services that made up GNP, manufacturing was a mere 18 percent. Savings fell and debt increased.

With prosperity based on consumption and debt, production simply diminished in national importance. As John Kenneth Galbraith has observed: "In the contemporary United States, the supply of bread remains plentiful . . . Having extended their bread consumption to the point [to where it is satisfied], people in the industrial countries have gone on to spend their income on other things . . . The effect of increasing affluence is to minimize the importance of economic goals. Production and productivity become less and less important." As noted, savings too took a back seat to consumption and as Ronald Wilcox has pointed out in the tax system was reformed to disfavor savings and investment and to encourage spending, as taxes on interest, dividends, capital gains and inheritances all increased.

By the end of the twentieth century, more than two-thirds of U.S. GNP was based on consumer spending. As noted, this generally was the result of mass production of affordable consumer products made possible by labor saving technology and inflationary fiscal policy. However, it is now apparent that this "affluence" masks the enormous amount of consumer debt and government borrowing that has sustained the consumption-based economy and that may now undermine the economic growth necessary to carry that debt over the long term. When Americans were producers borrowing was a decision made by a discerning consumer who calculated his or her ability to pay before making taking the plunge. This prudent consumer behavior may be traced to experiences of scarcity, particularly during the nineteen thirties, and echoes even further back to what Max Weber referred to as the Protestant Work Ethic. But more likely the producer knew that his pay was based on his production quota and therefore also knew that his purchasing power was limited by his physical capacity to produce. All things being equal, in a production economy consumer behavior struck a balance between meeting needs and, after much deliberation, springing for wants.

The economist John Maynard Keynes observed that the needs of human beings "fall within two classes—those needs which are absolute in the sense that we may feel them whatever the situation of our fellow human beings may be, and those which are relative only in that satisfaction lifts us above, makes us feel superior to, our fellows." Robert Frank, an economist at Cornell University, has re-popularized Keynes seminal observation and has observed that "keeping up with the Jones'" is the driving force of consumption. In many respects, the last decade of the twentieth century, with the Cold War seemingly won by the West, was an exercise in achieving superiority; the superiority of American innovation, its financial system, its affluence, the average American's very way of life, even the nation's military might, over the rest of the world. Individually, our possessions showed our superiority over our neighbors and friends. Our inalienable right to pursue happiness knew no bounds, as long as the cost of money was cheap. Americans identified themselves by brand names.

In *The Age of Abundance*, Brink Lindsey explains the gradual American transformation from a society of thrifty savers to one comprised of profligate consumers. As discussed, the shift accelerated dramatically after the Second World War when the United States was left with the world's only functioning economy. By 1955, an American worker produced most of what the rest of the world consumed. With widespread affluence came a voracious appetite for consumer goods. Even as the economy stalled in the 1970's, monetary and tax policy lead to a boom in transactional, paper wealth in the 1980's. All the while, the average American saved less and less and consumed more and more. The wealth boom reached

1. Drift or Mastery

its zenith in the 1990's, as thousands of paper-wealth millionaires were created overnight. "Are you a millionaire yet?" was an endlessly posed question. Did a millionaire live next door? Was your dad a millionaire? Even if the answer was "no" at least the average person could at least act like one—SUVs, Caribbean vacations, home-entertainment theaters, and cosmetic surgery where all purchased on easy credit terms. Maids, nannies and landscapers were paid cash but worked cheap as many were undocumented workers.

Yet there is something oddly undignified, even degrading, about waiting in a line for hours on Black Friday to purchase the latest electronic gadget, toy or article of clothing. Americans once viewed the sight of Russians waiting on long lines to purchase their consumer staples as pathetic. Such occurrences, Americans thought, were evidence of a society in economic and moral decay. Americans were convinced that the state-controlled Soviet economy had destroyed the human spirit and work ethic of the people. Russians had given up their liberties and freedom for the security of Communism even if it meant the lack of social mobility and the scarcity of consumer goods. Is the tradeoff between personal dignity and mindless consumption in the United States qualitatively different?

What about the water, the most basic of natural resources? Oddly a symbol of late twentieth century affluence, the ubiquitous plastic water became the basis of a booming $500 billion dollar industry. Companies pay little to nothing to extract hundreds of millions of gallons of groundwater per year, but rack up huge profits marketing and selling "natural" water. At the same time, according to the United Nations, the world is running out of water, which accounts for only three percent of the earth's water. Famine and draught threaten large swaths of the developing world and according to Maude Barlow, a United Nations water expert, water scarcity poses not just a public health risk, but a threat to global security. Currently, some 1.1 billion people, one-sixth of the world population, lack safe drinking water. Global water consumption is growing at unsustainable rates, doubling every 20 years, according to a March 2008 report by Goldman Sachs. A study by International Alert, a London-based conflict-resolution group, listed 46 countries with a combined population of 2.7 billion that have a "high risk" for violent conflict over water in the next two decades. Could consumption have reached a point where it threatens the planet?

37

Have Americans given up part of their work ethic tradition of prudence, saving and delayed gratification for the illusion of affluence at the expense of personal autonomy and freedom? As Brink Lindsey notes: "During the nineties, cultural pessimism was rampant on both sides of the ideological divide." Both Robert Bork and Al Gore inveighed against "an enfeebled, hedonistic" society that rejected the work ethic for "ravenous, insatiable" consumption. Condemning the spiritual sickness and dysfunction of a consumer society, Gore opined that "totalitarianism and consumptionism have led to a crisis peculiar to advanced industrial civilization: both are examples of alienation and technology run amok."

The social commentator and lawyer John Farmer, Jr. put the end of the twentieth century in perspective by observing alarmingly:

> So we've been, all of us, "supersized" in the past two decades. Everything from candy bars to fast food to fountain soda to the size of new homes has been juiced in one manner or another. We've become, in a word, enormous. We live, many of us, in enormous suburbs in enormous houses with enormous mortgages. We drive enormous leased cars, eat enormous food. We rent or own enormous homes down the Shore and ride around in enormous boats. Our children play enormously loud music and gain enormous weight. We all consume enormous amounts of gas and electricity and water, and produce enormous amounts of waste. We're nothing if not huge.

One also wonders whether consumption is directly related to obesity. If the endless parade of articles, television specials and the fad diet books aren't proof enough, the ominous warnings from the National Institute of Health, the Centers for Disease Control and Prevention, and the American Heart Association have determined that fully two-thirds of U.S. adults are officially overweight, and about half suffer from full-blown obesity. Among children between six and nineteen years old, 15 percent, or one in six, are overweight, and another 15 percent have serious health concerns relating to being overweight. Coinciding with rising consumer debt and cheap money, America's weight problem skyrocketed in the last decade of the twentieth century, riding from 50 percent of overweight adults to 66 percent in a decade. The total medical bill for illnesses related to obesity is $117 billion per year, and climbing, according to the U.S. Surgeon General. In fact, poor diet and physical inactivity has almost overtaken tobacco use as the leading cause of preventable death in the United States. According to Yale University public health expert David Katz, today's children may be the first generation in American history whose life expectancy is projected to be less than their parents.

Many critics continue to note the spiritual emptiness associated with excessive consumerism and many have bemoaned the apparent decline of the American work ethic, particularly among the youth who appear to be responding to the glamour and celebrity of affluence. But aping the rich and famous is not merely the pursuit of adolescents, who after all are struggling for identity. Rather, it was really the pursuit of adults living in prologue adolescence, adult who spend tens of millions of dollars on prescription drugs, cosmetic surgery, treatments, and other accoutrements of youth to live the "good life." In reaction, many condemn what is perceived as empty lifestyles that are eroding American civic life. As Edward Luttwak wryly notes in *Turbo-Capitalism*:

> Anti-pornography, anti-smoking, anti-fat, anti-beach nudity, anti-sex, anti-narcotic and anti-alcohol campaigns [were] vigorously advancing, while more prison terms, longer prison terms, mandatory life sentences, dozens of new death penalties, accelerated executions, ever-harsher prison conditions, and even a return to the chain gang, all reveal[ed] how economic insecurities [were] exposed. But of all the original Calvinist virtues saving, capital accumulation and investment instead of consumption, [was] the only one that remain[ed] forgotten."

Luttwak's opinions drip with condescension and loathing, as many critiques of contemporary affluence do. Indeed, self-loathing may be the primary preoccupation for some baby boomers. Even the rather affluent, according to Luttwak, feel a powerful sense of guilt for not earning enough money to meet their expectations. "Living in a country that so greatly respects and admires high-earning winners, losers find it hard to preserve their self-esteem. A great many merely lead lives of quiet desperation, searching for distractions, eager to amuse themselves in whatever will take their minds off their failure, from vehement religion to televised sports." While this type of social commentary smacks of routine, undergraduate criticism, Luttwak has a point when he characterizes many Americans as obese, cigarette smoking people with low self esteem caught in a vicious cycle of dysfunctional behavior.

Yet political leaders and corporate advertisers sell the same basic notion, whether framed as American exceptionalism or the pursuit of happiness, that American superiority is a birthright. At best, this belief is an exercise in national deception. At worst, the belief undermines the fundamental values that sustain communities and families—hard work and delayed gratification, which in turn lead to saving, investment and productive activity.

For most of the 1990's and well into the twenty first century, American savings rates actually fell below zero, as the nation went from having the biggest trade surplus in history to the biggest trade debt in history in only one generation. This deficit was the result of deliberate government policy. Borrowing and debt replaced production as the basis for economic prosperity. Debt bridged the gap between stagnating wages and a middle class lifestyle. It allowed increases in government spending without raising taxes. Debt created the illusion of upward mobility, even as jobs were being outsourced around the globe. As noted, encouraging consumer debt was a deliberate economic policy to deal with oversupply and to promote foreign trade. With China, Japan and many other foreign banks buying the debt paper of the United States, outsourcing too was, and is, viewed as just another part of free trade.

As it turns out, the profligate American consumer has created enormous wealth for the developing economies of China and throughout Asia and Africa that export their manufactured products to the U.S. That wealth enabled China and others to purchase U.S. government debt in enormous quantities. In short, the American consumer has not only created great wealth for the world but has enabled the U.S. government to pay for two wars, a financial sector bailout, health care for the poor and older Americans, and the entitlements of the welfare state through deficit spending. In that regard, the American consumer represents one of the great triumphs of free markets and has helped to define the course of human history. What other economic actor could have created so much global wealth and, at the same time, allowed the world's biggest economy to have both guns and butter at the same time for so long.

Since after the Second World War, American consumption supported the export economies of much of the world, first with easy credit, later with stock appreciation, only to be followed by home equity debt. Home equity debt alone amounted to $1.2 trillion dollars in 2008. To get the money to lend homeowners American banks borrowed from Asia and the Middle East. Loans were given even when borrowers lacked the ability to pay back the loan. Incredibly, a person making just $35,000 per year qualified for a sub-prime mortgage of $350,000. A huge market for mortgage-backed securities opened wide as financial institutions borrowed billions more from foreign banks and sovereign wealth funds to buy them. This entire arrangement was based on computer models that purportedly demonstrated an unbroken, endless upward trend of home appreciation. In other words, the value of the average American's home became inextricably linked to the economies of the world. Can it still be denied that Americans are now in a new era of economic and financial interconnectivity? Can Americans deny that hyper-linked global markets will redefine national sovereignty and shape national identity? Is there any doubt that globalization has brought America to an existential crossroads in the early twenty first century?

America's consumption society is the direct result of leadership choices, a century's worth of technological advance, societal restructuring, destruction and creation. When the U.S. economy was based primarily on production, most of the wealth was created capital investments in labor saving equipment. Most of the wealth went to the owners. Eventually, over production would lead to recession, trade tensions between nations and sometimes war. After the Second World War, easy credit, cheap money and government spending for both guns and butter spread excess goods more evenly throughout America's social strata. But nearing the end of the twentieth century, it was becoming apparent that consumption, as both a way of life and as the primary driver of the economy by far was reaching the point of diminishing returns.

There is no doubt that a select few Americans in this time of economic transformation have earned enormous financial rewards and that the income and wealth gaps have increased from 2000 to 2008 and beyond. For some the transition is painful and for most the pressure and insecurity is palpable. At the same time, the credit and debt burden has grown enormous, reducing public investments in education and job training. The tax burden on most Americans is also increasingly difficult to carry, thus limiting the ability of government to raise the resources to invest in education and training. Firms looking for skilled workers and low costs continue to outsource and shed jobs that add little knowledge value. In short, for the vast majority of Americans who are now about halfway through a profound economic and social transformation, the short-term reward is survival. However, the long-term fate of working Americans is contingent upon the ability of the United States to remain powerful in education, technology, and innovation. More than that, it will require Americans to spend less time consuming and more time re-tooling and learning. Assuming that government policies that are politically possible and affordable to achieve, this will require a substantial psychological, social and economic transformation.

For the people who have momentarily escaped the cycle of low skilled, low paying jobs and high personal debt, there is little appetite to bail out those who have made poor choices. In past eras of diminishing resources, a grim survival of the fittest mentality settled over the nation. Today, some have predicted that global economic and financial turmoil will scare Americans straight, that a new sense of frugality and sobriety will cause Americans to live within their means, to invest in their job skills, save more, and to prepare their children for global competition. In the end, however, a democratic government cannot change or direct the people, if the people do not want to changed or directed. While national governments can pass laws to redistribute wealth, they cannot stop technological advance and transnational global forces. In the final analysis, Americans may need to adjust to a world where the United States remains an immensely powerful nation but not necessarily the sole dominate power, a major power among other major powers.

The speed-up of change confronts individuals and organizations with new problems and to tackle these new problems requires new skills. This process is characterized by what some have called "cumulative circular causation." At some firms, the selection by employers of more knowledge-intensive employees and the natural selection of innovative firms accelerate further innovation and change. There is nothing to indicate that this process will be slowed down in the near future by government policies. Rather, there is every indication that this dynamic will continue, even accelerate, into the foreseeable future. At present, it is difficult to imagine the type of political leadership that can explain these complex phenomena to the American people and to move the nation to change voluntarily without the threat of imminent economic collapse. Even Franklin Roosevelt had the Great Depression to spur a national transformation from essentially a nineteenth century view of individualism and property rights to the acceptance that expansive government regulation could have a remedial impact on the harshest effects of market competition. At present, Americans *feel* that they are losing and many probably are. Welfare reform and an unprecedented number of legal and illegal immigrants have created a low skilled labor force to serve the middle class, whose wages have stagnated but who can still buy cheap goods from abroad on easy credit as their jobs are being outsourced. This situation is now becoming untenable for most middle class Americans. In 2008, the Pew Research Center survey showed that a growing number of middle-class Americans felt that they weren't better off than they were five years earlier. Their short-term assessment of personal progress, according to the survey, is the worst it's been in nearly half a century.

The survey paints a mixed picture for the 53 percent of adults in the country who define themselves as "middle class," with household incomes ranging from below $40,000 to more than $100,000. It found that a majority of Americans said they haven't progressed in the last five years. One in four, or 25 percent, said their economic situation had not improved, while 31 percent said they had fallen backward. Those numbers together are the highest since the survey question was first asked in 1964. Among the middle class, 54 percent said they had made no progress (26 percent) or fallen back (28 percent). Middle-class prosperity also lagged compared with richer Americans. From 1983 to 2004, the median net worth of upper-income families, defined as households with annual incomes above 150 percent of the median, grew by 123 percent, while the median net worth of middle-income families rose by just 29 percent.

In spite of this insecurity, many Americans remain relatively optimistic about the American Dream. Most report that in America a person can start out poor and end up rich. Nevertheless, in a nation of employees, most are ill prepared to take their place in the new knowledge economy. Still others appear oddly passive. In 2008, academics Daniel Kahneman, Alan Krueger, David Schkade, Norbert Schwarz and Arthur Stone published a study that may have opened a window on the American character in the beginning of the twenty first century. For the study, the five professors surveyed some 4,000 Americans, asking what they did the previous day and then quizzing them in detail about three randomly selected events from the day. Those surveyed were asked to rate the three episodes based on feelings such as pain, happiness, stress and sadness. All this was used to calculate what percentage of time people spent in an unpleasant state. The report concludes that Americans are little or no happier than they were four decades ago. Disturbingly, the report also measures a significant increase in the hours devoted to what the authors call "neutral downtime," which is mostly watching television. Women now spend 15 percent of their waking hours watching television, while men devote 17 percent.

Television, computers and cell phones may be low-stress and moderately enjoyable. But people aren't mentally engaged the way they are when they are exercising or perhaps learning new skills that may make them more competitive in the global economy. In short, many Americans have simply chosen to engage in mindless diversion. At some point, however, as the income and wealth gap widen further Americans may demand some kind of government action. Jonah Lehrer has reported that recent brain scan experiments suggest that people have a natural aversion to inequality. Lehrer and scientists conducting the experiments argue that brain activity demonstrates a human preference for equal distribution of income. This is called jealousy and envy and they are powerful human traits that have incited populist calls for redistribution since the first days of the Republic. But the forces unleashed by the global economy are too powerful for any one national government, even America's, to stave ff. In a democracy, it will be left to the people to freely choose production and active learning over passive consumption. A major policy objective, therefore, must be to contribute to the learning capability of firms, knowledge institutions and people and to promote innovation and adaptation. But experience teaches that it will difficult and costly to catch up once left behind.

1. Drift or Mastery

In *Gross National Happiness*, Arthur Brooks writes that most Americans report that they are happy with their individual circumstances, but one wonders whether an admission of unhappiness may equate with an admission of personal failure, which most people are reluctant to do. In any event, at least some percentage of "gross national happiness" appears inflated by the enormous amount of psychotropic drugs consumed by Americans; kind of like how a significant percentage of the stock market wealth during the nineteen nineties was inflated by crooked corporate bookkeeping or how the slugging percentage in Major League Baseball was inflated by steroids during that same period. The most widely prescribed drugs in America are antidepressants.

In 2007 alone doctors wrote 232 million prescriptions for such drugs, more than any other therapeutic class of medication, including prescriptions for pain, cholesterol management and hypertension. This represented an increase of 25 million prescriptions since 2003 and translates into an estimated 30 million patients in the United States who spent $12 billion on antidepressants, according to IMS Health, a market research firm. While the explosion in antidepressant prescriptions has set off a debate about what such widespread usage means, one thing is clear: many Americans appear depressed and are willing to take strong psychiatric medications that for decades had been prescribed for serious psychiatric problems. In the nineteen seventies, mood stabilizers such as lithium and Valium became widely available. They were followed in the ensuing decades by drugs such as Prozac, Paxil, Zoloft and a host of others that have been embraced by doctors and their patients. While there is no demonstrated cause and effect, it is interesting to note the transformation of the U.S. economy during this identical time frame. Manufacturing accounted for 25 percent of America's GDP in the nineteen seventies but just 12 percent in 2006. Financial services, which amounted to 12 percent of GDP in the seventies, amounted to 20 percent in 2006. Services account for nearly 84 percent of non-consumption based GNP. In other words, in a generation Americans have gone from manufacturing (the making of things) to providing services. While it could be as psychologically satisfying to provide a service as making a product, the stress associated with the occupational displacement to lower paying, but highly stressful, service jobs may account for some of the increase in prescription drug use.

In *Collapse*, Jared Diamond has examined the dynamics of societal change, specifically the factors contributing to the failures of group decision-making. Among other factors, groups may fail to anticipate a problem, primarily because of the lack of prior experience with the problem. In other cases, the interests of the decision-making elite in power clash with the interests of the rest of society. "Especially if the elite can insulate themselves from the consequences of their actions, they are likely to do things that profit themselves regardless of whether those actions hurt everyone else," Diamond observes. However, even with prior experience and when interests between groups are aligned, it does not necessarily mean that a group's reliance on past experience will result in a good decision to solve a similar problem. "For a year or two after the gas shortages of 1973 Gulf oil crisis, we Americans shied away from gas guzzling cars, but then we forgot that experience and are now embracing SUVs."

One hundred years ago, the United States was the world's leading producer of oil. Cheap oil has fueled the American economy for over a century. More energy use meant more production. Even with oil prices at all time highs in 2008, Americans still paid less at the pump than drivers anywhere else in the world, except for those countries where gasoline is heavily subsidized, like Venezuela. In fact, the United States is the only major industrialized nation to see its oil consumption surge since the oil shocks of the 1970s and 1980s, primarily because of cheap oil. By 1993, inflation-adjusted oil prices had fallen more than 75 percent, and the U.S. was consuming as much gasoline as before the shocks. Since 1980, oil consumption in the U.S. increased 22 percent, as compared to 2 percent in the United Kingdom and less than one percent in Japan. During the same period, Italy reduced its oil consumption by 13 percent, France by 14 percent and Germany by 20 percent. The spike in U.S. consumption can partly be explained by low gasoline prices, as compared to the rest of the industrialized economies, the SUVs manufactured by automakers, long commutes to work and low gas taxes.

America's expanding economy and increasing consumption increased living standards for most Americans in the twentieth century, even though the nation was in a virtual state of war for most of that time. This could not have been achieved without debt and deficit spending by government.

In the first decade of the twenty first century even decentralized warfare has been funded by deficit spending, not by the taxes that would require national sacrifice, and which could promote a sense of national purpose and identity. Thus, the long wars in Iraq, Afghanistan and Pakistan seem disconnected from daily experience. No doubt, the owner of a gas-guzzling SUV with a "Support Our Troops" decal slapped on its great big behind feels that he is supporting the "war effort" but he most likely has not realized the irony of his disconnected passivity. Of course, he supports the troops. But does he support the doctrine of preemptive war? Should America go to war for oil? Should America invest in a cap and trade system with or without China or India? Will he pay more for gas to invest in alternate energy sources? Is he willing to lower his consumption and perceived standard of living for a cleaner planet? Would he have a clue.

According to the U.S. Energy Department, the U.S. consumed about 21 million barrels of oil per day in 2007, nearly three times as much as China, which consumed about 7.8 million barrels per day. About 60 percent of U.S. oil consumption is imported, which is primarily paid for by borrowing money abroad, which in turn results in huge budget deficits and trade imbalances. Obligations owed to an aging population in the form of retirement and health insurance benefits also increase borrowing from abroad. As the rest of the world owns more and more of America's debt, it may well mean that the U.S. is placing its sovereignty and national security at risk. However, even the potential of these dire consequences has not provided the momentum for major economic change.

In the global economy, which is increasingly driven by knowledge, more than a clue is required. However, Americans are approximately as likely to believe in flying saucers as in evolution. Though fully modern human beings emerged about 180,000 years ago, more than half report that humankind just appeared 12,000 years ago. About one in five Americans believes that the sun orbits the Earth. In a 2006 poll, almost half of Americans said that it was not necessary to know the locations of countries where important news is made. Indeed, most Americans cannot identify Iraq, Afghanistan or Pakistan on a map, even though the U.S. has spent trillions of dollars and has lost thousands of lives in armed conflict in these countries since 2002. In the same poll, most Americans thought that the 9/11 terrorists were from Iraq. In fact by any measure, Americans as a whole are profoundly ignorant about world events and world geography. The fact that three of four applicants are rejected by the military is a sign that American is losing its edge. While the average American need not be an expert in foreign affairs, a global, knowledge-intensive outlook requires wider view, a change of habits, an acceptance that the rest of the world is becoming wealthier, sometimes at America's expense, and recognition that consumption based affluence has not guaranteed the autonomy, freedom and dignity necessary for a good, decent and meaningful life.

In any event, the world is not waiting for American consumers to change their habits. As wages begin to go up in China the price of imported consumer goods increase. Additionally as Chinese workers are better able to purchase more of what they make, a bigger market of consumers awaits both Chinese and foreign companies. This dynamic is occurring throughout the developing world. In other words, Americans will not be able to consume at a level that supports the U.S. economy unless they produce at home more of what the developing world wants to buy. The shift in momentum from consumption to production will be tumultuous and disruptive and the U.S. government cannot stop it. But it will require national purpose to make a reasonably successful transition, including massive capital investments in productivity and innovation from U.S. corporations in U.S. plants. Similarly, it will require public investments in education, training and infrastructure. Just as importantly, it will require the cooperation of foreign partners that have the cash to invest in U.S. firms and to buy U.S. securities. It will also require ethical leadership and a renewed work ethic to develop the intellectual and creative tools to manage complex social systems and to avert conflict. More than anything, it will require the energy and creative forces of an elite group of innovators and the willingness of the people to change. The sheer weight of inertia resists. Will it be drift or mastery?

2. The Knowledge Economy

America rushed toward the twenty first century, a new millennium, on all cylinders, or so it seemed. After decades of stagnating productivity, capital investments in computer and other technologies, together with liberal trade policies, were finally paying off for business and industry. In 1995, the nation's factories churned out $1.3 trillion in goods, up an inflation-adjusted 109 percent from 1970. This jump in production and productivity was accomplished with two million less production workers. Investments in knowledge capital also were paying off. In 1997, America's trade balance in high technology products, such as semiconductors, computer chips, lasers, imagers, displays, and data storage devices, stood at a surplus of $32 billion.

While the overall trade deficit reached a record $198 billion in 1997, as a percentage of an over trillion dollar economy, the amount was nearly negligible, particularly since the amount was offset by a $87.8 billion surplus in financial, engineering, technology and legal services. Additionally, the United States held a vast surplus in the value of intellectual property, evidence of an innovative, entrepreneurial culture well suited for success in the emerging, knowledge-intensive global economy that was taking hold.

Federal Reserve Chairman Alan Greenspan and others intoned that the United States was entering a "new age" economy of huge potential. The explosive expansion of the software industry and the spread of computer ownership and increasing Internet connectivity prompted a palpable sense of social and economic optimism. The stock market responded with a giddy run up of technology stocks. In 1997, Andrew Grove the chairman of Intel, was *Time's* Person of the Year. The microprocessor, the magazine proclaimed, was a "force for democracy and individual empowerment."

By 2000 trade policies promoted by the U.S. helped accelerate the economies in China, India, Brazil, Mexico and other developing countries increasing the amount of exports and imports to 25 percent of GNP, up from 17 percent in 1978. This exchange would have been inconceivable during the Cold War with potential markets closed off for ideological reasons. But with the end of the Cold War, the former communist countries opened up. To take advantage of the enormous potential to exploit new frontiers of wealth, wholesale deregulation occurred in the U.S. permitting capital to freely flow around the world. As American banks and corporations scoured the globe, foreign banks and corporations rushed to invest in the United States and buy assets. Annual capital flows into the U.S. for real estate, stocks, bonds, and government securities skyrocketed to $733.4 billion, up from $58 billion only twenty years earlier. By importing capital, the U.S. fueled a consumption binge, making America at the turn of the twentieth century a cornucopia of consumer goods, conveniences and personal comforts.

All of this money also fueled a record number of mergers and acquisitions that were achieved by leveraging debt. The rapid growth of dot com upstarts in the latter half of the 1990s proved a fertile breeding ground for mergers and acquisitions, reminiscent of what occurred in the automobile industry fifty years prior. For example, between 1996 and 1997 the number of Internet Service Providers (ISPs) in operation skyrocketed from roughly 1,500 to nearly 4,000. Because smaller ISPs were able to serve local markets less expensively than larger firms, the bigger firms in the domestic ISP market began consolidating in an effort to cut costs and achieve economies of scale. America Online Inc. (AOL) played a key role in this consolidation with its September 1997 purchase of the consumer online service CompuServe Corp. from WorldCom, Inc. The acquisition boosted AOL's subscriber base to over 10 million, pushing rivals like Microsoft, AT&T, and Prodigy to a distance second place. In a classic business strategy, AOL's size allowed it to lower its prices to better compete with the smaller firms. In turn, this prompted several up-starts to join forces in an effort to compete with industry leaders in terms of market share.

ISPs were not the only Internet players feeling pressure to grow via mergers and acquisitions, however. The intense competition between World Wide Web browser-makers Microsoft Corp. and Netscape Communications Corp. prompted both companies to seek Internet-related acquisitions as a means of keeping pace with the industry's continually evolving technology. Purchasing new technology meant neither firm had to spend the time and money necessary to develop its own products. In 1997 Netscape bought high-end Web server manufacturer KIVA Software Corp.; Internet commerce solutions provider Actra Corp.; Web graphics tools maker Digital Style Corp.; and messaging server technology vendor Portola Communications, Inc. That year, Microsoft acquired award-winning Web-based free e-mail service Hotmail; video streaming technology maker Vxtreme Inc; Java-based multimedia tools manufacturer Dimension X Inc.; Internet usage monitoring software vendor Interse Corp.; and WebTV Networks Inc.

Few if any of these firms had much in the way of tangible assets. None were profitable. Yet Microsoft and Netscape paid huge premiums for them. What they bought were intangible assets, intellectual property, the value of which far exceeded any other property. In short, these firms were competing for knowledge assets. But while John D. Rockefeller would not have understood paying such enormous sums for something that he could not take physical possession over, he would have understood how to take advantage of exclusive market arrangements to suppress competition.

In 1998 Netscape's shares of the Web browser market fall from 62 percent to less than 40 percent. Microsoft's decision in 1995, when Netscape's share of the browser market had hovered around 80 percent, to bundle its Internet Explorer browser with its Windows 95 platform had been effective. People who bought new computers used Internet Explorer simply because it was the browser software that had been pre-installed. In November of 1998 AOL offered $4.2 billion in stock for the struggling Netscape, an astronomical sum for a company that was hemorrhaging market share. Netscape's managers believed a merger with AOL could potentially boost Netscape's share of the browser market, especially if AOL changed its default browser from Internet Explorer to Netscape Navigator. The deal was also meant to increase both firms' positions in the e-commerce industry, which analysts predicted would be worth an estimated $4 billion by 2002. Netscape's Netcenter was already one of the leading full-service Web sites, offering users a gateway to the Internet, as well as online shopping and entertainment services, areas where AOL was looking to expand. Microsoft was also expected to compete extensively in these markets, and the merger would create a company that could potentially hold its own against the Microsoft. The deal was completed in early 1999, signaling the peak of the so-called "dot com bubble."

The big firms were basically paying premiums in many cases for nothing more than a good idea and a pro forma business plan. The people with the ideas and the plans became multi-millionaires over night. The enormous pool of foreign money which could be borrowed at low rate also fueled stock market frenzy, famously referred to as "irrational exuberance" by Federal Reserve Chairman Alan Greenspan. The average American wanted in on the act and did, some in a big way. A bull market driven by technology and "dot com" stocks expanded stock ownership, with the average American holding shares in index funds and 401(k) accounts. Web-based trading created a whole cottage industry of Americans who had given up their day jobs to become virtual stock market wizards. This general sense of ownership changed long held perceptions about Corporate America and Wall Street. When the federal government sued Microsoft for predatory and monopolistic practices, a poll showed that a majority of Americans still held the company in high regard. Its founder and CEO, Bill Gates, who was by then a multi-billionaire, was one of America's most admired people, second only to the Pope. For the first time in history the average American had a personal and emotional stake in the performance of the stock market. For many, the equity in their biggest asset, their home, was tapped to make bigger and sometimes riskier investments in the market. It was a time to get rich quick.

While Americans became speculators, the basic reality of working for a living always had a way of intruding on the dream. America was the world's biggest economy by far. By 2001 the U.S. produced about 22 percent of the world's output, a considerably higher percentage than the United

Kingdom had managed—8 percent—at the peak of its empire in 1913. Per capita GDP in constant dollars increased at an average rate of more than three percent per year between 1996 and 2000 and while the wealthy reaped most of the benefits from the global economy, higher productivity permitted wages to rise for the average American without sparking price inflation. For the first time in post-war history, the unemployment rate in the United States dipped below that of Japan, where government policies were geared toward full employment for life. Contemporaries marveled how America's low inflation and low unemployment could co-exist considering that the post-war consensus among experts was that high employment would trigger inflation. The U.S. had apparently achieved the impossible—a "Goldilocks" economy—hot enough to maintain employment levels yet cool enough to prevent inflation. Conventional economic views explained that this "virtuous cycle" was the result of technology and free trade, which caused America's workers to be more productive and America's businesses to be more competitive. And while many jobs, particularly manufacturing jobs, were being eliminated or outsourced overseas, many Americans felt that globalization was good for them and the country.

The tech companies demonstrated that knowledge was more valuable than land, physical plant, machinery and cash, the traditional indicia of valuing a firm's worth. The lenders endorsed this view and the American people wanted in large numbers. It was only a matter of time until this *new economy*, built on intangible assets like intellectual property, gave rise to a *new economics*. Unlike capital investments in the industrial economy that increased productivity but always reached a point of diminishing return as the output of goods eventually exceeded consumer demand capital investments in intellectual assets, primarily communications technology and robotics, reaped different rewards and had different results then investments in fixed assets such as land or machinery. In the industrial economy, capital invests always led to unemployment and dislocation, which caused weak consumer demand until inventories were reduced to a level that triggered hiring again. In this boom and bust cycle, wages could never rise beyond their marginal productivity. But in a *knowledge economy* built on the inexhaustibility of intellectual assets productivity could raise exponentially, which in turn could make extraordinary profit margins and vast new wealth for society possible for the foreseeable future.

In *The Third Side*, William Ury describes the new economy view that the inherent nature of knowledge creates its own intrinsic value. "Whereas land is a fixed pie lending itself to destructive fights over its division, the new basic resource [knowledge] is an expandable pie. More knowledge for you need not mean less knowledge for me; we can all partake in it . . . Knowledge is improved by sharing it." Ury points to Netscape, as the classic example of how knowledge is more valuable than physical assets. Netscape's assets were primarily intellectual in nature. "It consisted almost entirely of knowledge, ones and zeros of computer code. It cost the company next to nothing in the form of labor, machinery, or transport to create an almost infinite number of copies." It gave the code away for free, thereby unleashing innovative applications, which permitted the company to offer new products and services. Computer models were developed to test the theory that the expansion of knowledge and profits were potential without limit and when the upward trajectory exceeded the size of the computer screen, bigger monitors were installed.

Eliminating of the boom and bust cycle with investments in intangible assets was a radical theory but it provided the theoretical basis for the dot come era. Economists have always more or less agreed that new technologies tend to boost labor productivity. During the 1980s, productivity, as measured by nonfarm output per hour, averaged only about one percent per year, which followed essentially stagnant productivity during the prior decade. However, during the decade more of every investment dollar went into computer and related technology than to traditional machinery. Fifty percent of the investment in equipment, according to Joyce Kolko in *Restructuring of the World Economy*, which by the mid-eighties made up 73 percent of all fixed investment, was for microcomputers and communications technologies. As a result of these capital investments, productivity nearly doubled throughout the 1990s at the average rate of 3.28 percent per year. In retrospect, economists could have predicted this sustained improvement in productivity by looking at the key measures of technological progress, the types and amount of patents issued during the decade. While it is clear that under classical economic theory, investments in technology will increase productivity, so-called new economists posited that the knowledge content imbedded in the technology itself is an independent factor of production. Indeed, they argue that knowledge is a more critical input in production than labor or capital. As long as markets function properly and provide incentives for innovation and ingenuity, productivity will never reach diminishing returns because knowledge and ideas are inexhaustible resources. In short, markets can be relied upon to unleash vast quantities of ingenuity and innovation. Corporations will bid up the price incentivizing more innovation and free trade policies can be relied upon to create vast new consumers for new products, as the economies of developing countries rapidly expand to buy even more. The Internet and cellphone would seem to be the early twenty first century symbols for the knowledge economy.

In *Jump Point*, Tom Hayes explained how the world's leading cell phone companies predicted the world market for Internet users would triple by the end of the first decade of the twenty first century. What have been one billion wireless users in 2000 already had increased to two billion by the end of 2007. While three billion cell phone users by 2011 may be optimistic Hayes believes that the emergence of billions of consumers throughout the world will likely shake the global economy at its foundations. To observer Michael Malone: "We are about to experience the greatest and most culturally challenging consumer expansion since the discovery of the New World." Hayes and Malone see an explosion of new inventions, products, entrepreneurs, and companies, many coming from the most unlikely places, as knowledge-intensive firms learn to exploit the nonrivalrous nature of information.

The key to this explosive growth is the nature of information as a resource of production. In the *Ingenuity Gap*, Thomas Homer-Dixon explains how technology makes it easier and cheaper for firms to capitalize knowledge because ideas are inherently inexhaustible and once codified into a product, can be mass produced for next to nothing. The explosive expansion of the entertainment and software industries illustrate the power of knowledge. Creating musical content may be expensive but the cost of reproducing the content on a compact disc is minimal. Likewise, the tangible software itself is cheap to reproduce but the knowledge that goes into its creation can drive whole industries. Time Warner eventually purchased AOL for $180 billion. What was Time Warner expecting to get if not the knowledge capital of the Internet pioneer? Was the physical price of AOL's servers worth that much, or was it the innovation that was expected to launch Time Warner as a dominant player on the Internet?

Indeed, the same thinking about the Internet drove tech-obsessed buyers to purchase over priced "dot com" stocks throughout most of the 1990s. When the stock in Netscape, which had created a popular web browser, was offered to the public in 1995, its price per share went from $14 to $71 in one hour. Within four months, its capitalization exceeded that of Apple Computer. In 1999 alone, the tech-heavy NASDAQ boomed 86 percent. At the height of the boom, Americans added $260 billion to stock mutual funds. In retrospect, while the boom and bust of the dot-com bubble was the result of easy borrowing and a fair amount of irrationality, it nevertheless was a profound vote of confidence in the new, knowledge-based economy.

A "knowledge economy" is one in which the generation and exploitation of knowledge play the predominant part in the creation of wealth. To understand the concept, one must start with fundamental economic growth theories. In *The Wealth of Nations*, published in the transformative year of 1776, Adam Smith attributed economic growth and prosperity to the "multiplication of the productions of the different arts", which was the increasing division of labor into specialties, together with technological improvements and the accumulation of savings for capital investment. He believed, as many economists believe today, that these factors could produce "universal opulence" over time as long as government enforced property and contract rights, did not restrict commerce with monopoly patents, and provided for basic infrastructure and education.

However, as the decades progressed into the early stages of the Industrial Revolution, most of the population of England, France and Germany remained mired in poverty. Smith's theory seemed not to work. David Ricardo and Robert Malthus explained why. Ricardo argued that "diminishing returns" to the factors of production—such as land, labor and savings—would limit economic growth. For example, a farmer could try to increase the yield of his farm by hiring more hands, but beyond a certain point the additional crop yield produced by one more hand would start to decline. Eventually, more hands would not produce any more output at all. Taking this idea of diminishing returns to its logical conclusion, Malthus claimed that population growth was outstripping the productive capacity of the economy's physical resources, in particular productive land, and in the end would cause widespread misery and starvation. At the time Malthus made these observations, more than half of London's population were paupers, beggars or otherwise destitute. The strain on society's resources was so great, that the Malthusian theory provided the justification for mercantilism, colonization and war.

Of course, neither Ricardo nor Malthus was able to foresee the incredible and exponential expansion made possible by machinery and accelerated scientific advance. Machinery enabled English farmers to increase their yields per acre, thus transcending the limits of the land and labor. Machines, and later electricity, increased standards of living and fuelled long term growth by increasing output per worker, otherwise known as productivity. As economist Michael Scherer has pointed out, investments in more and better machinery have repeatedly throughout history "bailed humanity out of seemingly impending crisis from diminishing returns."

In the industrial economy, there are only two factors of production: machines and workers. But more machines could also lead to diminishing returns as they simply outstripped a worker's ability to operate them. Therefore, the driver of long-term economic growth was not simply more or machines, but better machines operated by smarter workers. In fact, in groundbreaking observations in 1955 and 1957, Robert Solow postulated that additional machines added only slightly more than 10 percent to labor productivity. Instead, the great force driving productivity and prosperity was better machines and smarter workers, what we now call innovation. In short, new technologies, and the knowledge and innovation embedded into the technology save us all from the Malthusian nightmare of diminishing returns. Stated another way, to transcend the crisis of diminishing returns, knowledge must be a factor of production. As such, ideas, in and of themselves, have the power to produce economic growth. For this insight, Solow won a Nobel Prize.

Intellectual assets have also created a whole new dynamic in world trade. For centuries, the economic view on trade was that countries export items that they have a comparative advantage in producing, and import items that they don't. As put forth by English economist David Ricardo in 1817, if in Portugal it takes less labor to produce wine than to produce cloth, and in England the opposite is true, Portugal will export wine to England and import cloth—and it will do this even if it can produce cloth with less labor than England can. This is what is known as "comparative advantage."

But in the modern world, economists have observed that trade hasn't followed the lines of specialization that Ricardo's theory suggests it should. The model based on Ricardo's insight predicted that trade would be based on such factors as the ratio of capital to labor, with "capital-rich" countries exporting capital-intensive goods and importing labor-intensive goods from "labor-rich" countries. This certainly has happened in trade between the U.S. and China. However, most international trade takes place between countries with roughly the same ratio of capital to labor. The auto industry in capital-intensive Sweden, for example, exported cars to capital-intensive America, while Swedish consumers also imported cars from America.

In 1979, economist Paul Krugman and others proposed a theory of trade that incorporated consumers' desire for diversity in their purchases. For example, some Americans will want European-made BMW motorcycles while some Europeans want American-made Harley-Davidsons; thus, the U.S. will simultaneously import and export motorcycles. Both BMW and Harley-Davidson will then be able to take advantage of economies of scale in building their brand of motorcycle, lowering costs so that consumers in both Europe and America will enjoy many choices at lower prices. In *Geography and Trade*, Krugman summarized his findings:

> Because of economies of scale, producers have an incentive to concentrate production of each good or service in a limited number of locations. Because of the cost of transacting across distance, the preferred locations for each individual producer are those where demand is large or supply of inputs is particularly convenient—which in general are the locations chosen by other producers. Thus [geographical] concentrations of industry, once established, tend to be self-sustaining.

Under Krugman's theory, firms face tradeoffs between concentrating in specific locations and incurring high transportation costs. The price of labor is relatively higher in developed economies but the skills of the workforce might be better than in the developed world. Transportation costs have decreased because of innovations in shipping and logistics, but the price of oil fluctuates. In the case of motorcycles consumers will be advantaged by free trade policies and quality and price being more or less equal, Harley-Davidson and BMW will compete primarily on brand loyalty.

Information changes the trade dynamic even further. Where information is the product being made, the production and transportation tradeoffs are frictionless. For example, starting in the last decade of the twentieth century, America's biggest technology companies, including IBM, Google, Intel and Microsoft opened research and development facilities in India and China. These locations offered well-educated engineers that work for lower wages than their American counterparts. Since what they are producing is essentially intellectual property, reproduction and transport costs are minimal. Thus, knowledge-intensive companies can act to their best advantage by locating R&D in India, production in China and distribution virtually. One possible downside, however, may be weak intellectual property protection in India or China but the information contained in a patent is often obvious or widely available. As far as cheap and easy distribution is concerned, Paul Goldstein has observed: "Far more than any earlier technology for distributing information, the Internet is emblematic of the nature of intellectual assets as an inexhaustible public good ... The Internet enables the simultaneous use of inventions, entertainment, and information by millions of users without hampering their use by millions of others."

The Internet's decentralized infrastructure has also enabled many people in remote locations to collaborate together on projects. The operating system Linux is but one of many important software programs that were created and improved by thousands of programmers voluntarily contributing their efforts on the Internet. Linux is freely available and distributed under a General Public License, which means that unlike commercial operating systems, its source code is freely available to the public. Although the open source code is non-commercial, it is used by many commercial firms and operates on software platforms incorporated by servers, computers and other products sold by many technology firms, including Hewlett-Packard, IBM, and Sun Microsystems.

These companies, along with many others, have also tapped into the open source network for creative talent. Open source software development provides a possible model of how horizontal structure and voluntary contributions by a network of knowledge workers can be mobilized to create value. So-called "open source communities" are based on the voluntary cooperation of developers in many different locations and from many different organizational affiliations around the world. The Internet enables open source projects to be organized around a stable group of core contributors who perform key tasks and who govern the project while coordinating the temporary efforts of a much larger group of volunteers.

The standard intellectual property strategy for firms that take advantage of open source platforms is to add some patentable or copyrighted content to the free code and to charge customers for the whole package. Marco Iansiti at the Harvard Business School and Gregory Richards, managing director of Keystone Strategy, Inc., an IT consulting firm, published a paper in 2006 classifying open source models in three ways. They discovered that "exploration-oriented" projects focus on pushing the front line of software development and are driven by a lead programmer or team. "Utility-oriented" projects have little centralized control and typically focus on de-bugging the underlying code to increase its functionality. "Service-oriented" projects focus on providing reliable services to all open source stakeholders and are usually led by a group with a specified governance structure.

The business case for the open source model is the development of consumer and content applications that typically do not compete with the firm's proprietary software, products or services. Firms may help distribute or market open source software and possibly provide technical support or they may directly support the open source software to run on proprietary products. Usually, the core group of programmers is comprised of employees from firms that have a financial interest in the project, not by owning it, but by generating indirect revenue from it. Essentially the enterprise resembles a membership organization, rather than a traditional command and control structure. The work by the non-core members, which can be complex and difficult, is rewarded by peer recognition, not by financial compensation. Copyright or patent laws do not necessarily protect their work product. IBM and others have nevertheless learned to leverage their work, primarily through the source code that supports other products. For example, in 1964, IBM introduced its System 1360 mainframe computer. The company released information about the structure and details of the operating system so that other firms could write applications to run on it. This feature proved to be an extraordinary draw for customers because the open platform attracted many other firms to create applications and enhancements for the platform well beyond the number and variety that IBM could have produced on its own. A market for upgrades was created immediately thereafter. Widely successful, by 1978 this open source strategy led to a 90 percent market share.

Similarly, in 1998 IBM decided to abandon its own work on software that runs servers to embrace the open source Apache software. Later it embraced the Linux operating system, which also runs severs. By 2006 the company had invested more than $1 billion in supporting and promoting this free software, generating revenue from services and related sales. Again, in 2007 IBM helped launch another software giveaway to compete with Microsoft's Office suite of products. Like Apache and Linux, the source code for Open Office is not subject to copyright or patent protection. It is free for the taking, although IBM supports it for a subscription fee.

Developing and providing free source code seems anomalous for an enterprise dedicated to monetizing every asset. But by supporting open source software, IBM is relieved of the burden of constantly improving it, since the volunteers are earnestly engaged in that activity. IBM is free to sell equipment and services, as an elite core of knowledge workers, some on IBM's payroll, continually increase the value of the code. These volunteers, who self-organize, monitor and govern their work, without the benefit of a traditional corporate organizational structure, fit Peter Drucker's profile of the ideal knowledge worker, more a voluntary member of an enterprise than an employee. Many are intrinsically motivated and aspire to add value because it gives meaning to their labor. They are not encumbered by the traditional employer-employee relationship and therefore owe their loyalty to themselves and their peers rather than to the firm.

For some, open source is redefining the institution of private property and provides a useful metaphor for the "knowledge commons." The open source movement, it is argued, will inevitably undermine the monopoly of intellectual property law. The movement's goal is to socialize all source code, paving the way for a wider knowledge commons comprised of information freely available to the public. In this way, the intellectual contributions of society are viewed as a public utility, but since the knowledge resources are not subject to the rule of scarcity, say like the physical resource of water, there is no risk of over consumption. In theory, the community members regulate the quality and integrity themselves primarily through transparency and peer pressure. The open source advocates do not however address the inevitable problems of incentives or specifically the lack of incentives for the potential army of "volunteers." In his research tracking 13,000 open source developers, the economist Josh Lerner found that less than one-tenth of one percent of them contributed nearly three-quarters of all code. Nearly 75 percent made only one contribution. Iansiti and Richards found that eight of ten open source developers they surveyed said that the reason they contributed was to learn new knowledge and skills, and half mentioned sharing knowledge and skills—two intrinsic motivators. At the same time, over half of the respondents mentioned getting paid for working on open source projects and getting help on developing a new software application as the primary reasons for contributing to open source projects—two extrinsic motivators. In other words, without the prospect of a suitable reward, it is unlikely that many people would contribute their best efforts to furthering open source development. As it follows, without an incentive most people would simply take from the open source community (or what some refer to as the "knowledge commons") as a precious few, elite contributors generate most of the innovation. At some point the contributors, like Atlas, will shrug.

Like the individual open source contributors, companies adopt open source strategies for many reasons, but in the end such strategies must enhance the bottom line. Oliver Alexy from the Techische Universitat Munchen Business School in Munich, Germany, has studied firms' stock performance before and after they announced that they were making proprietary software open source. According to Alexy's research, stock prices rose only if firms were able to clearly articulate how they expected their open source strategy to result in short term revenue. His conclusion: "Companies can't rely on vague assurances. For instance, promising to make their software an industry standard by giving it away free isn't enough to convince investors. Companies must also lay out a plan for bringing in cash in the near term."

In effect, companies are attempting to create an exchange system between two sets of consumers: an open source community—volunteers motivated by mutual contribution and knowledge sharing—and a mainstream market motivated by economic rewards. For example, let's say IBM makes source code that runs a serve freely available. The open source community contributes to the software by helping improve the design, functionality, quality, translations, and documentation of the software. The improved software attracts more customers that pay for support, services and training. In this model all three parties stand to gain. The community gains open source software they can use for their own purposes. This software has more functionality and more resources than a "pure" open source project could provide. In this way the community profits directly from IBM and its customers. The customers gain higher quality software at a better price. In turn, the customers profit from the open source community's ability to produce high quality software and IBM gains by growing and increasing its valuation as a result of keeping both sets of consumers' content.

Apple, Inc has also launched an open platform to increase the value of its popular iPhone. It has issued a "software roadmap" that allows independent programmers to build iPhone applications. Prior to the roadmap, Apple had only allowed developers to make software that ran though its web browser. Thus, iPhone users had been limited to applications that could only be used on the phone's wireless network. By giving the software away, Apple is allowing developers to come up with a compelling array of iPhone software, which will sell more phones. In short, Apple is exploiting the collaborative nature of software code by opening a clearinghouse, where users download applications for the iPhone. While most of these applications are free, Apple sells on average of $1 million a day in iPhone programs. Through the clearinghouse, the company acts as an intermediary of software to its phones. The phone's software is freely available and thousands of software developers compete to be included. Apple retains 30 percent of each download and, of course, sells the iPhone by the hundreds of millions.

Google too has initiated an open source initiative to circumvent what it considers the grip of monopoly power over wireless phone networks. In its quest to compete directly with the telecommunications giants in the cell phone market Google has gone open source. For example, in many parts in the world, buying a cell phone involves a trip to an electronics store where consumers can choose whatever phone they want. Then they pick a provider. In other words, the phone, loaded with software applications, can be used on any network. In the United States, however, big telecommunications companies like Verizon and AT&T have exercised control on what phones are offered. In effect, the big network and handset makers try to control what services customers can access and restrict software developers from developing new applications. Lobbied hard by Google and others, the Federal Communications Commission (FCC) threatened the big carriers with open access regulations and class action antitrust litigation organized and supported by the same companies forced Sprint-Nextel to "unlock" phone software so that the phones can be used when customers switch from other providers' networks. At the same time, Google entered the cell phone business by specifically leveraging its open source software.

Of course, the bare-knuckle strategy of lobbying, bullying and litigation is hidden by's brand of egalitarian coolness and Google like many companies take great care in nurturing its brand. In combination with handset makers, a few wireless providers, and other technology firms, Google has created a low cost mobile phone that incorporates the same applications and services that are on the Internet. By sharing the underlying source code, software developers create services that take advantage on the Internet's open platforms. Google's revenue is derived the same way as it is now by gathering user data to show targeted advertisements to cell phone users. In effect, software developers have open access to a host of tools to build new programs and services so that cell phones will evolve in the same way the Internet has, with no central control and little to no intellectual property protection for the source code. In 2008 pushed further by Google and others, the FCC expanded access further in a spectrum auction that conditioned additional bandwidth capacity for cellular networks on being open to all devices and software applications. In short, a block of airwaves was dedicated to open access use. Thus, the sustained combination of government prodding, litigation and threats of litigation, and the strategic uses of open source platforms, have threatened the telecommunications monopoly, spurred innovation and served as a model to open expand customer preferences. T-Mobile USA was the first U.S. network provider to bring a Google open platform-powered cell phone to market.

In turn, Verizon Wireless launched its open source initiative. Verizon, which previously restricted its network only to phones it sold through its retail stores or those of its distribution partners, made the shift in response to growing demands from regulators, consumers and technology companies for more "openness" in the wireless industry. Under the new policy, any company that wants to make a mobile device—either a cellphone or some other product—can bring it to market for Verizon's 65 million customers as long as it meets the carrier's minimum technical requirements. The device makers will be responsible for marketing and distributing the device on their own. They can either allow customers to have a direct relationship with Verizon or buy wholesale voice minutes and data capacity from the carrier and re-sell them to consumers under their own brands. "For Verizon to participate fully in the growth of the wireless industry we need to partner with the inventors and entrepreneurs who are creating these next generation products and services," announced Verizon Chairman and Chief Executive Ivan Seidenberg.

The lesson here is that intellectual property is not like physical property. If physical property is given away for free, it is consumed and exhausted. If intellectual property is given away for free thousands of innovators can use it all at once and it will never be exhausted. Physical property must be controlled and allocated from a central authority. Intellectual property is simply made available. Physical property is made productive by capital investments and labor that typically are located under one roof. Intellectual property does not require a localized presence and therefore challenges the definition of a "job." Clearly consumers will benefit from this openness and innovation. But where will the applications be developed and where will the phones be manufactured? The software is developed in a number of different places all over the world and Samsung Electronics and LG Electronics make the phones in Taiwan. The consumer wins but the worker is left to wonder whether he or she can even hold a traditional job.

When IBM announced plans to outsource 3,000 jobs overseas in 2004 one of its executives said, "[globalization] means shifting a lot of jobs, opening a lot of locations in places we had never dreamt of before, going where there's low-cost labor, low-cost competition, shifting jobs offshore." That same year, Nandan Nilekani, the chief executive of India-based Infosys Technologies, said at the World Economic Forum, "Everything you can send down a wire is up for grabs." Earlier, in testimony before Congress, Hewlett-Packard chief Carly Fiorina warned that "there is no job that is America's God-given right anymore." It's this last statement that chills the blood of many working Americans and causing them to feel anxious and suspicious about technologies and approaches that break down hierarchies.

The open source model as a way to innovate has moved beyond software development and the same collaborative approach is also revitalizing medical research. Begun formally in 1990, the U.S. Human Genome Project was a 13-year effort coordinated by the U.S. Department of Energy and the National Institutes of Health. Completed in 2003 the project has, among other things, identified all of the approximately 20,000 to 25,000 genes that make up human DNA and has stored the genetic roadmap on databases available on the Internet. During the project's lifespan, all of the data was placed in the public domain rather than allowing participant biotechnology firms to patent any of the results. Thus biology, like software, relies on teams of volunteers, notably graduate students and young professionals who have an incentive to get involved because it will enhance their professional reputations or establish expertise, many of whom are employed by universities and pharmaceutical firms.

Novartis, the Swiss drug company, uncovered which of the 20,000-plus genes identified by the U.S. Human Genome Project were likely associated with diabetes. It posted its findings on the Internet. Researchers worldwide are busily interpreting the data. However, the application of the open source model to drug development may prove more useful as an analogy than an application because different intellectual property rights apply. Software usually falls under copyright, which arises automatically and without cost to the creator. Drug discoveries on the other hand are generally protected by patents, which are costly to obtain. In short, the costs of open source outweigh the benefits.

Moreover, software innovation is quite different as compared to pharmaceutical innovation. Software innovation consists primarily of incremental improvements of proprietary systems. It incurs few costs. In contrast, drug discoveries are often measured in years and millions, sometimes billions, of dollars. Therefore, it may not be feasible for drug companies to use open source models in any significant way. This accounts for their powerful resistance to reform U.S. patent law. Tech companies want less protection, Big Pharma wants more. The current intellectual property regime fosters monopoly and therefore relies on hierarchy and secrecy which may be detrimental to a wider society that depends on a rich pool of sophisticated knowledge freely available to innovators. But intellectual property law has a proven track record of generating profits.

Usable knowledge produced by employees is codified and owned by their corporate employers. In turn corporations acquire smaller, innovative firms for their patents. From 2000 to 2006, IBM made 52 software acquisitions primarily for their patents. Patents allow corporations to extract as much usable knowledge as possible from public domain as they can. This monopoly concentration of knowledge works against the open source model of the knowledge commons. In effect, patents create an artificial scarcity of knowledge, thus driving up its costs. The costs of acquiring knowledge through higher education are also soaring, which in turn ensures a limited labor pool of high wage workers. Thus, even though knowledge is an inexhaustible resource, current law allocates it like any form of property which is subject to the market rules of supply and demand.

But the emerging story in the twenty first century is that knowledge work, not physical labor, provides the organizing structure for business success; the basis of corporate power; the overriding metaphor for society and its institutions; and the driving force of economic life. It began with the arrival of the so-called Information Age, but since each age produces is own world-altering breakthroughs that disrupt the status quo—think steam power of electricity—it's difficult to determine an actual starting point. In the 1840s, the telegraph revolutionized communications. The steam engine, the electric motor and the gasoline engine all dramatically transformed society. The first transcontinental cable in 1861 probably gave birth to the modern world. The story of a new information economy starts, perhaps arbitrarily, with the transistor, which was invented in 1948. The transistor opened up a new horizon for electronic communications. The integrated circuit followed in 1959. The computing machine was perfected. Soon thereafter predictions of the fully automated factory floor were in the air and it was anticipated that computers would be able to do the work of assembly line workers. As early as 1961, at least one technology theorist had noted that "in the second industrial revolution, the average human being of mediocre attainments or less has nothing to sell that is worth anyone's money to buy." Since that time, the economy has changed enormously. While such dynamism is a constant feature of a free economy, present observers have concluded that the United States is roughly halfway through a profound transformation from an industrial economy to a knowledge-intensive economy. The irony of this still evolving new economy is that for the majority of employees, employers provide little direct incentive for them to contribute what they know. For many organizations, even those that purport to be "innovative," efficiency and standardization are simply incompatible with innovation.

Thus, many workers in the first decade of twenty first century find themselves in a kind of vicious cycle. They must be more innovative and knowledge-intensive to compete but their employers insist that their work be as interchangeable as possible. Ill suited for a knowledge-intensive future, most American workers invest little to nothing in their own *learning*, and thus impair their *earning* potential. For many Americans, learning simply doesn't pay. As production work is outsourced to countries like China and India, Americans appear content to consume cheap, sometimes unsafe, goods produced by workers, some of whom are literally dying from the work they are performing. For some, consumption is viewed as a bona fide virtue, even patriotic, whatever the moral cost. Indeed, in the wake of the attacks on September 11, 2001, President George W. Bush, as well as the mayor of New York City and others, advised a stunned and anxious people to go about their daily routines, to go out, to shop, and to spend money least the terrorists would win. Retailers capitalized on the patriotic themes and for some shopping took on the trappings of a moral imperative, or at the very least, therapy.

Upscale purchasers may be able to pay a little more for products and services produced by firms that have environmentally sensitive brands or that have reputations for social responsibility. They are willing to pay more for the nice feeling. Is it any wonder that many Americans seem more loyal to corporate brands than to their jobs? Marketing gurus state that a successful brand functions as a store of values. The brand encapsulates a pool of attractive ideas that satisfy consumers' desire for meaning. To encourage loyalty to a brand, marketing must cultivate a sense of belonging and personal identification with the individual. In the past, such a sense of belonging was derived from a person's craft, later his or her profession or occupation. To this day the obituary pages begin by identifying the occupation of the deceased. In a more or less affluent society, or at least in an economy based more and more on services than manufacturing, consumption has supplanted production as the dominant social norm. Thus the social identity associated with being a producer, the job the craft, as been replaced by the social identity of the consumer, the brand, the massage.

But consumption and the debt that supports it have not increased wealth or security. Conventional theory suggests that if labor and technology remain constant, any additional investment in productive machinery and factories will eventually bring declining benefits because the market will become saturated with goods. Ultimately oversupply would create an economic bust, unless demand is expanded. Thus easy credit and government spending are ways of stimulating demand, more consumption. However, reliance on debt has masked the decline in production jobs. Two income households, cheap imports, easy credit make it easy to miss the one undeniable certainty of the new economy: that someone somewhere is trying to figure out how to eliminate some else's job. To survive, unskilled workers have had no choice but to work for less pay, no benefits, or both. Skilled workers, on the other hand, are safe to the extent that they can produce more with less. Communications technology has permitted them to do just that. From 1996 to 2000, per capita GNP increased at an average rate of 3 percent, an impressive sign of increased productivity. But the productivity boom inaugurated by inexpensive communication technologies more or less peaked at the moment of the dot-com bust in 2001. As a result, skilled workers too are faced with the grim prospect of working more for less.

Thus, two income families have become the norm. In 2006, the medium income of working-age husbands-wife couples (ages 25-59) was $73,765, two-thirds higher than medium family income. Eighty percent of these couples owned their own home. But increased family pressure, coupled with an increase in the number of hours worked during the workweek, is why one-third of workers report that they are burned out and stressed-out. Almost two-thirds of working Americans would like to work less. Forty percent sat their work loads are excessive and about the same percentage complain about excessive job stress. In 2001, a Cornell University report showed that the competing demands of work and family were creating extreme stress. Half of all women wished they could work part time, but only 2 in 10 actually did. Twenty percent of the men wished they could work part time as well. Only, 14 percent of the couples reported that they wanted both spouses to work full time.

In the first decade of the twenty first century, it appears that globalization has demanded more work from the average American to stay even, particularly given that hundreds of millions of workers around the world are ready, willing and able to perform the same amount of labor for less pay. In a series published by the *Wall Street Journal* in 2005 a decade's long wage and wealth gap was explored. Technology, globalization and unfettered markets tend to erode wages at the bottom and lift wages at the top. The series concluded that social mobility in America was at risk, even as most Americans wanted to desperately believe that their children at least had an opportunity for a better life. But by 2006 it was clear that middle-income families had lost ground to the highest-income group over two decades, as their average inflation-adjusted income grew less than half as much, or 27.9 percent. During this period, wages eroded for most workers.

Census data reports that median household income in 2006 was $48,201, just a bit ahead of its 1998 level of $48,034. In contrast, wage earners in the 90th percentile earned nearly nine times more than someone in the statistical middle. In the global economy, the demand for only highly educated, knowledge workers is exceeding supply, meaning that every one else was competing with equally talented people in other countries that worked for less. In short, it is the wealthiest tenth of wage earners that are reaping most of the benefits of globalization.

2. The Knowledge Economy

According to the World Economic Forum, the United States is the most competitive country in the world primarily because its laws strongly protect intellectual property and its is relatively easy to terminate workers as redundant. However, it appears that only the highly skilled, knowledge intensive workers seem poised to prosper in a knowledge-based economy. Despite promises by politicians to "empower" Americans, to the extent that government policy can encourage Americans to focus on learning new skills, no policy can succeed without the will and ambition of the people. Ultimately, whether America becomes a second rate economy depends on personal choice. To the extent that knowledge, and other intangible assets, become the indispensable ingredients for value-added, secure employment, the nature of the work and the social identity of the worker are changing. Because knowledge work tends to be modular and non-linear, the work can be performed without the necessity of a bureaucratic structure to command and control it. As such, knowledge work is guided less by a means (a job) to an end (consumption) than by concerns of autonomy, personal expression and intrinsic reward. Such autonomy, however, requires personal responsibility for producing or contributing something of value, ongoing and lifelong learning, and a strong ethical core to guide life style choices. Since most bureaucratic organizations do not value such autonomy, they are impediments to progress.

3. Work, Social Identity and Autonomy

We have been concerned throughout with social identity and the work ethic past, present and future, though a few words here on the nature or *naturalness* of work are warranted. In *Human Capital*, Thomas Davenport expresses a common view about work when he writes:

> If it hadn't been for Adam and Eve, we wouldn't worry so much about work. Genesis tells us that God gave the first two humans a pretty cushy deal. By providing then access to "every tree that is pleasing to sight and good for food," He fixed things so the first couple did not have to work at all.

Such is the common view that work equals punishment as Adam is later consigned to cultivate the ground from which he was taken and thus earn is bread by the sweat of his brow. However, a close reading of Genesis reveals that Adam from day one was required to till the Garden of Eden as the natural consequence of his existence. Thus work, in so far as Genesis is concerned, is the natural expression of humanity, more a blessing rather than a curse. Oddly, it was Marx who articulated the centrality of work to human nature most succinctly when he observed: "Milton produced *Paradise Lost* for the same reason that a silk worm produces silk. It was an activity of nature.'

From the beginnings of colonial America, work has been persistently glorified as something good in itself. Although the American work ethic has changed, it is still very strong. The idler, whether rich or poor, tends to be despised as a parasite. In *Work and Human Behavior*, Walter Neff attempted to formulate a psychological theory of why people work. Work, and as previously noted, particularly knowledge work, cannot be compelled by force. Yet, 140 million Americans voluntarily engage in work activity, which does not include the tens of millions more who engage in unpaid work. In the end, Neff concludes, "work is neither a blessing nor a curse, but simply one of the major conditions of man's existence . . . Work is still a major life-sphere, and will remain so indefinitely."

Of the 148 million people who work in the United States, over 114 million hold full-time jobs. More than 24 million people work part-time, another 3 million work on a contingent or temporary basis. Over 10 million Americans are self-employed. Eight and one half million people work as independent contractors.

Americas tend to work more hours per week than their European counterparts but they are much more likely to experience job satisfaction. Indeed, nearly half of the American workforce report a strong personal attachment to their employer and in an age of widespread corporate malfeasance, over 40% of the workforce still feels that their employer deserves their loyalty.

Americans engage in all manner of jobs and work is performed in every corner of the country. The typical American will spend about 15 percent his or her lifetime working at remunerative employment, much of that time condensed into about a thirty year timeframe. In addition to the work performed in factories, offices, or on the road, over 4 million people work from home. Even prison inmates are legally employed, 80 thousand of which hold jobs. GDP is only one measurement of this enormous amount of work. There is something else going on that can't be measured in mere statistics, since working in America is essentially an act of free-will, a voluntary exchange between employer and employee. Walt Whitman, the great American poet, perhaps captured the democratic sprit of work the best when he wrote:

3. Work, Social Identity and Autonomy

The hourly routine of your own life or
any man's life, the shop, yard, store or factory.
These shows all near you by day and night
Workman! Whoever you are, your daily life!

In the realities for you and
me, in them Poems for you
and me. (Excerpt from
Song for Occupations)

Studs Turkel also captured the spirit of working when he interviewed hundreds of Americans on the job and published them in *Working* in 1995. What comes through in these interviews is the unique nature of work in America and the level of satisfaction that most people have on the job. Perhaps it's because of job mobility, but most people believe that they have a choice. It is the uniquely voluntary nature of work that, in part, results in a legal system made up of a patchwork of rules, regulations and laws. Not that everyone chooses work over something else that they believe is meaningful. At any given time, six million adult Americans are not working or looking for work. Most have gone back to school, many, mostly women, are attending to responsibilities at home. Others are too ill or disabled to work and while there are no statistics on people who simply prefer to remain idle, perhaps Henry David Thoreau put it best when he wrote; *I sometimes wonder that we can be so frivolous to attend to the gross form of servitude called slavery . . . It is hard to have a Southern overseer; it is worse to have a Northern one; but worst of all when you are the slave-driver of yourself (Excerpt from Walden)*. Thoreau believed that the less labor a man did, the better for him and the community.

Most people, at least theoretically, have a choice as to whether to work or not. It's this "choice" that forms the legal foundation of "at-will employment," which will be discussed soon. Between eight and ten million undocumented workers are part of this voluntary workforce. They choose to violate federal law and to live in fear of deportation in exchange for wages. For many, the dominate feature of their choice is insecurity. They do not know how long their present work will last or, if they lose it, when they will get another job. They do not know when accident or sickness will hit them, and though they know that at some point age will restrict the full measure of their physical labor, they do not know what will happen to them between then and retirement, since an estimated $3 billion in social security benefits cannot be legally collected. Can it be said that these undocumented workers have a choice? Or what about people who are told to work on the threat of losing a welfare check? Can it be said that they too have exercised their free-will?

For most workers in the private economy, the voluntary nature of employment allows either party to the relationship, employer or employee alike, to legally end the relationship at any time, for any reason, with or without cause. This flexibility, however, would not pertain to the 20 million workers employed by state, local and federal governments and the 11 million workers in the private sector who belong to labor unions. Nevertheless, according to the World Bank, the at-will doctrine of employment makes the United States one of the easiest places in the world to fire a worker. Indeed, according to the World Bank, only in Hong Kong, Papua New Guinea, Singapore and Uruguay is it easier to fire a worker.

It is true that the at-will nature of employment in the private, non-unionized workplace means that an employer can fire any worker, at any time, for any reason or for no reason at all. In that respect, the World Bank is justified in ranking the United States as the sixth most flexible country for an employer to make a discharge decision. However, the absence of a fixed term contract does not represent the final word in this complicated area of employer-employee relations.

Writing in the 1940s, the economist Joseph Schumpeter (of "creative destruction" fame) noted that corporate organizations tended to suppress the "social function" of creativity and knowledge diffusion. He observed that that the specialization of functions in a corporation required the "bureau and committee work" that replaced individual action and decision-making. Schumpeter predicted that entrepreneurs would disappear as innovation became mechanized in corporate labs and that ultimately the very success of capitalism would beget socialism and central planning. However, it turns out that knowledge leaks and expands horizontally, fluidly across boundaries; not vertically where it gets trapped and horded on the way up to top management. Knowledge expands when it is freely shared among peers not subject to command and control rules. However, as a tool of hierarchical power, information is cramped, horded, rationed, and allocated to advance self-interest. Thus, in order to maintain an environment where employees can innovate, employers must by necessity give up a degree of control and secrecy so that ideas can be given free reign. As Lawrence Lessig notes in *The Future of Ideas*, "free resources, or resources held in common, sometimes create more wealth and opportunity for society than those resources held privately."

In his seminal work on post-war organizational culture, William Whyte astutely examined the mediocre results achieved by research and development departments' at most big corporations and the exceptions that balanced individualism with security and structure. In *The Organization Man*, Whyte noted the "great slough of mediocrity that is most corporate research." He observed two exceptions: General Electric and Bell Labs. The secret of their success was "their encouragement of individualism." They were "the most tolerant of individualism differences, the most patient with off-tangent ideas, the least given to immediate, closely supervised team project . . . [I]t is enough that the scientists do superbly well what they want to do." Profits, noted Whyte, came to these firms as long as the interests their autonomous knowledge workers and the company met at "some vital point."

Whyte, of course, was commenting on two corporate giants, both of which had near monopoly dominance of their respective markets. Therefore one could argue that without the extreme competition of a deregulated, globalized business environment, both companies had the luxury of allowing the creative freedom for an "off-tangent idea" that might, at some later time, lead to a profit-making breakthrough. However, it is reasonable to assume that non-hierarchical organizations tend to permit social learning where vertical relationships are formed, peers interact and knowledge is shared. Shared knowledge expands exponentially. At the same time, autonomy appears to complement knowledge work. "Autonomy", Greek for self-government, is about acting with a sense of choice, flexibility and personal freedom. It is the opposite of servitude or slavery. As noted above, knowledge is best nurtured in an environment where bureaucratic control has been loosened so that information can be easily and freely exchanged. Knowledge expands when more people have it and free information reinforces autonomous thinking and action. Command and control organizations abhor the free flow of information, believing that knowledge and autonomy will lead to chaos.

Recognizing this impediment to sharing and creativity, some companies are seeking to achieve social learning that can occur through peer-to-peer collaboration without having to radically dismantle the organization. This may be achievable through the implementation of social networking technologies. For example, at International Business Machines, some 26,000 IBM employees have registered blogs on the company's internal computer network where they share opinions and suggestions on technology and their work. Employees starting a new project routinely create information-sharing websites called "wikis" for posting memos as they build their teams. Thousands of IBM workers exchange lists of useful websites and corporate resources, using an IBM-developed program for social bookmarking.

Through this social network, IBM wants to enable each employee to borrow from a store of ideas generated by others, including customers who are permitted to log feedback and recommendations. The company wants its employees to create synergistic combinations of what were isolated, discrete ideas. Through this network too, the company wants employees to generate and distribute many more sets of instructions and know-how to solve problems.

All of this networking is, of course, subject to company guidelines. No employee is permitted to be anonymous online and it is easy to report inappropriate, scandalous, defamatory and subversive content. In short, IBM, and others, is seeking to codify the collective insight, know-how, intuition and tacit knowledge of its employees. This codification creates intellectual property that has the potential to expand indefinitely. The company hopes that it is feasible to direct this vast store of ever increasing knowledge for its competitive advantage. This advantage can be achieved, the company hopes, without jeopardizing IBM's disciplined hierarchy to carry out big tasks.

However, the fact of the matter is that despite enabling technologies, most big companies do not innovate well. Small firms produce about four times as many innovations per research and development dollar as medium-sized firms and about twenty-four times as many as large firms. Indeed, big corporations are seldom responsible for major advances in their industries. While there are exceptions, particularly in the pharmaceutical industry, big firms innovate best by leveraging their power: power of markets, over competitors, and over their employees.

As pointed out by David Korten in *When Corporations Rule the World*, the world's 500 largest industrial corporations control 25 percent of the world's economic output and the combined assets of the world's fifty largest commercial banks and diversified financial institutions amount to nearly 60 percent of the global stock of productive capital. According to Korten, the global trend is clearly toward greater concentration of the control of markets and productive assets, including intellectual property and knowledge assets. In the United States, Congress and the U.S. Patent Office have aided and abetted this concentration. Corporations routinely use the litigation machinery to advance their interests as well.

While Smith advocated for a regimented division of labor as the prerequisite of wealth creation wealth, he had also warned against the concentration of property and industrial production, which he observed would inevitably result in monopoly and oppress and dehumanize labor through specialization, regimentation and repetition. Rigidly organized work might lead to the "mental mutilation" of the worker, the result of narrowing the range of work and therefore personal liberty. Smith quite explicitly concluded that where the laborer was confined to simple, repetitive tasks, "he naturally therefore loses the habit of invention and generally becomes as stupid and ignorant as it is possible for a human creature to become."

Smith also explained that monotonous, piecework would render the workingman incapable of engaging in the affairs of citizenship and even incapable of defending the country in times of war. "But in every improved and civilized society this is the state into which the laboring poor, that is, the great body of the people, must necessarily fall, unless government takes some pains to prevent it," he observed.

As Paul Kennedy has explained in *The Rise and Fall of the Great Powers*, industrialization created permanent features of the modern age, including the "spectacular growth of an integrated global economy, which drew much of the world into transoceanic and transcontinental trading and a financial network centered in Western Europe, and in particular upon Great Britain . . . . The erosion of tariff barriers and other mercantilist devices, together with the widespread propagation of ideas about free trade and international harmony suggested that a new international order had arisen . . ."

Historians have compared the changes resulting from the "industrial revolution" to the transformation of savage Paleolithic hunting man to domesticated Neolithic farming man. According to Kennedy "[w]hat industrialization, and in particular the steam engine, did was to substitute inanimate for animate sources of power; by converting heat into work through the use of machines—rapid, regular, precise, tireless machines—mankind was able to exploit vast new sources of energy."

The consequences of machinery and the development of the factory system was stupendous, allowing industrial man to transcend the limitations of physical labor and unleashing unimagined productivity and wealth. This unprecedented increase in productivity also allowed industrial economies to transcend the natural law of scarcity that Malthus had observed. Before industrialization, productivity and technological innovation resulted in an increase in population, which in turn consumed the gains in production on the road to pauperism for the mass of laborers. In contrast, machines created "spectacular increases in production and wealth without succumbing to the weight of a fast-growing population."

Rapid industrialization in America also wrought dramatic social changes as well. While industrialization and the factory system created the need for an increasing population of laborers, wage labor, as well as the slave system in the South, quickly undermined the ideals of republican citizenship that were founded on self-directed labor and the independent judgment that such citizenship required. As noted earlier, Jefferson, who paraphrased Smith, argued that the factory system "bred a depravity and corruption of morals" as freemen reduced to working for wages became dependent and subservient; in short, nothing more than wage slaves who were unfit for republican citizenship.

In contrast, Hamilton advocated for an industrial state and viewed the factory system as an inevitable byproduct of property and progress. In view of republican opposition, however, Hamilton shrewdly reconciled factory work with liberty and property by advocating a paternalistic system reserved for women, children and servants who had been disenfranchised from the U.S. Constitution. In his report on establishing an American manufacturing sector submitted to the first Congress, Hamilton noted that women and children would make ideal factory workers and that "the husbandman himself would experience a new source of profit and support, from the increased industry of his wife and daughters, invited and stimulated by the demands of neighboring manufactories."

However, the concentration of capital required by the factory system, together with the labor saving machines that sent unskilled farm hands and immigrants to manufacturing centers in search of employment, undermined republican autonomy. As noted earlier, by the eighteen thirties, Alexis DeTocqueville observed the emergence of a new type of aristocracy in America. "The manufacturing aristocracy," he wrote, "first impoverishes and debases the men who serve it, and then abandons them to be supported by the charity of the public." This new force was "one of the harshest which ever existed in the world' and the lower wages fell "the more easily [laborers] were oppressed: they can never escape from this fatal circle of cause and consequence." Describing the freedom of the common laborer, DeTocqueville bleakly wrote: "The workmen must work day by day or they die, for their property is in their hands." He also described the wide chasm between capital and free labor, observing that the master and servant "meet on the factory floor, but know not each other elsewhere; and whilst they come into contact in one point, they stand very wide apart on all others. The manufacturer asks nothing of the workman but his labor; the workman expects nothing from him but his wages. The one contracts no obligation to protect, nor the other to defend; and they are not permanently connected either by habit or duty."

As the historian Thomas Fleming has written, "this new industrial aristocracy was in many ways worse than the hereditary aristocrats."

As Smith had concluded, Jefferson feared and DeTocqueville observed, the common wage laborer was dependent on his master for subsistence. This dependency and limited range of choice worsened when the Irish famine flooded American cities with impoverished immigrants in 1846. With indentured servitude on the wane, and with it the legal and moral obligation of the master to provide at least a minimal amount of care for his servant, the average period of employment for a wageworker was reduced to a week, or even a day or an hour, thus making wage labor more sensitive and flexible to the fluctuations of the market. If any single factor dominated the lives of these workers, it was insecurity.

By 1850, forty percent of working adults were working for wages and living in an industrial community. Like the great manufacturing cities of Europe, an industrial class had emerged in America. Indeed, according to many at the time, the wage laborer suffered more than the southern slave and was scarcely freer. Many Southerners continued to insist that Northern industrialism treated labor brutally and by comparison slaves were at least cared for by their masters. However, taken to its logical conclusion, this view led to slavery as the best condition of labor.

In reply, Abraham Lincoln justified wage labor by reaffirming the American civic creed. Lincoln believed that wage labor was superior to slave labor because the wage laborer in theory gave his consent and therefore exercised free will. Just as importantly, though thrift and ingenuity a wage laborer could hope one day to escape from his condition, whereas the slave could not. Lincoln's formulation was a clear expression of the labor theory of property.

However, the rapid increase in mechanization and industrialization after the civil war created deep anxiety among Americans who believed in the value of autonomy, individualism and craftwork. But labor-saving machines increased productivity, which was a natural outgrowth of private property. Also, the factory system appeared to reflect the notion of the evolution from a simple to a complex form, from uncivilized individualism to civilized interdependence, from simple tools to complex machines. As such, the factory was humankind's civilizing force. In a paper entitled *The Factory System as an Element of Civilization* delivered by Carroll D. Wright, the chief of the Massachusetts Bureau of Statistics of Labor, to the Social Science Association in 1882, the factory was portrayed as a force for "better morals, better sanitary conditions, better health and better wages." He concluded his paper with a call for the "Captains of Industry" to "carry the responsibility entrusted to them," for the "rich and powerful manufacturer is something more than a producer, he is the instrument of God for the upbuilding of the race."

From the beginning, industrialization had its critics, first Jefferson then other prominent Americans. In *Social Problems* written by Henry George in 1883, the labor-saving machines were "rendering the workman dependent; depriving him of skill and opportunities to acquire it; lessoning his control over his own condition and his hope of improving it; cramping his mind, and in many cases distorting and enervating his body." Moreover, the predetermined inevitability of social evolution and mechanization unsettled the Protestant belief in free will, the belief in the purposefulness of human effort, and especially in the belief in the value of human character. Nevertheless, a new American working class arose after the Civil War, making wage labor the unequivocal social experience. By the end of the nineteenth century, the industrial workforce expanded to more than a third of the overall population.

The frontier had always loomed large in the American mind and territorial expansion had always in theory been the prerequisite to preserving liberty and freedom. Since industrialization and concentration of property were inevitable, the freedom to leave the insecurity and oppressiveness of industrial work, or the contingencies of sharecropping, for the autonomy of land ownership acted as a safety valve. Western expansion preserved personal liberty and republican ideals but also exacerbated the conflict between free labor and slavery. The battle raged over whether each new territory would be slave or free and reached fever pitch when vast new lands were wrested from Mexico by war.

John C. Calhoun, the Senator from South Carolina, presidential candidate, and political economist, argued forcibly against what he considered the monopolization of the territories for free labor. His reading of history convinced him that all great civilizations were built on a permanent working class, what his contemporaries called a "mud-sill" class. To Calhoun, slavery represented a better condition of labor as compared to the brutal treatment of the industrial worker. However, as Hofstadter has pointed out, Calhoun's position, which represented large Southern property owners, fell by the weight of its own logic. "If there must always be a submerged and exploited class at the base of society, and if the Southern slaves, as such a class, were better off than Northern free workers, and if slavery was the safest and most durable base on which to found political institutions, then there seemed to be no reason why all workers, white and black, industrial or agrarian, should not be slave rather than free." This logic framed Abraham Lincoln's great postulation that a house divided against its self could not stand. "It will become all one thing or all the other," he said. "Either the opponents of slavery will arrest the further spread of [slavery], and place it where the public mind shall rest in their belief that it is in the course of ultimate extinction; or its advocates will push it forward, till it shall become alike lawful in all the states, old as well as new, North as well as South."

Secession of the slave-holding states from the Union was averted for a time through compromise and debate but the belief that two systems of labor were on a collision course persisted. Lincoln's election sealed the nation's fate. The Thirteenth Amendment abolished slavery and Fourteenth Amendment ensured that no state could deprive a citizen of life, liberty or property without due process of law or denied equal protection of the law. In short, Congress intended to protect identifiable classes of persons who were subject to discrimination solely because of their ancestry or ethnic characteristics, which obviously included former slaves, but also encompassed citizens of all nationalities and of any ancestry. In short, universal citizenship was established and the civil rights of "life, liberty and property" guaranteed to all citizens.

The free labor ideal had been vindicated by the Civil War and all Americans were free to sell their labor to their best advantage. All were entitled to pursue employment and own property on equal terms, free from the arbitrary, capricious and discriminatory hand of government. These universal rights of liberty and property belonged to employers as well. Moreover, the nation was expanding geographically and if workers grew tired of exchanging their labor for wages, they were free to seek new opportunities on the frontier as their forebears had done. Thus, the view that the frontier provided a safety valve for unemployment, poverty and wage slavery remained a precondition of liberty. But by 1870, America was a nation of wageworkers not pioneers, shopkeepers or farmers, and business conglomerates called trusts grew to enormous size. What followed was a wave of labor and business reform by the states. Underlying these laws was the recognition that the closing of the frontier, which Frederick Jackson Turner had announced in 1893, and large-scale industrialization had created a new social reality. Unlike the small farmers, merchants and artisans who preceded them, this first generation of wageworkers were dependent on others for the well being of themselves and their families. In theory only was the working person equal to their masters but in practice in was painfully obvious that these working people did not stand on equal footing with their employers. But so powerful was the pull of this theory that the U.S. Supreme Court spent a generation striking down all form of state reform laws.

In the most important of these decisions, *Lochner v. New York*, the Supreme Court struck down a law prohibiting the employment of bakery employees for more than sixty hours per week. "The general right to make a contract in relation to his business is part of the liberty protected by the [Constitution]," the Court held. New York's statute was "an illegal interference with the rights of individuals, both employers and employees, to make contracts regarding labor upon such terms as they think best." Laws "limiting the hours in which grown and intelligent men may labor to earn their living are mere meddlesome interferences with the rights of the individual," and so beyond the power of the legislature.

The *Lochner* decision the court incorporated the labor theory of property by maintaining the legal fiction that capital and labor were in perfect competition. As observed ob Henry Commanger in *The American Mind*, "That the sanctity of private property was ordained by natural law was assumed by economists in Europe and America alike; in America alone that assumption was transfigured into a doctrine of constitutional law." Prior the Civil War, in *Dred Scott v. Sanford*, the court reaffirmed the inviolate nature of private property as a doctrine binding Congress as well as the states and embraced property in slaves as well as land. With industrialization, the importance of competition grew paramount as a way of dealing with overpopulation and diminishing resources. In *The Affluent Society*, Galbraith sums up the approach, which was widely referred to as Social Darwinism, meaning "survival of the fittest": "Economic society was an area in which men met to compete. The terms of the struggle were established in the market. Those who won were rewarded with survival and, if they survived brilliantly, with riches. Those won lost were thrown to the lions. This competition not only selected the strong but developed their faculties and ensured their perpetuation. And in eliminating the weak, it ensured that they would not reproduce their kind. Thus the struggle was socially benign and, to a point at least, the more merciless, the more benign its effects, for the weaklings it combed out."

In his dissenting opinion, Justice Holmes protested that the majority had apparently incorporated "Mr. Herbert Spencer's *Social Statics*." It was Spencer, the celebrated and influential English political scientist, and not Charles Darwin, who coined the phrase "survival of the fittest." He believed that acquired as well as inherited traits were genetically predetermined. In *Social Statics*, he wrote: "Partly by weeding out those of the lowest development, and partly by subjecting those who remain to the never ceasing discipline of experience, nature secures the growth of the race who shall both understand the conditions of existence and be able to act upon them." Holmes' problem with the majority view was that it did not allow of experimentation by the state governments. A decade later a Virginia statute that promoted the sterilization of "mental defectives" was up for constitutional scrutiny. Now writing for the majority, Holmes declared that: "It was better for all the world, if instead of waiting to execute degenerate offspring for crime, or let them starve for their imbecility, society can prevent those who are manifestly unfit from continuing their kind." Justifying state legislation to promote the health and welfare of society, Holmes concluded: "The principle that sustains compulsory vaccination is broad enough to cover the Fallopian tubes. Three generations of imbeciles is enough."

By the end of the nineteenth century, classic laissez faire economic policies had hardened into eugenics, a pseudo-scientific doctrine that advocated the elimination of "unfit persons." Particularly persons with disabilities who were routinely labeled as "mere animals," "sub-human creatures" and "waste products" who were draining resources and producing only "pauperism, degeneracy, and crime." Eugenics caught on among many Americans. A combination civic-mindedness, a belief that science could solve societal problems, the imprimatur of progress, and racism led to the formation of the American Eugenics Society. Local eugenics societies and groups sprung up around the United States, with names like the Race Betterment Foundation. The movement quickly grew to 29 chapters around the country. At fairs and exhibitions, eugenicists spread the word and hosted "fitter family" and "better baby" competitions to award blue ribbons to the finest human stock. A poster at the Kansas State Fair illustrated the basic premise of Eugenics. It read: "you can improve your education, and even change your environment: but what you really ARE was settled *when your parents were born*. Selected parents will have better children. This is the great aim of Eugenics. More than half the states enacted sterilization laws inspired by eugenics ideals.

Shortly after deciding *Lochner*, the Supreme Court struck down a state law preventing companies from using the "yellow dog contract." Such contracts imposed a condition of employment whereby workers promised not to join a union. This agreement was legally binding and enforceable in state courts. The state of Kansas argued that the law abolishing such arrangements was necessary to prevent workers from being coerced by employers to withdraw from unions. The court disagreed, insisting that a worker faced with such a choice was nonetheless a "free agent." Given the alternative of quitting the union or losing his job, the worker was "at liberty to choose what was best from a standpoint of his own interests" and "free to exercise a voluntary choice."

The court found that the state of Kansas simply could not act to level the playing field between employer and employee. "[W]herever the right of private property and right to free contract coexist, each party when contracting is inevitably more or less influenced by the question whether he has much property, or little or none," the Court noted. Accordingly "unless all things are held in common, some persons must have more property than others. It is from the nature of things impossible to uphold freedom of contract and the right to private property without at the same time recognizing as legitimate those inequalities of fortune that are the necessary result of the exercise of those rights."

Coppage v. Kansas incorporated classic nineteenth century liberal economic theories about property, economic growth, and inequality. As land supply remained constant in quality and amount, labor and capital increased its productivity. Rents, as a result, increased and made the landowners wealthy. Wages on the other hand would basically rise only above subsistence level, unless a scarcity of workers drove up the price of labor. Likewise, in the factory, increased productivity, output per hour, would eventually increase wages as profits grew. But wages could not rise above a worker's productivity, for to do so would be to put his pay above his contribution. In other words, property, a fixed, tangible asset is a "rivalrous" resource; meaning that the use of the property by one person is at the expense of another. Attached to property are the legal rights of ownership and exclusion, which government is obliged to protect. When capital is mixed with labor, it becomes productive. The rents, i.e.: profits inure to the owner's benefit. However, worker productivity will eventually reach a point of diminishing returns; supply will exceed demand, thus increasing the labor pool with unemployed workers and therefore lowering wages. In short, unless held in common, property will always result in inequality.

Moreover, prior to the *Lochner* line of constitutional decisions, the legal doctrine of "employment at will" had gained common currency in the application of the common law. Since the employment contract was the result of a voluntary act of free will, a personal service contract could not be enforced in equity by specific performance. In other words, a court would not order compulsory labor for a breach of a personal service contract, the sole remedy being contract damages in an action at law. Unlike the presumption of a one-year contract under English law, in the absence of a duration, the employment contract was terminable "at will", at any time, for any reason, by either party without penalty. The assumption was that without a contract, both employer and employee were free agents, at liberty to exercise free choice to their best advantage. This meant that the employee could quit at any time. However, since this liberty was inalienable, the employer had the reciprocal right to terminate the employment without penalty. As one court explained: "All may dismiss their employees at will, be they many or few, for good cause, for no cause or even for cause morally wrong, without thereby being guilty of a legal wrong." In short, tradition and common law had codified the labor theory of property and the U.S. Constitution was the safeguard against legislative meddling in the affairs of free people. Inequality was the inevitable result of liberty and private property: some had more, others less, still others none.

Still, there must have been a certain cognitive dissonance facing the courts that believed in free labor yet nevertheless enforced arrangements impairing workers' ability to pursue a livelihood. As Henry George noted in his influential *Progress and Poverty*, written in 1879, competition between unequals was a deceit and a pretense. The freedom to contract obscured the harsher aspects of laissez-faire legal rules as applied to the emerging class of poorly paid wage earners. Former employees were routinely sued by their employers for unfair competition and misappropriation of trade secrets.

The transformation of craft knowledge into trade secrets codified Taylorism into common law, as courts expanded the definition of intellectual property and the use of non-compete agreements to protect employer control over proprietary knowledge gained by workers on the job and which was once considered an attribute of skilled craft workers and regulated by guilds or other associations. Guilds, in fact, promoted informal knowledge-sharing in arguing against the broad application of patent protection for inventions. However, as industrialization progressed courts increasingly rejected the artisanal tradition of knowledge diffusion in favor of exclusive corporate control of workplace knowledge. William Howard Taft provided one of the most articulate defenses of this new legal doctrine during his tenure as a state court judge. Taft, of course, is the only American to serve as both President and justice (later chief justice) of the U.S. Supreme Court.

In *Cincinnati Bell Foundry v. Dodds*, Taft held that the technique for making bells was a trade secret and therefore Dodds could be enjoined from using or disclosing it even in the absence of an express contract not to disclose or use his employer's secrets. This case signified the demise of the craft tradition of employee control over workplace know-how and tacit knowledge and the rise of the modern, corporate notion that an implied term of any employment relationship is employer control of value-added knowledge. In so doing, Taft mixed traditional notions of employees' duty of loyalty to his employer with the concept that employment was a matter of contractual obligations.

Several years after *Cincinnati Bell Foundry*, while on the sixth circuit court of appeals, Taft wrote the opinion in *United States v. Addyston Pipe & Steel Co.* Here the court enforced a covenant not to compete contained in a sale of a business. Since the question in *Addyston* was whether to enforce a contract, the case compelled Judge Taft to reconcile liberty of contract with freed to exercise private property (labor). Implicitly the court found that in the nature of corporate employment, knowledge and know-how were separable from human labor, thus transforming artisanal knowledge into corporate intellectual property. By the turn of the twentieth century, industrialism had supplanted local artisanal customs and traditions as the new foundational concept of labor and property. The liberty and freedom enshrined in the constitutional framework as bulwarks against government tyranny and mob rule had lead to the absolutism of capital.

Patent law also became a formidable basis for corporate power. Before the Civil War, patents were difficult to enforce and most inventors spent most of their time suing infringers and imitators. But as corporations replaced individuals as the primary holders of patents, courts more closely scrutinized infringement claims. Further, industrialization and technological and social changes caused by the concentration of capital and investment caused a shift in intellectual property law. Monopolies were generally recognized as the result of superior effort, skill and intellect and thus the law enabled the corporate inventor to enjoy the just benefits of its innovation. In the same unmediated way that natural selection drove evolution of the species, monopolies balanced the economy, maximized productivity and innovation, and propelled economic growth and social progress.

Today much of what we call "human capital", which is the value-added knowledge created by employees, belongs to the employer. Under these circumstances, getting employees to create valuable knowledge, even if they were motivated to do so, is extremely difficult. As Michael Perelman points out in *Steal This Idea*, the overwhelming majority of patents issued by the U.S. Patent Office go to corporations, not to individuals. Almost half of U.S. GNP involves some form of an intellectual property transaction, which represents enormous wealth. Thus, it is critical for business that the intellectual property created by an employee belongs to the business, including ideas that may not be patentable or copyrighted.

As Perelman states: "Ownership of the human capital allows the worker to earn a higher wage, but they have no more rights to the product that they produce then a machine does." Therefore, in information-intensive environments where employees are required to create new knowledge and share it freely with their employers, there appears to be a problem with incentives. To the extent that employees are expected to create and use value-added knowledge, it is codified and owned by their employers. Thereafter they may be discharged at will and prevented from using much of what they have learned on the job to earn a living in the future. The dirty little secret about the "new" economy is that employers view most employees as mere labor cost. They are not encouraged to increase their value because it would undermine efficiency and standardization. The goal is not to increase the information content of most jobs; rather the goal is to standardize as much knowledge as possible, so that jobs can be de-skilled or outsourced. For the elite worker that is actually paid to innovate, the law ensures that the fruits of that labor belong to the employer.

Current employment law is based essentially on property law and therefore favors capital. On the other hand, both federal and state governments have substantial authority to promote the health, welfare and safety of society. The states exercise their "police powers," although we have seen that those powers cab be narrowly construed by courts, and in addition to its power to tax and spend for the general welfare the Congress can enact laws that are necessary and proper to regulate activities that have a substantial affect on interstate or foreign commerce. The mass unemployment of the Great Recession of 2008-2010 left one in three workers unemployed for more than one year. And while most searched desperately for work, chronic unemployment and the receipt of government assistance has become widespread in the U.S. This absence of human capital from the economy, the depreciation of skills and the loss of productivity, compounded annually, represents an enormous problem for an economy that is in transition from an industrial stage to a knowledge intensive stage. In some economies compulsory labor would be a suitable, if not a short-term prescription, to the problem. In the U.S., however, fashioning a remedy consistent with basic notions of liberty and autonomy has been difficult.

Congress has consistently used its power of the purse to stimulate demand for workers through deficit spending and the Federal Reserve Bank has used its authority to regulate interest rates for the same purpose. Courts have expanded Congressional power to meet the needs of the public during economic emergencies but have stopped short of giving the federal government the power to directly order individuals to engage in the affirmative act of working by enforcing the Thirteenth Amendment's proscription against involuntary servitude.

Ironically, when Justice Holmes wrote: "It is better for all the world, if instead of writing to execute degenerate offspring for crime, or to let them starve for their imbecility, society can present those who are manifestly unfit from continuing their kind," the majority of the U.S. Supreme Court upheld the power of the state of Virginia to enact a law sterilizing "mental defectives." The state, the court held, had properly exercised its sovereign power to enact laws that promoted the health, safety, welfare and morals of its citizens. This power had been preserved within the constitutional framework and by 1935, nearly 20,000 forced eugenic sterilizations had been performed in the United States. As discussed, basically the same court invalidated state laws that purported to promote public health and safety by regulating working hours and labor-management relations. As previously noted, this apparent dichotomy was the result of social evolutionary theory, which still animates from eminent scholars today.

Peter Singer, Edward Wilson, and other evolutionary biologists believe that human nature tends toward hierarchy. Equality, they believe, is contrary to human nature, as it will inevitably require government coercion to achieve egalitarian outcomes. They point out that hierarchies exist in nature and that throughout history, humans created command-and-control organizations that concentrated power and structured an efficient division of labor. "The growth of large business is merely the survival of the fittest," John D. Rockefeller once told a Sunday school class. "It is merely the working out of a law of nature and law of God."

Curiously, social evolutionary theory—Social Darwinism—as a quasi-science actually undermined religious values and the secular creed of individualism and autonomy. As Henry Steele Commager has observed: "For evolution, operating remorselessly through cosmic laws, promised ultimately perfection, to be sure, but it was a perfection to which man could not make an independent contribution. Though it seemed at first glance far from exacting in its demands, it imposed in the end a price higher than that required by Calvinist predeterminism—the logical abandonment of free will. For having pushed God back to a first cause and denied Him the privilege, so carefully safeguarded by Calvinists, of being arbitrary, it proceeded to remove man from the controls, to reduce him to a passive element in nature rather than an active element in working out his own salvation. By subjecting the destinies of man to the inexorable operations of natural selection, it vetoed man's interposition and nullified his own efforts. Progress was sure, but the price was submission and conformity."

In short, the impact of social evolutionary thinking on the market was to diminish the power of the state to ensure the survival of the fittest. However, to advance the survival of the fittest, the doctrine paradoxically increased the power of the state to regulate procreation and social relations. This, of course, helped support and justify a governing elite of capital at the expense of labor, which was viewed interchangeably as God's will. Racial segregation and miscegenation laws were justified in the same manner.

Social Darwinism served both the interest of the market and the state. Its essential goal, like Taylorism, was efficiency, the efficient regulation of both material and human resources in an era of scarcity. Such regulation included the criminalization of contraception and abortion by the states as well. A particular virulent strain of social evolutionary thought took hold in Europe, particularly in Germany. When Hitler ascended to the chancellery, following legal, parliamentary elections, the race laws that followed were a natural extension of Western race ideology. The experimentation by Nazi doctors in genetics and state policies fostering a master race through procreation and child-rearing laws followed quickly. It is no coincidence, therefore, that Social Darwinism and eugenics fell quickly into disrepute after Nazi atrocities became widely known. This helped create a critical mass for constitutional change in America.

In 1942 the U.S. Supreme Court struck down Oklahoma's Habitual Criminal Sterilization Act, declaring, "marriage and procreation are fundamental to the very existence and survival of the race." In *Griswold v. Connecticut*, decided in 1965, the U.S. Supreme Court invalidated a Connecticut law that criminalized contraception between married couples. In so ruling, the court cobbled together a general protection against government invasions "of the sanctity of a man's home and the privacies of life." A so-called "zone of privacy" was created, enumerated by express constitutional protections, including the right to be free from unreasonable searches and seizures.

The dissenting opinion in *Griswold* would have been more deferential to the state's legislative judgment that the anti-contraception statute was needed to promote public morality, even though it conceded that the statute was "an uncommonly silly law" and "as a practical matter, obviously unenforceable." But the majority opinion discerned the central problem with the law, observing that the logic for upholding the law meant that if a state had the power to outlaw voluntary birth control by married couples, then, by the same reasoning a law requiring compulsory birth control was also valid. As it follows, if the power of the state could be used to promote birth, it could just as easily be used to promote sterilization or abortion, even euthanasia.

Roe v. Wade, which held that the state could not criminalize most abortions, was the logical extension of *Griswold*, finding a "right to privacy" in the decision to abort a fetus in the first trimester, although conceding that the state does have an important interest in preserving and protecting the health of pregnant women and in protecting the "potentiality for human life." But the undercurrent in *Griswold* remains: a government that can force a woman to bring a baby to term is the same government that can mandate an abortion, which is what the Chinese government had done in promoting its notorious one child policy.

Six years after *Roe v. Wade*, the New Jersey Supreme Court decided *In re Quinlan*, which held that the constitutional right to privacy encompassed the right to self-determination, "broad enough to encompass a patient's right to decline medical treatment under certain circumstances, in much the same way as it is broad enough to encompass a woman's decision to terminate a pregnancy under certain circumstances." The right to privacy or liberty, which ironically is derived from the same due process clause that was used to invalidate the fair labor laws during the height of nineteenth century free market capitalism, has been used to invalidate state laws restricting all manner of consensual adult behavior, including decisions about life and death.

Constitutionally speaking, as freedom has been constricted in the economic sphere allowing for more regulation, liberty has been expanded in the personal sphere. Thus there is no constitutional reason that reproductive liberty should not extend to using the same genetic tests that screen for diseases to target other genetic predispositions. What if prospective parents could screen for short or shy or blue-eyed or blond? What if prospective parents could screen for cognitive ability or creativity? This is largely an unregulated universe of treatment but as the secrets of the human genome become revealed almost daily, the ability to isolate specific genes and therefore identify specific physical and mental traits is becoming almost commonplace. It is entirely conceivable that prospective parents with the resources will be able to enhance genetic characteristics of their offspring, or even create additional ones. In other words, science and technology and the liberty to use them is redefining the American pursuit of happiness, creating a type of *artificial* selection.

Americans have long been preoccupied with the utopian notion of social perfection. Influential sociologists such as Lester Frank Ward, writing in the late nineteenth century, noted that liberty and human free will could repudiate natural selection by apply "art"—or that which is *artificial*. "The constant tendency," Ward wrote, "is to render everything more artificial, which means more and more perfect. Human institutions are not exempt from this all-pervading spirit of improvement. They, too, are artificial, conceived in the ingenious brain and wrought with mental skill born of inventive genius. Man's destiny is in his own hands . . . His power over nature is unlimited. He can make it its servant and appropriate to his own use all the mighty forces of the universe."

The implicit assumption here is that government can act as a human agent through collective action that can influence or even direct the trajectory of natural law and determine human destiny. Virginia's sterilization law was an example of how far government, in that case state government, could go to promote the public health and welfare and the Supreme Court decision that upheld that authority is an example of how far a court can go when evolutionary science is purportedly on its side.

Prominent anthropological biologists have advanced the theory that evolution favors cooperative traits over competitive ones in selecting for success. Darwin recognized this when he obverted that adaptation and change were the drivers of survival. For example, important information that increases the chances of survival is shared through cooperative systems. A person cannot be forced to share what they know through a compulsory system. Knowledge, the ultimate nonrivalrous resource, can be shared and every act of sharing can be multiplied exponentially. After twenty years of studying creativity in teams, Fritz Dressler puts it this way: "When connected together and lifted into a team mind, each individual mind becomes the interactive environment for every other mind . . . The creative magic that is the team mind resides in both the many parallel interactions and the larger actions common to all members."

This "team creativity", of course, can be easily leveraged through the Internet, which is not controlled from the center. Through the Internet, transaction costs, the costs involved in bringing a product to market, are thereby reduced. Since the purpose of a corporation, in part, is to concentrate capital and labor to reduce transaction costs, the economic basis for the corporate hierarchy is reduced. With the continual reduction of transaction costs, it is clear that individual success will depend much more on networks, small, inter-dependent organizations, and autonomous entrepreneurship.

In her book, *RenGen: The Rise of the Cultural Consumer and What It Means to Your Business*, Patricia Martin predicts a new era of entrepreneurship, "the largest class of entrepreneurs that the United States has seen in a long time. Not only are [a younger generation] driven to do original work, but they are going to want to live that out in originality designed careers. In order to do that, they will work hard to create their own enterprises because that is where they can realize their dreams. Most especially, for this generation, their agenda is to collaborate, to connect and to create." Thus, a new human evolutionary model, derived from teams and collaboration, may now be competing with the exiting model, derived from hierarchy and command-and-control structures. If knowledge is the most important resource, and it must have collaboration to thrive, hierarchy and top-down power structures have become the enemy of survival.

Additionally, if entrepreneurship and innovation are to remain dominant features of the *new* economy, property rights and access to capital are vital. America remains the most competitive nation in the world on these counts. However, American entrepreneurs will rely much more on foreign capital than ever before. The Panic of 2008 has laid the excesses of debt and consumption bare. The self-inflicted political wounds of sovereign debt default has undermined the role of the dollar as the world's primary currency. Writing in the *People's Daily*, Chinese economist Shi Jianxum has written: "The world urgently needs to create a diversified currency and financial system and fair and just financial order not dependent on the United States." The German Finance Minister Peer Steinbeck noted: "The U.S. will lose its status as the superpower of the global financial system . . . The global financial system will become more multipolar, with the dollar being supplemented by the yen, the euro and the Chinese yuan."

While an American nationalist might recoil from these foreigners, the immutable forces of globalization simply cannot be denied. Innovators will need to tap into foreign capital markets, meaning that the nationalist impulse to retreat from free trade will undermine American competitiveness. The impulse toward centralization will undermine cross-cultural collaboration. Nationality itself will need redefinition, as the concentration of power within the nation-state begins to decentralize among global markets. Liberty in the global economy not only means freedom from centralized corporate power but also freedom from the confines of national ideologies. Finally, liberty in the global economy also means freedom from the conventions that support social hierarchies, including the creeping nostalgia and fear that impair clear and practical thinking.

Thomas Friedman writing for the *New York Times* has observed: "In this age of globalization, government matters more than ever. Smart, fiscally strong governments are the ones best able to empower their people to compete and win." I respectfully disagree. In the knowledge-intensive global economy, smart, morally strong *people* will compete and at least have the best chance to win. Friedman hopes for a leader with the courage to tell the American people the truth so that they can make hard choices. However, as Jonathan Lethem has noted, in the long aftermath of 9/11, which calls out for a passion for truth and freedom, Americans instead have settled for passivity and silence. In other words, American exceptionalism does not necessarily extend to Americans being exceptional.

Peggy Noonan accurately reflected the mood of the American people near the end of the first decade of the twenty first century when she observed "a sense that our great institutions are faltering, that they've forgotten the mission; that the old America in which we were raised is receding, and something new and unknown is taking it's place." Ms. Noonan has called for a "patriotic grace" that "eschews the politically cheap and manipulative." For Mr. Friedman, hope serves as a substitute for effort. For Ms. Noonan nostalgia serves as history.

At the turn of the twentieth first century, the core values of capital and capitalism stood alone as the dominant force of society, east and west. In many ways industrial capitalism is running its course in the West, particularly in America, and a new, post-industrial capitalism is emerging, one that relies more on creating and leveraging information and less on the production of tangible goods. In nature, human creativity shares few constraints that limit the availability of capital and physical goods. But even as knowledge replaces physical assets as the primary means of production, creativity and innovation are not, in practice, subject to the egalitarian impulse of equal distribution or allocation.

Big organizations, particularly corporations, tend toward monopoly power whether in the old or *new* economy. Knowledge, while theoretically inexhaustible, remains the province of corporate elites and experts, partially due to how economic power is distributed and partially due to a stagnating sense of personal entitlement. The nature of work is becoming more knowledge-intensive, but many Americans are ill suited for the jobs that require creating and leveraging knowledge. In short, millions of Americans who assumed that twentieth century prosperity would deliver perpetual affluence risk being cast adrift without even a social identity on which to cling. In the heat of competition within the global economy, it is difficult to predict an outcome that will not be the result of wrenching change. But as John F. Kennedy observed: "Change is the law of life. And those who look only to the past or present are certain to miss the future."

In the midst of the Panic of 2008, David Wessel of the *Wall Street Journal* wrote: "Gone is the faith, shared by the nation's leadership with varying degrees of enthusiasm, that the best road to prosperity is to unleash financial markets to allocate capital, take risks, enjoy profits, and absorb losses. Erased is the hope that markets correct themselves when they overshoot. Also scrapped is the notion that government's role is to get out of the way." Again, I respectfully disagree to the extent that Wessel is expressing nostalgia for a return to a more muscular leadership of the nation-state, a reprise of the "greatest generation."

As big as the nearly $15 trillion U.S. economy is, the greed driven financial crisis that resulted from a 1999 deregulation law and the excessive leverage that left the U.S. in enormous debt required the resources of an international banking system to stem the tide of defaults and bankruptcies. In a $54 trillion world economy with vast pools of liquidity spread among free-trading markets, the United States needed a worldwide effort to support its financial system as the Federal Reserve depleted half of its assets to avert a full-fledged financial meltdown. To believe that the Panic of 2008 would result in the re-emergence of the strong nation-state, a "new nationalism" is to belie the reality that foreign banks and sovereign funds own much of the U.S. debt, including its junk debt, and that this inter-dependence motivated foreign central banks to inject billions of dollars into shaky U.S. and world markets. When Congress was urged to authorize the U.S. Treasury to sell bonds to replenish the Federal Reserve and to create a government agency to buy up bad debt, foreigners were expected to purchase the bonds.

The re-emergence of Russian belligerence in the Caucasus does not represent a credible threat to the immutable internationalization of labor and capital. While it true that Russia boosted its military spending by twenty five percent, its revanchist policies still appear incompatible with the open markets and small armies required by the economic leaders of the global economy. Simultaneous with Russia's splendid little war in Georgia, its stock market dropped 55 percent, a decline of $680 billion in value and foreign investors pulled more than $435 billion in assets from Russia's markets.

Nor will the Panic of 2008 and its aftermath result in "riots in the street," the implicit prediction of Doug Stumpf, the author of *Confessions of a Wall Street Shoeshine Boy*. True, all the big Wall Street firms that made fantastic profits on complex schemes and exotic transactions have engaged in an orgy of downsizing, which Stumpf describes with chilling post-modern detachment: "Your phone rings, and you're told to report to human resources. You stand up and announce to people in your row that it's all over. If they like you they applaud. In many cases, they'll be the ones to clean out your desk. Right after you get fired, you're marched out of the building by security." But the traders who were used to receiving six-figure annual bonuses will not be going on any bonus marches any time soon, at least not as long as the stash in the wine cellar holds out.

As the bailout plan was being hashed out, Americans complained about the risk of moral hazard. Others claimed the plan was socialism; others thought that the financial meltdown was God's will, or at least the result of the market's natural course. Still others opposed the plan as a bailout of the greedy rich. Some advocated caps on executive compensation and others oddly opposed the plan because it did nothing to fix the health care system. Perhaps this fractured dialogue is understandable. Average Americans gagged at the prospect of bailing out millionaires whose greed and stupidly brought the financial system to the bring collapse. But it also illustrates how little we know about global finance and how much our livelihood and way of life depends on globalization. Without global capital preventing a freeze on lending, every American would be severely and directly harmed. This reality, however, collides with the notion that American is the sole superpower, master of its own fate. This reality also lays bare the unsettling prospect that Americans are not up to the task to deal with the demands of the twenty first century.

In the industrial economy, when material wealth became concentrated in too few hands, thereby risking economic collapse, government was able to enact laws to promote competition on a more equal footing and to redistribute some of the wealth through tax and spend policies. But when wealth is based on intangible assets, such as intellectual property, broadly

3. Work, Social Identity and Autonomy

defined, what tools does government have to redistribute cognitive abilities, which are inherently unequal? What kind of power is necessary to redirect natural selection? And who decides?

A substantial portion of the population either distrusts or is disillusioned with the federal government. For them, the federal government is losing legitimacy. According to the American Enterprise Institute, during the Eisenhower and Kennedy administrations, about three about three quarters of Americans trusted the government to do the right thing most of the time. In 1995, one in two registered voters didn't bother to vote for president. By 1997 about three quarters of the population stated that they did not trust the government to do the right thing most of the time. For good reason: banking deregulation, NAFTA, and welfare reform created a huge wage and wealth gap. By 2005 the average salary at Goldman Sachs was about $600,000 per year; the minimum wage was $5.15 per hour; and the average hourly wage had not gone up in ten years, adjusted for inflation. By 2008 three in four Americans thought that the federal government was not competent to fix the economy, the same Americans who, ten years before, said that things were never better. In the face of this pessimism and disillusionment, nostalgia for a strong government led by visionary leaders who mobilize a virtuous citizenry has become the new civic religion.

That year Barack Obama emerged to play his part, campaigning on a platform of hope and nostalgia. The poisonous reaction to Obama was predictable given his support for national health care and the Employer Free Choice Act, which would have made union organizing easier. Unions are meant to counterbalance capital's power with labor power. Unions bargain for a greater share of the profits. They are perceived by capitalists in the harshest light and many owners would rather close shop than recognize a union as the exclusive bargaining representative of their employees. Even more than national health care which was supported by much of the health care and pharmaceutical industries, promotion of labor unions triggered a virulent attack against 'socialistic" government.

Ironically, as Americans have experienced more freedom in their social relations (single parenting, same-sex civil unions), bodily integrity (abortion, surrogate parenting, living wills), and personal expression (body art, transsexualism) we have experienced less control of our economic livelihoods. As the Panic of 2008 set in it was apparent almost immediately that capital had so fully and completely engulfed the American experience. All the shibboleths about free markets, frugality, prudent risk and self-reliance tumbled with the stock market. Americans were left unmoored and unstable, disconnected from the meaning of their labor, a profoundly unsettling feeling for a people who had been raised to believe that they were exceptional in the world, whose leaders had continually told them that they were the most free.

For Americans who profess a belief in liberty and autonomy, it is curious that so many have freely chosen meaningless work and dead end jobs. For a people who extol in creative change, it is curious that so many have settled for dull complacency. For a people who profess a belief in God, it is stunning that so many have lost faith in their ability to make a difference in their lives, and have instead adopted a grim, secular predetermined fate of working to consume.

The knowledge economy is placing an awesome premium on value-added knowledge work and devaluing most everything else, including professional, technical and administrative work. While these jobs may not be displaced wholesale, the modularization of many tasks may make these jobs permanently contingent in nature. As organizational direction and control loosens, so should the work for hire doctrine. However, the ability of the independent contractor to realize the full value of her human capital is cold comfort to the millions of workers who may not be able to transition to a contingent lifestyle.

As Daniel Pink points out in *Free Agent Nation*:

> In the end, security and loyalty have acquired new meanings. Security, once achieved through attachment to larger institutions, is now achieved by hedging risk and diversifying across several clients, customers and projects. Loyalty, which once ran vertically, has been turned on its side. It now runs horizontally-to colleagues, teams, professions and families. The result: For good or ill, the loyalty for security bargain

that defined the American workforce for several generations is gone.

However, Richard Sennett has argued that this lack of security and attachment tends to erode the work ethic and the ethical bounds between employer and employee. In *Corrosion of Character*, he concedes that workers no longer tethered to an organization are free, but it is "an amoral freedom," absent of social context. According to Sennet, a worker's identity concerns not so what a person does as where he belongs. In the knowledge economy, workers may not be able to county on the organization to set the pace and pattern of their lives. Instead, they may be subject to the vicissitudes of the market and technological forces beyond their control. For the average worker, this experience may be reminiscent of the upheavals wrought by the early stages of the industrial revolution.

To help employees focus and to bridge the knowledge gap, some companies have adopted a type of "happy talk" the purpose of which is to tap the wellspring of employee spirit. In many firms, "happyism" has taken hold of human resource departments. "No system, tool or methodology ... can beat the productivity boost you get from really, really enjoying your work," declares consultant Alexander Kjerulf, self-described "Chief Happiness Officer." HR journals brim with articles whose mood can be summed up in a passage from the May 2007 issue of *Personnel Today*: "The pursuit of true happiness has become a burning issue for politicians, economists and psychologists, and far from assuming that happiness is a personal matter, employers, too, should be doing far more to put smiles on the faces of staff."

In some firms, innovation has become a form of magical thinking. In their July 2003 Harvard Business Review article *Delusions of Success: How Optimism Undermines Executives' Decisions*, authors Dan Lovallo and Daniel Kahneman say that American companies "reward optimism and interpret pessimism as disloyalty." Thus, frank discussions of risk at many companies are interpreted as evidence of negativity; the risk-averse employee may be labeled a "gloom-and-doomer" and hear himself disparaged as "not a team player" during performance reviews. And where "delusional optimism" is prized, it becomes a risk factor in its own right. As Lovallo and Kahneman put it: "By exaggerating the likely benefits of a project and ignoring the potential pitfalls, [executives] lead their organizations into initiatives that are doomed to fall well short of expectations." Statistically, say the authors, positive-thinking managers tend to experience cost overruns and revenue shortfalls.

Nevertheless, enormous resources are devoted to fads, quacks and frauds. Of the $29 billion that companies invest in outsourced training, according to the American Society for Training & Development, a significant portion is earmarked for celebrity speakers, off-site seminars and "wilderness camps" designed to instill a positive outlook. In 2004, when Meeting Professionals International surveyed its membership, representing thousands of corporate and independent meeting planners, 81 percent noted a client preference for celebrity-delivered inspiration over skills-intensive training. In short, happiness has become the new social identity within Corporate America but there is no hard evidence that such induced positive thinking increases innovation, which still requires a depth of knowledge workers.

Peter Drucker coined the term "knowledge worker" in 1959, but left the definition rather circular. To Drucker, a knowledge worker is one who works primarily with information or one who develops and uses knowledge in the workplace. In *The Work of Nations* Robert Reich placed the knowledge worker into the narrower—but more carefully defined—category of "symbolic analyst." According to Reich, "symbolic analysts solve, identify, and broker problems by manipulating symbols." Their tools are "mathematical algorithms, legal arguments, financial gimmicks, scientific principles, psychological insights . . . systems of induction or deduction, or any other set of techniques for doing conceptual puzzles." For this type of worker, it's the input of knowledge and not the production process that adds value. "Final production is often the easiest part. The bulk of the time and cost (and, thus, real value) comes in conceptualizing the problem, devising a solution, and planning its execution."

Presumably, knowledge work (symbolic analysis) involves the creation of new knowledge—knowledge that would not exist without the worker's mental efforts. In reality, however, creating new knowledge is actually a fairly small part of the work. When the work pattern of knowledge workers is examined, there appears to be six, more or less, distinct types of work:

1. Routine work that is hard to separate from knowledge work. Formatting an article, for example, is work that might be done by a typist, but would be done by the knowledge worker when that takes less time than preparing the document and formatting instructions for the typist.

2. Networking, promoting, socializing.

3. Finding the data needed to produce the knowledge.

4. Creating what others have probably already created when this would take less time than to search, find, and appropriate what has been produced by others.

5. Truly original knowledge work—creating what has not been created before.

6. Communicating what has been produced or learned.

For firms that want to innovate, the most important distinction is the difference between types 4 and 5. Knowledge workers may spend much of the time creating knowledge that is new to them, but is the same or similar to the work product that has been created by other knowledge workers. Therefore, the work of most knowledge workers involves engaging in the process of reinvention and recombination. As previously explained, innovators rarely come up with new ideas. Instead they convert old ideas into new ones. They engage in "recombinant innovation", as ideas continually build on another, creating new forms and adaptations. Such work may well be pleasant and fulfilling. But the knowledge worker, as innovator, is only being paid for it because for his/her employer, reinventing, recombining and rearranging knowledge is cheaper than creating new knowledge. Likewise, for a large organization, it may be cheaper to acquire a small, innovative firm rather than to invent new knowledge. Indeed, the U.S. Small Business Administration reports that small firms generate 14 more patents per employee than large firms.

As discussed in earlier, even knowledge work can be outsourced. American firms have had to tap global labor markets for cheap, *skilled* labor. Simultaneously, they have employed software and other technology solutions within their own organizations to standardize as much administrative, technical and professional work as possible so that even higher-level work can be outsourced. What remains today is a small group of core employees who manage the corporate brand; market it's products; protect the corporate image; seek out and acquire smaller, more innovative firms; protect it's patents and other intellectual property; and who lobby legislatures for competitive advantage. Since most knowledge workers are vulnerable to outsourcing, they have no choice but to keep their options open. This divided attention is the bane of management.

In 2001 Aon Consulting survey a discrete group of knowledge workers to determine their level of commitment to their employer. According to the survey, 55% of high tech workers stated that they could be lured away by a job that paid less than 20% more than what they were making. Nearly 4 in 10 stated that they were underpaid, as compared to employees in similar jobs. About 56% agreed that they would stay at their current job if offered a similar job with only slightly higher pay.

Despite misconceptions, it appears that this sub-set of knowledge workers share the same values of their peers in other industries. The majority reported feeling somewhat or very connected to their organizations. Only 42% described committing to one employer as "foolish", although compensation was the most frequent reason given to leave an employer. This evidence appears to undermine the views of the common stereotype of tech workers as greedy and short-term minded. As observed previously, David Birch, an influential business consultant, observed that "the majority of people in college are into very much of a free-agency" with little expectation of a government-sponsored safety net. According to Birch, this free-agent status has eroded any expectation of job security and has made loyalty irrelevant. "What this means, he concludes, as an employer", he concludes, "is that you've got to start designing the things that you do, the skill sets, the nature of your work around that. It has got to be interchangeable parts. You've got to de-skill most of the things you do, so that any number of people who you hire can come in, in a relatively short period of time, and perform that job."

However, the evidence suggests that the "loyalty is dead" crowd may be off the mark, since job security remains a powerful driver of employee commitment, even among knowledge workers. While it may be true that these workers tend to be less interested than other workers in job security, the relentless outsourcing of knowledge work and the bursting of the dot com bubble in 2001 have caused increased concerns about job security, layoffs, personal finances, and hiring. Since that time, at least 800,000 high-tech jobs have been lost nationwide, sending unemployment rates among data processors and computer programmers shooting to nearly 11 percent in some areas of the country. A 2003 U.S. Commerce Department report confirmed that increasing numbers of technology jobs were moving from the United States to offshore spots including India, Ireland, the Philippines and China. In July 2003, for instance, IBM acknowledged that it was speeding up its schedule to shift three million service jobs to China and India. Microsoft Senior Vice President Brian Valentine admitted in a July 2002 presentation that IT work could be had in India at "two heads for the price of one." According 2007 Skills Survey of IT workers conducted by CNET News.com, a third of respondents to the survey agree or strongly agree with the statement "I feel that off—shoring is a threat to my current job", an increase from 2006's result, when 32 percent feared that their job could be sent abroad. One respondent wryly noted that "if (off-shoring) keeps up, we won't have an IT industry in this country, as the only people working in IT will be non-technically literate managers."

For Daniel Pink, the solution to this outsourcing, this mass dislocation, is independent contracting. In *Free Agent Nation*, Pink writes that knowledge workers can achieve security through diversification. "Security means investing human capital in several clients or projects rather than tying it up with a single company." With such an arrangement, "the free agent provides talent (productivity, services, advice) in exchange for opportunity (money, learning and connections). Independent contracting, however, is a rational economic choice only if a worker can realize the full value of labor without resort to the tools, resources and know-how provided by a traditional employer. A plumber, for example, can maximize his or her value separate and independent from the value-adding catalyst that only an organization can provide. But what of the technical support representative, software and database developer and programmer? The free agent and "Me, Inc." advocates believe that the skill sets held by these workers are sufficient to compete independently. However, in *The Culture of the New Capitalism*, Richard Sennett captured the disillusionment and despair of some high tech workers after the dot-com bubble burst. According to Sennett, the most common reaction among the laid off techies was that they felt suddenly alone. "It could be said" notes Sennett, "that the discovery is not too different from that of a machinist whose craft has disappeared; or in another way of the student tempted by a course in media studies, knowing that millions of other young people are similarly tempted. They all face the prospect of drift."

Competition is also fierce from both abroad and from knowledge workers arriving to the United States on a work visa. The H-1B visa is a non-immigrant visa that allows business professionals to work in the United States for a specific amount of time. The purpose of this visa is to give US employers the opportunity to hire foreign professionals if a US citizen or resident is not available. About 65,000 skilled workers enter the United States per year with this visa. On April 1, 2008, the *Wall Street Journal* published an editorial written by Matthew Slaughter, dean and professor at the Tuck School of Business at Dartmouth University. In it, he wrote that the U.S. was facing an "immigration gap." He also argued "U.S. companies today are crying out for more immigrants to satisfy their talent needs. The solution? Eliminate the cap on H-1B visas." The response was fast and furious. A highly skilled software developer from Parker, Colorado wrote:

> H-1B has been a disaster for workers like me. I understand the dynamics of supply and demand and the fact that no one owes anyone a guarantee. As a self-employed contractor I am earning about the same amount of money annually as I did in 1995. This is because the rates for the services I offer have been pressed downward by the increased flow of H-1B developers who are willing to work for far less money. It's getting to the point where I'll be going the way of the horse and buggy much faster if the number of H-1B visa issued each year is increased.

A senior project manager with an MBA from New Rochelle, New York, wrote about the intentional "dumbing down of the internal workforce" at many US companies and the impending crisis "if we don't build or learn things here anymore." He too raised the issue of skilled immigrants who are willing to work for less "with the bait of the green card." Another writer simply wanted Dean Slaughter to honestly explain, "that higher wages are one of the factors that harm U.S. competitiveness in a global economy."

For some, this prospect of drifting to the bottom has hardened into Social Darwinism. Michael Kinsley has written that the free agent movement has bred a generation of "smart loners" who "are convinced that they don't need society-nor should anyone else." While Kinsley concedes that he has generalized, it is no doubt true that labor that is devoid of social context as a different meaning than work that is the result of collective human effort. As Thomas Homer-Dixon has observed in *The Ingenuity Gap*, from the point of view of a worker who is detached physically but networked virtually, social and geographical reality is fragmented. "The Internet's fragmentation tends to supplant the shared public experience that is the key foundation of a society-wide sense of community." So perhaps for some work, a social context is not necessary. But if the objective is innovation and knowledge creation, even a simple brainstorming session requires a social context. Value added knowledge work requires much more. As previously explained, such activity requires collaboration and the resources of an organization. Rather than becoming the ascending presence in a free agent future, as Pink and Kinsley suggest, the "smart loner" is heading for extinction, as non-collaborative technical and data production work becomes increasing fragmented and de-skilled, thus being capable of being outsourced to any village or hamlet on the globe. In an odd paradox of language, for many workers in the globalized New Economy who simply cannot realize the full value of their labor, "free agency" means compelled redundancy. Additionally, as wireless technology spreads to the far corners of the globe, some predict a time where knowledge workers around the world are hired online by the minute to work on a project-to-project basis. Such work will resemble piecework and perhaps be assembled and packaged by a contract team.

Yet, *value-added* knowledge work requires commitment and engagement, a sense of responsibility for organizational success and to unrestrainedly pursue the objectives of the organization. Unlike production work, were efficiency and productivity can be measured, creating and sharing knowledge cannot be easily quantified. Moreover, such value-added knowledge work requires *voluntary* cooperation. It requires an employee to go beyond the call of duty and to exert effort, energy and initiative to the best of their abilities. It requires psychological engagement. In contrast, production work (whether of the blue or white collar variety) is performed consistent with rules, regulations, procedures and standards. Such work is subject to *compulsory* cooperation. It requires employees to be precise, efficient and productive but not necessarily engaged in what they are doing. The employer does not take valuable production time to ask the worker what he or she thinks. The worker feels no obligation to share his or her know-how. To produce just enough to avoid further compulsion, such as a verbal or written warning, is sufficient.

As previously explained, most firms give innovation lip service, only to rely on more command and control structures to get results. Consider the economic model that underlies traditional notions of supervision, the so-called "agency model," embodies the assumptions most common in the design of modern supervisory arrangements. The agency model presents supervision as a simple transaction consisting of a "principal" (the employer), an "agent" (the employee). The motivations of these actors are simple and as old as Adam Smith's dictum on the master-servant relationship. The agent dislikes expending effort but likes getting paid. The principal dislikes paying the agent but likes the work that the agent does. The objectives of principal and agent are thus diametrically opposed: The agent wants to be paid as much as possible for doing as little work as possible, whereas the principal wants to get as much work as possible from the agent while paying as little as possible. Supervision is complicated by the fact that the principal can't directly see how much effort the agent is expending but can only observe a result of the agent's work, which also depends on random factors. For example, a salesperson's total sales might depend not only on how hard he works but also on the weather during a given week. The primary conclusion of agency models is the importance of tying pay to performance, to provide employees with appropriate incentives.

However, there are several obvious problems with the agency model as it applies to knowledge work. First, the difficulties in observing knowledge work are more profound than those assumed by the model. Not only can't a supervisor observe effort directly in knowledge work, sometimes the supervisor can't understand what the worker is doing and may not be qualified to judge results. Because knowledge work cannot be easily measured, it is also more difficult to see causality and to attribute results to particular worker actions. Measurements of results often don't faithfully capture the results you really care about. Second, "agent" motivators appear inconsistent with those of knowledge workers. Knowledge workers are often interested in their work and motivated by a desire to do it well. The agency model suggests no way of leveraging these worker motivations. Third, the agency model posits the agent as a lone actor, bargaining or conniving for best advantage regardless of the peer pressure that is often brought on selfish employees to conform to cooperative values.

In 2007 the Gallup Management Journal surveyed a nationally representative sample of employed adults and found that less than one in three employees were actively engaged in their work. Most were not engaged, primarily putting in their time, maintaining just enough productivity to avoid negative consequences, and putting little energy or passion into their jobs. About 15% of the respondent's strongly agreed with the statement that their current job "brings out [their] most creative ideas." The researchers also explored the role of that workplace friendships played in promoting innovation. It has long been thought that friendships at work increase an employee's sense of job satisfaction and well-being. In his landmark *The Psychology of Work*, Walter Neff observed that the social context of work permitted friendships and a sense of belonging. The Gallup researchers found that about three-fourths of engaged employees, or about 21% of the total sample, strongly agreed with the statement "I have a friend at work that I share ideas with." The research strongly suggests that of the relatively few employees who generate ideas, group affiliation and friendship play important roles in staying engaged.

Knowledge is created through social interaction, sometimes referred to as collaboration. As noted in above, the traditional management strategies of a bureaucratic nature and the scientific management styles of controlling information and power, and seeking to direct workers might be counterproductive in relation to knowledge workers, and that a different management style which is less hierarchical and more flexible might be more appropriate. For the most part, managers who say that they value autonomy, innovation, creativity and flexibility are not prepared to grant autonomy to their staff and fail to consult, share information or encourage teamwork. Knowledge and expertise are often viewed as sources of power and as such are not easily shared. Ironically, this is even truer in a knowledge-intensive economy, which has unleashed the forces of globalization and where the premium and power attached to valuable knowledge escalate. In the absence of natural economic incentives and with the perceived power disincentives to diffuse knowledge, it follows that high-quality knowledge creation and collaboration will be stifled.

Moreover, value added knowledge work requires a greater degree of personal autonomy. Social networking technology, such as blogs and wikis can be useful tools for collaboration, personal expression and knowledge sharing within a large organization but without incentives to transcend the agency problem, the novelty of these technologies is insufficient to motivate people to contribute voluntarily. The irony of this emerging trend toward social networking at work is that for the majority of employees, employers provide little direct incentive for them to contribute what they know. Research indicates that sustained communication may go a long way in creating a social environment for innovation. According to researchers Kim and Mauborgne (1998) "the ability to express one's ideas or bilateral communication, which is the key element to engagement, implies the opportunity to voice one's perceptions, knowledge, and ideas, and the need to hear opposite parties out. This increases the likelihood that a high rate of knowledge and expertise will be diffused and shared."

In 2006 researchers at the university of Southern California and New York University published a noel theory to explain why humans seek out information, often for its own sake. Human beings, they wrote in *American Scientist* are designed to be "infovores" because knowledgeable people are more attractive mating partners, a fact that appears to be true across cultures, and because knowledge tends to increase the chances of survival. The researchers also found that when people acquire new knowledge the brain is rewarded with a morphine-like substance as it connects bits of information into a cohesive whole. Apparently, "knowledge high" is the result of the integrating and understanding new information.

Related to open communication is trust; in fact, trust is the foundation of communication. A world Values Survey that assesses basic values and beliefs in more than eighty counties, found that people care as much about fairness as they do about their own pecuniary interests. In commercial transactions, most people care about ethical values. Yet, a Watson Wyatt survey in 2004 indicated that about half the workforce simply didn't trust their employer. Most of this distrust centered on communication that is perceived as secretive or dishonest. When employees don't trust managers to make good decisions or to behave with integrity, their motivation is seriously compromised. Their distrust and attendant lack of engagement is a big, often unrecognized problem in many organizations. Of course the issue has always mattered, but it matters more in organizations that are dependent on the commitment and ideas of employees. Even Google, a company that receives a million resumes a year is experiencing defections. While some of these departures are the direct result of stock option vesting, the company have begun experimenting with an offsite "skunk works" to counteract the perceptions of cramped communication and secrecy within the larger organizational culture.

It appears therefore that there are intrinsic motivators that could transcend the agency problem. Researchers and commentators have opined that such motivators are what drive knowledge workers. The U.S. Department of Labor's most recent Longitudinal Survey on Job Satisfaction suggests that most working Americans are reasonable satisfied with their jobs. Among the factors that support high levels of job satisfaction are having responsibility for one's own work (52 percent), having a sense of worth in a job (42 percent), being recognized for individual contributions (40 percent), and the opportunity to make good use of skills and learning new skills (35 percent). It appears that autonomy, meaning, affiliation and learning may be the necessary ingredients to nurture value adding knowledge workers. To this end, several companies have created "communities of practice" groups of employees of similar professional or other interests that cross boundaries of departments and units. For example, Schlumberger, LTD is an oil and fuel services company with 52,000 employees spread over 80 countries that has created 23 communities ranging from chemistry to engineering, with about 140 special interest sub-groups. The company reports that 11,750 employees belong to a group. Uniquely, these communities elect their own leaders and govern themselves so that peer review and esteem remain powerful drivers of innovation and knowledge sharing. Make no mistake; while this environment can create competition and professional jealousy, the development of shared repositories and discussion databases that were actively managed by the community can foster a sense of mutual trust and obligation. In these shared spaces, individuals begin to evaluate who is making contributions to the greater community knowledge pool, and they began to judge the willingness of others to share the documents, templates, and other similar knowledge. The company spends about $1 million a year on these "Eureka" communities, as they are called, and compared to other knowledge initiatives, it is cost-effective.

While knowledge workers are, in part, motivated by the intrinsic nature of their work and the value of collaborative innovation, the corporate world is filled with moral ambiguities and knowledge workers have little control over the consequences of their work. In the end, most knowledge workers remain at will employees, agents of the corporate employer to which they owe a legal duty of loyalty and faithfulness. Knowledge workers are paid to perform services and their compensation will reflect only their own individual effort, although the value of the collective effort is much greater. The knowledge worker may receive extra compensation for his or her effort or the brilliant idea but the work is performed for hire and therefore the worker will have no ownership interest in the intellectual property that was created. Thus the knowledge worker's motivation and engagement will always be like any other worker at some undefined ethical point where the psychic costs associated with the lack of ownership and control over the consequences of the work outweighs the intrinsic reward gained by the work performed. Having reached this ethical tipping point, the at will knowledge worker can always voluntarily terminate employment but the obstacles to starting over, often with lower pay, may be too great to surmount. If the knowledge worker seeks control or ownership over the intellectual property he or she is sued for disloyalty or misappropriation. If the knowledge worker objects to the consequences of the intellectual property or how it is used, he or she can be terminated without legal recourse. The case of *Pierce v. Ortho Pharmaceutical* decided by the Supreme Court of New Jersey is illustrative.

This case presented the question of whether Dr. Pierce, an at will employee, had a cause of action against her employer to recover damages for the termination of her employment following her refusal to continue a research project she viewed as medically unethical. In 1973, Dr. Pierce became the Director of Medical Research/Therapeutics, one of three major sections of the Medical Research Department. Her primary responsibilities were to oversee development of therapeutic drugs and to establish procedures for testing those drugs for safety, effectiveness, and marketability.

In the spring of 1975, Dr. Pierce was the only medical doctor on a project team developing loperamide, a liquid drug for treatment of diarrhea in infants, children, and elderly persons. The proposed formulation contained saccharin. Although the concentration was consistent with the formula for loperamide marketed in Europe, the project team agreed that the formula was unsuitable for use in the United States. An alternative formulation containing less saccharin might have been developed within approximately three months. By March 28, however, the project team, except for Dr. Pierce, decided to continue with the development of loperamide. That decision was made in response to a directive from the Marketing Division of Ortho.

There came a time when Dr. Pierce felt that by continuing to work on loperamide she would violate her interpretation of the Hippocratic Oath. She concluded that the risk that saccharin might be harmful should preclude testing the formula on children or elderly persons, especially when an alternative formulation might soon be available. Ultimately, her ethical view conflicted with the Marketing Division's need to get the product to market, which would need the approval of the FDA. The conflicts eventually lead to Dr. Pierce's dismissal.

In upholding the dismissal, the court noted that employees who are professionals owe a special duty to abide not only by federal and state law, but also by the recognized codes of ethics of their professions. That duty may oblige them to decline to perform acts required by their employers.

However, the court observed that an employee should not have the right to prevent his or her employer from pursuing its business because the employee perceives that a particular business decision violates the employee's personal morals, as distinguished from the recognized code of ethics of the employee's profession.

According to the court "the controversy at Ortho involved a difference in medical opinions" and that to permit Dr. Pierce's suit to move forward would allow "a professional employee [to] redetermine the propriety of a research project even if the research did not involve a violation of a clear mandate of public policy. Chaos would result if a single doctor engaged in research were allowed to determine, according to his or her individual conscience, whether a project should continue." In sum, "an employee does not have a right to continued employment when he or she refuses to conduct research simply because it would contravene his or her personal morals. An employee at will who refuses to work for an employer in answer to a call of conscience should recognize that other employees and their employer might heed a different call."

No corporate worker, controls the consequences of their work. Maintaining ignorance of this fact or relying on the perpetual goodwill of the employer are untenable, particulary when work is highly vaulable. The employee is required to serve the master faithfully and can be terminated with or without cause at anytime. In return for the paycheck, even the knowledge worker gives up a big piece of his or her personality, their spirit, their intelligence and their physical labor when they are acting within the scope of their employment. There is no ownership interest in the product of the work. Pride of workmanship could serve as as a psychological substitute for ownership. The employee will never receive an equity share in the product, although performance incentives and stock ownership can serve as a resaonable facsimile. Thus, innovation and knowledge work do not directly solve the problem of unethical or fraudulent practices in the corporate world. However, environnements that foster innovation can be inherently more ethical if managed that way.

However, managers of knowledge workers often don't understand how best to manage their staff because ethical behavior is often not critical to the relationship. Firms that want to maximize the fullest potential of their knowledge workers must have effective collaborative environments (the best work is produced by means of teamwork, not by individual careerists), sharing of information (knowledge workers are listened to, trusted, and know what is going on), loose hierarchies (managers serve their staffs, not dominate them), and devolution of decision making (knowledge workers are trusted and trained to make decisions where the value is created—at the frontline). These environments tend to drive commitment and behaviors far beyond what could ever be written into a job description. Many traditional management techniques are not effective when dealing with work that is largely intellectual. In a knowledge-intensive organization, the role of management changes. Management becomes less about setting and policing rules for workers and more about establishing strategy, setting goals, showing leadership, and measuring results. Knowledge management is less about managing people and more about giving them the right goals, the right motivation, and the right tools, and clearly articulating how success or failure will be measured. Accessing the higher levels of human creativity and motivation in today's Knowledge Economy requires a sea change in thinking: a new mindset, a new skill set, a new toolset—in short, a whole new habit.

A recent Hewitt Associates survey of employees cited 28 attributes that they felt were important for their supervisors to have. The top five attributes were *Honesty* (which is not only avoiding the scapegoating of employees but also includes knowing when the supervisor is part of the problem); *Integrity* (which means being invested in the success of others and not hoarding information for personal advantage); *Caring* (which means understanding that most employees experience some difficulty balancing the demand of work with family responsibilities); *Fairness* (which means letting employees know what's expected and having an ethical foundation for the use of discipline; and *Approachability* (which means making the extra effort to maintain positive relationships and active listening). In short, supervisors in knowledge-intensive organizations must be leaders.

For most organizations, supervisors have no incentive to be leaders, that is, despite the corporate party line, management has no interest in supervision based on core values. The primary values for these organizations, many of which are competing globally, are efficiency, productivity, the elimination of waste, and reducing idleness. The primary role of the supervisor is to count time, apply procedures, and to justify discipline or discharge decisions in a well documented fashion. Since the exclusive focus is on production, supervisory training tends to cover how to follow the rules consistently and to avoid being abusive. In contrast, supervisory training in knowledge intensive organizations focuses on communication skills, conflict resolution, and the exercise of what Richard Florida terms "soft power." Soft power is the ability to get what you want by attracting and persuading others to adopt your goals. However, without acting form a core set of values, soft power is often an exercise in manipulation and deception. Thus all supervisory training in knowledge intensive environments starts with the clarification of individual and corporate values.

And what of the knowledge worker? A rough estimate of the percentage of truly indispensable workers at about one in one thousand, as measured narrowly by the skills and abilities that make a customer come back for more. The Gallup research suggests about 14 percent of workers are highly valued due not their extraordinary level of engagement, commitment and willingness to share what they know. They have their best ideas at work and in the knowledge intensive environment must be considered part of the organization's core. This, of course, is conjecture but experience and case studies lend more than an air of credence to this hypothesis. Research suggests that these core workers, what I have been calling throughout this discussion "value added knowledge workers" are motivated intrinsically, in various degrees, by autonomy, esteem and learning. The social science literature suggests that their work is a form of personal or creative expression, permitting them to "self-actualize." It is thought to be the highest form of social development.

In *The Human Condition*, Hannah Arendt distinguished between *Animal laborens* and *Homo faber*—between man as a worker, thoughtlessly and amorally lost in his labor's object, and man as a maker of society and its institutions, a builder of life in common. For Arendt, the maker had it all over the worker, who was, in her view, basically an indentured servant, alienated from his work and devoid of any social meaning. While this distinction is perhaps too contemptuous of practical life, the knowledge worker appears closer to a maker of his or her society and the institutions of the new economy. In many ways, the modern knowledge worker can be compared favorable to artisans and craftsmen. The work requires intense, constant involvement and ongoing learning. It often requires thousands of hours of what might be called an apprenticeship. In that regard, the elite knowledge worker is not alienated in the Marxian sense, since he or she *is* the means of production. Such a person is not engaged in uniform activity or the mere expenditure of energy, but rather is engaged in something psychologically meaningful, akin to a craft, where spontaneity, exuberance and freedom to perform make work and play nearly identical. The work is naturally creative. Such "free conscious activity constitutes the species-character" of the knowledge worker.

But unlike the craftsman whose identity was forged through a social or communal consciousness, the elite knowledge worker of today is released from the need for communion and instead finds meaning and context in an abstract self-fulfillment. Unlike the craft worker, who could see the fruits of his labor immediately—a chair, for example, it can be hard to find gratification from work that is largely intangible, or from delivering "goods" that are often symbolic. You can't even leave a permanent mark on a hard copy document in increasingly paperless offices. Thus, knowledge work is more or less intangible.

"Not only is abstract work harder to measure but it's also harder to define success," states Homa Bahrami, a senior lecturer in Organizational Behavior and Industrial Relations at UC Berkeley's Haas School of Business. "The work is intangible or invisible, and a lot of work gets done in teams so it's difficult to pinpoint individual productivity." She says knowledge workers measure their accomplishment in net worth, company reputation, networks of relationships, and the products and services they're associated with—elements that are more perceived and subjective than the output of a production quota.

Additionally, technology can obscure the full meaning of knowledge work and often results in the suppression of a human dimension. For example, computer-assisted design has largely replaced architectural drawing. It has, of course, increased efficiency and lowered costs. As Sennett has observed in *The Craftsman*, the architect, having no need to put pen to paper, now works in a condition of estrangement from the physical world and from the "relational" aspects of his or her work. The result, Richard Sennett explains, is poorly designed structures at odds with their surroundings and with the human needs of their inhabitants.

As previously noted, the idea that work was both ennobling and a path to salvation had its roots in the Protestant Reformation and, indeed, within the Judeo-Christian tradition as a whole. In 1991, Pope John Paul II in *Centesimus Annus* had summed up this tradition in the context of the emerging knowledge economy:

> The original source of all that is good is the very act of God, who created both the earth and man, and who gave the earth to man so that he might have dominion over it by his work and enjoy its fruits (Genesis, 1:28). God gave the earth to the whole human race for the sustenance of all its members, without excluding or favoring anyone . . . . But the earth does not yield its fruits without a particular human response to God's gift, that is to say, without work. It is through work that man, using his intelligence and exercising his freedom, succeeds in dominating the earth and making it a fitting home. In this way, he makes part of the earth his own, precisely the part which he has acquired through work; this is *the origin of individual property.*
>
> In history, these two factors—*work* and *the land*—are to be found at the beginning of every human society. However, they do not always stand in the same relationship to each other. At one time *the natural fruitfulness of the earth* appeared to be, and was in fact, the primary factor of wealth, while work was, as it were, the help and support for this fruitfulness. In our time, *the role of human work* is becoming increasingly important as the productive factor both of non-material and of material wealth. Moreover, it is becoming clearer how a person's work is naturally interrelated with the work of others. More than ever, work is *work with others* and *work for others*: it is a matter of doing something for someone else. Work becomes ever more fruitful and productive to the extent that people become more knowledgeable of the productive potentialities of the earth and more profoundly cognizant of the needs of those for whom their work is done.

> In our time, in particular, there exists another form of ownership, which is becoming no less important than land: *the possession of know-how, technology and skill.* The wealth of the industrialized nations is based much more on this kind of ownership than on natural resources. (Emphasis in the original)

The function of work was not to secure personal material wealth, but to discipline the soul and to serve God. By the Industrial Revolution, this creed had been secularized to mean prudence, frugality and delayed gratification. However, as pointed out by Brink Lindsey in *The Age of Abundance*, as a result of post-war and late twentieth century affluence, the pursuit of personal fulfillment is the governing creed of a generation that has never known privation. He pointedly sums up this creed in a single phrase, which is the title of the Robert Ringer book published in 1977, *Looking Out for Number One*. As explained by Ringer: "Looking out for number one is the conscious, rational effort to spend as much time as possible doing those things which bring you the greatest pleasure and less time on those which cause pain."

Of course, the Protestant Work Ethic could degenerate into rank greed and smug entitlement. Likewise the work ethic of the new economy could degenerate into rank selfishness and smug entitlement. Thus, freedom from production drudgery demands responsibility for maximizing one's talent and contributions to knowledge creation, a commitment to continuous learning, and the conviction and fortitude to prevail over disappointment, disillusionment and despair. This post-industrial secular desire for self-fulfillment is not without its profound spiritual quality. Whether a lifestyle or calling, or whether the reward comes in the here after or here and now, or whether the work performed is to serve God or to serve yourself, the bottom line is the same: be humbled by your talents, gifts and abilities and always strive to do your best.

The elite knowledge workers who are guided by a strong ethical and spiritual core will maximize their chances of success and happiness in the new economy. While they are still dependent on the catalytic effects of an organization, their value will ensure that organizations take care to nurture and retain them. But what about the majority of workers who simply work for a living or merely to survive? In the globalized new economy they will be continually haunted by the specter of underemployment and dislocation. They consume to salve the chronic ache of insecurity and float on a bubble of personal debt to keep up. Some have clearly made poor choices, unable to delay gratification or to anticipate change. Still others may have no meaningful choices to make, mired in poverty or addiction. The globalized new economy may leave them in a permanent state of insecurity or debt slavery. What role, if any, does government have in averting this dire outcome?

The implication of the new economic analysis is that there is currently no alternative way to prosperity than to make learning and knowledge-creation of prime importance. As explained previously, the non-rivalrous nature of ideas means that any particular idea can be used by an infinite number of people at the same time. As Jefferson famously wrote: "He who receives an idea from me, receives instructions himself without lessening mine." Human capital on the other hand is rival because skills cannot be separated from people. Thus, the skills of a group of highly skilled engineers employed by Google are not available to Microsoft. Accordingly, employers will exercise their property and contract rights to ensure that at least some of the human capital that they employ remains rivalrous.

In contrast to people, machines are more durable and ideas are more durable than machines. When a person leaves a company, he takes his skills with him but any knowledge that the person may have created—a scientific calculation, software or a blueprint—lives on after the person is gone. Again, firms will use property and contract rights to retain ownership over that knowledge. However, because technological innovations are continually being over thrown by new ideas, the spectre of diminishing returns is kept at bay. Thus, the logic of the new economy dictates that a country's capacity to take advantage of innovation depends on how well it diffuses knowledge and how quickly it can become a "learning society". Learning means not only using new technologies to access global knowledge, it also means using them to communicate with other people about innovation. In the knowledge economy individuals, firms, and countries will be able to create wealth in proportion to their capacity to share knowledge and learn how to innovate.

4. Reengineering and the Changing Nature of Work

A lot is at stake for individuals and organizations. In 2005, one estimate had intellectual property-based industries accounting for nearly 20 percent of the total private sector contribution to GNP. In addition, because these industries are growing faster than the overall economy, they may account for 40 percent of real economic growth. Moreover, because they depend on knowledgeable workers, knowledge-based firms pay, on average, 40 percent more than the average wage paid to U.S. workers.

The wage gap between a highly paid knowledge worker and that of a low skilled day laborer is vast, as is the gap between the highly skilled professional and the office administrator. According to Thomas Homer-Dixon, the ability of firms to exploit the nature of ideas and knowledge has increased this gap. "As a result, the ideas of the very best idea-generators (whether individuals, groups, or corporations) can be brought to a much larger market than before, and these people can therefore reap much larger rewards. In large, highly competitive, highly efficient markets, the difference between the rewards received by the best and the second-best idea-generators is immense." As economist Robert Frank writes: "Developments in communications, manufacturing technology, and transportation costs . . . have enabled the most talented performers to serve ever broader markets, which has increased the value

123

of their services." Those changes "have sharply increased the value of the top performers relative to their lesser ranked rivals."

Homer-Dixon cites research that strongly suggest that occupations that increasingly require cognitive complexity will continue to pay the biggest rewards as other occupations will pay increasingly less. He points out that this type of functioning is not evenly distributed among the population and "those who are very good at managing complexity will be in high demand." Thus, the new knowledge economy "boosts the incomes of our societies' cognitive elites. In other words, [the knowledge economy] reinforces the stark divisions of wealth [that] are a reality of modern life."

Additionally, highly knowledge-intensive workers tend to be more mobile and better able to negotiate the challenges of an economy in transition. According to a Rand Study (2005), "knowledge-based workers have increasingly become independent contractors to capitalize on the demand for their specialized services in order to take charge of their economic destinies." Indeed, an increasing number of self-employed people desire the benefits of becoming independent contractors, including being their own boss and being able to work from home on flexible schedules. "[T]here is little evidence that workers are forced to leave their regular, full-time jobs to start working for themselves as freelancers."

At the same time, it is clear that during the last three decades corporate restructuring, reorganizations, downsizing and outsourcing have driven tens of thousands of professionals and skilled technicians to seek opportunities as independent contractors, consultants and freelancers. Between 1979 and 1984, 10.8 million Americans were permanently laid off or dismissed. Most of these layoffs reflected permanent changes in the manufacturing sector. However, by the mid-1980's, most firms had learned to use information technologies to reduce the number of white collar and middle management jobs. To be sure, many workers prefer flexible, short-term work assignments but critics of the practice of deconstructing full time jobs into be short term, project-specific jobs, is creating a two-tiered work force. Those in the first tier work full-time receive health care and other benefits and have an expectation of continued employment. In contrast, workers is the second tier are part of a growing pool of workers and move from job to job, often making less money and rarely receiving benefits. Indeed, so-called "contingent" jobs earn on average eighty-two percent of what there "regular" counterparts earn. The data suggests a similar picture for benefits. Those that are employed in contingent arrangements are less likely than other workers to have health insurance from any source. While almost three-fifths of workers holding traditional jobs have group health care insurance (about 129 million employees and their dependents), only one in two contingent workers have such coverage.

If the "value" of an employee's work is defined as the talent, experience and knowledge that accentuates the strengths of the organization, then the hard reality is that most white-collar work adds little knowledge value to an organization. This does not mean that the work or the people performing the work are not valuable. They have, of course, intrinsic value as human beings and the work that they perform has dignity. However, efficient white-collar production requires standardized data inputs, systematic but routine data processing and predictable outcomes, leaving only a narrow range of discretionary judgment to the white-collar worker. To the extent that such judgment is necessary, it is aided by a software solution. In short, most white-collar administrative work is interchangeable, if not dispensable.

Moreover, advancements in communication technology have made many management functions redundant. The traditional role of middle management in a corporate hierarchy had been to collect, verifies and assemble information from below, organize it, and push it up the chain of command. However, "groupware" and "office suites" that organize information and facilitate peer-to-peer interaction has, literally, cut out the need for the "middleman," thus leaving managers of white collar production workers vulnerable to organizational consolidation and reengineering. According to Catalyst, a research and advocacy firm restructuring has reached even the executive sites of corporate America. From 2002 to 2007, the total number of corporate-officer positions declined 21 percent.

"Reengineering eliminates not just waste, but non-value adding work as well," observed Hammer and Champy in the best-selling *Reengineering the Corporation*. "Most of the checking, reconciling, waiting, tracking, monitoring-the unproductive work that exists because boundaries within an organization—is eliminated by reengineering, which means that people will spend more time doing *real* work." (Emphasis in the original). Presumably, the "real" work means knowledge-intensive work and "since workers in reengineered processes spend more time on value-adding work and less time on work that adds no value," knowledge workers should enjoy more job security. However, as noted, most white-collar production work constitutes little more than non-value added labor cost. Accordingly, by 1990, of America's largest one hundred companies, 77 percent of all layoffs involved white-collar workers, many of them older workers. As a result, nearly six million people over the age of fifty who remain working are self-employed. Many are transitioning to retirement and while some of those laid off have been able to go on to more satisfying, more lucrative work, many have experienced lower wages, either as contractors or consultants, or because the jobs that they have landed pay less.

It is undeniable that the biggest cause of rising income inequality in the United States over the past two decades has been the erosion of wages for the 70 percent of the U.S. workers with less than a college education. These workers' incomes have been eroded by long periods of unemployment, dislocation, economic globalization, and the shift from manufacturing jobs to lower paying service jobs. During that same period, the wages of workers' with at least some college education has gone up by 35 percent. But as demonstrated in a report issued by the Center on Budget and Policy Priorities (2006), "more recently, even college-educated workers have experienced real declines in wages, in part because of offshore competition." For example, Intel Corporation, the giant chip manufacturer opened a plant and research center in Shanghai, China in 2000, primarily to be closer to suppliers and to be near a steady flow of workers educated at local universities. In 2007, it broke ground for a $2.5 billion state-of-the-art manufacturing center in Dilian, about 800 miles west of Shanghai. The factory will employ 1,200 workers.

Intel has noted that much of its highly sensitive information will be protected but the unremitting evolution of the new economy appears to be following the same trend as pharmaceutical outsourcing. Big pharmaceutical firms have been outsourcing research and development functions for nearly two decades, primarily to India and China. Industry insiders state that this outsourcing is following a natural progression as research and development firms gain basic knowledge, resources and skills necessary for drug discovery. Such firms are inching closer to becoming *discovers* rather than just fabricators and copiers. While the loss of trade secrets and other intellectual property is always a concern, the quality of the work performed at the low cost and high speed is worth the risk for many companies. For now, highly sensitive information remains a closely held secret, making such jobs part of a firm's core function, and therefore less likely to outsourcing. Likewise, employees engaged in such sensitive work, such as research physicians and chemists, will command the salary and benefits befitting the value of their work. All others are competing against tens of thousands of skilled researchers in India and China.

Thus, investments in research and development are declining in the United States, even though the nation continues to spend more on such activities than any other country. Research and development spending as a proportion of GNP puts the United States sixth worldwide, following Israel, Sweden, Finland, Japan and Iceland. In 2000, India spent $20 billion on research and development activity, seventh worldwide, and china invested nearly $72 billion, placing it third in worldwide expenditures that year. While more foreign firms continue to invest more in research and development in the United States through their subsidiaries, more U.S. firms are investing in research and development in other counties. In 2002, U.S. firms invested $21.2 billion abroad in such activity. In short, even knowledge in subject to the same global supply and demand rules as goods and services. Thus, knowledge workers are in the same competition with foreign labor as their brethren on the production floor.

More than 25 million Americans (almost one-third of all white collar workers and 19 percent of the total workforce) are professionals and highly skilled technicians. But even these "knowledge workers" experience profound job insecurity in the new economy. The reality is that the global economy has driven most firms to focus intensely on their core competencies and to find alternative staffing arrangements to perform non-core, albeit highly skilled, functions. For most organizations, highly skilled lawyers, accountants, information technology administrators, and labor relations' specialists represent non-core functions that can be outsourced. In short, even highly skilled professionals and technicians can find themselves part of the contingent workforce. According to the Rand study, "most of the research on alternative workforces attributes technological change, heightened international competition, new management paradigms, deregulation, and the increasing costs of taxes and benefits as leading economic factors generating growth of the alternative workforce." These alternatives include independent contracting, freelancing and temporary work assignments.

Indeed, for some, any job is preferable to unemployment. In his book *Turbo Capitalism*, Edward Luttwak notes the rarity of long-term unemployment because of the absence of long-term government assistance. Perhaps owing to a vestige of rugged individualism, Americans are more likely than Europeans to accept work of lower status. "At any one time, depending on how each industry is faring, can find ex-insurance company middle managers delivering pizza to the door in New Jersey, or aerospace engineers driving taxis in Los Angeles. It helps that few occupations are foreclosed by licensing and permits."

In the *Rise of the Creative Class*, Richard Florida glibly paraphrases Peter Drucker and notes that knowledge workers are increasingly becoming owners of their know-how because "more workers than ever control the means of production, because it's inside their head." However, very rarely can the value of what's inside a person's head be realized outside the catalytic effects of the organization. Quite often, it is an employer that provides the preconditions for generating the idea in the first place. The employer provides the tools and location where employees can brainstorm. The employer nurtures an environment of innovation. The employer provides incentives and opportunities to invent. The employer recruits and retains the best and the brightest so that ideas, like stars, can be born and shine bright. In short, the organization is, more often than not, the catalyst, if not the proximate cause of the idea. As Drucker explained: "Only the organization can provide the basic continuity that knowledge workers need in order to be effective. Only the organization can convert specialized knowledge into performance."

The individual needs the organization and the organization needs the individual. "Even the smartest people in the world need a mechanism to assemble, package, promote and distribute the fruits of their thinking," says

Thomas Stewart in *Intellectual Capital*. "Like a blast furnace that converts iron and coke into steel, the organization concentrates, processes, and reifies knowledge work" he adds. While copyright law may not confer any ownership rights over the employee's idea, the employer lays claim over the intangible property on the basis of providing the essential ingredients and preconditions for the idea's genesis. Take for example, a magazine article. When an article is written for a magazine, it is accomplished as a work for hire. As such, the magazine owns the copyright. The writer, however, remains the owner of the knowledge that went into producing the article. When someone reads the article, they too possess the knowledge contained in the article. In that the regard, an employer and employee may be co-creators of the idea and therein lays the potential problem because when the relationship breaks up a custody battle over the intellectual property is sure to follow when the idea is a really good one.

Aside from the problem of ownership, creating value seems to be the prerequisite to job security. Hammer and Champy, writing in 1993, have suggested that employees who add value are required not follow rules, but rather to exercise judgment on the job in order to do the right thing. 'In companies that have reengineered," they argued, "the emphasis shifts from training to *education*—or to hiring the educated. Training increases skills and competence and teaches employees the 'how' of a job. Education increases their insight and understanding and teaches the 'why.'" (Emphasis in the original.). Time has proven Hammer & Champy both wrong and right. As noted, as white-collar work grows more software "solutioned" employees are simply not paid to ask "why." They are not paid for their insight and understanding into work processes. They are paid to execute with the fewest mistakes possible. Having no incentive to demonstrate insight and understanding, few seek out leaning opportunities that do not have a direct impact on their day-to-day job duties.

Post-World War II corporate leaders did little to undermine this status quo. The post-war corporations had grown so enormous that many came to resemble nation states, operated like autonomous governments. Some corporations engaged in the equivalent of a foreign policy. As Galbraith has pointed out, corporate size served not only monopoly power and the economies of scale, but also served the purpose of planning. "And for planning-control of supply, control of demand, provision of capital, minimization of risk-there was no clear upper limit to the desirable size." The number of white-collar professionals, technicians and administrators increased enormously. Designed for a period of heavy and growing demand and therefore accelerated growth, this form of corporate organization suited the circumstances of the post war times perfectly." Most college graduates had one simple goal: the big corporation and, as observed by Jack Beatty, "conformity in the school and workplace complemented oligopoly in the domestic marketplace and US hegemony in the world economy."

Corporate executives viewed themselves as great statesmen and leaders, stewards of the public trust. They were venerated for their virtue and judgment. They expected little in the way of creativity from the rank and file employee. Instead, executives demanded and received loyalty in exchange for job security. Employment at a corporation during this time was secure. Nonunion employers, who wanted to maintain the right to remain union-free, matched or exceeded union wages and benefits. Under this social compact, workers gave their loyalty and the most productive years of their lives to their employers. In return, employers promised job security and wage growth. America's post-war dominance of the world economy was unprecedented in modern history and there was no reason not to think that the social compact could not endure indefinitely. To many job security in an ever expanding economy was more or less a given, an entitlement of citizenship. To many, a job was not merely a *privilege* of citizenship; it was an *entitlement* of citizenship, with job security and rising wages, more or less, expected.

That sense of entitlement emerged after World War II and was first articulated by Franklin Roosevelt. In 1944, as the war economy continued operating on all cylinders but as the death toll swelled, the President laid out a post-war vision to for the war weary nation in his last State of the Union message to Congress. In a way seeking to justify the world war, he called this new platform an "economic bill of rights." The political rights enumerated in the Constitution proved inadequate to assure freedom. New social and economic rights were necessary to achieve "true individual freedom." Among these rights were "the right to a useful and remunerative job . . . the right to earn enough to provide adequate food and clothing and recreation . . . The right of every family to a decent home, the right to adequate health care ... the right to adequate protection from economic fears of old age, sickness, accident, and unemployment ... the right to a good education." It was a post-war agenda on which both big business and big labor could agree, as long as business remained dominate in the world.

In retrospect, generally speaking, it is apparent that the captains of industry who had grown dependent on government protection from disruptive competition during the war had grossly miscalculated their ability to control events after the war. The social compact that they openly encouraged could not endure in a free globalized enterprise system. The rest of the world quickly increased their standards of living by adopting, more or less, the American model of free trade. This created a global market for goods and services, but also a global labor market that required workers to be more flexible and information-intensive in the work that they performed. But the post-war social compact which exchanged loyalty for security, and which was reinforced by union contracts and government policy, had severely limited the freedom of choice for millions of Americans. As William Whyte has noted, the "organization man" traded his individuality for a secure place in the corporate cocoon. "The corporation's emphasis on teamwork, conformity, groupness, pliancy and the rest of the bureaucratic virtues, had spread across the economy." It had created a population of blue and white-collar employees, particularly in the bureaucratic corporations, who lacked the flexibility and transferability of skills necessary to find jobs of comparable worth within the wider economy. They had performed their jobs "the company way." The skills that they developed were the skills particular to moving up a specific corporate ladder.

Unions perpetuated the worst features of Taylorism. By 1950, over 14 million of the nation's 62 million workers were union members. Many union contracts resembled Taylor's time and motion studies. In its collective bargaining agreement with the United Auto Workers, General Motors divided the hour into six-minute periods. Work was fragmented to fit these periods and the worker was paid by the number of tenths of an hour worked. At the same time, the staffs of corporate controllers, planners and auditors increased tremendously, as the American corporate model spread rapidly to Europe and Japan. As Galbraith has noted, American industry was designed for a period of heavy and growing demand and therefore suited the circumstances of the postwar times perfectly.

In addition to the fragmented work on the shop floor, much of the white-collar work was also monotonous and repetitive, but efficiencies that resulted from this the division of labor increased profits and living standards. The big corporation, while employing only 10% of the working population, nevertheless became a dominant social institution. There was no clear limit to its desirable size. The corporation was glorified as the nation's steward and caretaker. It produced its apostles and high priests. One of the most devout, Peter Drucker, proselytized that the big corporation was the institution that set "the standard for the way of life and the mode of living of our citizens; which leads, moulds, directs; which determines our perspective on our society; around which crystallize our problems and to which we look for our solutions."

However, as observed by Whyte, the immediate post-war generation was not entirely comfortable with surrendering their autonomy to the corporate way of life. Having been raised during a time when rugged individualism was venerated, they experienced anxiety and guilt when giving up their individuality. It was a difficult choice: freedom and opportunity versus conformity and security. Everything that this generation had been taught weighed in favor of freedom and independence as the dominant social values. No longer able to express individuality through autonomous self-directed work, the corporation man submerged his ego and directed his energies instead to consumption. In the past, self worth was measured by individual achievement, what an individual made of himself. Without that avenue of self-actualization, the self worth of the corporation man became inevitably measured by what he consumed not by what he created. At the core of this relationship between corporate employee and the corporation lay a moral ambiguity. The organization not only suppressed autonomy and free will but also diffused personal responsibility throughout the bureaucracy. Long-term tenure, a good salary, bonuses and benefits had gone a long way to compensate for the anxiety caused by this moral uncertainty and lack of purpose.

Indeed, wage labor had long imposed a moral and political dilemma. Adam Smith argued that a segmented division of wage labor would increase productivity and therefore national wealth. However, large-scale wage labor called for larger concentrations of capital that tended to suppress wages. Smith's theory of the "wage fund" purported to demonstrate the deleterious effects of raising wages because such wage inflation would lower the standard of living. In short, Smith's perfect economy was based on a regimented division of wage labor, which would increase productivity, thereby allowing wages to increase naturally as the greater productivity increased wealth. Dismal? Yes. Exquisite? Yes. One wonders whether Smith kept bees as a hobby.

To Thomas Jefferson, however, large-scale manufacturing betrayed the values of the American Revolution. True independence could only be achieved when Americans were able to meet the demands of republican citizenship through the autonomous, self-directed labor and independent judgment that such citizenship required. As argued forcefully in the *Notes on the State of Virginia*, "dependence begets subservience and venality, suffocates the germ of virtue, and prepares fit tools for the designs of ambitions." According to Jefferson, wage labor generally and factory work in particular, bred a "depravity and corruption of morals" as it had done in London, Glasgow, St. Etienne, and Frankfurt.

Ironically, for a nation given birth by the rejection of an aristocracy, unfettered capitalism created a powerful elite. By the 1830's Alexis DeTocqueville documented the emergence of a "manufacturing aristocracy." This aristocracy "first impoverishes and debases the men who serve it, and then abandons them to be supported by the charity of the public. It is one of the harshest which ever existed in the world." The lower wages fell "the more easily [laborers] were oppressed; they can never escape from this fatal circle of cause and consequence." DeTocqueville's chilling observation of the American scene: "The workman is generally dependent on the master: these two men meet in the factory, but know not each other elsewhere; and whilst they come into contact in one point, they stand very wide apart on all others. The manufacturer asks nothing of the workmen but his labor; the workman expects nothing from him but his wages. The one contracts no obligation to protect, nor other to defend; they are not permanently connected either by habit or duty."

Perils of Prosperity

In *Capital City*, Thomas Kessner sums up nineteenth century industrialism as follows: "As technology transformed the working process, reducing many to low-skilled ciphers in a mechanized manufacturing system, industrialists adopted the self-serving view point that labor was to be dealt with like machines and raw materials, as simple costs of production. And like any other cost, it had to be brought down as low as cold be gotten." Despite skyrocketing profits, owners continued to push wages down.

As pointed out by Eric Hobsbawm in *The Age of Capital*, by the mid-nineteeth century "it was perfectly evident that most workers would remain workers all of their lives, and indeed the economic system required them to do so." Nearing the end of the century, America had become a nation of employees. In short, the industrial economy had evolved at odds with the civic conception of freedom and liberty. Military and bureaucratic methods of organizing work demanded conformity. Some employers provided uniforms, a company song, and company script, which could be used as legal tender in the company town. But this sense of belonging was preferably to the fear and anxiety of job insecurity. "If any single factor dominated the lives of nineteenth century workers it was *insecurity*. They did not know at the beginning of the week how much they would bring home at the end. They did not know how long their present work would last or, if they lost it, when they would get another job under what conditions. They did not know when accident or sickness would hit them, and though they knew that some time in middle age, they would become incapable of doing a full measure of adult physical labor, they did not know what would happen to them between then and death."

This hand-to-mouth insecurity created enormous stress and social pathology. During the pre-war worldwide economic depression (the "Great Depression"), the nation learned a stark lesson in mass unemployment. In a landmark study concluded in 1938, researchers Eisenberg and Lazersfield documented that long term unemployed workers experienced fear, feelings of inferiority and shame. They explained the progressive stages of unemployment:

> First there is shock, which is followed by an active hunt for a job, during which the individual is still optimistic and unresigned;

4. Reengineering and the Changing Nature of Work

he still maintains and unbroken attitude. Second, when all efforts fail, the individual becomes pessimistic, anxious, and suffers active distress; this is the most crucial state of all. And third, the individual becomes fatalistic and adopts himself to his new state but with a narrower scope. He now has a broken attitude.

This powerful description of the "broken man" was later supported by psychological studies demonstrating that job loss ranks just behind death of a loved one, discovery of a serious disease and divorce as a producer of serious psychological stress. Moreover, suicide, crime, depression and other personal and social problems were associated with prolonged job loss. The post-war "organization man" remembered growing up during the Depression. As children, many were dislocated. Others watched silently perhaps as their own parents became broken. The profound sense of insecurity and fear left an indelible mark on this generation. Still others deferred their domestic pursuits to serve during the war. The concepts of freedom and liberty were abstractions for this generation. In the choice between freedom and security, security was the preferable state, even if resulted in a kind of existential drift. Besides, the sheer amount of time devoted to the job, and the consumption of material goods that followed a good salary seemed more than adequate to fill the moral void. Ultimately, however, the lack of autonomy bred by dependence and conformity formed a poor foundation to compete in the world. In the end, the well-meaning promise of corporate security without the moral responsibility to adapt to a changing world was illusory and for many the capacity to change, evolve and adapt to changing circumstances simply atrophied. With all of their eggs having been placed in one basket, they became the victims of their own complacency and hardened sense of entitlement. They are now the victims of the global economy.

5. The Knowledge Firm

The ongoing transformation of the U.S. economy is conventionally measured by the shift from a manufacturing (production) to a service (consumption) economy. It is plainly characterized by an explosion of data and codified knowledge, propelled by a revolution in information and communication technologies, but the changes go much deeper. Intellectual property, in all its forms, has become perhaps the leading product of the U.S. economy, even though it is "produced" by relatively few people. The shift from a manufacturing economy to a service economy is evidenced by the fact that 60 percent of the today's workforce is comprised of white-collar office workers, up from just 18 percent one hundred years earlier. About 8 and 10 of these workers are nonexempt administrators, professionals and technicians who are carrying out tasks of various complexities under the direction and control of others. While the knowledge content of their jobs is apparent, particularly with the need to utilize various technologies, the depth and scope of this knowledge is relatively modest. Nevertheless, the service economy (and most of U.S. manufacturing today) is plainly characterized by an explosion of data and codified knowledge, propelled by a revolution in information and communication technologies. But the transformative changes go much deeper. Intellectual property, in all its forms, has become perhaps the leading product of the U.S. economy, even though it is "produced" by relatively few people.

The prevailing view is that an ever-growing percentage of people in the service economy are "knowledge workers", that is, they add value with their brainpower, not their physical labor power. In reality, the modern global economy, which may have commenced with the formation of the General Agreement on Tariffs and Trade in 1947, went into hyper-drive with the fall of Communism in 1989, and later ratcheted up by the formal acceptance of China into the World Trade Organization at the end of 2001, has flooded the world labor market with potentially tens of millions of skilled, knowledgeable workers and potentially billions of new lower skilled producers and consumers. While the purpose of outsourcing routine production jobs is to cut costs, American firms have also had to tap global labor markets for lower paid, *skilled* labor to remain competitive. Simultaneously, they have employed software and other technology solutions within their own organizations to standardize as much administrative, technical and professional work as possible so that even higher-level work can be outsourced. What remains at the core of many corporations today is an elite cadre of employees who manage the corporate brand; market its products; protect the corporate image; manage consultants; diversify investments and holdings; make deals; nurture relationships within the finance community; explore exotic financial arrangements; engage in research and development projects; seek out and acquire smaller, more innovative firms; protect the firm's patents and other intellectual property; figure out ways to attract and retain core talent and eliminate non-core functions; and who lobby legislatures for competitive advantage and special favors. Many core employees are not producing anything tangible, anything that exists as a material object. Instead they are engaging in knowledge-intensive tasks, or as Robert Reich has noted, they are engaging in "symbolic analysis" such as solving, identifying, and brokering problems by manipulating symbols. They simplify reality into abstract images that can be rearranged, juggled, experimented with, communicated to other specialists, and then, eventually, transformed back into reality. The manipulations are done with analytic tools, sharpened by experience. These tools may be mathematical algorithms, legal arguments, financial gimmicks, scientific principles, psychological insights about how to persuade or to amuse, systems of induction or deduction, or any other set of techniques for doing conceptual puzzles.

According to economists Robert Shapiro and Kevin Hasset, the total value of all this knowledge to the overall economy was about $5 trillion in 2005. In short, most of the value of most corporations is based on intangible, knowledge assets and a relatively few employees are responsible for maximizing the value of these assets. The value of knowledge assets is increasing. In contrast, the value of production assets, such as machinery, physical plant, cash and cash equivalent, and production labor, are declining. Witness the erosion of manufacturing jobs in the United States, which have been declining for nearly two generations, primarily due to automation and outsourcing to lower wage countries. In January 2004, the number of such jobs stood at 14.3 million, down by 3 million jobs, or 17.5 percent, since July 2000 and about 5.2 million since the historical peak in 1979. By 2007, employment in manufacturing was at it's lowest since July 1950. As a result, the U.S. makes less what the rest of the world takes, insofar as the manufacturer of consumer goods are concerned. Even so, the manufacturing jobs that do remain, are more value added and knowledge intensive, such as customized engineering, supply chain integration and product service. Thus, manufacturing survives in the United States by being more knowledge intensive, and the jobs that remain require far more than simply efficient production; that is, physical labor. But becoming more knowledge-intensive has not been easy for tens of thousands of workers, particularly for those whose sense of entitlement has outweighed their commitment to learning and re-tooling.

The transformation from an industrial economy based on production and physical labor and to more knowledge intensive, *new* economy is reflected in America's trade imbalance. In 2007 the nation's international deficit in goods and services was $711.6 billion. Chinese exports to the U.S. outpace U.S. exports to China six to one. For all the ingenuity and innovation that Americans can muster, there is not enough knowledge content in what the typical America firm exports to balance the trade debt. But one element of the trade picture is beneficial to the truly knowledge intensive firm. The U.S. has a large *surplus* in intellectual property. By the end of the twentieth century, U.S. exports in the form of royalties and licensing revenue exceeded $37 billion, topping aircraft exports or telecommunications equipment. The competition for global dominance of knowledge assets is fierce. Governments around the world are actively trying to prod their leading multinational firms and universities to develop ideas, cutting-age designs and processes that can be patented and protected.

Thus, America's innovation edge is being challenged. In fact, the ratio of receipts and fees generated by the exporting of intellectual property to the payments for intellectual property created abroad has been declining since 2000. In 1999, the ratio of receipts to payments was about 3:1. By 2002, the ratio of receipts to payments dropped to 2:1. The National Science Foundation's Science and Engineering Industries 2000 report concludes, "These trends suggest both a growing internationalization of U.S. business and a growing reliance on intellectual property overseas." Even as receipts from all forms of intellectual property from abroad have increased, the rest of the world is taking advantage of the same knowledge-intensive technologies as the US and thus quickly bridging the knowledge gap.

In 2005, the number of intellectual property applications filed from China rose nearly by half over the previous year, placing that country ahead of Australia, Canada and Italy for the first time. While such a jump could be the reaction to sustained allegations of rampant intellectual property theft (the U.S. Chamber of Commerce estimates that intellectual property theft from China costs U.S. business about $250 billion annually), China nevertheless is developing the capacity to export products that where once the sole province of more knowledge-intensive economies. In 2005, the United States was sixth in patents per million people, after Switzerland, Finland, Japan, Sweden and Germany; and eighth in patents in relation to GNP, after Finland, Switzerland, Japan, Sweden, Germany, Netherlands and Israel.

The mantra for this globalized, knowledge-intensive economy is, of course, "innovation" but according to Douglas Solomon, chief technology strategist at IDEO, an innovation-consulting firm, "corporations inherently have antibodies that come out and they envelop and kill innovation." To most big corporations innovation means acquiring innovative firms, engaging in patent and copyright litigation and ensuring that employees do not misuse or misappropriate trade secrets and other confidential and proprietary information. To the extent that technology, biomedical, pharmaceutical and other "innovative" firms engage in invention and discovery, it remains the sole province of an elite core of employees who are paid well. As a matter of property law, they are basically well-paid servants. Everyone else, regardless of what the corporate creed says, is labor cost. But unlike the industrial worker, the knowledge worker owns the means of production, his or her own brainpower. This observation has driven some thought leaders, such as Richard Florida, to declare the end of history; that is the end of the economic friction between capital and labor, and the beginning of a new era of free market bliss. However, before we become too giddy with the notion that the new economy will eventually transform the masses into clever, affluent and free people, it is best to pause and remember that, in our time, work is increasingly subject to market forces, requiring individuals to make lifelong investments in their skills and knowledge base. Without these "capital investments" in the stock of skills and know-how, both the individual and society will reach a dead end. While the new economy tends to increase the value of knowledge, it is relentlessly generating its share of haves and have-nots. Forrester Research, Inc. predicts that 3.3 million U.S. jobs will be sent offshore by 2015, accounting for 2 percent of the entire workforce and $136 billion in wages. At the same time, for the employees that are adding value with their knowledge, wages are going up.

Current intellectual property law limits the expandable nature of knowledge because it creates a type of monopoly. The purpose of a profit-making firm is to dominate its market, to create, whenever feasible a monopoly, and to exploit that monopoly for as long as possible; in other words to use its property rights of ownership and exclusion. Intellectual property, while intangible and theoretically infinite, is still, as a matter of law, property and like all property, it increases in value when demand exceeds supply. Therefore, knowledge-intensive firms must own as much intangible, intellectual property as possible, such as patents, copyrights, trade secrets, ideas, even employee-know-how, so that it can be hoarded, allocated and exploited. Since for most big corporations today, survival is based on the monopoly control of knowledge, it would be terribly naive to think that truly valuable knowledge would be shared or managed as if this resource was a public utility.

Yet even while whole industries are powered by information, today's intellectual property, labor, employment, and contract law remain bound to nineteenth century property law. These legal rules make certain that value-added information remains a scarce, private and, therefore, an exploitable resource. These rules also make certain that most, if not all, of an employee's work product, including intangible, knowledge "products" is owned by his or her employer. In short, when it comes to knowledge as intellectual property, we have a twenty first century economy governed, in part, by nineteenth century legal rules. The foundation of these rules rests on traditional notions of liberty, property and free will. Wage labor is "free" because it is essentially an act of free will, a voluntary exchange between employer and employee. The output of this exchange, labor, legally belongs to the person who is paying for it, the employer. Thus the fruit of this labor, whether tangible or intangible, creates a property interest that vest with the employer. The ownership of intellectual property in the new knowledge economy will determine whether firms and their employees can thrive in the global economy.

When a chief executive says, "people are our most important asset" he (almost always "he" since by 2008, still only 12 of the Fortune 500 companies had CEOs who were women) is really speaking of a small percentage of the firm's employees. Everyone else is merely labor cost. As such, for most companies, "knowledge management" is nothing more than squeezing standardized inputs into a template to achieve predictable outcomes. In *The New Pioneers*, Thomas Petzinger calls "knowledge management" a "great oxymoron" since for most corporations it amounts to nothing more than creating a database of best practices that gives employees a menu of responses from which to choose. He notes that firms have learned to "Taylorize" white-collar work. Frederick Taylor published the *Principles of Scientific Management* in 1911. Taylor's methods reshaped the very nature of industrial work and revolutionized how it would be organized. According to Taylor, "scientific management involves a complete mental revolution on the part of the workmen . . . and it involves the equally complete revolution on the part of management's side. For now on, workers were told not to take any initiative, just "do your job", least they waste time in doing the job the "right way."

For Taylor, time was of the essence. In study after study, he broke down every operation on the factory floor into its simplest tasks and then timed each to find the most economical way of performing it. His concepts of time study and his notion of the elementary task soon became the organizational paradigm of the great manufacturing enterprises. Following these principles, manufacturers perfected mass production, nowhere more dramatically than in the automobile industry. Ford Motor Company improved on Taylor's concept of dividing work into simple, repetitive tasks by creating an assembly line. On this line, a worker would install a simple part with one basic, uncomplicated task. Thousands of workers simply repeated thousands of simply tasks, a thousand times a day. Sophisticated management systems followed to maintain efficiency and productivity. In short, workers were interchangeable, like the gears of a machine.

In *The Triumph of Conservatism*, Gabriel Kolko observes: "Scientific management was a thoroughly totalitarian philosophy, and merely a rationale for cutting costs. In the last analysis, its success depended on workers working harder and the elimination of loafers. Taylor's reputation and fame were based on his promise of lower labor costs for businessmen." But while lowering labor costs and increasing efficiency may have been the primary reasons for firms to adopt scientific management principles, Taylor made explicit the core of his program: to take possession for management of the "mass of traditional knowledge" once held by workers themselves, the "knowledge handed down to them by word of mouth, through the many years in which their trade has been developed from the primitive condition."

As Alan Trachtenberg has observed in *The Incorporation of America*, "the social distribution of knowledge begins a major shift with a transference (as far as technology and techniques are concerned) from bottom to top." Scientific management had provided a rationale and methodology to transfer control of the knowledge content of work from the employee to the employer "and in so doing to complete the process inherent in industrialization: the appropriation of inherited craft skills by industrial capital. In short order, big corporate and government research dominates innovation and the majority of patent holders become corporations.

In a perverse irony of language, most "knowledge workers" today are not paid to innovate or even think outside the box. They are paid to support the small fraction of the workforce, perhaps 1 in 1,000 that add knowledge value. This is why most firms invest as little as possible in work that customers do not value and whose workers' skills are easy to replace, automating what they can, outsourcing the rest. With service and sales jobs that cannot be outsourced, the "human capital management" business generated $7.2 billion in revenue in 2007. Such management systems are nothing more than a Taylorized time breakdown, usually in thirty-second intervals, of key functions, such as speaking with a customer on the phone. These time standards are used to schedule efficient workers during peak hours, increasing competition between sales people and boosted sales per hour. For the average retail worker, human capital management has transformed the relational dimension of the sales transaction into a time-sensitive grind.

In the global economy, knowledge, rather than physical labor or tangible property, may be the most critical asset "owned" by employees and the firms that employ them. In that regard, the transformation of work and organizations is radically changing the way Americans labor and is realigning the social and legal relationship between employers and employees. Some commentators believe that this post-industrial restructuring has unleashed social Darwinian forces, creating the environment where only those with superior skills will survive. Others see rapid structural change as an opportunity to unleash the dormant forces of individualism and self-fulfillment. Whichever the case, when knowledge is the indispensable asset for innovation and success, and where labor can be purchased anywhere in the world, no individual is immune from the demand to increase their individual intellectual asset portfolio and no organization is immune from obsolescence. Since most people took post-war prosperity and affluence for granted, the pressure and stress of this new form of competition is shocking. Moreover, even big corporations are vulnerable, thereby increasing the need to attract and retain value-added employees and to outsource labor costs.

Consider Google, Inc., arguably the most powerful company on the Internet. There is no reason to doubt Google's belief that its people are its most important assets. The company is famous for its lavish employee perks, which include top-flight chefs in the cafeteria and free massages for stress-out engineers. But in what the *New York Times* (June 3, 2007) calls the company's "inner sanctum" a team of engineers are creating real value. In the "search quality" department, Amit Singhal and hundreds of other engineers, computer scientists, psychologists, and linguists working in small teams are constantly engaged in small innovations to perfect "the magical, mathematical brew inside millions of black boxes that power [Google's] search engine. Their work is veiled in secrecy.

Google values Mr. Singhal and his team for basic competitive reasons. Their work leaves searchers satisfied with Google's results, making it less likely that users will go to Yahoo or Microsoft, thus "preserving the tidy advertising gold mine that search represents." Google recruited Mr. Singhal from AT&T labs. AT&T recruited him from Yahoo, where he was that firm's chief scientist, which, in turn, recruited him from Amazon. Google is keenly aware of the importance of value-added human capital and will relentlessly, perhaps ruthlessly, find and retain it. At the same time, Google will freely outsource less value added work to China, India, Viet Nam and the Philippines. Thousands of code writers, data analysts and software engineers in these countries perform important knowledge work for the company. In the new economy, even a "cool" company, one that seeks to do no evil, understands that its survival of the fittest. Mr. Singhal too may operate under this Darwinian assumption, for without the catalytic effects of the organization, what is his real value? Stated another way, if every person was able to receive the full value of his ideas and know-how, there would be no employees. Instead, there would be only independent contractors and free agents. However, most people who have been part of the economy for the last century and a half, including Mr. Singhal, cannot readily receive the full value of his knowledge since full value is only realized when he works together within his engineering group, thereby creating something greater than the sum of his individual effort. But for the synergies of the group, Mr. Singhal's knowledge surely has much less value.

As Singhal's efforts becomes catalytic within his team and within the wider organization, knowledge creation takes on communal dimensions. The knowledge contained within the "inner sanctum" can remain secret only for so long. At some point it must be codified into code and monetized if possible. At that point it's secret status becomes public and is subject to reverse engineering by competitors. In 2011 as Google was defending itself from allegations that it was systematically engaging in monopoly practices on the Internet, Singhal stated publicly that "Google's search algorithm is actually one of the world's worst kept secrets. PageRank, one of our allegedly 'secret ingredients,' is a formula that can be found in its entirety everywhere from academic journals to Wikipedia. We provide more information about our ranking signals than any other search engine. We operate a webmaster forum, provide tips and YouTube videos, and offer diagnostic tools that help websites identify problems"

The dynamic and challenge of knowledge intensive work is that the person's intellectual work product must be shared to have value. Information that is hoarded or fenced in like land or other physical assets has no value to an employer. At some point the knowledge imbedded in a product or service becomes public, requiring an ongoing investment in creating new knowledge, innovation and improvement. As America adjusts to the new realities of a knowledge intensive, technologically enabled economy, new conflicts emerge. In the new economy, employees are ill served by growing dependent on one employer or letting their skills become stale. Self-directed workers who have transcended the zero-sum struggle over non-value added jobs have taken responsibility for their own development and employability. They are responsible for increasing the value of their labor through expanding their knowledge and honing their skills. In the new economy, their knowledge adds value to their employer's products and services. However, as Galbraith has noted, corporations are driven to own, or at least control, everything. In an industrial economy, this monopolistic tendency meant controlling the market. It meant concentrating industrial capital at the expense of eliminating or displacing labor. In the new economy, it means owning or controlling knowledge, including employees' knowledge. Taken to its conclusion, this relentless drive to own and control as much knowledge power as possible creates a monopoly over knowledge that could seriously impair the progress of a society and undermine the fundamental human right to pursue a livelihood and earn a living. Left to develop on its current trajectory, the new economy will result in displacement and drift for tens of millions or American workers.

Consider the software giant Oracle. It has aggressively acquired PeopleSoft, Siebal Systems and BEA Associates. The conventional wisdom has been that talented knowledge workers had to treated delicately or risk their running out the door to waiting competitors. Brilliant engineers and their sales teams can't be pushed around with impunity, or so the thinking went. But the financial success of Oracle cannot be ignored. After acquiring

PeopleSoft in 2005 the company let go 5,000 employees and steered customers to alternative Oracle products. Company stock soared nearly 70 percent. Larry Ellison, Oracle's CEO makes a simple point: "We want to be number one in all segments." It's hard to argue with this sentiment but other firms have revised their innovation strategies to account for the risk of losing top-flight talent as they seek to break into the next big market.

Cisco Systems, the giant computer networking company, spent $2.5 billion on acquiring 44 firms in its core switch and router business. But to break into the twenty first century Internet market, it spent about $11 billion on a handful of innovative firms. Its prior acquisition strategy was based on the fast incorporation of firms it had gobbled up, replacing their leadership teams with Cisco employees and quickly absorbing individual firm identities into the Cisco brand. But in 2003 Cisco began experimenting with a hands off approach to handle the highly valuable talent it was acquiring. Cisco consciously decided that the more innovative firms could keep its management team and, in some cases, to maintain their own brand and the corporate culture that nurtured it. In short, to successfully crack the Internet market, Cisco took care to give up some of its autocratic control to ensure that value added knowledge workers felt at home.

Aside from Oracle's aggressive approach to succeeding in the software industry, it's Microsoft's unsolicited, unfriendly, and ultimately unsuccessful $44.6 billion bid for Yahoo that has the potential for permanently altering the rules of the new economy because it represents the acknowledgement that talented, knowledge intensive employees will be sacrificed *en mass* to ensure the firm's survival. For the most part, because of the reluctance to disrupt talented employees, hostile takeovers were taboo among technology firms. Companies focused on new growth rather than cost savings, developing and nurturing innovation from within. Indeed, much of Microsoft's early success was based on its ability to win the "ground wars" as it engineers built new techniques from scratch and improved them on an ongoing basis. Apple, Inc. too has won its share of the innovation and improvement wars. In Microsoft's case, pushing the antitrust envelope by bundling its products to become the de facto industry standard ensured stable growth.

By going after Yahoo!, not just poaching its talent, but also going after the entire company, Microsoft consciously changed its innovation strategy. Microsoft's CEO, Steve Ballmer acknowledged that by combing the two giants, two billion dollars could be saved by eliminating overlapping operations. According to the *Wall Street Journal* (February 2, 2008), "unsolicited bids, especially for people-intensive companies like Yahoo, tend to scare away those human assets. There will be much carnage before this is over ... Still, in a world where users, not companies, are continually innovating and upending the business world, creating an ever-larger bureaucracy doesn't seem like a guarantee of anything."

6. A Digression on Private Property

While a universal free labor ethic was established after the Civil War, the origin of voluntary or free labor goes back at least to the Enlightenment when English philosophers such as John Locke imagined new possibilities for achieving liberty, freedom and happiness. Locke, a Puritan, closely followed the Book of Genesis in developing what would be referred to as the labor theory of property. To Locke: "God, when he gave the world in common to all mankind, commanded man also to labor, to improve it for the benefit of life, and therein lay out something upon it that was his own, his labor." The right to property began whenever a person "mixed" his labor with something, thereby removing it from its natural state. He theorized that labor conveyed ownership of property and that political liberty itself rested on the individual's control over the fruits of his own labor. Locke opposed slavery, which he defined as the state in which individual's no longer controlled their labor, as a violation of natural law but found no fault with indentured servitude, since the servant gave up his freedom only until such time as his debt was repaid to his master. In theory at least, the servant could one day become a master.

Locke's labor theory of property formed the bedrock of an emerging free exchange economy and once codified by English common law, became the driving force from an economic system controlled through royal prerogative and toward a free market economy. No less than Edward

Coke ruled, in 1603, against the royal prerogative to grant a monopoly in *Darcy v. Allen*. Darcy, a groom in the Queen's privy chamber was granted a 21-year monopoly patent over the manufacture, import and sales of playing cards throughout all of England. Allen, a London merchant, infringed the patent, and suit was brought.

Allen enjoyed considerable support from the merchant class of London, who chaffed under the abuses of the royal monopoly system. But it was God who trumped the Queen. "The Ordinance of God is, that every man should live by labor, and that he who will not labor, let him not eat," argued Allen's counsel. As it followed, "a restraint of a man's trade is against God's law. Now therefore, Letters of Patent against the laws of God are void." This biblical justification of free labor greatly influenced the court to rule in favor of Allen, although the court's holding was based primarily on the deleterious impact of the monopoly on "the freedom and liberty of the subject to engage in the lawful trade of his choice."

In determining an ownership right to an intangible, knowledge asset, one might return to Locke's labor theory of property. No one has a monopoly over ideas and know-how. Such absolute control would violate natural law. As with physical property, humankind is commanded to improve and apply the idea through effort. When labor is mixed with the idea, ownership is created. According to Locke, each person plainly has "a property in his own person," including the labor of his body, and the work of his hands." He continues by explaining "a freeman makes himself a servant to another by selling him, for a certain time, the service he undertakes to do in exchange for wages he is to receive." Thereafter, that labor no longer belongs to the free man but to the master. "Thus," writes Locke "the turfs my servant has cut, I have a right to them and it is my property without the assignment or consent of anybody. The [servant's] labor has fixed my property in them." It appears therefore that an idea belongs to everyone in common but when someone takes that common knowledge and expresses it in a tangible form (or a "teaching" in the parlance of patent law), a property right is created. If that property is created within an employer-employee relationship, the property belongs to the employer.

6. A Digression on Private Property

For nearly three centuries, workers have contributed their physical labor in exchange for wages. The general rule in the industrial economy was that the employer owned the means of production and the worker was not paid to think. However, information technology has made at least some work increasingly more information intensive. Value-added knowledge is more critical still. In the knowledge economy, property is less tangible; rather it is "intellectual property" broadly defined. Take the case of Dr. Kai-Fu Lee, Microsoft and Google. Dr. Lee was working at Microsoft as vice president of a division overseeing technologies for speech recognition, search and language processing. He held a doctorate in computer science from Carnegie Mellon University, where he worked as an assistant professor before joining Apple Computer. He spent six years at Apple and worked at Silicon Graphics, Inc. before joining Microsoft.

At some point during his employment with Microsoft, Dr. Lee signed an employment agreement, which provided in relevant part:

> While employed at Microsoft and for a period of one year thereafter, I will not . . . engage in activities competitive with products, services or projects (including actual or demonstrably anticipated research or development) on which I worked or about which I learned confidential or proprietary information or trade secrets while employed at Microsoft . . .

The agreement further provided:

> Confidential or proprietary information or trade secrets means all data and information in whatever form, tangible or intangible, that is not generally known to the public and that relates to the business, technology, practices, products, marketing, sales, services, finances, or legal affairs of Microsoft . . .

Dr. Lee is credited with establishing Microsoft's research and development center in Beijing, which houses about 380 researchers. Upon his return from a short sabbatical, Dr. Lee gave notice to Microsoft that he was leaving for a job at Google as president of that company's China operations in charge of establishing a research center there. Microsoft's lawsuit quickly followed, alleging that Dr. Lee had violated his employment agreement and seeking a court order enjoining him from setting up Google's shop in China. In short, Microsoft was saying that Dr. Lee was not free to leverage knowledge gained in its employ. Its justification too was based on 300-year old property law.

America's early colonial experience seemed to bear out Locke's moral imperative regarding property, temporary servitude and wage labor. England's master-servant laws were feudal in nature and bound servant to his master, and master to servant, for a prolonged period of time. The master was legally obliged to provide for the care and instruction of his servant. For his or her part, the servant was bound to serve the full term of the indenture under threat of physical punishment and legal sanctions, including imprisonment. However, the difficult and expansive terrain of the New World's frontier required early settlers to adapt social and legal arrangements. Indentures were not easily enforceable where servants could simply relocate to another location to find work, as did Benjamin Franklin who escaped his printing trade indenture in Massachusetts to seek new opportunity in Pennsylvania.

In particular, the social structure of Puritan New England resulted in flexible labor arrangements. For one, the harsh New England terrain required maximum effort by every able-bodied citizen. Moreover, work was considered an act of devotion. The Puritan worked to glorify God and the twin doctrines of calling and improvement meant that every adult was compelled to achieve salvation through meaningful work. Puritans did not work to live, they lived to work. As summarized by Stephen Innes: "Work for the saints was the warrant and source of all wealth: God gave the use of the world to the industrious and rational; title to property came principally from work; the fruits of labor belonged to the worker; men and women had only a right to what they actually could use. Puritans were equal before God, each driven by a calling to improve their own lot, thereby contributing to the common good. Communal capitalism was born in Puritan New England. So was the profit motive.

Adolph Berle in the *American Economic Republic* observed how the Protestant work ethic deeply informed labor and commerce in early America. "Man's chief end was to glorify God, and to serve and praise Him forever. This he could do with every human action, in every phase of his life. He glorified God by worshipping in Church, or by making a first-rate pair of shoes, or by performing services in such a fashion that he made his employer and his associates and those around him happier." In short, maximizing one's economic value was consistent with serving the Lord. Doing well was further evidence of virtue. "That the merchant should accumulate a fortune was entirely in accord with the theory that the laborer was worthy of his hire, and that the Lord would forward the fortunes of his faithful servants." By the time of the Revolution, free enterprise had been the American way of life for nearly a century.

American revolutionary thought closely followed Locke's formulation of the labor theory of property. So close was the Declaration of Independence to Locke's writings in form and substance that Thomas Jefferson was accused of copying Locke's *Second Treatise of Government*, which was published in 1690. In sum, Locke defined property as more than tangible objects, but also "as property that men have in their persons as well as goods." Adopting this concept of autonomy and self-ownership, the Declaration clarifies the fundamental property right, the ownership of oneself, and combines it with the inalienable rights to secure life and liberty and to pursue happiness.

A republican form of government or what is often called "liberal democracy" was viewed as the best political system to preserve life, liberty and property. However, Adam Smith's *Wealth of Nations*, first published in 1776, the same year as the Declaration of Independence was no less revolutionary that the colonists' statements of grievance and separation. It has been observed that Smith's theory of limited government and individual freedom founded on natural, unalienable property rights established the political framework for the modern free enterprise system. Smith too opposed slavery, as well as government monopolies, trade unions, industry cartels, long apprenticeships and any other restrictions on free enterprise and interferences with the free market. To Smith, all such restrictions on labor and commerce were immoral and violated "the just liberty both of the workmen and those who might be disposed to employ him. As it hinders the one from working at what he thinks proper, so it hinders the other from employing who they think proper."

Smith, like Locke, viewed labor as an extension of property. To Smith, "the property which every man has in his own labor, as it is the original foundation of all other property . . . is the most sacred and inviolable." For the laboring poor, that property "lies in the strength and dexterity of his hands." No matter how unequal, the master-servant relationship was not inconsistent with freedom, liberty and free will because it was, at least in theory, the result of a voluntary exchange of property. As long as government stood out of the way, this voluntary exchange was subject to simple bargaining rules: "The workmen desire to get as much, the master to give as little as possible."

The U.S. Constitution does not define property, leaving that to the states to define under common law. However, it is clear that the drafters viewed property in Lockean terms. During the ratification debates, James Madison paraphrased Locke, arguing that the term "property" embraced "everything to which man may attach value and have a right, including the labor that acquires daily subsistence." As observed by Richard Hofstadter in *The American Political Tradition*, the founders expressly linked liberty to property. "They wanted freedom from fiscal uncertainty and irregularities in the currency, from trade wars among the states, from economic discrimination by more powerful foreign governments, from attacks on the creditor class or on property from popular insurrection. They aimed to create a government that would act as an honest broker among a variety of propertied enemies and preventing anyone of them from becoming too powerful."

According to Hofstadter, the founders probably would have accepted the declaration that "all men were created equal" but only as a legal, not a social or political, proposition. Even Jefferson believed in the existence of a "natural aristocracy" based on private property, but, as Hofstadter has noted, "dread of the propertyless masses" was all but universal among the men who founded the national government. What encouraged them, however, was the broad dispersion of land. Small landowners had a stake in the government and even tough merchants, bankers and large landowners would dominate the government, small property owners would have an independent and far from negligible voice. Thus property ownership became for basis of suffrage: consent of "the people" meant property owners, small and large. Accordingly, the survival of the new

Republic was based on the wide dispersion of property accomplished by a government with its chief purpose to protect property rights. The arbitrary redistribution of property would have been viewed as tyrannical. The rights derived from Nature's law, the right to life, liberty and property would be preserved, as self-autonomy would give free reign to human ingenuity and ambition. In this regard, the drafters also recognized the connection between human ingenuity and prosperity when they authorized Congress to grant authors and inventors a limited monopoly over their intellectual property, thus creating ownership rights in intangible property.

After a hearing a Washington State judge permitted Dr. Lee to begin working for Google in a limited capacity but ordered him not to work on "products, services or projects" that compete with Microsoft, including Internet searching and speech technologies. In short, the court found that Microsoft did not own Dr. Lee's reputation and his academic contacts. His reputation and contacts were not Microsoft products, services or projects. Accordingly, Dr. Lee was allowed to leverage his reputation and relationships to further Google's interests by recruiting personnel, working with the Chinese government, and by offering non-technical advice about how to do business in China.

Because the court found that Dr. Lee's reputation and academic relationships did not belong to Microsoft, it did not need to decide whether "intangible information related to Microsoft's business" could be deemed proprietary to the company. Dr. Lee was permitted to exercise his intellect and other "human capital" to make a living. But what about Dr. Lee's ideas and know-how; did Dr. Lee or Microsoft own them? Surely, Microsoft has a legitimate interest in protecting confidential information, such as trade secrets, customer lists, formulae, designs, code, and customer good will. Microsoft may also have a protectable interest where Dr. Lee's services were special, unique or extraordinary, and the loss of which to Google might expose Microsoft to irreparable harm. Certainly, tangible information is "owned" by the employer and therefore the employer is entitled to protect and defend its ownership rights. An idea or an employee's know-how, however, is intangible, but may nevertheless constitute a "trade secret." It can be just as valuable as a customer list. In a knowledge-based business, it is becoming more and more important to reduce the amount of time between developing an idea and the protection of it. An employer does not want to have a great idea come up, only to have it be the one that got away. Therefore, the employer may insist that the idea, i.e.: trade secret, remain secret until such time as it can be transformed into a copyright or patent. Secrecy however can be counterproductive in the knowledge economy since knowledge can only expand from a process of sharing, exchange and openness. Organization's that compete on the value of their copyrights, patents and other intellectual property are beset by the conflict between creativity and expression, on the one hand, and control and secrecy on the other.

The conventional wisdom in the West is that the balance between expression and secrecy, freedom and security is best struck with a republican form of government, which is sometimes referred to a "liberal democracy." As such, many in the West view liberal democracy as an indispensable ingredient to support free markets. But this assumption is not supported by the facts, considering that non-republican forms of government have been compatible with capitalism. Indeed, as previously noted, leading economist believe that authoritarian regimes can foster markets as long as workers have some way of venting their frustration with government economic policies and can influence at least indirectly government decision making. This is basically the case in China today. Economic policies are formulated from the top, primarily in secrecy, and carried out through state instrumentalities. Through civil disturbances and acts of disobedience the Chinese people protest land use policies and local government corruption. Bloggers, although monitored, are permitted to criticize the pace and pattern of economic development and other policies. Thus, it can be said that informal democratic processes are at work in China, a one-party state that trades freely.

Indeed, the evolutionary economists from von Mises to Hayek to Singer and Wilson argue that trade predates history, that is markets predate liberal democracy by thousands of years. This view of liberty as an extension of property lies at the heart of today's fierce struggle over the role of government and the public debt. Shortly after the 2011 compromise to raise the U.S. government's so-called debt ceiling, which brought the federal government close to defaulting on its sovereign debt, Eric Cantor, the chief negotiator for the House Republicans define the political battle over the federal government's debt as between adherents of the "welfare state" and "capitalism." (*Wall Street Journal*, August 6, 2011). He described the policies of the welfare state as "taking from those who create and giving to those who don't." But arguably, welfare programs are the result of the progressive impulse that springs from liberal democracy. Indeed, the U.S. Constitution gives Congress the power to enact laws necessary to regulate interstate commerce and to tax and spend for the general welfare, which has required it from time to time to enact laws that have addressed dangerous levels of income inequality. Thus, it may be liberal democracy itself that is the problem for those who would dismantle the welfare state. An authoritarian regime can protect property just as well as a liberal democracy, as long as it is not rotted with corruption.

Would Dr. Lee have fared as well in China? He has since left his job as president of Google China to form Innovation Works and investment incubator that encourages Chinese entrepreneurs in China. Sarah Lacy a tech writer and blogger notes that if Dr. Lee "convinces more Chinese entrepreneurs to start businesses, that's good for China and the tech world globally." And it would be a sign that Chinese law protects property to the extent it is beneficial to the government's overall economic plans.

I would argue, however, that to compete in the knowledge economy, employers must be able to tap employees' creativity throughout the organization. But the command and control structure of a typical vertically organized corporation tends to stifle creativity; worse, this type of organization can breed conformity, mediocrity dishonesty and corruption. In other words, property without liberty may work in an industrial economy but may not get optimal results in the knowledge economy.

7. The Protection of Intellectual Property

Ideas are enormously valuable resources in the new economy. They form the basis for innovation and are incorporated in new technology. In 2004, the information technology industry alone contributed $445 billion to U.S. GDP. While it is widely understood that the use of new technologies in production and in delivering services increases productivity, it may be that innovative ideas embodied in new technologies play an important, independent role. In a free market economy, increasing productivity, output per labor hour, is the key to rising living standards, as it allows wages to increase without inflationary pressures on prices. Productivity is the key to competing in the global economy, since it allows firms to produce more with less. However, investments in productivity, such as new machinery or higher skilled labor, are subject to diminishing returns. As some point the increased production outstrips demand, leaving unused inventory and reduced profits, making layoffs necessary.

Ideas, on the other hand, may represent an input that expands indefinitely. Ideas can be used over and over again, by skilled people, originating in firms but leaking into the wider economy. One firm's use of the idea does not exhaust the resource. Instead the resource spreads to other firms, raising the productivity of their machines and people. "Thus," according to Thomas Homer-Dixon in *The Ingenuity Gap*, "if an economy is well-endowed with human capital, it can exploit the inexhaustible nature of technological ideas to counteract the natural tendency of capital investments to produce diminishing returns." In essence, ideas, unlike labor or capital, can be a factor of production that can actually exhibit increasing returns. In other words, the economic benefits derived from investment in the production of useful ideas do not decline over time. As a freely available resource, ideas are literally inexhaustible.

This availability ensures innovation. According to Professor Hargadon in *How Breakthroughs Happen*, innovators rarely come up with new ideas. Instead they convert old ideas into new ones. He calls this "recombinant innovation", as ideas continually build on another, creating new forms and adaptations. In practice, even patents hardly ever represent truly unique art or science. In a study based on 630,000 U.S. patents, the Israel Institute of Technology found that "innovation is essentially a process of coupling." Or as illuminated by economist Mark White: "Every time technologists discover a single new material, humanity then has the potential to make every known object in a new and potentially quite useful way. In turn, these individual objects combine with human assemblies of subjects to create further new possibilities. These possibilities then radiate out into the complements and substitutes for all known objects and object assemblies, creating further possibilities. Each and every new material expands the entire scope of human technology."

Professor Gilson has written persuasively in the *New York University Law Review* (1999) that in locally concentrated knowledge industries, such as California's Silicon Valley and Boston's Route 128 corridor, firms have benefited from greater innovation where knowledge workers are free to leave employers and bring their know-how and ingenuity to new employers or start up firms. Such mobility accelerates recombinant innovation and has led to repeated breakthroughs in the cumulative technology of computer components and software. In short, job mobility and knowledge sharing creates a public stock of knowledge that benefits all concerned. However, if firms can simply replicate ideas from a public stock of knowledge, then they may not have an incentive to innovate. In such a case, maintaining secrecy of an idea before it becomes public knowledge is essential. For example, it is legally permissible for a firm to take a competitor's product apart with the view to discovering how it was made even though this reverse engineering may reveal secrets of the competitor's production processes. But if the underlying ideas that are embedded into the product are "free," the problem is not whether there is demand to consume it; rather the problem is whether there are enough incentives to produce it. In addition to secrecy, Patent and Copyright law provide the remedy to this problem by giving creators an exclusive right to control some of the uses of their work for a limited period of time. This monopoly and the time to exploit the idea provide the incentive for organizations to innovate.

As previously noted, the U.S. Constitution gives Congress the power "to promote the progress of science and the useful arts, by securing for limited times to authors and inventors the exclusive right to their respective writings and discoveries." This is the formal source of federal power over patents and copyrights, and the allied area of trademark law. This constitutional provision was modeled on the Statute of Anne (1557) that was enacted by the Parliament to "encourage learning" and to break the royal monopoly on bookselling and publishing. The Federalist Papers make only the briefest of mention of this congressional authority. Madison in Federalist No. 43 merely mentions this "miscellaneous power", the utility of which "will scarcely be questioned." He simply notes that copyright has been recognized by English common law and to allow the states to devise their own legal systems would be highly inefficient.

The authority to enact laws that granted limited duration patent and copyright protection to foster the arts and sciences reflected a practical solution to the problem of who should own and control ideas, particularly ideas that were useful to the community. According to Thomas Jefferson, an individual could exclusively own an idea as long as he kept in to himself "but the moment it is divulged, it forces itself into the possession of everyone, and the receiver cannot dispossess himself of it ... That ideas should freely spread from one to another over the globe, for the moral and mutual instruction of man, and improvement of his condition, seems to have been peculiarly and benevolently designed by nature ... Inventions then cannot, in nature, be subject to property." Lincoln, on the other had viewed patent rights as indistinguishable from other property rights. In his Second Lecture on Discoveries and Inventions in 1859, he observed: "the patent system added the fuel of interest to the fire of genius, in the discovery and production of new and useful things."

As noted earlier, an idea, once shared, does not render it exhausted. In fact, innovation is created when people build on someone else's idea. In the state of nature knowledge expands and is inexhaustible. In this state, there would be no need for a "patent," since patents are granted for "inventions" and inventions in nature cannot be subject to property. However, Jefferson, who would be the nation's first patent commissioner, was if nothing else a realist. Man did not live in the state of nature; he lived in the material world of positive law. In fact, a government had just been instituted based on the consent of the governed and the governed wanted to make a profit on their ideas. The inventor believed that if he or she did not have the exclusive right to exploit the invention, there would be no incentive to invent. Without a patent, an idea could simply be taken, benefiting the taker without incurring any cost by inventing. This state of affairs would provide a disincentive to invent, thus progress would be impaired. In short, fueling progress was the constitutional aim of patents and copyrights. They were indispensable ways of enabling innovation in a free market system. In short, patent and copyright laws are designed as a barrier against idea theft, so that inventors have an incentive to invest in their ideas.

In *Bonito Boats, Inc. v. Thunder Craft Boats, Inc.* (1989), the U.S. Supreme Court made clear that the states could not undermine the Patent Act. In this case, Thunder Craft developed a hull design for a fiberglass recreational boat that it marketed under the trade name Bonito Boat Model 5VBR. The manufacturing process involved creating a hardwood model that was then sprayed with fiberglass to create a mold. The mold then served to produce the finished fiberglass boats for sale. No patent application was filed to protect the utilitarian or design aspects of the hull or the manufacturing process by which the finished boats were produced. After the Bonito 5VBR had been on the market for six years, the Florida Legislature enacted a statute that prohibits the use of a direct molding process to duplicate unpatented boat hulls, and forbids the knowing sale of hulls so duplicated.

Earlier decisions made clear that state regulation of intellectual property must yield to the extent that it clashes with the federal patent statute's balance between public right and private monopoly designed to promote certain creative activity. The efficient operation of the federal patent system depends upon substantially free trade in publicly known, unpatented design and utilitarian conceptions. A state law that interferes with the enjoyment of such a conception contravenes the ultimate goal of public disclosure and use that is the centerpiece of federal patent policy. Moreover, through the creation of patent-like rights, the States could essentially redirect inventive efforts away from the careful criteria of patentability developed by Congress over the last two hundred years. By offering patent-like protection for ideas deemed unprotected under the federal patent scheme, the court held that the Florida statute conflicted with the "strong federal policy favoring free competition in ideas which do not merit patent protection." In short, the patent law creates no affirmative right supporting a cause of action against a competitor to assert a right to make or copy what is in the public domain and excluded from patent protection.

On the other hand, copyright protection may be extended to nearly any written material, including computer code. Notwithstanding this protection, the public may engage in the "fair use" of a copyrighted work, including reproduction for the purpose of criticism, comment, news reporting, teaching, scholarship or research. Violators of a copyright are subject to a private right of action for infringement.

Generally speaking, an idea may have intrinsic value, but maximum value cannot be realized until it can be expressed in a tangible way, as a song, a poem or as software. Unlike the sole creation of an artist, an originator of new software may lack the resources to transform the idea into a tangible application. Others may be needed to contribute the resources to bring the idea to fruition. More often than not, others are part of an organization. Modern copyright law, which does not allow for the ownership of any ideas, only distinctive ways of expressing them, recognizes that the fruits of employees' ideas and know-how belong to the employer under the "work for hire" doctrine.

Work for hire is a special term used in the Copyright Act. Normally, when a person or group creates a copyrightable work, whether a song or a computer program or a sculpture, the person or persons creating the work have a copyright in the work. Thus, the creators can exploit the work and receive money for their creative energies. However, a work for hire is when a person creates a copyrightable work but does not own it. The Copyright Act allows for the copyright to go not to the creator but to the person who hired the creator to make the work. In short, the employer legally owns the copyright in exchange for wages.

In 1998 Congress extended the term of existing copyrights by twenty years. While Congress changed the term of copyright just once in the first hundred years of the Copyright Act, and once again in the next fifty years, it has extended the term of subsisting copyrights eleven times in the past forty years. The last extension meant that works that were to fall into the public domain in 1999 would now not be free until 2019.

Critics labeled the 1998 extension the "Mickey Mouse law" because the copyright to the venerable mouse was set to enter the public domain in 2004, with his best known animated pals following shortly afterward. One reason Disney Corporation put its weight behind the 1998 legislation was to keep Mickey and the gang out of the public domain. Opponents subsequently adopted a *Free the Mouse* campaign that included a lawsuit challenging the copyright extension brought by Eric Eldred, an online publisher of books that had fallen into the public domain. In effect, the extension bottled up for another generation public domain works that Eldred was about to publish. He filed his suit in the federal court, arguing that the First Amendment to the U.S. Constitution, which guarantees freedom of speech and of the press, limits Congress' power to extend copyrights indefinitely. According to Eldred, since existing copyrights protect work that is already created, extending the terms of this work restricts speech without any expectation of future creativity. In other words, the extension would suppress creative enterprise, thereby undermining the purpose of the copyright law, which is to create an incentive to create.

The U.S. Supreme Court upheld the 1998 extension, holding that the Constitution did not limit Congress to a single "limited time." Congress was free to grant extensions, as long as the extensions themselves were limited. In theory then, Congress could incrementally grant a perpetual monopoly on copyrighted works. As observed by Lawrence Lessig in *The Future of Ideas*, "[t]he freedom to build upon and create new works is increasingly, and almost perpetually, restricted under existing law [and] that control has been concentrated in the hands of holders of copyrights-increasingly large media companies."

Viewed from one angle, the *Eldred* case presented the narrow issue of whether Congress had the unfettered power to enact copyright extensions. By holding that the enactment of the copyright extension fell within the broad grant of Congress' constitutional authority, the U.S. Supreme Court followed the tradition of deference to a co-branch of government. The Court did not wade into the debate between two starkly different views of the public domain. One view holds that the public domain lacks value because there is no incentive to invest in preserving and distributing public domain works. The alternative view is that the public domain is a vast repository of raw material, out of which new creations are made, thus adding to society's cultural heritage form which all should be able to draw after the expiration of a copyright. The Court's reluctant to overrule Congress is a signal that it will not disrupt, at least presently, intellectual property jurisprudence which permits ownership of intangible property as if it were a physical object. As such, the economic rule of scarcity applies. As long as the copyright holder can control the supply of the copyrighted works, the price of access will be high.

The problem of access, or the lack thereof, cannot be entirely addressed by the moral argument that all should have equal access to the "knowledge commons." Jefferson's view that legal (monopoly) protection of intellectual property may impede, rather than advance, progress has been cited widely by advocates, such as Lawrence Lessig, who argue that intellectual property law is illegitimate in many cases because intangible objects are not naturally subject to the rules of scarcity because they can be simultaneously consumed by everyone without reducing the available supply. This is especially true when the content is expressed electronically. In that regard, the Internet is challenging the traditional economic rules of supply and demand, and the legal foundation on which these rules are supported.

In *Metro-Goldwyn-Mayer Studios v. Grokster* (2005), the U.S. Supreme Court addressed the liability of peer-to-peer technology providers. Each month, billions of electronic files are shared across peer-to-peer networks without the necessity of being routed through a central server. In this case, Grokster, a file sharing provider which have its software out for free, was aware that its users employed the software primarily to download and share copyrighted material, although since there was no central server, the networks were so decentralized it was impossible to discover which files were copied and when. Grokster received no revenue from its users. Its revenue was derived solely from the sale of advertising space and streaming advertising directly to users. In effect, Grokster (and Napster, another file sharing network) had facilitated the creation of an information commons, where intellectual property, 90 percent of which was copyrighted material, was accessible and freely available, but without the permission of the copyright holders.

Here, the U.S. Supreme Court acknowledged the tension between the competing values of supporting creativity through copyright protection and promoting technological innovation by limiting infringement liability. Indeed, the court noted:

> The tension between the two values is the subject of this case, with its claim that digital distribution of copyrighted material threatens copyright holders as never before, because every copy is identical to the original, copying is easy, and many people (especially the young) use filesharing software to download copyrighted works. This very breadth of the software's use may well draw the public directly into the debate over copyright policy.

While most of Grokster's users shared copyrighted material, the networks had other non-infringing uses. Some music performers gained new audiences by distributing their copyrighted work for free, and some distributors of public domain content also used the peer-to-peer networks to disseminate files. "The more artistic protection is favored, the more technological innovation may be discouraged," the Court noted. It set out to balance this tradeoff by holding Grokster liable for aiding and abetting the infringement of others, observing:

> The argument for imposing indirect liability in this case is, however, a powerful one, given the number of infringing downloads that occur every day using Grokster's software.

When a widely shared service or product is used to commit infringement, it may be impossible to enforce rights in the protected work effectively against all direct infringers, the only practical alternative being to go against the distributor of the copying device for secondary liability on a theory of contributory or vicarious infringement.

In the end, according to the Court, unlike a home recording device, the preponderance of the evidence demonstrated that Grokster's service was "good for nothing else but infringement."

In 2007 media conglomerate Viacom, the owner of MTV, Nickelodeon, and Paramount Film Studios, among many other television and film companies, sued Google and its video sharing website YouTube. Basing its suit, in part, on the *Grokster* decision, it is seeking one billion dollars in damages and an injunction to prevent what it calls "massive copyright infringement." When Google acquired YouTube, it held back some of the purchase price in anticipation of the lawsuit.

The underlying dispute is about the 1998 Digital Millennium Copyright Act (DMCA) and whether YouTube enjoys immunity under the Act's safe harbor provisions. Like Grokster, YouTube does not have direct knowledge of copyright infringement, although Viacom alleges that it could discover infringements if it wanted to since, unlike Grokster, YouTube's networks are routed through central servers. Also, like Grokster, YouTube does not receive direct revenue from file sharing but uses instead Google's advertising methods. In addition to file sharing, YouTube permits users to create and post their own videos and to rank and critique the videos of others. Under the DMCA, however, a website provider cannot be held liable for the infringement of its users if it takes down the copyrighted material once it has been notified by the copyright holder. YouTube claims it enjoys this safe harbor because it immediately responses to the take down notices issued by Viacom, which is devoting substantial resources to combing the billions of video clips that users post.

According to Philippe Dauman, Viacom's president and CEO, "its more efficient for [YouTube] to screen the content. For [Viacom] its like finding a needle in a haystack because [YouTube] doesn't make available what is posted. It's very expensive." However, presumably Congress did not what to unduly burden innovative technology, since the DMCA does not require websites to actively monitor content for potential copyright infringement. Thus Viacom is seeking to stretch the law or, alternatively, to apply the *Grokster* holding to this situation. In either case, this litigation represents an important confrontation between technological innovators and copyright holders.

A great deal is at stake. Google profits greatly from the knowledge commons that it has created and continues to expand. The intellectual property that it provides is free for the taking and shared many times over. On the other hand, Viacom's business model, which is based on the ownership and control of copyrighted content, is vulnerable to unrestricted file sharing. After negotiations for revenue sharing broke down, Viacom filed its suit, which now represents a battle of the titans, pitting old economy property rights against new economy technologies that are smashing away at the foundations of intellectual property law. Unless the parties agree to a revenue sharing deal, which is predictable, the outcome of this battle will set the rules for a long time. Should Google prevail, it will most likely shake loose the moorings of nineteenth century property law. Similarly, if Viacom prevails, it potentially sets the stage for a rethinking of how the knowledge economy should be regulated, since Viacom's argument that it should be the sole provider of is intellectual property is remarkably similar to the policy behind assuring a single provider for a physical property product. A core notion for the regulation of public utilities is that such firms form natural monopolies and entry into these businesses should be restricted to assure the existence of a single provider that can achieve economies of scale. Competition could be destructive, the argument goes, leading to the failure of many firms as prices fall to marginal costs. Competition might also undermine universal service to the detriment of consumers.

Ironically, Viacom's complaint is based on a policy that treats the media conglomerate as a public utility, a classic stance taken by old economy firms to justify court-ordered or government-imposed limitations on competition. Viacom wants to retain its monopoly control over the intellectual property it owns and wants to exclude a new form of competition, except that it does not want the burden of regulations associated with public utilities that are enacted to protect the public interest. The inherent inconsistency in Viacom's position may fall by the weight of its own illogic, so its lawsuit begs for time; time to make a deal with Google, time to master a new technology, time to acquire competing firms, and above all else, time to lobby Congress to change the law in its favor. But time in the *new* economy seems to move faster, and time may or may not be on Viacom's side.

Unlike the Google—Viacom litigation which is subject to contentious settlement discussions, the Authors Guild, the Association of American Publishers (AAP), and Google announced a groundbreaking settlement agreement in 2008 on behalf of a broad class of authors and publishers worldwide that would expand online access to millions of in-copyright books and other written materials in the U.S. from the collections of a number of major U.S. libraries participating in Google Book Search. The agreement, reached after two years of negotiations, resolved a class-action lawsuit brought by book authors and the Authors Guild, as well as a separate lawsuit filed by five large publishers as representatives of the AAP's membership.

Under the agreement, Google is required to make payments totaling $125 million. The money will be used to establish the Book Rights Registry, to resolve existing claims by authors and publishers and to cover legal fees. The agreement promises to benefit readers and researchers, and enhance the ability of authors and publishers to distribute their content in digital form, by significantly expanding online access to works through Google Book Search, an ambitious effort to make millions of books searchable via the Internet. The agreement acknowledges the rights and interests of copyright owners, provides an efficient means for them to control how their intellectual property is accessed online and enables them to receive compensation for online access to their works.

The contentiousness of the Google—Viacom litigation means not only that there is much more money involved than with Google's Book Search, but also that the law currently favors Google For example, in a similar case, eBay won a significant victory in 2008 over jeweler Tiffany & Co. in a federal court ruling that set a clear limit on how far online retailers have to go in policing trademarks on U.S. websites. In this case, Tiffany sued eBay for facilitating the sale of counterfeit Tiffany jewelry. However, the court found that eBay responded appropriately in removing listed items once notified of their illegal nature. Tiffany, like Viacom, contended that eBay should have taken greater responsibility by refusing to post listings it could have "reasonably anticipated" were counterfeit.

In ruling that the DMCA placed the entire burden on trademark holders of policing their intellectual property on the Internet, the court noted that congress had created a policy of favoring online sellers. According to the judge in the case, eBay could not be liable for trademark infringement "based solely on their generalized knowledge that trademark infringement might be occurring on their Web sites." EBay removed listings when Tiffany notified it of suspected counterfeit goods, but refused to go further and preemptively take down listings before any such notification.

While Tiffany pursues its appeal, the company, like Viacom, lobbies Congress to shift more of the burden of the brand name and copyright policing on to online sellers. But comprehensive regulation of the Internet may take a treaty to harmonize conflicting law enforcement. eBay lost nearly the identical case against Louis Vuittan, when a French court ordered it to pay $61 million for enabling the sale of knockoff bags.

In addition to copyright law, patent law also provides protection for intellectual property. Inventions subject to patent protection can be devices as well as processes. A patent application must describe the invention with reasonable specificity, must explain how the invention meets the statutory requirements of being novel, useful and non-obvious, and must identify the true inventor. A patent lasts for a term of ten years and entitles the patent owner a monopoly to make, use and sell devices and/or processes that are claimed by the patent.

In contrast to the Copyright Act, the Patent Act says nothing about the ownership of patents produced by employees. While the Patent Act provides for the assignment of a patent upon issuance, state law governs the validity of assignments. When the patentee or person identified in the patent application as the true inventor is an employee, state employment law governs the rights of the patent. In addition to financial considerations, the struggles over ownership are about dignitary and autonomy issues.

7. The Protection of Intellectual Property

For inventors, control over their patents is control over their creativity, and owning their patents is often as much about receiving credit for that creativity as it is about money. Just as employment for some people is as much about a paycheck, so too, is control over intellectual property. Inventions usually belong to the inventor. Therefore, employees are often required to assign inventions over to his/her employer as a condition of being employed.

A typical assignment gives up an employee's "entire right, title and interests to all inventions and designs" that he/she may "make, conceive, develop or perfect" during the course of employment and for a designated time period after employment has ended. The reasonableness and therefore the enforceability of such agreements depend on various factors.

One of the seminal decisions dealing with the enforceability of patent assignments is *Ingersoll-Rand v. Ciavatta*, decided by the New Jersey Supreme Court in 1983, although Armand Ciavatta's story was not unique. While working as a research program manager for Ingersoll-Rand, he submitted a dozen ideas for new products. The company rejected them all. After Ciavatta was fired after a dispute with his boss over the quality of a mine roof stabilizer, he had an idea for an improved stabilizer. After tinkering with the idea at home, he developed a prototype stabilizer with kitchen utensils borrowed from his wife. Investing his life savings along with money borrowed from a bank and from his brother, Ciavatta patented his stabilizer and started his own business to market his invention. When Ingersoll-Rand learned of Ciavatta's invention it examined whether the device was feasible and, if so, whether it infringed on any of the company's existing patents. The company also discussed whether Ciavatta's device could be a competitive threat. After the stabilizer caught on in the market, Ingersoll-Rand sued Ciavatta in a New Jersey state court for an order to relinquish the patent, alleging that he had violated a pre-invention assignment agreement, which required him to assign any patent over to the company. The case presented a question about the limits on such agreements.

While ultimately ruling in Ciavatta's favor, the court sought to balance three distinct interests: the employee's interest in "enjoying the benefits of his or her creation," the employer's interest "in protecting confidential information, trade secrets, and, more generally, its time and expenditures in training and imparting skills and knowledge to its paid workforce" and the public's "enormously strong interest in both fostering ingenuity and innovation of the inventor and maintaining adequate protection and incentives to corporations to undertake long-range and extremely costly research and development programs." These cases are often fact sensitive and usually turn on whether the employee was hired, explicitly or implicitly, to invent. If the employee was hired to invent, the mandatory assignment to the employer will be enforced. Similarly, if an invention was created on company time or through the utilization of company tools or resources, even if the employee was not hired to invent, the assignment of the invention in favor of the employer will be generally enforceable. If on the other hand, the employee produces an invention on his or her own time, using general skill and knowledge, the employee will generally be given ownership rights, and therefore the mandatory assignment will not be enforced. In short, under patent law, the employer will own an invention produced in the context of the employer-employee relationship. In contrast, if the invention is produced as the result of the inventor's general skill and knowledge, without using the employer's resources, and with technology widely known to the industry, the invention will belong to the employee.

In addition to the statutory protection of intellectual property under the Copyright and Patent Acts, secrecy too plays an important role in controlling information and protecting intellectual property, particularly where the information takes the form of trade secrets. Trade secrets are not governed by federal statute and the legal definition varies from state to state. The term has considerably wide scope and applicability and my cover any information used in the company's business that gives the company an advantage over its competitors, and is not readily discoverable by people outside the company through ordinary means. Trade secrets may include tangible material such as customer lists, research results, designs and specifications, marketing and financial data.

In *The Economics of Justice*, Judge Richard Posner has discussed the importance of secrecy to innovation. The law provided broad protection for business secrets. "Almost any knowledge or information used in the conduct of one's business may be held by the possessor in secret."

Secrecy plays a critical role in encouraging the protection of information, especially where the nature of the information is not subject to copyright or patent protection. An idea can be appropriated easily and often the costs of tracing an idea to its origin preclude reliance on a property-rights system. "If ideas as such as distinct from the sorts of concretely embodied ideas protected by patent and copyright laws, could be patented or copyrighted, the scope of, and difficulty of determining, infringement would be excessive." Thus compelling employees' adherence to secrecy guidelines and monitoring employees' communications both in within and without the organization, is an important management function in knowledge-intensive companies.

Keeping track of information inside a company has been a daunting task because published information resides in so many disparate places: emails, handwritten notes, documents stored of PCs and shared servers, laptops, even cell phones. This does not even include the information that employees collect over time that they keep in their heads, information that they may take when they leave. Consequently, resources are not only invested in creating and nurturing knowledge, they are also expended in safeguarding and protecting knowledge. Safeguarding knowledge is a difficult task. As pointed out by William Easterly in *The Elusive Quest for Growth*, knowledge leaks. "Useful knowledge about how to produce things at low cost-that is, how to get rich-is hard to keep secret," he says. "People have an incentive to observe what you are doing. People who work with you have a high incentive to leave and do what you are doing to get rich." But for employees who may be impatient with waiting downstream to acquire knowledge leaks may resort to other means to accelerate the process. A 2006 study polled more than 800 companies about data security issues. The respondents rated the top two data security risks as the misappropriation of trade secrets and security breaches resulting in the disclosure of private information. Short of breaching their duty of loyalty or committing a crime, employees should be figuring out ways to leverage their knowledge, since the financial rewards in the information economy are flowing to knowledge workers. Employers, on the other hand, are trying to plug the knowledge leaks. Consider the typical employment policy regarding "confidential information." In exchange for the job, the employee agrees to use confidential information solely for the company's benefit. The policy states, in relevant part:

Perils of Prosperity

> Confidential information means any Company proprietary information, technical data, trade secrets or know-how, including, but not limited to, research, product plans, products, services, customer lists and customers, markets, software, developments, inventions, processes, formulae, technology, designs, drawings, engineering, hardware configuration, marketing, finances, or other business information disclosed to me by the Company, either directly or indirectly, by writing, graphics, orally, electronically or through observation, or which I have learned as the result of my employment.

Consider also the policy that requires employees to assign intellectual property to the employer by:

> Promptly making full written disclosure to the Company, and holding in trust for the sole right and benefit of the Company, and assigning to the Company, or its designee, all my right, title, and interest in any and all inventions, original works of authorship, developments, concepts, improvements, designs, discoveries, ideas, trademarks or trade secrets, whether or not patentable or registrable under copyright or similar laws, which I may solely or jointly conceive or develop or reduce to practice, or caused to be conceived or developed or reduced to practice, during the period of time I am employed by the company.

And that provides, in relevant part, that:

> All original works of authorship made, solely or jointly, within the scope of my employment with the Company are "works for hire" as that term is defined in the US Copyright Act.

It is clear that these terms create a property interest in both tangible and intangible knowledge assets, which are owned solely by the company. The purpose of these policies is to facilitate the exchange of knowledge, ideas and know-how among employees for the benefit of the company without risk of misappropriation. For the employee's part, the knowledge community to which she is part and plays an active role enables her to optimize the performance of her duties owed to the company. But the policy to which she must adhere may restrict her ability to earn a living in the future. What the company is saying with this policy is that the company, as evidenced by the intellectual property created by the employee, owns the "human capital" in the same way that it owns machinery and real estate. While this assertion seems inimical within a free enterprise system, the ethical and legal justification for this ownership right rests on 300-year old principles.

As noted, no business wants to have a great idea come up, only to have it be the one that got away. Therefore, the employer may insist that the idea, i.e.: trade secret, remain secret until such time as it can be transformed into a copyright or patent. Secrecy however can be counterproductive in the knowledge economy since knowledge can only expand from a process of sharing, exchange and openness. Organization's that compete on the value of their copyrights, patents and other intellectual property are beset by the conflict between creativity and expression, on the one hand, and control and secrecy on the other.

8. The Role of Government

Because the government does not collect data on outsourcing, nobody knows for sure how many jobs have gone offshore. As previously noted, the IT research firm Forrester estimates that some 400,000 American service jobs have been moved overseas since 2000. This figure may not appear so serious in a country with 130 million workers, but it is the possibility of future job loss that has Americans worried. About 11 percent of the $1.7 trillion spent on technology worldwide in 2007 was sent to technology out sources. Forrester estimates that 3.3 million American service jobs will be off shored by 2015. Add to that the forecasts for robust job growth in India and China and one has the makings of a serious problem. A report by the McKinsey Global Institute predicted that by 2008 IT services and back-office work in India will grow fivefold, employing four million people. Not surprisingly, a plethora of anti-outsourcing legislation has been introduced into state legislatures, and the US Senate is considering banning the outsourcing of government-funded projects.

In a way, this most recent outsourcing phase is simply a result of the deregulation of the telecommunications industry and the dot com era that followed. Thousands of kilometers of fiber optic cable and high bandwidth connections laid during the boom years have united much of the world in high-speed connectivity. Relentless growth in storage capacity and high-speed transmission (digital scanning is currently at 200 pages a minute) has meant that anything can be digitized and sent anywhere for processing. This new and cheap capacity has emerged at a time when corporations, emerging from recession, are desperate for cost-cutting measures to boost profits. With manufacturing transferred overseas, high-speed imaging and communication technology can help cut costs even further, particularly in software applications, data processing, accounting, and customer service. Many large US corporations have become "virtual" manufacturers. Although their product design and marketing is done in the U.S., the actual production work is carried out in lower cost locations like China or Mexico. As noted earlier, even research and development work is being outsourced, even at the risk of losing some protection over intellectual property.

Countries like India have moved into the twenty-first century by setting up high-speed networks, effectively turning their cyberspace into virtual office space for the West. Now an employee sitting in Chennai can examine the image of a medical insurance claim on his computer screen and fill in the form for processing. As Andrew Grove, the CEO of Intel Corporation, said in a speech, "From a technical and productivity standpoint, the engineer sitting 6,000 miles away might as well be in the next cubicle and on the local area network." Moving a customer service center to India cuts costs by 45% on average. It is that invisible worker, ready to work for a tenth of the average US salary that is beginning to scare the American middle class.

In addition to fast-developing infrastructure, there has also been a sharp rise in the number of English-speaking engineers, accountants, and business students graduating from Indian and Chinese universities, as well as other developing nations. In the new economy, money follows brains. Another survey by the McKinsey Global Institute shows that while $56.1 trillion, or one-third of the world's financial assets were held in the US in 2006, the total held by emerging markets reached $23.6 trillion. And their assets are growing twice as fast as those of developed countries.

However, in *Competing for the Future*, Henry Kressel and Thomas Lento point out that the outsourcing of valued-added manufacturing jobs undermines innovation. According to the authors, where manufacturing processes are automated, labor is a relatively minor component of the total cost of production. In short, "labor costs are not a major competitive issue in the world of high-tech." On the other hand, they write: "high-tech product innovation is closely tied to the manufacturing process. In new industries such as nano technology, solar energy and semiconductors, product designers and production engineers have to work together from initial concept right up to devising the production process. It's the only way to be sure the product can be successfully manufactured at low cost. In addition, if you're in an advanced industry and you abandon manufacturing, you also abandon future innovation, because the talent to create innovations eventually follows the production facility."

What is certain in the knowledge-intensive, global economy is that money will follow innovation. For example, the dot com boom was initiated by huge investments in innovative Internet firms. Similarly, the Chinese Internet industry is, in part, being driven by Western venture capital. Intel's venture capital arm, Intel Capital, invested $200 million in 2005 in more than twenty-eight companies in China. In 2008, the firm created an additional $500 million fund to invest in technology start-ups. In *Silicon Dragon*, Rebecca Fannin explains how Silicon Valley is migrating to China. She states that money raised for Chinese venture funds soared from $3.4 billion in 2006 to $3.7 billion in the first half of 2007. Big U.S. venture capital firms like Sequoia have set up shop in China and homegrown firms are also investing large sums in small innovative firms. It is estimated that China represents the biggest Internet user base in the world, particularly for video and the world's largest cell phone market by number of accounts. In contrast, Kressel and Lento observe that the capital for creating flexible, high-tech manufacturing in the US is simply not a national priority. As they write: "We do not manufacture displays, although they were invented here, and we are rapidly losing our semiconductor manufacturing plants as these migrate to Asia. We are becoming consumers, not producers, buying products on credit with ever cheaper dollars. Reversing this trend is difficult. Once the cycle of outsourcing to offshore providers has begun, domestic supplier networks atrophy and labor skills disappear."

Advocates of outsourcing argue that companies can achieve improved levels of efficiency. Even an extremely conservative estimate places the savings by outsourcing at a healthy nine percent. Lower production costs lead to a decreased price for the consumer in a competitive market.

That frees up more of the consumer's income to purchase other goods and services. The world reaps enormous benefits from letting countries specialize in what they do best and most cheaply, they say. Not only does this system increase efficiency and achieve economies of scale, both of which lead to a drop in costs, but also it lays the groundwork for even more path breaking technological changes in processes and products. Future generations are the biggest beneficiaries of the dynamic gains from outsourcing brought on by technological advances. And they argue that the United States cannot morally end outsourcing simply because local jobs are lost; outsourcing has an immense upside in its effect on the lives of people around the world. They insist that it presents a unique opportunity to assist people mired in poverty. Their view is that the best and most enduring form of assistance the United States and other developed countries can give to poor nations is not in direct grants, or even loans, but in open markets.

As discussed by Joyce Kulko and others, the kinds of economic activity that have emerged in the last decades of the twentieth century have diverted most investment production to sophisticated financial schemes aimed at squeezing the highest possible profits out of existing assets, almost invariably at the expense of the average worker. In the United States, corporate mergers and raiding, made possible by unprecedented credit imported and underwritten increasingly from foreign banks and sovereign wealth funds, have became far more profitable in the short term than building new production sites. Ultimately, the pace and pattern of capital investment is directly influenced by political considerations, specifically to taxation.

Those who want to cut tax rates find support in the supply-side school of economics. The intellectual firepower beneath the supply-side school comes from the Austrian economists, Ludwig von Mises and Friedrich Hayek. As noted earlier, Hayek in particular, believed that wealth creation starts with entrepreneurial activity—new ideas for goods or services, new and more efficient production techniques and new technologies. Lower tax rates stimulate this activity by increasing incentives for saving, investment, risk taking, and work effort.

Those who oppose these supply-side tax cuts generally follow the teachings of John Maynard Keynes. Keynes emerged during the Great Depression as an advocate for government spending. In short, he argued that consumers saved too much and spent too little. This view, of course, was implicitly critical of the values of thrift and frugality. Therefore, according to Keynes, the government should spend and run a federal budget deficit. In effect, he argued that demand-side stimulus, not supply-side stimulus is what an economy needs when it is not investing enough in production.

According to Richard Gale at the Urban Institute tax cuts have ambiguous effects on economic growth in the long run. A tax cut will affect labor supply, human capital accumulation, saving, investment, entrepreneurship, he says, but the reduction in revenues will raise the federal deficit (unless matched by spending reductions) and therefore reduce national saving. This theory suggests that deficits "crowd out" private investment, putting upward pressure on interest rates. In other words, tax cuts increase government borrowing, which in turn eats up the available pool of capital. But an equally persuasive case can be made that government spending "crowds out" investment. Spending must be financed by either borrowing or taxation. Borrowing is voluntary. In contrast, taxation is compulsory. Thus, borrowing is always the most politically acceptable way to finance investments. In either case, whether the government spends or cuts taxes, there will be a deficit, as long as expenses exceed revenue.

But do deficits really matter? A deficit of $300 to $500 billion, or more, is relatively insignificant in the pool of global capital markets. In the U.S. alone, capital markets were $30 trillion dollars deep in 2002, for the world as whole capital markets approached $100 trillion. Deficits of the size projected in the early decades of the twentieth first century may not have the impact on interest rates that many fear. Thus on balance, tax cuts may be preferable than government spending to spur domestic business investment, as opposed to making those investments abroad. As for funding the tax cuts, if spending cuts cannot offset them, the difference will need to be borrowed from abroad. In short, the deficit matters a great deal as a political issue and as a proxy war between capital and labor and over the role of government and national identity.

What nurtures innovation, of course, is private property, more specifically intellectual property rights, which reward inventor and entrepreneur alike with monopoly power. However, Michael Perelman in *Steal This Idea* observes that "the tightening grip of intellectual property rights widen the gap between rich and poor, making the rich richer and the poor poorer. To the extent that government strengthens the hold on intellectual property rights even further, still ore wealth and income will shift away from the rest of society to the powerful few that now control the bulk of intellectual property." In other words, intellectual property law has made information a rivalrous resource. Unless such property is held in common, as discussed earlier, capital like labor is compensated at a rate corresponding to marginal productivity. If a few individuals owned property in large amounts, it would be to these individuals that income would accrue. In a developed economy, increased production is an alternative to redistributing resources that are rivalrous. As Galbraith has pointed out, productivity "has been the great solvent of the tensions associated with inequality." The increased production of goods, however, will ultimately reach a level of diminishing returns, making income inequality worse as a result. As supply exceeds demand, layoffs occur and profits decline. It is during these times that government "primes the pump" by stimulating demand either by government spending in excess of taxation or cutting taxes in excess of spending. In addition, the Federal Reserve Bank expands the money supply by buying U.S. Treasury bonds with the intent of making money cheap to borrow. Moreover, as the Federal Reserve devalues the dollar against foreign currencies, manufacturers are able to gain an export windfall. Thus, there is a powerful argument that monetary and fiscal policies alleviate the need for government to embark on any big, centralized program that would reallocate or redistribute tangible or intangible property, or for government to change the nature of property, or for courts to redefine the legal protection of property. Thus, the new knowledge economy should be allowed to evolve naturally under the norms and rules of competition and free enterprise.

Because monetary and fiscal policies are shrouded in technicalities and buried in regulations, most Americans are unaware of the monetary policies mentioned above and therefore do not make the connection that government is already deeply involved in the economy and that such polices can mitigate against severe recession and ruinous inflation. Indeed,

Americans as a whole demonstrate little or no interest in macroeconomics. However, most show a skeptical view of government intervention. Thus, public opinion appears to support a limited role for government in the economy. A 2007 poll conducted by Democracy Corps reported that 57 percent of respondents agreed that "government makes it harder for people to get ahead in life," and 54 percent thought, "government mostly gets in the way of the economy and job growth."

Labor unions have long attempted to create a viable exception to doing nothing but they too have confronted obsolescence in the global economy. The Wagner Act, a New Deal enactment, protects the right of workers to organize into labor unions and to bargain collectively over wages and working conditions. The Wagner Act framework permits labor unions to counter corporate power so that bargaining can take place, more or less between equals. In practice, collective bargaining has become a zero-sum game in the new economy—one parties' gain is another parties' loss. Locked in endless power struggles, often exacerbated by inflammatory class-war rhetoric, the law's most devout adherents have presided over the de-industrialization of America. When economic forces required cooperation between management and labor to maintain the skill level of the workforce or to save a facility from closing or leaving the country, the doctrinaire defenders of the faith continued to act like macho gladiators. Tenured professors with nothing to lose were also prime offenders, as they continued to provide an endless stream of class conscious politics disguised as scholarship. The result of this fruitless and endless struggle has been the loss of millions of manufacturing jobs during the last quarter of the twentieth century. At the same time, management has learned to produce more with less. Manufacturing GDP remains about 14 percent, but this percentage has been maintained over the last two decades with about one third less manpower.

With labor's limited ability to influence corporate behavior, in some industries the strike remains a last resort weapon, if only to remind the consuming public that management and labor are still capable of mutually assured destruction. However, these struggles have not had much impact on the public mind, to the frustration of union leaders who feel, perhaps justifiably, that they are fighting the battle for all producers. So while the Goldilocks economy was casting its aura of well being and complacency, organized labor used the strike, which ultimately taped a latent anxiety about the global economy. In 1997 over one hundred and eighty five thousand members of the teamsters' Union walked off their jobs at United Parcel Service of America (UPS) in a dispute over higher wages and pension benefits. The union added demands to cover part-time employees and to create more full time jobs. Strategically, the union positioned the strike, which inconvenienced the public, as standing up for exploited part-timers, a position that resonated widely with the public. Poll after poll taken during the strike revealed a deep anxiety over job security and a widespread belief that the economic expansion was not being shared equitably with the workforce.

The fifteen-day strike settled with a public relations windfall for the union and a settlement that required UPS to create two thousand additional full time jobs. However, almost a year to the day that the settlement was reached, UPS repudiated that part of the agreement which required it to create the new jobs. Optimism about the strike revitalizing the labor movement quickly faded.

In 1998 nine thousand members of the United Auto Workers (UAW) walked off their jobs at two General Motors stamping plants purportedly in protest of health and safety conditions. But below the surface, the struggle pitted GM's competitive drive to cut costs against the union's efforts to save jobs. National labor leaders argued that there was no need for GM, a company that was operating in the red, to relocate manufacturing facilities abroad. The company argued that under the Wagner Act, making investments in plants abroad was not a subject of mandatory bargaining. The stamping plants were strategically chosen by the union because of the vital role they played in GM's word wide production operations. It was thought that a crippling strike would end quickly, well in time for the UAW's annual convention in Hawaii. The strike lingered for weeks and affected tens of thousands of workers nationwide, as assembly plants and suppliers closed. In the end, the parties reached a stalemate, costing the workers a billion dollars in wages and the company two billion dollars in lost profits. According to the UAW president, "nobody really won. We had to strike over what we had already negotiated for."

8. The Role of Government

By 2000 the UAW was beginning to acquiesce to the evitable, that a two-tiered wage scale was necessary to keep domestic industry viable. In 2006, Big Three automakers reached deals with the UAW that would let them hire a group of workers that receive lower pay and benefits. Auto suppliers had negotiated similar plans. Once the bastion of high paying jobs, manufacturing has succumbed to the pressure of global competition, as the Wagner Act has not been readily adaptable to the new economy. For example, unions have not had much success in recruiting workers in the service industries. Also, contracting and project work has made it difficult to identify a bargaining unit, which is a legal prerequisite to forming a union. Ironically, it is the continued reliance on the Wagner Act framework more than anything else that has undermined the importance of organized labor in the global economy.

Nevertheless, organized labor has resisted legislative efforts to amend labor laws. The so-called Flex-Time Act would allow hourly employees to work up to eighty hours over a two-week period in ways that best meet their family or personal commitments. For example, an employee could work a 50-hour week the first week, without overtime pay, but work a 30-hour week the second week. Similarly, the so-called Teamwork for Employees and Managers Act would allow employers and employees to form committees to address "matters of mutual interest." Both of these proposals have been criticized as undermining worker protections to overtime pay and the right to collectively bargain free of employer control.

On the other hand, organized labor has aggressively promoted the Employee Free Choice Act, which would permit employees to more easily organize labor unions. Under current federal law, unions must win elections to become legally recognized as a bargaining unit. While labor unions lost much of the time, many believe that the results are skewed by the flagrant intimidation engaged in by employers. The Employee Free Choice Act purports to level the playing field by making elections unnecessary if the union can demonstrate that 51 percent of the identified bargaining unit agrees in writing to be represented by the union. If this occurs, the Act would require mandatory bargaining and arbitration if a collective bargaining agreement cannot be achieved. The Employee Free Choice Act is controversial, as it eliminates the employer's right to speak against the union during an election campaign, since there would be no campaign. However, the employer's right to freely and fairly campaign against union recognition is constitutionally guaranteed. Therefore, "card check" recognition of a labor union is dubious as a matter of constitutional law, particularly if the employer refuses in good faith to recognize the union's majority status based on authorization cards alone and insists instead on exercising its First Amendment right to an open and fair election. In short, if enacted, it is relatively uncertain whether the Employee Free Choice Act would apply to any employer in the private sector.

Should the demands of the global economy alter the nature of federal labor law, and thus the fundamental nature of private employment, corporate America would have failed to meet its most basic obligation: to manage corporate affairs in a way that preserves its assets and maximizes shareholder return. It is clear that corporate America has an obligation to create a fairer and more equitable economy for no other reason than self-preservation. In a 2008 *Business Week*/Harris poll, only about half of employees surveyed thought that layoffs were necessary for business to become more efficient and prepare for future growth. A staggering 95 percent of the respondents stated that employers should sometimes sacrifice profits for the sake of making things better for their workers and communities. Sixty seven percent indicated that government should punish employers that unfairly eliminate jobs.

While Congress has the enormous power of the purse, it cannot simply order American corporations to use their $1.3 trillion cash surplus to create jobs in the U.S. Congress can only use its tax and spend authority for the general welfare, which means making investments in infrastructure and promising new technologies that can create jobs in the future. In 2008 automobile manufacturers were loaned money to build new factories and re-toll assembly lines to build electric cars. Electric battery companies received research grants and consumers became eligible for subsidies to buy the electric cars. In 2008, these policies were designed as investments in future growth not necessarily to increase demand as was the case during the 1930s.

8. The Role of Government

To this day, economists and historians are still tiring to explain the Crash of 1929 and the Great Depression and continued recession that followed. How did the industrial machine that had dazzled the world and provided millions of working men and women with the highest standard of living in history collapse? Another try is not warranted here and, in any event, it is unnecessary, although the consensus view is that the Federal Reserve failed to lower interest rates and inflate the currency to keep enough dollars in circulation and Congress obsessed with the federal budget deficit and national debt failed to increase spending. Fearing the ruinous inflation that had ravaged Europe, particularly Germany, after the First World War, policy makers bet that the economy would respond to balancing the federal budget and the enactment of high trade tariffs which, they thought, would eventually absorb excess supply and cause employers to begin hiring again.

Throughout the nineteen twenties, production and productivity grew steadily: between 1919 to 1929, output per worker in manufacturing industries increased by 43 percent. Wages increased, but generally these productivity gains were not passed on to the over thirty million Americans that worked for daily or weekly wages at the time. Although estimates of the minimum living wage were about $2,000 per year, the average American worker never made more than $1,500.

Seventy eight percent of American families had income of less than $3,000 per year. Forty percent had incomes of less than $1,500. Only 2.3 percent of the population enjoyed incomes of over $10,000 per year. Sixty-thousand American families, in the highest income brackets, held savings which amounted to the total held at the bottom twenty-five million families. Five percent of the population with the highest incomes received approximately one half of all personal income.

As wages stagnated and the costs of production decreased, industry became increasingly more productive. With only a small percentage of the population able to direct excess income into consumption of goods, easy credit and installment purchase terms were offered to middle class consumers to increase mass production. Sophisticated advertising techniques developed during the war increased demand as well. Eventually, efficient mass production out-paced consumer demand, thus reaching the point of diminishing return. Excess inventory led to a recession and the feverish pace of production and consumption slowed dramatically.

As noted the national banks, led by the Federal Reserve, decided to let the bust cycle cure itself but by 1930, 4 million workers were unemployed. Consumer spending continued to decline causing manufacturers to cancel their orders and layoff more workers. Stock prices, which were already over valued due to speculation through most of the twenties, dropped. By then 1.5 million Americans owned stock, primarily through mutual and insurance funds but large institutional investors, corporations and holding companies dominated the stock market. As stock prices plummeted and loan defaults increased, banks, financial institutions and other institutional investors found themselves holding worthless paper. As depositors rushed to withdraw their savings from banks, the national banking system reached the breaking point. The stock market followed.

American firms could not export their way out of the recession because of the Smoot-Hartley Act, which penalized imports into America, and which set off a worldwide round of tariff increases in 1931, making a dire economic situation even worse. Most historians view Congress' irrational stampede to balanced budgets and trade protectionism as a massive self-inflicted political wound. By 1932 14 million Americans were unemployed, about one in four working Americans. National income declined by half and Gross National Product by one third. There was little in the way of a safety net for the unemployed and displaced, as they attempted to make ends meet on meager savings, odd jobs and public charity. As the bottom fell out of farm prices, farmers slaughtered livestock and burned crops to prop up prices, this at the same time as soup kitchen sprung up in every city to feed the hungry. Food riots, labor violence and communist propaganda gripped many Americans in fear and panic and a fierce struggle between capital and labor disrupted the economy further with destructive strikes.

Perhaps it's too simple to suggest that unrestrained greed caused the nation's worst economic calamity in the twentieth century. In actuality, bad government policies played the dominate role. After the stock market crash, the Hoover administration, with Congressional support, raised taxes to narrow a budget deficit; tariffs were raised to protect domestic producers from foreign competition; and industry-labor cartels were promoted to fix prices and wages. The Roosevelt administration adopted these policies as a palliative to what had become a worldwide recession. It seemed reasonable at the time. After all the system worked predictably well given the economic rules of the time. After a century of minimally regulated industrial capitalism based on the labor theory of property the rule of marginal productivity, a relatively small portion of the population were left owning the means of production, while the majority of the population worked to produce goods for their own consumption. The iron rule of wages ensured that workers could subsist to produce and to consume when they were productive.

However, as conditions got worse and became more dire still, the dual creeds of laissez faire and Social Darwinism were eventually swept away by the palpable fear of economic and social collapse. As pointed out by Hofstadler, by the time Franklin Roosevelt took office in 1933, "a silent revolution had taken place in public opinion . . . that henceforth, for the purposes of the recovery, the federal government was to be responsible for the condition of the labor market as part of its concern with the industrial problem as a whole. Congress and the president suspended the antitrust law; that is they agreed with business cartels that monopoly produced greater societal benefits than unrestrained competition. Business groups and trade associations were permitted to set prices and to develop codes of "fair competition." In return, workers were guaranteed the legal right to collectively bargain with their employers. In part, the fear of right-wing and other radical-populist solutions led to the passage of the Social Security Act provided Americans with a wide but still shallow safety net. It was opposed by many business leaders as reckless and irresponsible, and by some as an act of dictatorship.

After a generation of invalidating laws that impaired private property, the U.S. Supreme Court upheld almost all of this remedial legislation, which also included changes in the tax laws and the regulation of the stock market and banking and finance industries. In a stunning reversal of its prior decisions on private property, the court observed: "The community is not bound to provide what is in effect a subsidy for unconscionable employers. The community may direct its law-making power to correct the abuse which springs from their selfish disregard of the public interest."

The New Deal did not end the Great Depression. World War II and its aftermath ultimately did that.

As Richard Rumelt has discussed, in 1939, before the U.S. entered the war, about 15 percent of the workforce was unemployed. In 1940 about 11 percent of workers were conscripted into military service. By 1943 another five percent of the workforce was directly employed by the government as support personnel. Government spending increased 400 percent and the U.S. had reached full employment. Wages increased but because of rationing and high consumption taxes living standards stayed at Depression-era levels. Savings and purchases of government bonds skyrocketed. Eventually nearly twenty years of pent up consumer demand exploded—one might say that this was the Big Bang of the post-war consumer society.

With the exception of the New Deal and some smaller Great Society programs that followed a generation later, private employment has not been created directly by public expense. While the impersonal and sometimes harsh nature of the free market has been tempered somewhat by federal and state regulation, private employment, as a transaction between private parties, retains its special status as being indispensable to a free society. As such, it remains subject to individual, contractual relations, rather than to collective, government dictates. While employment is clearly a social good, how work is organized and allocated remains essentially a private matter guided by market forces. In other words, while employment is a social good, like other property, it is not allocated by government as a public good. It is this essential nature of private employment, that it is allocated by market forces, that makes the United States competitive, according to the World Economic Forum.

However, it is beyond dispute that meaningful work for the greatest number advances the public good. William Julius Wilson states this maxim this way: "Work is not simply a way to make a living and support one's family. It also constitutes a framework for daily behavior ... Regular employment determines where you are going to be and when you are going to be there. In the absence of regular employment, life, including family life, becomes less coherent. Indeed, the studies conducted during the Depression suggested that the children of chronically unemployed adults became emotionally unstable and did poorly in school. Family relationships deteriorated and violence within the family increased.

An alternative to private employment is the social welfare model of employment. This model suggest that given the long-term of the global economy, workers will have no choice but to take advantage of a wide variety of contingent and part-time work options, supported by publicly supported programs such as wage insurance and subsidies for health care and child care. This model is being used by most states, with the assistance of federal funds, to employ people who have left welfare and move private employment one step closer to a public entitlement. Many advocate, including Jeremy Rifkind that this model should serve as a framework for work in the future.

Public entitlement alternatives to private employment would obviously transform the employer-employee relationship, as some of the basic employment decisions that are now guided by the market, such as wages, would be influenced by quasi-governmental, third-party intermediaries. Layoff decisions would be governed by rigid formulas, causing high transaction costs and the type of inflexible labor markets that are the case in most of Europe. America has come close to establishing this social model.

There are always several proposals in Congress at any one time to transform the nature of private employment, to treat it as a public good. One proposal is to create a New Deal-style public works program to help the U.S. deal more effectively with environmental degradation and which would guarantee many Americans a job and be funded by a broad-based tax or combination of taxes. Other bills would require greater job security, mandatory severance payments for laid off workers, and taxing companies that outsource jobs. But what about creating knowledge-intensive jobs? This requires a fully functioning market with access to capital.

Also, as discussed earlier, government policy can have an impact on breaking the monopoly on ideas and facilitating open source innovation. But the resulting upheaval may actually undermine the more or less secure jobs in the software industry. Also, as suggested, courts can scrutinize agreements that restrict knowledge sharing with an eye toward whether the protection of corporate property rights harms the public by suppressing competition. Such an approach could encourage increased cooperation between firms aimed at sharing tacit knowledge, in the form of technological alliances, formation of business networks and closer linkages between suppliers and customers. Changes in immigration policy may be part of the solution as well.

Additionally, as previously observed, a substantial portion of the nation's legal and illegal immigrants lack a high school diploma. According to Jason Riley in his book *Let Them In*: "The reason that immigrant workers tend not to elbow aside natives for jobs and depress wages has to do with the education and skills that foreigners typically bring to the US labor market. Most immigrants fall within one of two categories: low skilled laborers or high skilled professionals." At the same time, talented immigrants who are educated in the United States are forced to leave. Foreign-born students holding temporary visas received 35 percent of all research doctorates awarded by US universities in 2006. That number climbed from 25 percent in 2001. As fewer native born students major in science and technology in favor of the humanities and education, American universities have recruited abroad. By 2006, foreign students comprised 44 percent of science and engineering doctorates issued in the United States. Given this reality, about 42 percent of Ph.D.s working in U.S. scientific and engineering occupations are foreign born, up from 24 percent in 1990. In 2006, 62 percent of doctoral degrees in engineering went to foreign nationals. Yet most foreign-born graduates from US universities are required to leave the country after their student visa expires. So-called H-1B visas are capped. In short, American universities are educating the next generation of innovators only to see them leave after graduation.

Arguments opposed to lifting the cap claim that foreigners will take well-paid knowledge work away from Americans or will work for lower salaries if these graduates are not forced to leave the country. But does it make sense to import unskilled labor and, at the same time, deport knowledge-intensive workers? A 2005 McKinsey report surveyed hundreds of senior finance executives and found that their single most important concern was the availability of professional workers. Other counties, such as United Kingdom, have enacted policies that enable employers to import MBA graduates with little red tape. Any one who graduates from a select school can automatically work in the U.K. for at least one year. Exporting this value added human capital makes little sense under present circumstances.

Never in history have so many races, nationalities and cultures mixed. There has been a sharp rise in the rate of intermarriage in the last decades of the twentieth century, as immigrants with temporary work visa marry U.S. citizens and gain citizenship status themselves. In the U.S. according to a forecast by the Urban Institute, marriages between some combination of black, Hispanic, white and Asian will triple to 21 percent of total weddings by 2050. To those who celebrate ethnic identity and cultural diversity, the idea of the large scale mixing of the races raises the specter of homogenization or of a generic culture. Certainly that is the tendency of transnational corporations that market brands across cultures.

In *Who Are We?*, Samuel Huntington has worried that bilingualism, dual citizenship, religious diversity and multiculturalism risk undermining distinctly American ideals—including the creed that holds out the promise of freedom and opportunity. However, U.S. power in the twenty first century will rest largely on shared values among people around the world, notably the faith in openness, which enables the United States to adopt the best qualities from around the world as its own and, in turn, spread those qualities everywhere else. The nation-state, and therefore nationality, is based on a contiguous territory, with a single or dominate language and shared traditions. But the nation-state itself is being drawn into the global economy, as Americans or ever more inter-dependent on the rest of the world, particularly since foreign money has fueled American consumption and therefore supported American living standards.

Accordingly, in addition to open trade and open borders, resources must be shifted from consumption to investments in learning. The average American household owes more than its yearly income. A national sales tax could replace the income tax, although this reform carries substantial risk, considering that two-thirds of the GNP is based on consumer spending. In other words, much of the present economy is based on consumer spending, so that any policy that promotes savings at the expense of consumption will likely slow the economy, thereby increasing the national debt. To pay down the debt, the income tax burden would need to be heavier. However, the top one percent of wage earners already carries 40 percent of the tax burden and the top 10 percent carry 71 percent of the country's tax burden. In fact, the single largest group of taxpayers in the upper income tax brackets are subchapter S corporations and limited liability corporations, which pay at a personal rate, including manufacturers, professional service firms and technology companies. In contrast, the bottom 60 percent of income earners pay less than one percent of federal income taxes. The middle 20 percent pays 4.4 percent of federal income taxes.

But many Americans are fed up with raising inequality, or at least the *perception* of inequality. A 2007 Gallup poll found that 66 percent of Americans believe upper-income people do not pay enough taxes. On the other hand, they fear paying too much themselves. A 2008 Kauffman Foundation survey asked respondents about what posed the greatest economic threat to their well being. "Higher taxes" was the most frequently cited worry, with 50 percent saying it was their first or second concern. Only 20 percent believed that the federal budget deficit was their top worry. So it appears that raising taxes to pay down the national debt is not a priority. However, raising taxes on the wealthy seems vaguely fair, when the average American has experienced stagnant wages.

An alternative to raising taxes is to continue borrowing from other countries, using U.S. assets—corporations, real estate, and other revenue producing assets—as collateral. This debt inevitably lowers the net wages for the average worker, which requires more cheap goods from abroad so that the average American can maintain his or her standard of living. However, at the same time that debt maintains consumption, it decreases wealth, as it becomes exported or collateralized. The worst-case scenario is a spiraling down of wages as more jobs get outsourced and increasing income for the elite cadre of knowledge workers with superior skills that are able to compete and thrive in the global economy. This, of course, is a prescription for social upheaval, but oddly is the program that both left and right wing academics have been advocating for generations—that is, transferring wealth to developing nations as a form of economic reparations, or as the natural result of free markets.

8. The Role of Government

The federal government spends about $30 billion a year through various programs for worker training and readjustment. In many cases, this money amounts to nothing more than supplemental insurance for lost wages. The fact of the matter is that the federal government is very good at mailing checks to people in a timely matter and very bad at creating private sector job. Currently, federal wage insurance is a pilot program for a small subset of workers, age 50 or older, which lose their jobs to trade competition. Under the program, a worker who takes a lower-paying replacement job can receive a government subsidy for two years, equal to 50 percent of the difference in earnings up to a total of $10,000, provided the new job pays less than $50,000 a year. Wage insurance could provide an important tool in a broader set of policies designed to help American middle class families insure against disruptive income fluctuations. According to McKinsey Global Institute, companies exploring offshore outsourcing to cut costs could offer wage insurance to full-time employees, much the same way as they might offer severance pay, for less than 5 percent of the savings companies realized from the outsourcing. The government could provide financial incentives to encourage employers to offer these plans. Because payouts would be time-limited, there would be little risk that companies would be saddled with long-term legacy costs, although employer-provided wage insurance would mean higher costs. As such, the U.S. could experiment with pilot programs that offered workers the voluntary option of paying a small premium to receive extensive wage insurance. While such an optional program runs the risk of drawing only the most vulnerable workers, such an option could be popular with a broad spectrum of workers.

American firms and their employees are, of course, competing in a global economy that is becoming ever more interconnected under free trade policies and the integrated markets that such polices create and maintain. Today, IBM is one of the most aggressive firms when seeking out global opportunities. In 2007, the company derived 65 percent of its business from outside the United States. This means investing in local neighborhoods, developing school curricula, providing volunteers, and hiring the best, brightest and most politically connected professionals in the host country. In other words, IBM is a global citizen, not an *American* company, but a *global* company. As more corporate talent and resources are redirected globally, what, if anything, does IBM owe America?

Recognizing that opportunity is shifting from America to the rest of the world, the company has established "learning accounts" for employees who may be facing displacement. These accounts are used as a tuition savings plan so that workers can learn new skills.

While employment remains a private transaction, some industries may be able to engage in some form of collective action to address the nation's most pressing workforce concerns, including job security, career preparedness, training and education. In 1996, an inter-industry group of corporations, including AT&T, DuPont, GTE, Johnson & Johnson, the former Lucent Technologies, and NCR Corporation, created the *Talent Alliance*. The organization was privately funded and was an attempt to find jobs for the thousands of AT&T employees who were being laid off at the time. Ultimately, the organization petered out, primarily because its members were unable to commit sufficient staff and resources to realize its full potential. Nevertheless, the concept remains valid. Corporate members contribute resources for training and education and create a talent bank that matches employees with open jobs within the membership. For their part, employees are expected to take advantage of the training opportunities and to be flexible enough to move across firms to work on a project basis if necessary.

Employees will even need to adapt to a new architecture of work, as workspace gets redefined. Already, companies have eliminated offices, even the ubiquitous cubicles in favor of team rooms and unassigned desks. With the explosion of mobile devices, business is transacted literally from anywhere, and any place could be a workspace. Together, with the intangible, interconnected nature of the work itself, worker flexibility has fast become a fundamental prerequisite in the global economy. This model creates a new social compact, but like the *Talent Alliance* experiment, may require collaborative effort across firms in order to maintain a secure social fabric. Accordingly, the model, which would be based on individual liberty and mobility, and fused together by collaborative networks across many firms, could be the prototype of how a global, interconnected labor market would function.

However, liberty and mobility assume that individuals have the resources to be autonomous and that they can express their freedom within open, equally accessible markets. Rivalry over resources will, of course, create winners and losers but there are times when the sheer number of losers, when too much inequality, endangers the entire community. Since over 140 million Americans receive health care benefits through an employer-sponsored plan, flexible, mobile employment arrangements will most certainly add to the 50 million Americans who lacked health insurance in 2008 alone. Health care in the U.S., while heavily regulated by state governments, is essentially subject to private transaction, a form of private property, which by its nature will create inequality for those people who are left out of the market. One obvious solution is for government to take over the private health care market and treat health care as a public good, subject to government allocation. A purely government-run system will by necessity require enforced quotas and substantial administrative costs, much the same as market-driven managed health care operates now. Since liberty requires choice, a government system based on rationing would obviously limit that choice. But employers and insurance companies already severely limit choice. In short, the so-called private system of delivering health care in America is perhaps more inefficient and as limiting as any government system could be. Assuming that flexible, mobile and contingent project work will be the norm for most working Americans, the rational approach would be to dismantle the so-called private market for health care, treat health care as a public good, and let the federal government play a greater role, such as a public program that is similar to Medicare and Medicaid, which in 2008 took up about 4 percent of U.S. GDP.

Among the developed economies, Americans spend twice as much on health care; yet, for all the money it pays on health care, America is not the healthiest nation. In 2007, the CIA World Fact Book listed the U.S. as 45th for life expectancy. Infant mortalities rates in the United States are the highest among the developed economies. The U.S. ranked 29th lowest in infant mortality rates, down from 12th lowest in 1960. The U.S. also has the highest percentage of uninsured residents among the developed world, which increases the costs health care insurance. The uninsured typically put off attending to problems until they are severe. The longer the patient waits to take care of a health problem, the greater likelihood the disease will involve complications that make it more difficult and expensive to treat. Many uninsured suffer from chronic diseases. Chronic diseases account for more than 75 cents of heath care spending, according to the Centers for Disease Control and Prevention. Of course, life expectancy and infant mortality is associated with many factors, including health and economic status, race and ethnicity, access to quality medical care, and cultural problems of obesity, drug use and life styles that make chronic conditions worse. But it's clear that treating the uninsured increases costs across the board.

Americans are ambivalent. Most are covered under an employer plan. Employers shop for the coverage, negotiate the insurance and offer it to employees on a take-it-or-leave-it basis. The employer subsidizes the premium 80% on average. The employee contribution is often unnoticed through incremental deductions from a paycheck. At the point of service, the employee pays about 10 cents for every dollar of health care that is consumed. This, ironically, is socialized medicine and Americans understandably love it. The illusion is that employer-sponsored health care can be consumed as virtually a free resource with little or no incentive to maintain healthy lifestyles or to consume wisely.

Similarly, Medicare and Medicaid are single-payer, government health care programs. Understandably, health care providers and patients strongly endorse these programs too, particularly Medicare, even though tens of billions of dollars are spent on over treatment every year. The illusion here is that as a public entitlement, health care is virtually free and inexhaustible. As over utilized as employer-sponsored health care is, Medicare utilization is roughly 50 percent higher than that, even after adjusting for age and medical condition. In other words, given two individuals with similar health care needs a Medicare beneficiary will consume nearly 50 per cent more health care. Health care providers, pharmaceutical firms, medical device manufacturers and others have a vested interest in the current "free" health care system.

In short, at least on some level, most Americans believe that health care is a basic public entitlement, like "free" public education, and that limitations imposed either by government or corporations are unfair, illegitimate, or both. However, health care is not free and it is paid for by shifting the costs and government borrowing and it appears that the current hybrid private-public system has resulted in the overconsumption health care in the U.S. In fact, in a 2008 study issued by the National Institutes on Health, about half of the surveyed internists and rheumatologists reported prescribing placebo treatments to their patients on a regular basis. Replacing the current system with a government-sponsored universal health insurance program may result in some form of price controls and rationing. But on balance a government-sponsored program could be just as good if not better than the current system, which already practices managed care rationing at exorbitant prices to achieve mediocre outcomes. An employer and individual mandate would require healthy people be part of the insurance pool, thus mitigating premium increases for the sick.

The individual mandate, which requires individuals to obtain health care insurance or pay a penalty, is subject to much litigation. As previously noted, under Article I in the U.S. Constitution Congress has the right to impose taxes for the general welfare but it cannot tax what it can't regulate. Clearly, the health care delivery system in the U.S. is national in scope and the health care insurance contract constitutes interstate commerce, which Congress has the power to regulate. But is the individual mandate necessary and proper to regulate the health insurance industry. As previously noted, the U.S. Supreme Court has extended Congress' power to regulate activities that have a substantial impact on interstate commerce. At least one circuit court of appeals has ruled that Congress has a rational basis for concluding that the individual mandate is essential to regulating the national markets in health care delivery and health insurance.

Of course, Congress' great Article I powers are not without limitation and federal courts are split on whether the personal mandate exceeds congressional authority. The Fifth Amendment provides that "no person shall be deprived of life, liberty or property without due process of law." Presumably the liberty interest at stake with the individual mandate is the autonomous choice to forgo health care insurance, analogous perhaps to the right possessed by a competent adult to refuse medical treatment at the end of life or a woman who chooses to abort a fetus in the first or second trimester. But the word "liberty" presumes at least two concomitant principles; the first being that the individual exercising their free choice is presumed to be guided by reason. Second, the individual's rational choice is not made outside a social context.

If one becomes ill and requires medical treatment or can prevent illness with a consultation from a health care provider but refuses and chooses instead to become gravely ill, the individual may be exercising his free will to suffer and die but conventional norms would deem such a choice irrational or the result of mental illness or incompetency. The rational choice would be to seek available treatment. At that point the costs of the medical care provided to the uninsured individual is shifted onto the community in the form of higher premiums for the insured. Thus, the libertarian choice to remain uninsured is mere license to engage in an anti-social act, void of the personal responsibility presumed in the term "liberty." Just as the conscientious objector is required to pay his or her taxes knowing that a portion will fund a war effort, requiring an individual to purchase health care or pay a penalty does not violate liberty without due process of law. Since the personal mandate serves the purpose of increasing the health insurance pool without violating anyone's liberty, it is moral.

Another argument against the individual mandate is that Congress has usurped the inherent power of the state to regulate health care. While the states have what is often called "police powers" to enact laws that promote the health and welfare of its citizens (limited by the Fourteenth Amendment), the structure of the Constitution limits Congress to "enumerated" powers. Thus it is argued that the individual mandate infringes on state prerogatives—so-called states' rights.

In 2007 the U.S. Supreme Court in *Gonzales v. Carhart* upheld a federal law prohibiting a form of late-term abortion presuming that Congress had the power to enact the law under the commerce clause of Article I. Dicta in recent federalism jurisprudence, however, has suggested that the balance between state and federal authority should primarily serve the important function of protecting personal liberty by checking and balancing the power of the national government. As dicta, the observation that principles of federalism serve personal freedom is axiomatic. However, as noted above, ordered liberty would not support guaranteeing to the individual the right to make irrational or anti-social choices. What authority then does the state of Virginia, let's say, have to codify the individual choice to become gravely ill and to shift the responsibility for paying for treatment onto the public? In the abstract it can be argued that the state of Virginia is entitled to pass any law it wants, or no law at all, as long as its legislature has deemed the action a promotion of the public welfare, even if it is irrational or anti-social such as segregation based on race in places of public accommodations. But such state action (or inaction) would strongly promote a grave national problem of racial inequality. As such, Congress enacted the Civil Rights Act of 1964 which prohibited unequal treatment based on race in places of public accommodations and the U.S. Supreme Court upheld the law as a proper exercise of Congress' power to regulate interstate commerce. In short, race segregation is not dissimilar to other forms of state promoted protectionism and monopoly. Both racial segregation and laws to protect in state business from outside competition are designed to maintain the status quo of local prerogatives, prejudice and pride.

It is beyond dispute that widespread medical insurance constitutes interstate commerce. The commercial transaction based on the third party payer system has irrevocably separated the physician from the patient. While the code of medical ethics ensures that the vast majority of patients receive competent care, the third-party payment system has ruptured the moral dimension of the face-to-face market transaction. It is difficult to look a patient in the eye and recommend unnecessary treatments when the patient is paying the full freight. It is quite another thing to submit the bill to Medicare or an insurance company for payment. The remoteness of the payer facilities over consumption by the patient and fraud by the provider but the insurance industry has socialized risk, in turn creating a trillion dollar industry with millions of providers and patients dependent upon it. Government has a legitimate role in regulating this national industry and Congress has deemed the individual mandate indispensable to spreading the risks more broadly. The individual mandate will not necessarily make the market transaction more personal or moral but as federal government policies have facilitated the global economy by sweeping away local business practices and labor markets, health care delivery warrants a national approach. At the heart of the federalism argument is "trust"—can the American consumer trust the federal government to allocate resources fairly when it is obvious that "free" medical care is no longer sustainable. As medical technology moves forward and new techniques can measure outcomes, the practice of medicine is becoming less an art and more a science. Computers compile vast amounts of data so that treatments can be based on best evidence. Best outcomes can be rewarded and third-party payments can be based on the quality of outcomes rather than on the quantity of treatments. Where government is the payer that engages in this type of cost-benefit analysis it is called rationing and his generally viewed with hostility. When insurance companies engage in the identical practice of rationing it is called the free market at work and is generally viewed as acceptable. Government rationing can be subject to the democratic process, which can be messy, noisy and unpredictable. When the market rations resources it does so by one simple, easily understandable rule—whatever the market will bear.

Another federal government program is Social Security. About 80 percent of today's retirees receive more than half their income from social security. However, people in the lower fifth of the income scale count on social security for eighty percent of their retirement income. The system pays benefits to retirees that have paid into the system during their working years and to "survivors" that have outlived their working spouses. Moreover, the system pays benefits to millions of people who are disabled. In short, the social security system is the cornerstone of the nation's social safety net.

Social security income was invented in Germany in the late nineteenth century. When the German government set the retirement age at sixty-five in the government-sponsored pension system in 1891, the average German lived to be less than forty-five. When social security was enacted in the United States in 1935, the retirement age was also set at sixty-five and the average worker was expected to live to the ripe old age of about fifty-three. Today, men age sixty-five can expect to live another 16 years; women, another 19 years. In short, the social security system will be paying out more money than its creators ever envisioned.

The good news, of course, is that we are living longer. But for the social security system, the bad news is that it may be going bankrupt. As noted in the previous article, social security pays retirement, disability and survivorship benefits to 48 million Americans and collects payroll taxes from 144 million workers and employers. The ratio of workers to social security recipients is currently 3.3 to 1. While the social security fund is solvent, obligations already exceed $11 trillion dollars, or more than six times the federal budget.

While the system is solvent today, already 76 million Americans are beginning to retire. In a few years social security will be paying out more than it brings in. By 2030, the ratio of workers to recipients will be 2 to 1 and the system will be near bankruptcy. There simply will not be enough workers to carry the nation's retirement burden.

The social security system has come under fire because of its inherent unfairness. For example, since social security benefits are based on lifetime earnings, women receive lower benefits than men because they are paid less and are more likely to leave the work force to care for family members. Also, one controversial report concludes that African-Americans collect fewer benefits during retirement than retired whites because their life spans are shorter. Such is the case with the poor as well. The amount of benefits a person receives from social security depends on how long the person lives. Since the poor generally have shorter life spans than the affluent, poor people may pay into the system throughout their working lives but receive almost no benefits.

The Social Security system has also been criticized for its low rates of return. Under the existing system, employers and employees pay a payroll tax, which is then invested in Treasury bonds that have about a 2 percent rate of return. Critics have noted that investing the payroll tax in a conservative mutual fund instead would yield more than twice the current returns.

Until recently, proposals to redirect a portion of the payroll tax into self-directed pension accounts have been fueled by a booming stock market. For almost a decade preceding the dot com bust, the Dow Jones Industrial Index posted a gain of more than twenty percent a year. Reportedly, this stock run added 12.5 trillion dollars to household net worth. However, with the recent stock market crash during the Panic of 2008, advocates of privatizing social security are a bit more cautious but nevertheless point out that even during the Great Depression, the stock market has always out-performed social security.

While there appears to be a consensus to at least partially privatize social security, it is unclear how Corporate America will respond when literally every working American and retiree becomes a stockholder. What, if any, impact will generational conflicts have on the stock market and corporate decision-making? For example, the interests of retirees could conflict with the interests of workers, particularly when layoffs and other forms of restructuring tend to increase the value of the company's stock. To date, the challenge of maintaining a social safety in a free market economy has been met with a publicly financed system. Whether privatizing the system will exacerbate generational conflict and the tension between the haves and have-nots, or create a fairer, more equitable retirement system remains to be seen. At present, the benefits weigh in favor of maintaining the current system if the inequities can be corrected.

As the role of government begins to take shape in the first decade of the twenty first century, the global, interconnected economy presents other enormous challenges as well. The United States buys about a fifth of all goods and services traded worldwide, importing about $2.63 trillion worth of the world's products in 2007 alone. The U.S. remains the world's biggest economy, producing about a quarter of global economic output. Exports were over $1 trillion in 2007, supporting over 800,000 jobs. Thus, in addition to advancing policies that encourage investment and learning, the role of the federal government is to open up markets through trade agreements. Phillip Bobbitt has referred to this function as the fundamental role of the "market-state." In *The Shield of Achilles: War, Peace and the Course of History*, Bobbitt has argued that the function of the modern nation state, which was to increase the national wealth of a nation's people and to allocate resources fairly, is changing as information, not territory, becomes the driver of national wealth and power. The purpose of the merging market-state is to *increase* wealth, not merely to allocate scare resources. Thus, the role for government, according to Bobbitt, is not to deliver material well being directly but to maximize people's opportunities to advance themselves and to get out of the way.

In 1990 trade represented about 40 percent of world GDP. By 2004, trade exceeded 65 percent of world GDP and the global economy expanded by half. In effect, Bobbitt is advocating for another great wave of market re-regulation and free trade that would create most of the economic incentives for investment and growth. This is of course classic liberal economic theory which everyone Bobbitt believes will surely recognize its fundamental validity. But the market-state faces at least three fundamental challenges in the global economy. The consequences of America's enormous

8. *The Role of Government*

need for foreign capital to fund its human capital and technological investments may create a balance of payments crisis, which over the long haul may make America poorer. Thus, America must remain attractive to foreign capital. This means that valuable U.S. assets—companies, ports, technology, intellectual property and real property—must continue to attract buyers from cash-rich economies, presently from Asia and the Middle East. From 2003 to 2008, foreign-led mergers and acquisitions increased more than six-fold. In 2007, there were over 2,000 foreign-led acquisitions of U.S. companies in deals worth $405.4 billion, twice the value of deals in 2006 and up from $60.8 billion in 2003, according to Thomson Reuters. Restrictive trade policies would slow the inflow of foreign money, and could ultimately lead to crushing interest payments, which relates to the second big challenge of the market-state: the rise of nationalism both among American borrowers and foreign lenders, particularly China.

As discussed in a *World Street Journal* essay (June 7, 2008), modern Chinese nationalism has its roots in ancient grievances against the West. Patriotism has replaced communism, justifying the legitimacy of the ruling class. Indeed, not standing up vigorously enough to foreign pressure is a common accusation made against Chinese officials by students and intellectuals. China, in short, is not a market-state and cannot be counted on to act in the interests of multinational corporations and financial institutions if trading or lending practices ever threatened its sovereignty. On the other hand, from 1997 to 2007, Americans doubled their purchase of imported consumer products, with about 42 percent coming from China. Because China exports more than it imports, it holds the largest foreign-exchange reserves in the world—$1.81 trillion by mid-2008. China's foreign exchange increases by about $40 billion per month. As a result of its prolific exporting and massive infrastructure investments, China's economy has been growing more than 10 percent per year for a decade. Relatively low interest rates have hedged against price and wage inflation, maintaining high rates of employment, which is the government's goal.

In short, the economies of China and the United States are inextricably linked and at present the well being of each nation depends, in large part, on the other. America has exported vast amounts of its wealth to China and China has exported affordable products to America. Since the nineteen seventies, China has engaged in the largest migration in human history. In *Factory Girls*, Leslie Chung has observed that three times the number of people who immigrated to America from Europe over a century have migrated from Chinese rural areas for industrial centers in just thirty years. Among other things, this massive demographic shift is causing extreme ecological stress. Seventy-five percent of the surface water in China is too polluted to drink. Thus, China must continue to export and modernize. It has nothing to gain and every thing to lose should it stop buying U.S. debt securities, which would cause hyperinflation for the United States. China has nothing to gain and everything to lose should it dump U.S. securities on the market, thus creating a deep recession in the U.S. and most of the rest of the world. China has nothing to gain and everything to lose should it trigger the events that would send the United States into bankruptcy. Nevertheless, as China's economy grows, demographers predict that the elderly population will grow from 100 million people older than sixty years of age in 2008 to 334 million people by 2050, including a staggering 100 million eighty years or older. In short, China's prosperity is a slow-motion Malthusian nightmare in the making unless it continues to make the investments in productivity necessary to create a modern welfare state. This development alone will change the nature of the Chinese-U.S. relationship as both national destinies appear to be linked for many generations to come.

Neoclassical, liberal economic theories, like that advanced by Bobbitt and others, suggest that in a free market living standards for poor and rich societies should converge over time. This appears to be happening globally, as developing economies begin to bridge the wealth gap with free markets. Indeed, larger disparities of wealth and opportunity do not presage a peaceful twenty first century. Therefore, Americans should welcome the gradual narrowing of the global wealth gap. But without exponential growth, competition from the world's economic resources remains a zero-sum game subject to the rule of scarcity. In the first decade of the twenty first century, the developing world's gains have come, in part, at the expense of the American worker who produces less and less of what the world is willing to buy. In times of past economic and social crisis, Americans have felt fear and envy and have exhibited prejudice and ill will. Americans, who supposedly believe in freedom and small government, have demanded centralized and command-driven intervention, often as a precursor to war. When the free market faced its most profound challenge in the past century, the Great Depression of the nineteen thirties, the market wasn't allowed to fix itself. Instead, the nation-state directed government intervention. It is a quaint notion today to think that any national government could re-direct the global economy. Worse, demagogues may actually try, setting off a trade or other war to the detriment of the entire world.

But multinational corporations that maintain global brands care little for the sovereignty of any nation state. Benjamin Barber has observed in *Atlantic Monthly* (March 1992) that "common markets demand a common language, as well as a common currency, and they produce common behaviors of the kind bred by cosmopolitan city life everywhere." International knowledge workers—bankers, media specialists, professionals—"compose a new breed of men and women for whom religion, culture, and nationality can seem only marginal elements in a working identity." To transnational corporations, nationality is irrelevant. Unlike Chinese companies, American corporations are not national champions and will promote patriotic themes only if it sells its products. At present, nationalistic impulses in the U.S. are largely based on race, which drives the building of the security fence along the Mexican broader. Mainstream shareholders still admire big business, even as it exports American jobs. Moreover, in return for foreign capital investment, the U.S, is exporting a great deal of intellectual property in return, the same intellectual property that forms the foundation of American competitiveness.

In the last decade of the twentieth century, President Bill Clinton advocated the passage of the North American Free Trade Agreement (NAFTA) and other trade agreements, convinced that free trade was a prerequisite for American prosperity. The export of so-called blue-collar factory jobs was inevitable but as a palliative, welfare was reformed, which required welfare recipients to eventually find work. As production jobs were outsourced requiring dislocated workers to find lower paying jobs in the service economy, their resentment and anger were quelled somewhat with the realization that at least the "welfare queens" and other dead beats were forced to find and hold a job, regardless of how low paying the job might be. This triangulation, essentially race bating as official policy, obscured a massive transfer of wealth from labor to capital. Likewise, tax cuts advocated by President George W. Bush and enacted by the Congress furthered the same trend, creating the biggest wage and wealth gaps since the nineteen twenties. To avoid widespread discontent, America relied on foreign money to support the average American's standard of living. In addition, new pools of money were plumbed in the housing market and more money was literally manufactured by bundling gimmicks.

American's strategic challenge in the first decades of the twenty first century lay in its increasing dependence upon international trade and, more importantly, international finance, without irrevocably placing its economic destiny in the hands of foreigners abroad or demigods at home. A recent study on globalization commissioned by the Financial Services Forum, an association of chief executives of twenty big financial firms, observed a backlash against globalization. The study suggests that governments and businesses must come up with new ways to spread the benefits of globalization more widely and to assist those who become unemployed or dislocated due to economic change. These firms see rising public anxiety about globalization as a threat and realize that advocating comparative advantage, ie: Social Darwinism isn't going to win the debate. According to the report: "Making the case for trade and globalization requires a list of specific, meaningful, practical, cost-efficient, and effective public and private sector responses to the reality that while the aggregate benefits of free trade and globalization are tremendous, it can sometimes bring with it painful dislocations for individuals, families, towns, regions, even entire industries."

The study lists a range of ideas, such as raising taxes on the wealthy to address income disparities to insuring individuals and communities against "sudden economic dislocation" caused by a plant shutdown. In other words, insofar as the Financial Services Forum is concerned, some of the biggest beneficiaries of globalization—global financial institutions—have reaffirmed the role of government to redistribute wealth and to allocate resources fairly under the traditional rules of scarcity. Recognizing that workforce training will do little to help struggling workers in the near term, the study concedes a robust welfare state. Promoting labor unions that might leverage their collective bargaining power is not mentioned as a possible way to ease the economic transformation of workers.

The inability to provide job security or mobility and the acquiescence to lower wages, has left labor unions with little value in exchange for union dues. Among knowledge workers, however, labor's relevancy may lie in its pre-Wagner Act past. In Silicon Valley, some technology workers have set up a clearinghouse for job training, certification and job placement. These "virtual unions" are also beginning to administer portable health and pension benefits. This approach harkens back to pre-Taylorism and is analogous to the old craft unions. They may be more adaptable to the demands of the knowledge economy and de-emphasizes the zero-sum struggle of the Wagner Act framework.

If there is an employment problem in the new economy, some say that it is a supply of labor problem. It is not a lack of jobs, but a lack of workers with the skills that are needed and prized by the information economy. Business journalists Bob Davis and David Wessel in *Prosperity: the Coming Twenty-Year Boom and What It Means to You*, find growing inequality and lack of job opportunities for the "unknowledgeable" to be an education problem. Moreover, it is an education problem that the United States is rapidly solving through our dynamic and flexible network of community colleges. One of their chapters is even subtitled "How Community Colleges Will Foster Prosperity and Equality." However, according to Thomas Homer-Dixon, "given the distribution of natural aptitudes and abilities in our society, not everyone can be educated or trained to be an information worker or knowledge producer. A knowledge-based economy privileges certain abilities over others, and only a relatively thin stratum of the society has those abilities in abundance ... Some people are going to be left behind, and societies with rapidly widening inequalities can't be politically stable for long."

Robert Reich also finds inequality and limited job opportunities to be primarily an education problem. But he is less optimistic than Davis and Wessel. Reich sees evidence that the richest fifth of the U.S. population is "seceding" from the rest of the country. They send their children to private schools then they oppose adequate funding of public schools. They live in residential enclaves with private guards and oppose the taxes needed to support police departments. Giving every child with the intelligence to become a symbolic analyst the education that it takes to become one should be a national priority. But Reich is skeptical that it will. Indeed, the top-tier private universities in the U.S. are enjoying unprecedented wealth, as endowments and gifts have soared. This contrasts with the growing financial pressures at many state universities, which educate three of four U.S. college students. Enrollments at colleges are increasing as state governments are curtailing budgets for higher education.

For the last one hundred years, government has defined and allocated education as a rivalrous resource, rather than as the nonrivalrous resource that education really is. The rationale for government to allocate finite resources is to avoid depletion. This is the dynamic that Garrett Hardin termed "the tragedy of the commons." "Picture a pasture open to all," Hardin writes, and consider the expected behavior of "herdsmen" who roam that pasture. Each herdsman must decide to add one more animal to their herd in order to increase their wealth. In making a decision to do so, Hardin writes, the herdsman reaps the benefit while everyone else suffers. The herdsman gets the benefit of one more animal, yet everyone suffers the cost, because the pasture has one more consuming animal. And this defines the problem: while the benefits of adding another animal are enjoyed by only the one herdsman, the costs will be borne by the others. Therefore, each herdsman has an incentive to add more animals than the pasture as a whole can bear. As Hardin describes the dynamic: "Therein is the tragedy. Each man is locked into a system that compels him to increase his herd without limit—in a world that is limited. Ruin is the destination toward which all men rush, each pursuing his own best interest in a society that believes in the freedom of the commons. Freedom in the commons brings ruin to all."

To avoid ruin, men and women form governments to regulate the commons. However, where consumption does not result in depletion, there is little need to regulate the commons. In other words, there is no ruin when the resources in the common are nonrivalrous. Education is such a resource; it cannot be over consumed or depleted. However, since nonrivalrous goods exist "free" in the commons, there is little incentive to improve it or to create more. The solution to this problem is to privatize the resource, thus creating incentives to create more and better education. Of course, government will continue to play a vital role in protecting consumers from education fraud, ensuring equal access, and guaranteeing transparency and accountability.

Similarly, American taxpayers fund billions of dollars worth of research every year, thereby creating incentives to create and disseminate knowledge. The majority of university research is sponsored by government agencies and is not targeted to specific commercial markets or end products—it is, by definition, basic research. However, since it is the nature of research to identify and test new ideas, its results often lead to the expansion of scientific knowledge as well as to the development of new technologies and products which benefit the public. Through the National Institute of Health alone, taxpayers funnel more than $428 billion per year into medical research. However, until 2008, much of this research was available only through costly subscriptions to medical journals. Realizing that placing information into the public domain will advance scientific discovery, Congress has made available the roughly 80,000 NIH-sponsored research papers for free on a website. Many universities have followed suit and have posted scholarly papers online in free, searchable databases. This "free" research can then be privatized in order to crate the incentives to innovate. Opening up the research produced by American universities via the Internet is probably one of the most cost-effective ways of helping competitive economic advantage. As recognized by the Founders, the dissemination of knowledge is critical to the creation of wealth and it need not be monopolized in all cases by patent protection.

Other government policies may tap the world's need to reduce greenhouse gas emissions. The potential for "green collar" jobs, which are defined as blue-collar work force opportunities created by firms and organizations whose mission is to improve environmental quality, could be very large in the second decade of the twentieth century and beyond. Such green collar jobs include highly educated engineers, but also organic food industry workers, solar panel manufacturers and installers, wind turbine repair jobs and "green home" retrofitters. Nationwide, the American Solar Energy Society estimates that as of 2008 there are about 8.5 million jobs in the so-called "clean tech" sector, which it projects could grow to 40 million in the United States by 2030 with strong and aggressive measures form federal and state governments. Investors appear to be taking notice of profit opportunities. Venture capital opportunities in the sector hit $5.18 billion in 2007, up 44 percent from the year before. Silicon Valley, where a combination of California's environmental policies, scientific talent and entrepreneurial culture has given birth to dozens of start ups.

Similarly, new recycling laws may require brand name companies to re-invest in US plants. With little fanfare, the New York City Council passed an ordinance in 2008 that holds computer, television and MP3-player manufacturers responsible for collecting and recycling their products once consumers discard them. According to the United Nations, 93 percent of a product's environmental impact is determined before purchase, in the extraction of resources and the manufacturing process, packaging and shipping. There is already an electronic waste law in the European Union and the purpose of the New York City ordinance is to divert millions of tons of toxic materials from landfills and incinerators.

To date, U.S. firms have found it cheaper to outsource manufacturing jobs than to retrofit U.S. plants. However, should the United States enact an electronic waste law similar to the European Union, the design and production of electronic computer products will need to be made in a ready-to-recycle way. Foreign manufactures, particularly in China, many of which cannot even make safe toys, may not have the processes to meet this need. American and foreign electronic firms may need to invest in high-end manufacturing closer to the consumer, which of course would include the massive U.S. market.

Government can also define property in other ways. For example, air is the ultimate nonrivalrous resource. As long as air is free, renewable energy will never supplant fossil fuels. But if government put a price on carbon, the alternatives start looking better. Corporations like General Electric, General Motors, Dow Chemical and DuPont, argue that the most feasible way to do this is through a "cap and trade" system that sets ceilings for carbon output and lets companies that come under the limit sell credits to those that don't. The hope is that overall carbon levels fall, even though profits are made from selling credits. The goals is to drive investment, research and development with this system, as government sets and enforces standards and also makes a big profit acting as broker, which in turn gets invested in more research and development.

The Venture Capital Association makes the case that if the U.S. science budget for cap and trade technologies, including renewable and energy efficiency technologies, were brought in line with that of the National Institutes of Health—about 29 billion—an explosion of projects and jobs would occur. The 1997 Kyoto Protocol was an early attempt at a cap and trade system, with an aim of having developed nations reduce their carbon emissions an average of 5 percent below 1990 levels by 2012. The accords were meant to drive cuts in greenhouse gases and promote investment in clean technologies through carbon trading. But when China, India and Indonesia were excused from the protocol, the United States refused to sign on, eventually abandoning the protocol altogether in 2001.

The cap and trade system commenced within the Euro Zone has had mixed results but some experts believe that when most of the world eventually assigns a price to carbon, the demand for cheap carbon-free electricity will increase exponentially. In short, world governments have the wherewithal to create the next big technological burst, creating the legal and regulatory framework to advance innovation for a long time to come. It starts with the carbon value tax, that is, a tax on each product's "carbon footprint."

Take the automobile, for instance. For every mile it travels, the average car in the U.S. emits about one pound of carbon dioxide. Given typical distances and fuel-economy numbers, that translates into about five tons of carbon dioxide per car, per year. A study by the university of Michigan's Center for Sustainable Systems found that, over its expected 120,000-mile life, an American-made midsize automobile emits the equivalent of about sixty-three tons of carbon dioxide. That number includes all emissions from the production of the car's raw materials, such as steel and plastic, through the shedding of the car once it is junked. At each point over a government-imposed limit, the carbon value would be taxed, thus creating an incentive to purchase a more efficient car.

According to the International Energy Agency, American consumers produce about nineteen tons of carbon dioxide emissions per capita, as compared to 4.28 tons on average for the rest of the world. The reality is that nearly the entire production, transportation and energy infrastructure of the United States hinges on fossil fuels, which is why oil, gas and coal are subsidized and wind, solar and alternative power sources are not. Reshaping a market to make Americans use less electricity and make power companies buy energy from cleaner sources will require an entirely new regime of taxes, incentives and price signals set by the federal government. Taxing carbon and shifting subsidies from fossil fuels to alternative sources of power would, of course, raise the price of nearly everything that Americans buy. Under continuing global pressure, it is likely that real wages for most Americans may continue to stagnate for at least another generation or more. In essence, a "Green Economy" will require the current generation of Americans to accept lower living standards so that the next generation can have a cleaner, and perhaps a more prosperous, economy. According to Curt Carlson chief executive officer of SRI International in Menlo Park, Calif., the nonprofit parent research institute that owns Sarnoff Corporation: "This is a 50-to 100-year problem, not a 10-year problem like our politicians say. Over the next 20 years, it will be slow going until we see the technologies we need ... They have to start by investing in what really matters. What you see in the mainstream media does not show the scale of the problem. It is going to take everything we [have] to do it."

The present generation, however, is the same one that voraciously consumed itself into unsustainable levels of debt by essentially passing onto future generations its obligation to pay it off. Many have not shown the inclination or temperament for such sacrifice, nor have they embraced such a national mission. The fossil fuel-based economy's hunger for energy is dangerous not only because of global warming, but also because it is depleting biodiversity, destroying a unique species every twenty minutes. It also means that the governments and corporations that control the world's oil and gas reserves are able to concentrate more power in fewer hands, threatening democratic institutions in the United States and elsewhere.

In *Hot, Flat, and Crowded*, Thomas Friedman argues that what is needed is the executive leadership of an Abraham Lincoln or Franklin Roosevelt to create a single, national system that would shift resources, reallocate incentives and release the pent-up innovation and creativity that exists in the market. Both Lincoln and Roosevelt led during life and death circumstances for the nation. Both amassed enormous executive power during wartime. Both were accused of being dictators and both died in office—Lincoln, of course, from an assassin's bullet, but Roosevelt too was nearly shot by an assassin—but while in office both were able to communicate an authentic national mission and credible reasons for Americans to sacrifice. But their leadership was augmented by compulsory national and military service, the temporary suspension of some civil liberties, and wartime profiteering. That type of state power might exit in state-capitalist economies but does not yet currently exist in the U.S.

The current generation of Americans, enabled by their leaders, have basically diverted resources from future generations without laying the foundation for growth. They have not borrowed to build schools and to make a college education universal. Instead, they have borrowed against future earnings to finance their consumption. In the case of households, debt rose from about 50 percent of GNP in 1980 to a peak of 100 percent in 2006. By 2008, households owed as much as the entire U.S. economy can produce in a year, or $14 trillion. Debt enabled consumption far exceeded what was produced. From 1983 to 2008, total debt, private and public, increased by $45.1 trillion, GDP only $10.9 trillion. In many respects, this generation of Americans has merely met the economic expectations of their era, which was to compel economic growth through consumption, rather than through production. But schools, roads, airports and the nation's medical systems have all suffered, starved for the investment that would ensure future prosperity. In retrospect, the combination of shortsightedness, selfishness and greed is reprehensible. This generation even expects their children to pay for their longer life spans, the same children that were subject to 1.7 million reports of abuse and neglect in 2010. Less than one in four workers age 55 and older—just 23 percent—has savings and investments totally $250,000 or more, according to a study published in 2008 by the Employee Benefit Research Institute. About 60 percent have less than $100,000. With the coming explosion in Medicare costs, the federal budget deficit may eventually get so large that foreign investors would need to find safer havens. Were that to happen, and the United States was left struggling to attract financing, the country's assets would be up for the biggest fire sale in history.

The investments necessary to create a knowledge-intensive, green economy will require enormous sums. If that money is borrowed from abroad, more American jobs and assets will be exported in return. Moreover, to the extent that the money from sovereign wealth funds is needed, concern about the political motives of these government institutions may be heightened, raising suspicions about foreign influence. If the Federal Reserve buys Treasury notes, in effect printing more money, the U.S. dollar could be seriously compromised. However, the jobs that remain and the many that could eventually be created will be more knowledge-intensive and only a small percentage of Americans may be qualified to fill them unless investments in education and training are also made. In short, moving aggressively away from fossil fuels to cleaner energy represents an enormous gamble in innovation and growth, so big, in fact, that the developed economies will need to work in concert.

The market is potentially enormous. In a 2007 report, the U.S. Department of Energy concluded that the United States could make wind energy the source of one-fifth of its electricity by 2020, up from 2 percent in 2008. That would require neatly one-half billion dollars in new construction and would add more than three million jobs, estimates the report. As of 2008 Germany had already created a quarter of a million jobs in renewal energy. Assuming that executive leadership at all levels emerges to articulate why Americans should transform its economy to be more knowledge-intensive and greener, it would be the first time that Americans would be asked to voluntarily lower their standards of living and to willingly sacrifice their consumption habits to pursue a national mission during peacetime. For all the tub-thumping and flag waving emotionalism and expressions of patriotism, the majority of Americans has never once acted out of authentic national purpose. To be sure, some marched for civil rights and to end the Vietnam War, and a heroic few put their lives on the line in Viet Nam or in Birmingham. But the majority stayed at home or in the dorm, watching events unfold on their television sets. Simply put, embracing regulations aimed at curbing global warming that would force coal-fired electricity plants to pay for the pollution that they emit would raise energy costs for at least a generation. Similarly, a carbon-value tax would raise prices on nearly everything that is made or transported. However, in the long run wind, solar and other alternative fuels would become competitive over time. There may be vast amounts of money to be made retooling and supplying the world with new energy sources. Thus, the knowledge-intensive, green revolution must be driven in the same way as all other revolutions—by charismatic, visionary leaders, a zealous cadre of elite, young true-believers, the curtailment of some liberties, and a strong dose of profiteering. Like all other revolutions, it will surely be driven by excess.

9. The Role of Markets

Under the pressure of political and social reform, Congress enacted the Sherman Antitrust Act in 1890. Defenders of monopoly argued that the concentration of property was the result of natural forces and that any intervention by the national government would be a step on the road to serfdom. However, it became clear after the Civil War that concentrated corporate power was undermining the free enterprise system. Two years earlier, no less than President Grover Cleveland, delivered a broadside to Congress. It is worth repeating at length:

> We find the wealth and luxury of our cities mingled with poverty and wretchedness and unrenumerative toil. We discover that the fortunes realized by our manufacturers are no longer solely the reward of sturdy industry and enlightened foresight, but the result from a discriminatory favour of the government, and were largely built upon undue exactions from the masses of our people. The gulf between employers and the employed is constantly widening, and classes are rapidly forming, one comprising the very rich and powerful, while another are found the toiling poor. We discover the existence of trusts, combinations, and monopolies, while the citizen struggling far in the rear, or is trampled to death beneath the iron heel. Corporations, which should be carefully restrained creatures of the law and the servants of the people, are fast becoming the people's masters.

Cleveland's apocalyptic vision of class warfare was meant to justify the use of national power to regulate the excesses of the market, chief among them the widening, and in his view, the unsustainable wealth gap. Then, as now, it was the American middle class that held the entire economic system together. Their belief in private property, enterprise and opportunity constituted the bedrock of the free enterprise system. If the system, which was built on millions of Americans believing in the system's virtue, was to be saved by its own excesses, the national government would need to act. Cleveland's tactic created the momentum for the antitrust law, which declared illegal "every contract, combination in the form of trust or otherwise, or conspiracy, in restraint of trade." Portrayed as socialism by the entrenched business interests of the time, the law's passage merely reflected longstanding, Adam Smith-type liberal economic orthodoxy: that competition was the cornerstone of free enterprise. As Galbraith noted, the antitrust law "addressed the one conceded flaw in an otherwise perfect system."

However, as previously explained, the profit value of knowledge can be measured by its scarcity and the completive edge for most firms is to monopolize, not share knowledge. Thus, big corporations are driven by the dual objectives of controlling and suppressing knowledge, to take out as much knowledge from the public domain as possible and to privatize it. By creating this property interest in knowledge, innovation can be stifled and knowledge itself could be subject to diminishing returns. But as a matter of public policy, monopolies can either be regulated or broken up. As discussed in earlier, *United States v. Microsoft* may serve as the *Standard Oil* case of the new knowledge economy. In *Microsoft*, the Antitrust Division of the U.S. Justice Department prosecuted the software giant, believing that an intellectual property monopoly was neither inevitable nor desirable. The government alleged that Microsoft had willfully maintained a monopoly position in the operating system market through a variety of tactics aimed at suppressing the development of a layer of software, called middleware, that works between Microsoft's Windows operating system and software applications. Ultimately the remedies that were fashioned by the federal court were precisely the remedies available in many public utility cases—a duty to provide access on reasonable, nondiscriminatory terms.

Of course, a patent is not a monopoly, per se. A monopoly is something in the public domain that the government takes from the public and gives to a person (like in the famous British case of the playing cards). An invention is something that did not exist before and was not in the public domain. It is something novel, that upon publication via the grant of the patent has the potential of enriching the public domain with the knowledge of the invention, and upon expiration of the patent, enters into the public domain, free to be used by anyone. Under federal patent law, a patent is considered "personal property", like any other personal property (35 United States Code, section 261). In other words, a patent is a right to exclude. But such a right does not necessarily create a monopoly over a market. People other than the inventor can compete with a patented product; they need only use products based on different ideas. Thus, a patent behaves like a grant of real property, in that the owner of a house may exclude others from using it, but the owner does not have a monopoly over the real estate market. According to the 1995 U.S. Department of Justice/Federal Trade Commission Antitrust Guidelines, patents are "comparable to any other form of property," are not "presumed to create market power" and licensing patents is "generally pro-competitive."

Nevertheless, Microsoft decided to settle its antitrust litigation with the European Union by paying an initial fine of $1.35 billion. A European antitrust commission found that Microsoft had abused its near-monopoly position by bundling a media player with its Windows operating system and denying competitors information needed to make their computers work with Microsoft's ubiquitous Windows software. The commission found specifically that Microsoft hadn't proved that sharing its technology with rivals would "have a significant negative effect on its incentives to innovate." Under a deal reached after nine years of litigation, Microsoft agreed to slash the cost it was charging to license the interoperability information needed to make software work well with its Windows software. Additionally, Microsoft agreed to license all of its intellectual property, except patents, necessary for competitors to work with a version of Windows used on business servers. Competitors will now pay a one-time fee for the license, rather than royalties. In effect, the company agreed to license information that competitors need to make their software work better with certain versions of Windows. It had long resisted doing so, saying the information comprised fruits of its intellectual labors that it should be able to keep secret. Given the global nature of technology, and the global nature of most big technology customers, the settlement is likely to mean that the interoperability information will spread to companies doing business outside of Europe.

The ruling suggests that dominant knowledge intensive companies have special responsibilities if they have a product, like Windows, which is indispensable to innovation in other markets. By requiring Microsoft to disclose communications protocols to help competitors make products that work with Windows and to offer versions of Windows without media player software it had bundled with the operating system, it is hoped that the ruling will result in a victory for innovation and innovators by making it easier for small firms to compete with dominant firms by forbidding dominant firms from taking actions that exclude them from the market. This could mean more innovation that dominant firms can't control.

Traditionally, the central concerns of antitrust enforcement has been to detect and deter cartel behavior, usually price fixing, bid rigging, and market division-and to block horizontal mergers that lead to high levels of concentration and then to coordinated price and non-price competition. In practical terms, that means that government puts most of its resources into anti-cartel and anti-merger review and enforcement. However, antitrust enforcement is equally essential to innovation and economic growth. The fact that the pace of technological innovation is constantly accelerating makes it more, rather than less, important to sustain the right balance between reward and rivalry. The reality is that fear of being left behind is more likely to spur innovation than is complacency bred of stable market power.

Robert Hahn and Peter Passel from the Milken Institute have observed that market power is short lived in the world of high tech. "The real story here is the ever briefer period in which companies with clear leads in technology and marketing seem able to sustain their advantages. As a consequence, antitrust policy built around traditional tests of market power is at best a way to keep lawyers well remunerated and, more likely, a significant barrier to productive change."

9. The Role of Markets

Hahn and Passel point out the expensive irony of Microsoft's decades-long battle with the U.S. Department of Justice and other antitrust authorities on two other continents. Whatever market power Microsoft acquired by building its Internet Explorer at no extra cost to its ubiquitous PC operating system was already ebbing by the time the corporation became mired in its antitrust battles. The researchers cite the startling rise of free, open source software as one of Microsoft's biggest competitive challenges, noting the wide use of Linux in operating systems. "The Nightmare on the horizon, though—the one that prompted Microsoft to offer a 62 % premium to Yahoo! shareholders—is Google and the Internet 'cloud,'" meaning that hand-held devices and the systems that operate them, will be the next big battleground for Microsoft, Google, Facebook and other knowledge-intensive firms that want to build the next great platform for the Internet.

A platform is the software code on which third-party applications function. IBM dominated the first commercial platform with its expensive mainframe and operating systems aimed at corporate users. Like Microsoft, IBM engaged in decades-long antitrust litigation with the U.S. Department of Justice and again the federal government was behind the technological wave. Having nothing to do with IBM's eventual settlement of its antitrust litigation, Microsoft and the Windows operating system supplanted Big Blue as the PC revolution took hold.

Similarly, open source platform software enables innovation on the part of thousands of firms and millions of people who will build the applications for which consumers will pay. Whichever corporation dominates the platform(s) will reap the enormous benefits, making billions of dollars selling devices, advertisements and services. In fact, Google has relied on the open Internet to make its entire business, building revenue primarily from advertisements, but also from selling various services and web-based products. The company vigorously opposes proprietary platforms on the Internet for this very reason as it spins its lobbying efforts as advocacy for innovation. However, innovation itself can and does take many forms. The term is applied to basic scientific breakthroughs, important commercial inventions, product modifications and new production techniques. All are important to society. Whether in the form of improved product quality and variety, or production efficiency that allows lower prices, innovation is a powerful engine for enhanced consumer welfare. By prohibiting private restraints that impede entry or mute rivalry, antitrust enforcement seeks to create the conditions in which entrepreneurial initiative can flourish and in which opportunities for bringing innovations to market can continue to be exploited by a multitude of private actors in a free market. But for those that believe the Internet creates a new paradigm for antitrust enforcement, the competition to create the dominant platform may be doing a sufficient job. In 2008 Google launched Chrome, a web browser to rival Microsoft's Explorer and in 2010 Microsoft launched Bing as a rival search engine to Google. The battle between Facebook, Google and others over social networking revenue also demonstrates how an "open" Internet is fueling robust competition.

Nevertheless, Google's dominate role in Internet advertising—it accounts for 70 percent of U.S. searches—and its decision to strike a deal with Yahoo to combine advertising strengths has resulted in serious antitrust concerns. a group of major advertisers complained to the department about the deal. The Association of National Advertisers, which represents major advertisers such as Procter & Gamble and General Motors has warned that the deal could lead to higher prices and limited opportunities for Internet advertisers. Predictably, Microsoft has also objected to the deal, saying it would unfairly foreclose competition on the Internet. In Senate hearings in July, 2008, Microsoft's general counsel testified that "if search is the gateway to the Internet, and most people believe that it is, this deal will put Google in position to own that gateway and the information that flows through it."

While in truth, open source Internet platforms are redefining the definition of "property" in the new, information-intensive economy Microsoft and others contend that Google is aggressively seeking to fence the information commons. To some extent, the Internet commons provided the ethical rationale for Grokster's business model and, to a lesser extent, supports Google's position against Viacom. However, as the goal of Google like any corporation is to make a profit by dominating its market it simply shifts gears and supports the opposite position when convenient and necessary.

Actually, the Internet commons does have moral and legal precedent in the material world. Locke's formulation on acquiring and owning property, which was given to mankind by God "in common", rested on creating a property interest in one's labor as long as there remained enough resources for others to use. As it follows, English common law recognized grazing, hunting and fishing rights and other such easements on the uncultivated or unused lands of others.

Since there are limits in the material world of scarcity to how much can be removed from available resources while ensuring enough is left for others, as a moral principle, everyone has a moral right to use the resources of the commons. However, the Internet commons, unlike the land commons, is not a resource already stocked by nature waiting to be made into private property by someone's labor. In contrast, according to Kenneth Hemma of Seattle Pacific University, the Internet commons "is stocked by and only by the activity of human beings. People cannot make land, but they can (and do) make novels, music, proofs, theories, etc: and if someone does not make a particular novel, it is not available for human consumption." In other words, content providers need incentives, such as a revenue stream form sales or from advertising.

In 2010 Google found itself in the same predicament as Microsoft, accused of being a monopoly gatekeeper, this time to the Internet commons. Under formal investigation by the U.S. Department of Justice, there have been a growing number of complaints in the U.S. and Europe that the company has used its search monopoly to exclude actual and potential rivals by lowering their rankings in Google searches. Such "click rigging" can fence out content by ensuring that competitor's search engines are never reached by consumers. Google of course denies these allegations but unlike Microsoft it has not advanced an argument that its search practices promote innovation or customer choice. According to industry observers, Google's inability to formulate a coherent ethical basis for its business practices has left the company with a superficial defense, merely "expressing indignation that anyone would deign to question such a hip, warm and fuzzy company." But Google's public persona is simply not a moral justification for monopoly practices and has left the company vulnerable to accusations of amorality. On the one hand the company advocates for a "free" Internet and lobbies for so-called net neutrality. On the other, it may be using its power to engage in search rigging. Unless it can be shown that consumers are independently savvy enough to maximize their search choices regardless of Google rankings, Google's market dominance may warrant regulating the company's search rankings as a matter of antitrust law.

10. The Economics of Knowledge

The globalized, new economy has driven corporations to downsize, right size and upsize, outsource and in-source, reengineer, restructure and reinvent. They have tried decentralizing, deregulating and divesting. In the end, most corporations have become a bit flatter, but the dead hand of bureaucracy, like mortgage debt, is not easily eliminated. Moreover, the control and command structure of many organizations still plays an important role in insulating and protecting management from taking personal responsibility for business decisions that don't pan out. Nevertheless, when there is no more people to outsource, the relentless demands of the knowledge economy will require most organizations to become even more horizontal and decentralized, or perhaps even *un*organized.

Google has taken a different track to scale the problem of maximizing value-adding behavior with a type of *in*-sourcing solution. In just nine years it has built the dominant Internet search engine, redefined advertising and boasts a $160 billion market capitalization. To tap into the drive and innovation of its people, the company is decentralized into small, self-managing teams. Additionally, engineers are encouraged to experiment with offbeat products to foster what might be major breakthroughs. The culture appears to produce many ideas but as pointed out by Peters and Waterman in *The Search for Excellence*, ideas are a dime a dozen unless there are people who have the know-how, energy, daring and staying power to implement them and even at Google their appears to be serious problems converting ideas into competitive advantage.

According to Laszlo Bock, Google's human resources manager, "creativity comes out of people bumping into each other and not knowing where to go." Sounds cool. But former employees describe the creative culture at Google as chaotic, disorganized and unstructured with the chances that an idea generated by the average employee being implemented "basically zero." An attempt to tap the talent pool for innovation may be backfiring. Dubbed the "20 percent" time rule," every employee is able to spend one-fifth of his or her time exploring any new idea. On the surface, this rule makes a great deal of sense. Since the average Google employee easily spends 20 percent of their time on unproductive activity or being idle, why not have them spend time on "exploring" an idea. However, according to former employees, in practice the 20 percent time rule works out to be more of a 120% time rule, since no one actually gets around to completing assigned projects. The result of this "innovation" is that nearly every Google employee works seven days a week.

Google, of course, is just another corporation that is challenged to unleash employee creativity. Even though it dominates the Internet, it still has only one proven revenue stream and most of the big innovations, such as YouTube and Google Earth, have come through acquisitions. According to Douglas Merrill, Google's chief information officer, some of the firm's most interesting ideas have come from unexpected places within the organization. For example, members of the finance department suggested improvements to Google's content publishing system. However, when it came time to compete with Microsoft's PowerPoint in 2007 it acquired Tonic Systems.

Worse for Google and other Internet companies, revenue growth slowed dramatically after the Dot Com Bust. The company's rapid growth was fueled almost entirely by its sales of search ads and its attempts at innovation have more likely than not petered out. By 2008 thousands of projects were cancelled or streamlined and engineers were asked for the first time to make a business case before their project could get funded. Also, the company has pared down hundreds of promising innovations that cannot be justified by the bottom line. But perhaps the most telling fact of Google's ability to unleash innovation is the jettisoning of one of the company's most cherished values—network neutrality.

Since the company's inception, Google, as well as Microsoft, Yahoo, Amazon.com and others, have stood firmly behind keeping the Internet open to all traffic on an equal basis. In fact, in 2006 Google declared:

> Network neutrality is the principle that Internet users should be in control of what content they view and what applications they use on the Internet. The Internet has operated according to this neutrality principle since its earliest days . . . Fundamentally, net neutrality is about equal access to the Internet. In our view, the broadband carriers should not be permitted to use their market power to discriminate against competing applications or content. Just as telephone companies are not permitted to tell consumers who they can call or what they can say, broadband carriers should not be allowed to use their market power to control activity online.

As a follow up, Microsoft wrote Congress declaring that ensuring network security "could dictate whether the U.S. will continue to lead the world in Internet-related technologies." Realizing, however, that a revenue stream could be created by partnering with Comcast and other broadband carriers, both Google and Microsoft now advocate that the Internet should be tiered, with faster and easier access to the Internet given to firms that can afford it, potentially choking off the competition and innovation from smaller, less heeled firms. Once the anti-Microsoft, Google's checkered innovation record has ensured that it will become just like Microsoft. Since it is clear that Google's innovation strategy is based, in part, on lobbying and acquisitions, Google's talent search is similarly based, in part, on raiding other companies for value adding knowledge workers. As previously noted, Dr. Kai-Fu Lee was the case in point.

Dr. Lee was poached by Google from Microsoft because of his unique talents and experience and the Washington state court permitted him, with some limitations, to work for Google in China. Dr. Lee eventually left Google only to compete with his former employer. His reputation, skills and abilities, his own human capital, his "property", was leveraged within the context of a free exchange for compensation and other valuable consideration. Thus, property, with its associated right of control, exclusion, exchange and exploitation, provided the basic ingredient to Dr. Lee's happiness and personal fulfillment. In short, private property provides the foundation for liberty in a free market society, although all this Silicon Valley talent poaching did lead to an agreement on anti-poaching guidelines among several firms which triggered antitrust scrutiny by the U.S. Justice Department.

Likewise, intellectual property protection, which included Microsoft's trade secrets, provided the incentives for the company to invent new technology applications, which benefited society. If all such property were socialized as part of a knowledge commons, human nature would ensure that the motivation to create new applications would diminish, thereby hurting society. Human capital and intellectual property ownership, therefore, provides the fundamental precondition for success in the knowledge economy. Without it, dependence and serfdom are assured.

However, as we have seen, the property tends to concentrate in too few hands. This concentration is enabled by the work for hire doctrine and the by the broad protection of knowledge under the trade secret doctrine. But if otherwise productive people are to thrive in the knowledge economy, a balance must be struck between absolute control of intellectual property, broadly defined, and the knowledge available in the public domain. Innovations must have a fighting chance to succeed and others must be able to at least survive the insecurities of contingent work.

In 2011 Google paid a big premium for 17,000 patents from Motorola Mobility Holdings so that it could compete with Apple's smart phone. The bulk purchase actually was a fallback plan sine the company was outbid by a consortium of companies, including Apple that purchased bulk patents from Nortel Networks. The purchasing price of $4.5 billion of the Nortel patents signals a race to control as much intellectual property as possible in the battle for smart phones, a market that is projected to reach 2 billion within a decade. The consortium also reflects a model for firms to share patents without resorting to costly and time consuming patent litigation.

As discussed, copyright and patent law, and contractual restrictions on competition, tend to create monopoly power. Monopolies can either be regulated or broken up. In *United States v. Microsoft*, the Antitrust Division of the U.S. Justice Department prosecuted the software giant, believing that an intellectual property monopoly was neither inevitable nor desirable. The government alleged that Microsoft had willfully maintained a monopoly position in the operating system market through a variety of tactics aimed at suppressing the development of a layer of software, called middleware, which works between Microsoft's Windows operating system and software applications. Ultimately the remedies that were fashioned by the federal court were precisely the remedies available in many public utility cases—a duty to provide access on reasonable, nondiscriminatory terms.

In the past, government was slow to act because business lobbied hard against regulation and antitrust enforcement. Crisis often ensued. When government did act, the courts were often hostile to reform. To date, the federal government has similarly taken hands off approach and it is unlikely that government intervention can change the overall trajectory of the knowledge economy. Intellectual property protection and the free market bargain between employer and employee will remain the norm, even as the difficult transition of the knowledge economy accelerates. Private property, free labor and free enterprise have been the fount of societal benefits, not a threat to it. However, excessive concentration of knowledge capital, and therefore wealth, poses grave dangers. Education reform, tuition assistance, universal health care, retirement savings reform, perhaps even wage assistance, are but some of the important and necessary initiatives that should be on the legislative agenda.

Eventually the courts will have to accommodate the law of tangible and intangible property to the new realities of the knowledge economy as it did in the past to accommodate industrialism. After a generation of striking down legislation attempting to regulate the economy and the employer-employee relationship in the name of liberty and economic utility, the U.S. Supreme Court reversed itself and upheld New Deal reforms in 1937. In *West Coast Hotel v. Parrish*, the court found that economic collapse required government relief. Remarkably, it stated that it was unnecessary "to cite official statistics to establish what common knowledge through the length and breath of the land ... The community is not bound to provide what is in effect a subsidy for unconscionable employers. The community may direct its law-making power to correct the abuse which springs from the selfish disregard for the public interest."

Moreover, after nearly a generation of economic libertarianism, the need for government oversight of business became obvious. In 1938, Congress created the Temporary National Economic Committee in response to President Roosevelt's belief that the concentration of economic power among just a few hundred manufacturers, banks and investment trusts was creating a negative impact on the U.S. economy. Among the Committee's recommendations was amending the Patent Act to prevent the monopolization of innovation and the adoption of compulsory licenses to prevent the suppression of competition.

The Committee's recommendations did not go unnoticed by the U.S. Supreme Court. In 1941, the court decided *Cuno Engineering v. Automatic Devices*, which dealt with the nonobvious requirement under the Patent act. According to the court, for a patent to be nonobvious, the inventor must evidence a "flash of creative genius," a very stringent standard to uphold a patent. The court cited the Committee's work to justify such a high threshold in order to create a disincentive to a "class of speculative schemers who make it their business to watch the advancing wave of improvement, and gather its foam in the form of patent monoplies." Today, these speculators are often referred to as "patent trolls," firms that file and own patents with no intention of practicing the art, waiting instead to file an infringement suit against companies that actually apply the art to products and services.

Eventually, the iron grip of economic predetermination and Social Darwinism gave way to remedial governmental and judicial intervention. In *The American Mind*, Henry Commager has observed that the restless American character played an important role in upholding the principle that government could intervene, direct and, perhaps mold, the economic rules of nature. Americans he wrote "were logically and psychologically precluded from believing in a progress to which they made no contribution and which was divorced from their control." Moreover, unbridled competition over scarce resources threatened republican, democratic institutions and in many cases led to violence and civil unrest and violence. The American experience with mass unemployment, foreclosures, bank runs, and lack of purchasing power had taught many legislators and academics that the natural boom and bust cycle could one day led to long-term economic collapse and anarchy, which could only be quelled by a police state. As observed by Hofstadter, "industrial society was to be humanized through law," first by reforms enacted by the states and eventually by the federal government.

If American workers are to take full advantage of the nonrivalrous nature of information in the knowledge economy, the economic law of scarcity may need to give way to a rule of reason. Is it reasonable to expect employees to compete successfully in the knowledge economy when corporations own and control all the most important assets? Should non-competition and confidentiality agreements be subject to antitrust scrutiny? Should employers meet a higher burden of proof to enforce such agreements? Should copyright holders be allowed to suppress First Amendment speech rights? Should patent holders with no intention of practicing the art taught by the patent be permitted to extort large sums of money from firms that want to innovate? These are just a few issues of public policy that will inform judicial decision-making.

Firms such as IBM and Texas instruments have built big licensing businesses by charging other companies royalties for using their patents. Pure patent-licensing firms, sometimes referred to as "trolls" or "sharks" represents a sizable expansion of a controversial business, which companies acquire patents with the sole purpose of licensing them to others, without ever producing a product. For many in the technology business, a wake-up call came in 2006 when BlackBerry-maker Research in Motion paid a $612.5 million settlement to Virginia-based NTP, Inc. following a four-year legal battle that nearly shut down the wireless email service.

Given the nature of constitutional jurisprudence and the political realities of judicial selection, it is expected that the courts will move incrementally to better calibrate the competing demands of innovation and intellectual property protection. In 2006 the U.S. Supreme Court decided two cases that reflect awareness that patent monopoly may undermine innovation.

In *EBay v. MercExchange*, the Court held that patent holders are required to demonstrate that the alleged infringer caused "irreparable harm" before being awarded a temporary restraining order. While on the surface, this decision turns on a technical application of equity law, the underlying policy is clear: before suppressing the innovation of another, the patent holder must meet an extraordinary burden of proof.

In *MercExchange*, a Virginia company that owned several patents for the sole purpose of excluding others from practicing the patent's art, filed suit alleging that EBay infringed its "Buy It Now" patent. The patent covered an electronic commerce feature, which allowed buyers to purchase an item directly without bidding. The court found that EBay had infringed the patent but the judge refused to issue an order enjoining EBay from using the patent, finding that MercExchange's licensing of the patent to Ebay was better for consumers. The federal court of appeals reversed the trial judge and ordered it to issue an injunction, holding that the power of the injunction, which would have enabled MercExchange to put EBay's direct purchase operations out of business, was "a natural consequence of the right to exclude" even if MercExchange had no intention of practicing the patent's art. Thus, the patent's monopoly power gave the patent troll enormous leverage over firms looking to serve consumers better and more conveniently.

When the U.S. Supreme Court agreed to hear the case, Adobe, Apple, Intel, Yahoo, Google, Microsoft and Cisco Systems, among other firms, lined up behind eBay and filed a brief in support of the trial court's denial of the injunction. The group noted that technology products typically consist of hundreds or thousands of patented components. Because it is impossible for technology companies to investigate all of the patents, and pending patent applications, these firms are vulnerable to costly patent litigation. Since the litigation is mostly commenced after standards are adopted, designing around the claim is often not a realistic option. An automatic injunction gives the patent holder enormous bargaining power, forcing infringers to sometimes pay exorbitant settlements to stay in business. Innovation suffers when firms think twice about invention or forgoes the invention entirely. The U.S. Justice Department and others sided with MercExchange. The Supreme Court overturned the circuit court's approval of the injunction, holding that nothing in the Patent

Act eliminated the traditional reliance on weighing the equitable factors considered in determining whether an injunction should issue. But it also ruled that the trail court erred in denying an injunction on the basis that MercExchange does not itself practice the patented invention.

In *KSR International v. Teleflex*, the court held that obvious improvements to existing patents do not enjoy patent protection. While the prosecution of a patent has always required a showing of "non-obviousness," the court made it easier for lower court judges and the federal patent court to call inventions "obvious" and therefore ineligible for monopoly protection. Patentees have long had the upper hand in patent litigation but the *KSR* decision has shifted the balance of power back to innovators. In this case, the court rejected a rigid application of existing tests for obviousness in favor of a more expansive and flexible approach that gives judges more discretion. According to the court, "if a person of ordinary skill in the relevant subject area would be able to fit the teaching of multiple patents together like a puzzle" then the patent is obvious. "Granting patent protection to advances that would occur in the ordinary course without real innovation retards progress."

Like the New Deal court in 1937, the present court does not need statistics to prove what is common knowledge. The United States is in the midst of the most entrepreneurial era of its history, with more than 500,000 Americans involved in launching their own companies each year. New patents often lead to the creation of those companies. These entrepreneurs, like Bill Gates and Steve Jobs, often create the jobs and industries of the future. Patents, however, grant monopolies. As long as intellectual property remains subject to private ownership, the court will be required to maintain a balance between competing demands.

In 2008 the U.S. Court of Appeals for the Federal Circuit made it much harder for companies and individuals to get patent protection on abstract processes developed for businesses, such as tax strategies and investment methods. In the case of *In re Bilski*, the court upheld a ruling made by the Board of Patent Appeals and Interferences, which denied a patent for a method of hedging risks of sudden changes in energy costs. While patent law specifically allows the patenting of processes, the court ruled that this protection doesn't extend to all abstract strategies of doing business.

The court, in a 9-3 decision, wrote that in order for a process to receive patent protection, it has to either "transform [an] article to a different state or thing" or be "tied to a particular machine." The risk-hedging strategy, the court ruled, did not fall into either category. The court stated "transformations or manipulations of . . . business risks, or other such abstractions cannot meet the test because they are not physical objects or substances . . ."

The plaintiffs, Bernard Bilski and Rand Warsaw, had developed a hedging strategy used by several utilities to smooth out revenues in a sector where prices often gyrate. They argued that the utilities should have to license the right to use the method, citing *State Street Bank v. Signature Financial Group*, a 1998 court decision which largely allowed so-called "business method patents. Yet, the patent office denied their request and the plaintiffs appealed. *Bilski* has largely disavowed the highly controversial *State Street Bank*, which had granted protection to a system for managing mutual fund accounts. The *State Street* decision was widely cheered by the financial-services and software industries, among others. But ever since its issuance, the case has been a lightning rod among patent practitioners, with detractors largely arguing that it led to a glut of weak patents.

For the great majority of issued patents, a significant concern posed by *KSR* will be its general sentiment that patents have been too easily granted and that they should therefore be more closely scrutinized. In large part, the Supreme Court was reacting to an already existing public disdain for weak patents and it is therefore difficult to predict the precise role *KSR* will have in advancing innovation. What's certain, however, is that the costs and uncertainties of patent litigations will become even more expensive and time consuming than they already are. The law's complexities are pitting corporations against each other in high stakes competition. For the corporation that knowingly infringes a questionable patent as a strategy for obtaining a license, the litigation is merely a business decision measured by costs and benefits.

As previously explained, the U.S. Supreme Court appeared to have shifted its patent jurisprudence in favor of innovation. In *KSR International v. Teleflex*, the court held that obvious improvements to existing patents do not enjoy patent protection. While the prosecution of a patent has always required a showing of "non-obviousness," the Court made it easier for lower court judges and the federal patent court to call inventions "obvious" and therefore ineligible for monopoly protection. Patentees have long had the upper hand in patent litigation but the *KSR* decision has shifted the balance of power back to innovators. In this case, the court rejected a rigid application of existing tests for obviousness in favor of a more expansive and flexible approach that gives judges more discretion. According to the court, "if a person of ordinary skill in the relevant subject area would be able to fit the teaching of multiple patents together like a puzzle" then the patent is obvious. "Granting patent protection to advances that would occur in the ordinary course without real innovation retards progress," the court says. Microsoft and Cisco filed "friends of the court" papers in the suit. They are also pursuing a lobbying strategy to statutorily codify of the *KSR* decision.

Microsoft and other advocates explain that the problems with the current patent system are especially harmful to the information technology industry. Low bars to patentability, a presumption of validity for issued patents and unlimited range of patentable subject matter ensure that an excessive number of patents are issued. In the IT industry, a single product may contain a number of patented technologies, perhaps thousands of them. A new version of a software program virtually always builds upon pre-existing technology, adding new features based on new innovations but incorporating a great deal of prior technology as well. Companies such as Microsoft and Oracle have been vocal advocates for patent reform. Microsoft has been especially critical of a legal framework that has caused it to spend $100 million a year defending itself against 35 to 40 lawsuits at any one time. Microsoft has gone on the legislative offensive after a jury awarded Eolas Technologies $565 million in damages, a decision that has been partially reversed, in a patent dispute over Internet Explorer.

In contrast, the pharmaceutical industry which may have a single patent to cover ten years of research at a cost of hundreds of millions and sometimes billions of dollars wants as much protection in as many ways as possible for a patent. A new drug usually constitutes a separate and distinct invention protected by a few patents relating solely to the substance. The drug companies take advantage of this characteristic to file multiple versions of the same patent to figure out what is the most valuable part of the patent to protect. They could keep the patent process going by filing multiple continuations until they found the best way to defend it. The pharmaceutical industry does not want the test for obviousness to change, although the *KSR* decision was a major blow to the industry. In any event, critics charge that many patents awarded today are overly broad or fail to take notice of "prior art", a legal term indicating that somebody else invented a product before the patent applicant. For Big Pharma, however, the expiration of a patent for a block buster drug, or the inability to extend the life of such a patent with a somewhat obvious improvement, can cost tens of thousands of jobs. In 2008 alone, nine of the biggest pharmaceutical firms announced the elimination of more than 45 thousand jobs over a five-year, primarily due to competition from generic drug producers.

For many software developers, this reform does not really go to the root of the problem. They say that it is still too easy to get a patent on software. The patent office grants roughly 2,000 software patents each year. This figure is large in comparison to the number of major innovations that occur in the software industry. Software is developed by building on the work of others; seeing what products already exists and then trying to build something better. Software patents, therefore, often impose an expensive legal delay to innovation; and since software is comprised essentially of intangible knowledge, it has a nonrivalrous nature. Consequently any novel idea is liable to have been thought of hundreds of times before. When the idea becomes appropriate for incorporation into a product the chances are it would already have been patented.

IBM has a very strong software patent portfolio. It is over size even in proportion to the size of IBM itself. This is a result of IBM's patenting every single idea every employee ever comes up with, rather than having any great propensity to be truly innovative. Certainly, IBM has never been considered synonymous with innovative software. IBM even has a patent, 5,247,661, on a software application to permit employees to automatically document ideas for later patenting. When the company was being investigated for anti-trust violations in the late 1970's and early 1980's it eventually agreed to a consent decree permitting the automatic licensing of its patent portfolio. That decree, of course, created the precedent for the Microsoft decree. Now, as mentioned earlier, IBM is a proponent of open source software development.

Similar to trolls are the so-called "patent sharks," firms with hidden intellectual property that surface, threatening to sue, when its rights are inadvertently infringed. Most of the time the lawsuit is a surprise, since the target firm is usually not able to identify the shark until after the suit is filed. For example, Intel paid Intergraph Corporation $675 million for infringement of its clipper processor patents, even though Intergraph stopped manufacturing hardware years before the infringement suit was filed and never used some of the patents for products. But the U.S. Supreme Court will weigh in again in a case that Microsoft and other tech companies hope will make it easier to challenge the validity of a patent that a shark might hold.

A $290 million patent infringement judgment against Microsoft in 2009 has barred the company from selling certain versions of its Word Software. A key question in this case is whether proving a patent invalid should require "clear and convincing evidence" as opposed to "a preponderance of the evidence." Most federal courts use the stricter "clear and convincing" evidentiary standard which favors the patent holder. In this case, i4i Inc., a Toronto-based technology company, persuaded a jury that recent versions of Microsoft Word infringed the firm's software patent that deals with manipulating documents.

While federal patent law does not state a standard for challenging the validity of a patent, Microsoft is arguing that the U.S. patent office does not consider all of the evidence before issuing a patent; in short that the Patent Office too easily grants patents thus hindering innovation and consumer choice. The U.S. Supreme Court will deliver what will appear to the layperson as a technical decision on a burden of proof but the stakes are high for technology companies.

For consumers and the wider society, innovation is fast becoming the sole province of corporations. In turn, work is becoming more modular, raising important issues of identity and ethics. In an industrial economy, a person's work identity lay in the consequences of his or her labor. An organizational affiliation provided social context and meaning. Paradoxically, open source, modular work, which requires "social software" to perform, requires little tangible organizational context. Indeed, there is no need for a tangible organization at all. The work and organizational context are virtual, the experience more personal than social. Less a force for social identity, knowledge work tends to be a force for personal expression. In effect, many firms in the global, information-intensive economy are privatizing knowledge and diminishing the social function of the work that creates and uses it. Knowledge and knowledge work are being pulled from the public domain, guided less by social concerns and more by private concerns of autonomy and personal identity. Where the organization provided the vehicle for group thinking and a reason for relinquishing personal responsibility in favor of corporate decision making, this new identity, and the autonomy that goes with it, will require responsibility and accountability, and a strong ethical core to guide the lifestyle choices of the, chief among them a personal commitment to lifelong learning and wellness. Ultimately, this new work ethic, this new work life identity, may be the most profound consequence of the knowledge economy.

11. Deregulation and Decentralization

The security of the post-war social compact of lifetime employment and guaranteed wage increases could not be sustained when workers in other countries were ready and willing to work for far less than American workers. What had been missing in these countries was investment in both material and human capital. This occurred with the end of the Cold War when the communist inspired slave labor systems abruptly ended in many countries.

In 1985 a passionate reformer Mikhail Gorbachev came to power in the Soviet Union. While socially and politically, the Soviet empire was relatively stable, its economy could not support the demands of a military superpower. With the prospect of permanent economic stagnation, reformers sought a "better socialism," one in which the economy remained centrally planned but was more responsive to market pricing, profits and loss. Meaningful discussions about the fuller integration of the European Union, with a common currency, and the prospect that the United States would be the primary beneficiary of borderless European trade fueled reformers' the sense of urgency. China's move toward controlled capitalism also created an impetus for change.

Gorbachev launched his campaign to modernize socialism with two interrelated platforms: *perestroika*, or restructuring (both of the economy and political structures) and *glasnost*, or freedom of information. But as Hobsbawm observed in the *Age of Extremes*, "there was what turned out to be an insoluble conflict between them." The Soviet Union's command and control economy required reform from the top, but the "top", communist party leaders and government bureaucrats (the *nomenklatura*) were the chief obstacles to transforming the system that it had created and controlled. While reformers wanted a "socialist market"—that is, the advantages of capitalism without losing those of socialism where risk taking, entrepreneurship and the profit motive could thrive without creating a wealth gap—"nobody had the slightest idea of how, in practice, the transition from a centralized state economy to the new system was to be made." A free-market ideology, it was thought, was the shock therapy needed to transform the sclerotic Soviet economy into a modern system capable of competing with the United States, China and a unified Europe.

While there may have been an arms race between the superpowers, the real race was for economic preeminence. During this time, in the United States and Britain, economic policy was driven by the deregulation of *de facto* monopolies. Prior to deregulation, the U.S. economy was rigid but relatively stable. A great many industries—airlines, banking, natural gas, electricity, and telecommunications—were subject to strict regulations and others, like the auto industry, enjoyed tariffs that protected their domestic market. Markets were stable and, absent management-labor conflict, so was the labor force. Growth was incremental but steady. Wages increased and customers paid higher prices. Inflation was moderated by the Federal Reserve Bank, which manipulated interest rates to increase unemployment at the first sign of inflationary wage and price increases. By and large, the boom and bust cycle was an artifact of government policy. Stable employment, incremental increases in wages and profits, and relatively low inflation was the great post-war achievement of big corporations and the federal government working hand-in-glove.

New thinking in China accelerated the transformation toward globalization. Deng Xiaoping had initiated his own economic and social reforms to position China for an emerging global economy. China was well suited for globalization. Within a decade, China achieved almost unprecedented growth, rivaling that of the United States in the later stages of industrialization. Capitalism took root unleashing the natural entrepreneurialism of the Chinese people. Millions of people were mobilized for factory work and land, formerly held collectively by the state, was privatized. Peasant riots were suppressed and mandatory birth control imposed. However, unlike the Soviet Union, capitalism was introduced from the top without relinquishing any political power. When a student uprising threatened the legitimacy of the communist regime, it was brutally beaten down. In the waning days of the twentieth century, the United States normalized trade relations with China, opening up a potential huge market for goods and services.

Since China's entrance to the World Trade Organization, financial and insurance firms, banks and manufacturers have rushed to get closer to an enormous amount of savings and potential customers. Technically, this is not outsourcing. Rather, it is a deliberate corporate decision to invest abroad. In 2006, IBM sold its personal computer division to Lenovo Group, the Chinese computer giant. Two year later, Big Blue opened its first supply-chain research facility in China to meet the growing demands of companies that are expanding their global trading networks. The facility is located in Beijing and it represents the future of global supply chains. According to Sanjeev Nagrath, IBM's Global Business Services' supply chain manager: "China is a key link in the global supply chain, from a major procurement center for sourcing activities to a manufacturing center to now even an R&D center. For any company operating on a global level, China is very much a part of their supply chain, or their supplier's supply chain in an expanded sense." By 2008, U.S. firms have invested more than $22 billion in China.

In 1991, India also took the great leap forward. Even after its leader Rajiv Gandhi was assassinated, his Congress Party released the world's biggest democracy from such economic shackles as strict industrial licensing and overly complicated import licensing. With in decade, India emerged as a destination of global back office outsourcing, including technical and legal services, and a hub of research and development for the computer industry. As Americans became pitted against workers from around the globe, the financial payoff of a higher education became more apparent. Starting a long term that is continuing well into the twenty first century, medium weekly earnings on an inflation-adjusted basis have trended upward for college graduates while declining for workers with lower educational levels, particularly among high-school dropouts. By the first decade of the twenty first century, the earnings of even college graduates began to stagnate, thus evidencing the importance that value added, knowledge-intensive work was having on income.

The eventual collapse of the Soviet Union naturally drew attention to the failures of over regulation of the economy by government. It accelerated deregulation in the United States and in the wake of the dismantling of the Berlin Wall, the almost theological faith in an economic system in which resources were allocated by an unrestricted market spread around the globe. As James Patterson has noted in *Restless Giant*: "American champions of globalization—that is, market friendly expansion of free trade and easy flows of money, goods, communications, and people across international borders—hailed it as a boon to exporters, and consumers, and as forwarding the 'knowledge economy.'"

For American firms, global competition demanded that they find and exploit new markets. But expanding into new products and services was difficult for many of the big post war firms that had embraced the predictability and security of government regulated monopolies. Thus, many made the strategic decision to deliberately deconstructive their monopoly power. As strange as it seems, companies like AT&T argued that consumers would benefit if the government would deregulate its telephone monopoly. The deregulation of the telecommunications spawned a booming industry that grew rapidly, creating new firms like WorldCom, and created the catalyst for the dot-com era. Deregulation also led to the demise of the big telecom giants, which employed tens of thousands of employees that had enjoyed essentially lifetime employment.

Perhaps the restructuring of AT&T in the waning days of the twentieth century demonstrates the most dramatic example of this new corporate-induced reality. In January 1996, anticipating the enactment of the Telecommunications Act later that year, the New Jersey-based telecommunications giant stunned the nation when it announced a reorganization plan accompanied by the elimination of 40,000 jobs in three years. Later the company issued an internal memorandum to its employees, explaining "the reality of today's marketplace demands that we must be able to respond swiftly to market growth opportunities and relentless competitive pressures. If we are to win in the marketplace the company must become a more efficient, effective and profitable business . . . As a result we will introduce an involuntary workforce management program in selected organizations."

AT&T's announcement of its "involuntary workforce management program" caused the price of its stock to soar. By the end of 1996, the company announced $75.53 billion in earnings. A restructuring of this size was unusually since workers were generally laid off during slow economic times, not during big earnings years. However, according to *Fortune Magazine*, the old rules were inapplicable as "the companies of the Fortune 55 have reconstructed, reengineered, refinanced, downsized, laid off, split up, and merged their way to prosperity." By June of that year, the *Personnel Journal* speculated on what many American employees were feeling: that the biggest contributor to downsizing was the growing pressure on corporations to net increasingly larger stockholder returns, at any expense. The top ten American corporations earned almost a trillion dollars in 1996, a year when tens of thousands of jobs were eliminated permanently.

AT&T's vice president of human resources codified management's thinking on this "new deal" for American workers. Instead of the employer-employee relationship being based on an exchange of loyalty for security, the executive explained that employees would have to prepare themselves to move from job to job. Instead of "living in the past" and concentrating on lost jobs, she explained that employees should train themselves to offer the best skills so that employers could hire and retain the "very best workers." In the new economy she declared, "all workers were contingent."

In sharp contrast to the millions of "contingent" workers, the "very best workers" like Mr. Singhal of who are adding value, and for others who are paid for their insight and understanding, their well-being and happiness depends primarily on their desire to acquire and leverage knowledge. For those who aspire to be like them, it is clear that their success depends on two things. First, success and happiness will depend on the individual's desire, commitment and motivation. Second, there must be a wide

243

diffusion of knowledge within organizations and through the wider business community. However, the breakdown of the post-war social compact may ironically be perpetuating the interchangeability of work, a kind of hyper-Taylorism, which undermines job mobility. For example, in 2000, David Birch, an influential futurist and business consultant, was interviewed by the *Wall Street Journal*, during which he observed that "the majority of people in college are into very much of a free-agency" with little expectation of a government-sponsored safety net. According to Birch, this free-agent status has eroded any expectation of job security and has made loyalty irrelevant. "What this means as an employer is that you've got to start designing the things that you do, the skill sets, the nature of your work around that. It has got to be interchangeable parts. You've got to de-skill most of the things you do, so that any number of people who you hire can come in, in a relatively short period of time, and perform that job."

De-skilling means that anyone can perform a task anytime, anywhere. Thus, firms are free to base their hiring decision almost entirely on cost. This, thousands of information technology jobs have been "de-skilled," resulting in hundreds of call centers being located throughout the world, where relatively knowledgeable technicians, using knowledge management tools, perform interchangeable tasks. Wages are low, adding little value to the local economy. At the same time, value-added knowledge workers are fast becoming an elite group. They generate the ideas and create the other intellectual property that fuels their employer's success. Birch is wary of these value-added workers. They are selfish and greedy, he says, and have little interest in the company's success. Instead, "they have an interest in how much money they get paid and what the benefits are. And they care about having a good time [at the company.]." He would prefer that all knowledge work resemble "a Lego game, of red and blue pieces and yellow pieces."

In sharp contrast to Birch's freewheeling view of knowledge workers, particularly younger workers, is Drucker's observation that such workers are really "de facto volunteers", bound to a firm by its mission. "What motivates knowledge workers" notes Drucker, "is what motivates volunteers. Volunteers, we know, have to get satisfaction from their work more than paid employees precisely because they do not get a paycheck." Indeed,

Florida's optimism knows no bounds. While citing Drucker favorably, he posits that knowledge workers do not really work for the money; rather they work "for the challenge, the responsibility, for recognition and the respect it brings."

A cynic might think that Drucker and Florida are merely obscuring the social Darwinism of the global economy, cheerleading for corporate ruthlessness. But there is no reason to doubt their sincerity. Apparently they fervently believe that the knowledge economy will create autonomous, free workers who pursue interesting projects for the challenge and status that it represents. It will, of course, for an elite group of people, but no more or less than when the industrial economy produced inventors and artists. In other words, each age will produce its share of creators and discoverers, but it is unlikely that the knowledge economy will produce them wholesale. In any event, value-added knowledge work requires a social context, an environment where in-depth collaboration occurs spontaneously, where a red piece can interact with a blue piece in a seamless way. But where value-added knowledge, rather than physical labor or white-collar, interchangeable work, is what is being exchanged between employer and employee, the conflict over who owns and controls this asset is really an age-old conflict about liberty and freedom versus dependence and servitude.

12. On The Nature of Leadership

If Enron, WorldCom and other corporations managed essentially as racketeering enterprises are any indication of what passes as executive leadership in the modern corporation, the average corporate executive in America is a grossly over paid bureaucrat, whose every decision and act violates the fiduciary duty of care owed to the organization and its shareholders. The executive's cynicism and corruption infects his inner circle of well-paid lackeys and degrades the spirit of every employee. Of course, the leadership at Enron and WorldCom represents only a tiny fraction of American executives, but the probability of corruption, unethical practices and criminality is high in most corporate environments, primarily because managers almost always act in their own interests at the expense of the firm's interest. Such is the case because executive and management leadership poses inherent conflicts of interest. As Adam Smith described, "managers of other people's money [rarely] watch over it with the same anxious vigilance with which . . . [they] watch over their own . . . [T]hey very easily give themselves a dispensation. Negligence and profusion must always prevail."

Adolf Berle and Gardiner Means coined the phrase "the separation of ownership and control" in their landmark 1932 book *The Modern Corporation and Private Property,* and it remains the most widely used expression in the voluminous literature on corporate governance. It refers to their observation that during the nineteen twenties the structure of ownership in large corporations changed from the traditional arrangement of owners managing their own companies to one in which shareholders had become so numerous and dispersed that they were no longer willing or able to manage the corporations they owned.

The authors warned that the separation of ownership from control might enable controlling managers to increase their own wealth at the shareholders' expense, and that warning became the focus of fifty years of subsequent research in the economics literature. However, those same fifty years also witnessed dramatic changes in ownership concentration, stock trading strategies, and theories of corporate governance. Generally, most shareholders are not interested in being involved in the firm's business activities. These shareholders act like investors, not owners. The difference is subtle, but important. An owner is focused on the business performance of the firm. An investor is focused on the risk and return of his or her stock portfolio. Harold Williams, the former chairman of the Securities and Exchange Commission, was more direct in his observation of shareholder responsibility and the long-term interests of the corporation when he stated "the traditional concept of the investor is becoming obsolete. The linkage between ownership and participation in the equity markets is to put it mildly—strained. Increasingly, the so-called investor is often nothing more than a short-term speculator in the company's income stream."

The shareholders of a corporation are the principals, and the managers who run the company are the agents. If shareholders cannot effectively monitor the managers' behavior, then the managers may be tempted to use the firm's assets to increase their own lifestyle. Or, as James Burnham put it in his 1941 book *The Managerial Revolution*, managers will behave as if they are the owners. Executives may enjoy perks such as liberally charging the corporate expense account, chartering the company jet, ordering top-grain leather office equipment, and so on at the expense of shareholders. Of course, the criminal abuses of the last decade of the twenty century and beyond make these examples seem almost quaint.

Solutions to this problem tend to come in two categories: incentives and monitoring. The incentive solution is to create situations in which the executive's wealth is tied to the wealth of the shareholders. That way, the executives and the shareholders want the same thing. This is called aligning executive incentives with the shareholders. Executives would then act and behave in a way that is also best for the other shareholders. For most U.S. companies, executives are given stock and/or stock options as a significant component of their pay. Executives who are rewarded in this way experience increasing pay packages as the value of the firm's stock goes up. For nearly two decades, which ended in the Panic of 2008, much of the value of a wide swath of American corporations was highly leveraged, based on money borrowed against future earnings. Executives made out handsomely as such borrowing inflated stock prices, making a mockery of such quaint notions of investing for production. With nothing really to produce other than financial returns, borrowing finally reached unsustainable levels, as the market ruthlessly re-evaluated and re-priced stocks, telling each executive what their real value to the firm really was.

The demise of WorldCom and its chief executive officer Bernard Ebbers presaged this massive market realignment and demonstrate how modern corporate structure turns "corporate ethics" into an oxymoron. As legend has it, in 1983 partners led by Ebbers, a former basketball coach, sketched out their idea for a long distance company on a napkin in a coffee shop in Hattiesburg, Mississippi. Their company Long Distance Discount Service (LDDS) began providing service as a long distance reseller in 1984. For fifteen years it grew quickly through acquisitions and mergers. Ebbers was named chief executive officer in 1985 and the company went public in August 1989. Its $40 billion merger with MCI in 1998 was the largest in history at the time. In 1999, WorldCom's stock reached its highest price at $96.75 per share. Both the company and its chief executive officer were highly celebrated. With one hundred dollars invested in 1989, an investor would have enjoyed a return $6,000 only a decade later. In 1998 alone, the company's stock appreciated 137 percent. A year later Fortune and the Wall Street Journal declared the company and its chief executive officer a great American success story.

In October 1999, WorldCom attempted to purchase Sprint in a stock buyout for $129 billion in stock and debt. The deal was vetoed by the U.S. Department of Justice. At the same time, WorldCom's "success" began to unravel with the accumulation of debt and expenses, the fall of the stock market, long distance rates and revenue. Within a few years, WorldCom stock fell below one dollar per share and the company filed at the time the biggest bankruptcy in history.

WorldCom had improperly booked $3.8 billion as capital expenditures, boosting cash flow and profit over at least five quarters. This disguised the actual net loss for 2001 and the first quarter of 2002. In simple terms WorldCom did not account for expenses when it incurred them, but hid the expenses by pushing them into the future, giving the appearance of spending less and therefore making more money. In 2003, a court-appointed bankruptcy examiner described the company as having a "culture of greed." Additionally, a special investigation committee report asked why no one disclosed or complained about management misconduct. The report averred: "the answer seems to lie partly in the culture."

But in many respects, WorldCom's culture resembled that of any other corporation where the interests of shareholders and executive leadership were aligned. The company's mission statement was straightforward: "Our mission is to be the most profitable, single-source provider of communications services to customers around the world'—in other words, the mission of the firm was to increase shareholder value. Organizational goals were aligned with this mission. Each department had to meet financial goals and wherever possible, individual managers would be held responsible for not meeting his or her quarterly numbers.

Departments were organized as cost centers, competing against each other over budgets and other resources. Sharing resources across departments was not encouraged unless it could be billed against the other. If managers missed goals for one month, they were warned. Three consecutive months of missing revenue targets resulted in discharge. According to the Committee report, managers' performance evaluations were based on achieving the "right results" with no emphasis on whether these results were achieved the "right way." In short, executive leadership was deterministic and results-oriented. The underlying philosophy was the "ends justify the means." The executive team's moral justification for this philosophy was essentially utilitarian—the greater good was served by countless individual acts of deceit. And like most corporations, the organizational structure was hierarchical and command-and-control. Management's primary tool for control was power and primary methods of motivation were external rewards and punishment. The company was a big hit with investors and Wall Street analysts.

At WorldCom, as is the case at many corporations, employees worked for material reward. As such, the relationship that most managers had to their work had no higher purpose than a paycheck. While perhaps leaving employees disconcerted or disconnected, their work life flowed from bureaucratic rules, without space for free will. Thus when Betty Vinson, a mid-level accountant pleaded guilty to securities fraud her lawyer described her as a "victim of unscrupulous higher managers." She was only following orders. She lacked the autonomy to make an independent decision.

The word autonomy has several usages in philosophical contexts. In ethics, autonomy refers to a person's capacity for self-determination in the context of moral choices. Kant argued that autonomy is demonstrated by a person who decides on a course of action out of respect for moral duty. That is, an autonomous person acts morally solely for the sake of doing "good", independently of other incentives. In his *Groundwork of the Metaphysic of Morals*, Kant applied this concept to create a definition of personhood. He suggested that such compliance with moral law creates the essence of human dignity. In metaphysical philosophy, the concept of autonomy is referenced in discussions about free will, fatalism, determinism, and agency.

Conformity can be viewed as a model society which argues that the best world is one in which there are few disruptions, where conflict is rare or even nonexistent. The best way to achieve this is for people to conform to particular ideals or ways of acting. The goal is for smooth, undisrupted functioning. Since corporations insist on conformity, autonomy, can be, and usually is to one extent or another, waived to another authority, such as by agreeing to follow governing laws. In a corporation, an employee may cede autonomy and agree to conform as a condition of employment. Further, the free will of an employee can be restricted by a more powerful authority, such as when the boss makes a demand to work over time. The decisions of employees can also be coerced and the actions of employees' can be forced. Thus, when Betty Vinson, a mid-level accountant at WorldCom pleaded guilty to securities fraud her lawyer described her as a "victim of unscrupulous higher managers." She was only following orders. She had no choice, no capacity to decide.

But what of the human desire for morality? Lawrence Kohlberg (1971) has focused on moral development and has proposed a stage theory of moral thinking from childhood to adulthood. In Kohlberg's first stage, the child assumes that powerful authorities hand down a fixed set of rules which he or she must unquestioningly obey. At this stage, the child defers to superior power or prestige. In other words, the child conforms. There is no substantive notion of free will or self-determination. His or her primary concern is receiving rewards and avoiding punishment.

Viewed through the lenses of Kant and Kohlberg, Vinson lacked free will and was operating at the moral level of a child. However, within WorldCom's culture, Vinson was also acting rationally. She as well as her co-conspirators simply calculated that that the damage caused by their unethical and criminal actions to each shareholder was minuscule while the benefits to them were enormous. In other words, unethical acts at most corporations are the rational, self-interested, things to do. Moreover, the managers' and shareholders' interest are aligned because the paramount interest of both shareholders and managers is to increase the value of the stock—regardless of the true value of the firm. Both are concerned with the performance of the share—rather than the performance of the firm. Both are preoccupied with boosting the share's price—rather than the company's value.

Excessive CEO compensation has, of course, been fueled by this paper wealth. In 1980, the ratio of executive compensation to the pay of the average workers was 40 to 1. By 2008, the ration was 300 to 1. CEO's made about ten times the compensation of even the second-highest executive in the firm. Advocates for such high compensation argue that boards of directors are paying CEO's for their return of value to shareholders. But over the quarter century, the U.S. economy has been awash in cash. In turn, stock prices were heavily influenced by speculators' expectations that other speculators would continue to bid a stock up. In this way, stock prices are not related to value at all. Thus, many CEO's are not paid to create long term value; instead they are paid to achieve short term returns. Of course, these returns represent a big piece of executive compensation.

Most top executives are not entrepreneurs. In fact, most corporate executives have been groomed since business school to please the boss

12. On The Nature of Leadership

and follow the crowd. While the corporate mantra may be *innovation* and *leadership*, most executives are subject to "groupthink." In his classic book, *Groupthink*, Irving L. Janis, the Yale psychologist, explained how panels of experts could make colossal mistakes. People on these panels, he observed, are forever worrying about their personal relevance and effectiveness, and feel that if they deviate too far from the consensus, they will not be given a relevant role. They self-censor doubts about the group consensus and eventually conform to the assumptions held by the group.

Once the executive becomes part of the inner circle, the pressure to conform is more powerful still. Since the executive's performance is evaluated more and more on predetermined outcomes, pleasing the boss becomes more important that doing a good job. Thus, creating a good impression with the boss is scored higher than competence. In the end, the executive that is promoted is the one that has expressed the most inauthentic behavior and deception. During their entire corporate careers they have spun all facts and viewpoints in directions they believe will most please the boss. In short, "corporate ethics" becomes an oxymoron as much of what passes as executive development, particularly the performance improvement process, is inherently unethical. As noted by Samuel Culvert, a professor of management at UCLA:

> I believe it's immoral to maintain the facade that annual pay and performance reviews lead to corporate improvement, when it's clear they lead to more bogus activities than valid ones. Instead of energizing individuals, they are dispiriting and create cynicism. Instead of stimulating corporate effectiveness, they lead to just-in-case and cover-your-behind activities that reduce the amount of time that could be put to productive use. Instead of promoting directness, honesty and candor, they stimulate inauthentic conversations in which people cast self-interested pursuits as essential company activities.
>
> The net result is a resource violation, and I think citations should be issued. If it's a publicly held company, shareholder value gets decreased. If it's a governmental organization, time is lost that could be spent in pursuit of the public good.

In is wholly unclear that given the culture and organizational structure of corporations and other bureaucracies whether high level executives are capable of acting at a high moral level. For example, corporate executives do not invest their own money. They take no risks with their own money. With lucrative severance agreements, their risk of failure becomes a certainty for reward. By 2007 the U.S. financial industry debt was equivalent to 116 percent of GNP, compared with a mere 21 percent in 1980. Having accumulated debts beyond what were sustainable, financial institutions were forced to reduce them, leading to $1 trillion in write-downs in 2008 alone. As credit markets, the lifeblood of the economy froze, the federal government took the unprecedented step of taking equity stakes in the nation's largest financial institutions in return for cash, to some extent nationalizing a segment of the banking industry. In return for the infusion of capital, banks were required, among other things, to limit incentives for the top five executives, accept clawbacks for financial irregularities, and prohibit the use of so-called golden parachute payments for executives.

Clearly, while these dramatic measures have been improvised to stabilize financial markets in time of crisis, an open question is whether this partial nationalization of the banking industry has created a new model to influence corporate governance. While the federal government has limited voting rights as a preferred equity shareholder of, say Bank of America, it took an eighty percent equity stake in AIG, the giant insurance company, and appointed two board members. It is expected that the federal government would be guided by ordinary fiduciary duties owed to the taxpayers, who will ultimately foot the bill. Such a duty of care should prevent the government-appointed Board members from promoting a political agenda that would be inimical to shareholder/taxpayer interests. But the federal government is not an ordinary fiduciary; it is a democratic institution representing the sovereignty of the nation and is constitutionally obliged to promote the public welfare. As such, government-appointed board members may indeed pursue agendas that promote important government interests, such as greater financial transparency or limits on executive compensation. And if board appointments and other corporate policies can be imposed as conditions of an equity infusion, why not a government loan?

In 2008 the U.S. auto industry lobbied Congress hard for a $28 billion loan for the retooling that was necessary to build the next generation of fuel-efficient vehicles. At the same time, General Motors was closing a truck plant in Michigan and a metal stamping plant in Wisconsin. What meaningful distinction can be made between bailing out the banking industry with equity stakes and bailing out the auto industry with a loan? Couldn't the federal government condition the loan on achieving some public purpose, such as reevaluating the possibility of keeping the truck and metal stamping plant open, thereby saving American jobs? The Big Three automakers have conceded unprecedented federal oversight as a condition for an industry-wide bailout. Afterall, if welfare recipients are told to find work as a condition of a government handout, why should a corporation get a handout with no strings attached?

In addition to the Congressional spending power, the power of the executive order is also available. About 300,000 companies do $200 billion worth of business annually under a government contract with the federal government. Current federal rules require federal contract officers to evaluate whether would-be contractors can demonstrate a satisfactory record of integrity and business ethics. The evaluation criteria can be expended to include investment in training and other programs that demonstrate a concern for human resource management. Further, just as an executive order requires government contractors to practice affirmative action in exchange for a contract, an order can be issued that urges contractors to invest in employee re-training as an alternative to off-sourcing; or off-shoring can be banned outright in connection with the work being performed under the contract.

It could be that in saving the financial markets, which many called socialistic, the federal government has created a new legal framework for directly influencing corporate governance and executive leadership, requiring leaders to conscientiously balance the conflicting and converging interests of shareholders, management, employees and other stakeholders, rather than simply giving this balance lip service as they have done in the past. Corporate executives will need more than ever to be transparent and collaborative in understanding and achieving mutually shared goals. They will also need to have even a higher degree of integrity than what the law otherwise requires to gain the trust necessary to manage complex relationships and to find the win-win solutions needed for success.

"There's a lot of grotesque greed underneath this crisis," noted Paul Krugman, the 2008 Nobel Prize winning economist, but "greed isn't illegal." Nor is honesty legally required at most corporations. Nevertheless, in the aftermath of the Panic of 2008, Judy Shelton predicts a rebirth of capitalism, an "honest capitalism" built on "trust achieved though transparency." "With freedom comes choice; with choice comes responsibility. What is true within one's own life and one's own community should be true for the world at large. Integrity matters, competence counts, and earnest effort finds reward." And so it is within firms that innovate for survival. Corporate hierarchy suppresses free will and defuses responsibility, reducing flesh and blood managers to mere instrumentalities who carry out the orders of higher-level functionaries.

American International Group (AIG) is a stupendous example of corporate group think and management guided by automatic pilot. AIG devised computer models to gauge risk in more than $4000 billion of complicated deals called credit-default swaps. Executives relied on those models to help figure out which of these swap deals were safe. Firm leaders praised the computer models as extremely reliable and highly conservative, reassuring shareholders that such swaps were a "money-good portfolio."

Highly paid consultants were retained to build the computer models. Consultants are often used as substitutes for executive leadership and allow corporate executives to shift responsibility for decision making. As it turned out, the AIG consultants used overly optimistic theories about real life situations. Executives simply abdicated decision making to the predeterminism of the computers. Richard Feynman, the American physicist known for the path integral formulation of quantum mechanics, referred to the giving up of human free will to the computer as a disease. The science novelist and movie director Michael Crichton observed that sophisticated computer models create their own reality with data, simulations and projections. AIG's executives accepted the reality created by the computer model with an exceptionally high degree of religiosity. Few challenged the group's faith, for fear of being branded a disbeliever. Even when confronted with evidence of a decade long stagnation in wages making credit defaults likely, the faith of the true believers never wavered.

In their book *Built to Last*, James Collins and Jerry Porras, observed that successful, visionary companies were "cult-like." Their observation did not connote a negative image; rather they were attempting to describe a set of practices that "vigorously screen out those who do not fit the ideology . . . [and] . . . instill an intense sense of loyalty and influence the behavior of those remaining inside the company to be congruent with the core ideology, consistent over time, and carried out by zealots." Thus, for better or worse, the cult-like firm will reject nonconformists and embrace group thinkers and sycophants. No one at AIG dissented from the form's core ideology—like WorldCom, the only ideology was to make money. Few dissented from AIG executives' faith and optimism in the computer models, choosing instead to follow the party line of easy money, even when losses could have been easily anticipated.

The federal government takeover of AIG, one of the world's biggest insurance firms, has fanned skepticism about computer models that financial firms use to mange risks. But the more critical problem is how AIG's executives were lulled into such an unshakable belief in easy money even when evidence to the contrary proved otherwise. As a criminal probe was launched to determine whether AIG executives misled investors and the firm's outside auditors, it is clear that the company's risk-management mistakes were based on management complacency. Managers were aware that the computer models did not measure the risk of future collateral write downs but nevertheless simply went along.

A similar religious experience transpired at Merrill Lynch during its head long race to become the biggest mortgage player on Wall Street. Again, group think interfered with management's ability to understand the risks. Dissenting managers were simply replaced, inquisition-style, with yes men. In a *New York Times* expose (November 9, 2008), Gretchen Morgenstern quotes former executives that managers were "more concerned about achieving their superiors' profit goals, than about monitoring the firm's risks." In a particularly strange twist, the corporate governance and internal controls personnel became the leaders in rooting out traders that questioned the firm's risk taking gambits. Such traders were chastised and intimidated and eventually reassigned.

In sum, what passes for executive leadership, in most cases, simply ensures mediocrity. Over the long haul, executive leadership dooms most firms to failure, sometimes spectacularly. However, since the aim of management is self-preservation, business will always ask government for help when necessary. When a foothold can be made in a new market or when the runway needs to be cleared for a new product, executives will seek deregulation. When competition becomes too great, they will seek ways to restrict and protect their market share with new regulations. In short, business leaders are apolitical and will become a crony to government leaders when they are able.

As one media wag has put it, "unlike in Europe, where cronyism appears to be an academic major in business schools", big national government arose in America after big corporations were already in place. In other words, big government was born in reaction to big business. The result was a struggle for power, with corporations defending positions and government from time to time seeking to reduce it. In the last quarter century of the twentieth century and continuing into the twenty first, the balance of power has weighed heavily in favor of corporations. While many suggest that such corporate influence over political decisions is the result of enormous campaign contributions and lobbying, it is more likely that globalization itself has increased corporate power. At least since the end of the Cold War, global markets have increasingly more independent from many of the limitations imposed by nation states. Indeed, the deleveraging of global financial markets in the first decade of the twenty first century has laid bare the complex and fluid financial networks that have been forged as the precipitous drop in American home values triggered a tidal wave of default worldwide.

The 2008 government bailout of the financial industry and the partial nationalization of the banking system may mark the return of greater government influence over corporate affairs. As previously suggested, such government assistance may come with many undesirable strings. For example, in a lawsuit brought by 12 states, several cities and a dozen pro-environment organizations against the federal government, the U.S.

Supreme Court held that Clean Air Act specifically authorizes the U.S. Environmental Protection Agency to enforce regulations that reduce carbon emissions in order to protect the public and effect clean air standards. The ruling in *Massachusetts v. U.S. Environmental Protection Agency* means that inaction to find and punish violations of standards set by the Clean Air Act runs contrary to the EPA mandate. The lawsuit was brought by states that saw their own budgetary considerations, public health and fieldwork capabilities strained by the extra work their administrators were being asked to do in order to comply with federal clean air provisions.

While overstating the regulatory consequences of this decision, the *Wall Street Journal* (October 20, 2008) put its editorial finger on a rising tide of regulation when it stated:

> The EPA hasn't made a secret of how it would like to centrally plan the U.S. economy under the 1970 Clean Air Act. In a blueprint released in July, the agency didn't exactly say it'd collectivize the farms—but pretty close, down to the "grass clippings." The EPA would monitor and regulate the carbon emissions of "lawn and garden equipment" as well as everything with an engine, like cars, planes and boats. Eco-bureaucrats envision thousands of other emissions limits on all types of energy. Coal-fired power and other fossil fuels would be ruled out of existence, while all other prices would rise as the huge economic costs of the new regime were passed down the energy chain to consumers.

Whether out of self-preservation or profit, or both, corporate leaders must develop a rationale for preempting massive government intervention in corporate affairs, particularly if they are to rely upon that same government to ensure against their failure. In *Built to Last*, Collins and Porras also observed how the more corporate executives espoused a particular point of view, the more they were likely to behave consistently with that point of view even if they did not previously hold that view. The authors systematically studied visionary companies that struggled to live up to their core values. Their central observation was that core values enable firms to commit themselves to increasing innovation. Their core values not only anchor them, they say, but release them. Their conclusion: corporations should stand for something nobler than profits.

The reality of the first decade of the twenty first century and beyond is that if corporations want government to do less, they will have to do more. Executive leaders will need to incorporate a new model for responsibility, one that considers the impact of the enterprise ion the world around it. While it is true that Milton Friedman once referred to executives' "social responsibility" as "spending someone else's money for a general social interest," the run up to the Panic of 2008 showed that executives were spending someone else's money for their own personal interest. In any event, it is becoming clear that global economic, environmental and political factors are eclipsing nineteen century notions of property rights. Wal-Mart, the company people love to hate, understands this reality perfectly. In 2007, Wal-Mart announced a plan to ask suppliers for data on their energy efficiency and is monitoring emissions on some suppliers. Since then, at least six of the world's largest companies are banding together to press their suppliers to release data about carbon emissions and climate-change mitigation strategies.

Dell is also improving its energy efficiency, claiming carbon neutrality mostly by purchasing environmental credits. These are financial instruments that fund environmental improvements made by others, such as running wind turbines or planting forests. Dell reasons that these credits cancel out its carbon footprint, which includes carbon emissions associated with its suppliers and customers. Other companies pledging to become carbon neutral include Google and Yahoo, both of which are working to become more energy-efficient and are also buying offsets. Both companies include in their footprints such things as their facilities' electricity use and their employees' commuting and business air travel. Google also includes the emissions produced in the manufacturing of the servers that its data centers use.

Indeed, a growing number of firms around the world are setting ambitious targets for performance in not only financial terms but also in environmental and social terms. According to a 2007 McKinsey report, ninety percent of companies said that they were doing more than they were five years ago to incorporate environmental, social and governance issues into their core strategies. Moreover, it appears that transparency and responsibility may be consistent with successful innovation. Hierarchical, command-and-control organizations do not innovate well because they cannot free up the lateral communication and sharing that is necessary to promote creativity. In their book *The Naked Corporation*, Donald Tapscott and David Ticoll use the concept of "open enterprise" to describe an organization that is actively transparent, but also carefully manages critical competitive information. In this model, the organization builds the loyalty of knowledge workers through openness and sees these people as investors of intellectual capital. Transparency enables the creation of trust for internal audiences and external customers. "Corporations should undress for success," they write. "Knowledge liberation is about making the unknown known to both executives and employees." Further, as social networking technologies are adopted by organizations to promote innovation, previously unimaginable levels of transparency may be achieved.

But most corporate executives either are caught in or actively perpetuate a vicious cycle of degradation, secrecy and abuse of power. According to IBM's 2010 Global CEO Study, "creativity" was selected as the most critical factor for future success. The CEO's that were interviewed told researchers that the global business environment is volatile, uncertain and increasingly complex. They also stated that the complexity of an interconnected world is aggravated by a number of factors which requires "a great deal of creativity as e re-invent ourselves to truly thrive in the new economy." However, every corporate structure sows the seeds of WorldCom because corporate execution is accomplished with a robust exercise of power which instills conformity and suppresses creativity.

Thus the corporate executive must pursue monopoly power in all aspects of his role and whenever possible gain special privileges from government regulators and when necessary labor unions. But this symbiotic relationship between Big Business, Big Government and, at times, Big Labor is dangerous to both innovation and individual autonomy. According to the Business Trust Survey released by the World Economic Forum in 2010 only 37 percent trusted government to do the "right thing" and only 45 percent trusted business. Government and business is often viewed in cahoots to preserve monopolies and to suppress competition until the status quo needs disruption through deregulation.

Gordon Crovitz suggests "with such low trust in government, corporate executives would be better off keeping a safe distance from politics." But this is wishful thinking because corporate leaders are legally obliged to advance corporate interests. If this means rationalizing political contributions and lobbying as First Amendment speech in the U.S. and at the same time justifying the suppression of political speech abroad as incremental social progress, the leader will do what it takes. Few can take the risk of taking a principled stand—the game must be played under the existing rules.

What employees expect from executive leaders is usually rooted in the basic interpersonal operation of the employer-employee relationship, where personal connections are made through trust, reliability, care, and appreciation. Once this relationship is established and maintained, leaders can deliver the rest of what they have to offer—their talents—and innovation may flourish. However, when leaders do not succeed in building a healthy relationship, the connection with employees is weak, and there is little chance to move to a higher level of innovation and success. AIG and Merrill Lynch are examples of closed systems built on the WorldCom model of external rewards and punishments, dominance, zealous conformity, and a religious devotion to money making.

Nevertheless, there appears to be a connection between high integrity governance, peer-to-peer communication, social responsibility and innovation. With more transparency and teamwork, organizations benefit from a more efficient process of decision making and tactical execution, as employees are more informed, operations speed up, and problems are identified more readily along the way. To achieve these outcomes, leaders must try to build trust and experience and a more finely tuned collaboration with their peers and employees. And both the organization as a whole and the individual leader are perceived as having a higher level of credibility in the process. But in the modern corporation ethical challenges are everywhere. In the knowledge-intensive, economy these ethical dilemmas are magnified and globalized. In the struggle over intellectual assets and the concentration of knowledge power that results, monumental decisions about whether and how to share and expand resources will need to be made, a role that will be played more and more by government and big corporations.

13. Information Ethics

"Corporation ethics" like "knowledge management" is an oxymoron. A corporation is a legal entity, a fictitious person. It is controlled by officers who report to directors elected by shareholders. Under U.S. corporation law, the shareholders are owners. In the common law, ownership connotes a corresponding responsibility inasmuch as ownership, as a social matter, implies free will. In the classic *The Common Law*, Oliver Wendell Holmes cites Kant's imperative that freedom of the will is the essence of personhood. Thus, ownership "is to be protected because a man by taking possession of an object has brought it within the sphere of his will. He has extended his personality onto or over that object." Ownership of property is the objective realization of free will which, in turn, requires personal responsibility for the consequences of that freedom, the essence of autonomy and human dignity. Indeed, the American constitutional structure is based on this idea—that property cannot be separated from person, who has an inherent moral agency, and thus the first purpose of government is to protect property.

Shareholders are legal owners of the corporation but they do not possess corporate assets nor do they exercise ownership control over corporate property. Since corporate law separates ownership from control, shareholders are not legally liable for the debts or liabilities of the organization. Stated another way, shareholders are owners without any ethical obligation for the consequences of corporate acts.

Directors are the legal representatives of the shareholders and must fulfill their responsibilities as fiduciaries, with the utmost duty of care and trust. As agents of the shareholders they are expected to hire and fire corporate officers, approve important decisions, distribute profits and ensure that the shareholders are given adequate information about the business affairs of the company. As representatives acting with the scope of their official capacities, directors must discharge their official duties on behalf of the shareholders. As agents, not owners in their own right, they do not exercise the type of free will that would be expected of owners under the common law. They are instead fiduciaries of the shareholders who own the corporation without the burden of the moral or ethical responsible of ownership, from which the directors are twice removed.

Corporate officers are also agents and fiduciaries but their duty of care is owed to the corporation, the fictitious legal person. But obviously the decisions made by the officers have a direct and immediate impact on their own wellbeing, such as decisions about executive compensation or whether or not to merge with another firm. Thus, corporate officers have an inherent conflict of interest because they serve two masters—the shareholders and themselves. For example, a decision to merge may be beneficial to the corporation but may threaten the long term position of the officer. Or a excessively generous compensation package for the officer may provide a perverse disincentive for the officer to take calculated risks on behalf of the corporation.

Since no person really "owns" the corporation and the legal entity lacks the moral core at the center of personhood, the corporation cannot have a morality. In short, the corporate entity is more a machine than a person. Moreover, since the corporation must as a matter of law indemnify officers and directors when they are acting within the scope of their agency it is difficult to fix personal responsibility for the consequences of corporate acts. This, of course, permits executives to take risks on behalf of the corporation that they would not otherwise take if they were to be personally liable, say for pushing the envelope of antitrust law or violating the patent of a competitor or conducting business in a country that engages in widespread human rights violations. Thus, a corporation and the individuals that work within them, always have the potential to engage in unethical acts and practices.

Indeed, since many organizations are shot through with ethical dilemmas and conflicts of interest, it is not difficult to understand the reality of widespread corporate fraud and malfeasance. Often written off as "greed," a personal failing, unethical practices are actually the result of separating ownership from morality. Mandatory ethics training for managers cannot put the genie back in the bottle and therefore is not designed to probe or examine this conundrum. The organizational structure and the law that supports it are what they are; they cannot be modified or changed by the directors or anyone else except Congress. The buffer zone of agency often combined with the pressure from above and from within the team to achieve a financial target permits otherwise good and decent people to engage in unethical or illegal acts. More widespread are the smaller, but no less destructive, acts of employee disengagement from the job which results from the lack of personal ownership and responsibility within the organization.

Ethics training raises awareness of applicable laws and codes but the agent's duty to further corporate interests sometimes outweighs the personal sense of right and wrong. Therefore the main purpose of corporate ethics training is to mitigate penalties against the company after the fraud has been uncovered or disclosed but it really prevents the wrongdoing in the first instance; that is, of course, unless a knowledgeable person often acting out of a pecuniary interest blows the whistle.

For some technology firms in the global economy, serious ethical dilemmas abound, among them the possibility of knowingly violating civil liberties at home and human rights abroad. For the most part, American consumers have willingly given much of what would have been considered in the past personal or private information over to firms as the price of a frictionless electronic transaction. Opt out features are rarely displayed conspicuously but the public nature of the new media has created a no-holds-bar attitude when it comes to letting it all hang out. In 1988 *Newsweek* reported the results of a poll that showed Americans' top social concern was loss of privacy. Twenty years later that concern had fallen off the top-five list. Nevertheless, the quantity and quality of personally indentifying information that is collected and whether the collector should provide notice has emerged as an important ethical issue because the collection and use of such information is driving whole businesses.

In a *Wall Street Journal* interview (August 14, 2010), Google's then-CEO Eric Schmidt discussed the future of businesses built on self-directed consumer Internet search. "I actually think most people don't want Google to answer their questions. They want Google to tell them what they should be doing next." Because of the information Google currently collects from users of its various search, email, phone and other services "we know roughly who you are, roughly what you care about, roughly who your friends are," he added. As the company works feverishly on artificial intelligence software, Mr. Schmidt predicts that "the technology will be so good it will be very hard for people to watch or consume something that has not in some sense been tailored for them."

When humans predict the wants and needs of another to manipulate or direct behavior it requires a great deal of information built on experience and intuition and a reading of the other person's desires, fears and vulnerabilities. This usually occurs within the context of a relationship and is informed by voluminous amounts of verbal and nonverbal communication. For AI software to utilize this type of intuition it would conceivably require not only vast amounts of information about a person's preferences but it would also require the codification of emotional and psychological data as well. And that is the essence of targeted advertising, which requires a profound intrusion upon an individual's habits, feelings and thought processes. The psychologists, cognitive technologists and AI software engineers employed by Google and other researchers supported by the company and others have purportedly uncovered that human behavior is eminently predicable. Therefore the corporate goal is to collect as much personally identifiable information about consumers as possible so that the individual can be adequately prompted, or told, "what to do next."

In 1963 the U.S. Supreme Court observed that "the fantastic advances in the field of electronic communications constitute a great danger to the privacy of the individual." The court was concerned about warrantless electronic eavesdropping by the government. The court could not have imagined a time when an individual would knowingly engage a media device that collects information on his or her job, hobbies, family, friends, politics, health and more. Applications contained in Google and Apple phones track the location of users and other "regularities" of behavior.

Researchers study the data as patterns emerge that can predict not only movements but how an individual interacts at work and home, with friends and during leisure time. "you have zero privacy," Sun Microsystems CEO states. "Get over it." But Google, Apple and other collectors, aggregators and users of information know that their brand matters and that is indispensable to project "trust"—an intangible but powerful connection and a product has with a person that is hard to gain but easy to lose. Thus many firms find it necessary to engage in an ethical slight-of-hand.

In 2006 the U.S. Department of Justice was sued by the American Civil Liberties Union (ACLU) alleging violations of civil liberties in connection with government surveillance of U.S. citizens under the USA Patriot Act, which was quickly enacted after the September 11th attacks to permit the Justice Department to monitor electronic communications and web searches. In aid of the Justice Department's defense, government lawyers subpoenaed Google, Microsoft, Yahoo and America Online and demanded that the companies compile and produce information from search indices and inquires entered by users. After some negotiation and agreement over a protective order, Microsoft, Yahoo and America Online complied with the Justice Department's demand. Google resisted on various grounds, objecting to the burdensome nature of the demand. Significantly, Google took the position that compliance with the subpoena would result in the loss of user trust in Google's ability to protect their privacy. According to Google, users trusted the company "because of the privacy and anonymity of the service." While Google lost the motion to quash the government's subpoena, it won the public relations war by positioning itself as the principled defender of user privacy.

At the same time, Google scientists were making major breakthroughs in collection and tracking software and it was clear that the Google phone would contain applications that would collect personally identifiable information about users. Google was also trying to penetrate the search market in China, the world's biggest, but a market filled with ethical landmines. In 2007 Yahoo responded to a demand by the Chinese Internet officials to disclose private information on political dissidents, including Wang Xiaoming and his wife Yu Ling. Yahoo complied and its disclosure lead directly to Mr. Wang's arrest and alleged torture, followed by high visibility ligation and a Congressional hearing portraying the company as

Perils of Prosperity

evil. That accusation of malice caught the attention of Google executives considering that company's credo proclaimed the Google's goodness and that another Yahoo-type crisis was only a matter of time.

While Google "gatekeepers" long censored web searches and video content in foreign markets, Google co-founder Sergey Brin was purportedly uneasy about China's censorship laws and how government officials used the Internet for political repression. Still Google moved aggressively in to Chinese market but after two years total company search revenue generated in China was less than 5 percent. To compete, however, Google compromised on its published credo and engaged in "voluntary" censorship. But fearing a reprise of the Yahoo public relations disaster, Google executives lobbied the U.S. State Department hard to run interference for the company. As a result, State Department officials pushed their Chinese counterparts repeatedly on trying to accommodate Google and other U.S. firms. For a time, Google and the Chinese government avoided public confrontations and quietly resolved government requests for information on a case-by-case basis. But neither side was satisfied with the arrangement. Chinese officials resented Google's power to keep them at arm's length and Google was having a great deal of difficulty protecting the integrity of its systems.

Cyberattacks traced to Chinese hackers were launched repeatedly on Google's servers, as well as on the servers of other U.S. firms. After more than two years trying to cash in on the Chinese search market, Google partially withdrew its operations from the mainland. Mr. Brin reportedly found the experience of entering the Chinese market as personally troubling, describing the Chinese government's Internet laws as approximating "totalitarianism." While it is true that corporations as such have no morality, the individuals within them are moral human agents. Mr. Brin, who came to the U.S. from Russia at the age of six in 1979, was no doubt raised by parents who felt degraded and dehumanized living in a totalitarian state and instilled in their son a suspicion for unchecked central authority. According to Mr. Brin, the Cyberattacks on Google's servers and the theft of intellectual property was the "straw that broke the camel's back" for the company.

Yet even though the Google has moved its servers out of mainland China and no longer offers a censored version of Google-China, the company remains on the mainland and is aggressively penetrating the cell phone market and the market for other services. Technology companies and significant segments of the U.S. government believe that web technologies and social networks will have a democratizing influence long term on authoritarian regimes and this belief has become part of U.S. foreign policy. Their belief is founded on the faith that information freely shared and disseminated will engage the citizenry and enlighten despots. But these technologies cut both ways. Firms such as Nokia, Siemens and Cisco Systems sell surveillance tools to authoritarian governments from Iran to China. Like gun manufacturers, these companies claim no responsibility for the consequences of how their products are used.

One may argue that an ethical line can be drawn between the voluntary commercial nature of surveillance and data collection in the U.S. and the compulsory nature of such surveillance and how it is used by authoritarian regimes. Within the context of a online commercial transaction imbedded in the fine print one can find a consumer notice that personally identifiable information will be collected and used for legal purposes. This means, among other things, using sophisticated data mining software to profile consumers and to send them messages about what to purchase. With artificial intelligence software the goal is to take the next step and instruct the consumer on how to act, think and feel. When government seeks to express free will with a law or regulation, citizens have recourse to constitutional litigation. In contrast, it is possible, that an individual can expressly or implicitly waive free within a commercial context with some limitations. For example, when a non-competition agreement entered into by an employer and employee is overbroad, it will be set aside. When privacy is invaded and emotional distress is caused, the common law recognizes a cause of action. And in Europe, where there is far more sensitivity to invasions of privacy than in the U.S., codes are enacted to prevent such invasions for commercial purposes.

But surely Mr. Brin knows that a reason why he is in the U.S. is because a political system negated human autonomy, which included the right to privacy and personal integrity. Personhood as expressed by free will remains at the center of a humane and democratic economy and this moral imperative cannot be necessarily be measured by the bottom line. At present, Google and the other technology companies are essentially self-regulated on privacy issues and have voluntarily adopted codes of conduct. In 2011 the ACLU sued several firms for invasion of privacy and consumer fraud and Congress has held hearings on whether to introduce formal regulations. At some point it will serve the industry's interest to promote formal regulations in order to preempt civil litigation and to keep competitors in line. When that happens Google will once again proclaim the moral high ground and reaffirm its credo to always do good.

Of course, the faith in democracy among corporations is evidenced by the amount of corporate money that floods the political system. In 2010, without having to determine the corporation's status as a "person" under the U.S. Constitution, the U.S. Supreme Court purportedly provided a textual reading of the First Amendment that ensured unlimited corporate participation in the political process. In *Citizens United v. Federal Election Commission*, the court invalidated a provision of a federal campaign finance law that, among other things, disallowed certain corporate contributions to political advocacy groups. In so doing, the court built upon the standard corporate law that views shareholders as owners of the corporation and the agents of the corporation as the proxies for the shareholders. But again, this right to free speech, like sharehoders' rights of ownership is derivative and is therefore disconnected from the free agency that would otherwise demand moral accountability. Thus, corporations and other organizations like labor unions are able to contribute unlimited amounts of money to political advocacy groups on an anonymous basis. Notably, the Supreme Court has refashioned the First Amendment to act as both a sword and shield for corporations such as the *Lochner* court did with the due process clause, thus overruling the legislative enactment of a co-equal branch of government.

With the enormous amounts of special interest money following into political campaigns and the rank gerrymandering that it encouragers the average American, depending on the election, does not even bother to vote. Excessive executive compensation when a company performs poorly or even when the federal government bails out the company has left many Americans feeling that the game is rigged. It has also bred cynicism about whether an education and hard work is worth it. To be sure, there will always be some that act as predators, taking as much from the system by hook or by crook. But it was at a similar point of spiritual bankruptcy that Mikhail Gorbachev and others within the elite of the Politburo realized that the governing structure of the Soviet Union needed reform.

Corporate faith in democracy is relative. The degree of corporate influence over the governance structures of the U.S. is a direct consequence of the power of property and is relative to what it may be in, say China or Turkey. True, the First Amendment protects individual expression and the right to be free from unreasonable intrusions by government but personal information used to advertise and manipulate human behavior may suppress the ability of the consumer of free choice. Mr. Schmidt expects that what Americans really want is to be "told what to do next." Google believes it will reach this social tipping point soon with ever more sophisticated technology. This is, of course, another conspiracy to restrain trade, another form of monopoly. As such, for a corporation there is really no moral or ethical line to be crossed when doing business in a country that requires compromise on civil liberties. The corporate decision to enter the market is merely a business decision, albeit one that has the potential to cause a public relations debacle. Therefore the relationship must be managed carefully and with subtlety, using government auspices when possible. Google, the fictitious legal person, has no morality. Eric Schmidt, the corporate agent is amoral when acting within the scope of his agency—exactly the way shareholders want and expect them to be and what corporate law requires. Such is the state of information ethics in the global economy.

14. We the People

According to the World Economic Forum, in 2008 the United States remained the most competitive nation in the world, but was heading for major problems. According to the report:

> Despite the financial crisis, the United States continues to be the most competitive economy in the world. This is because it is endowed with many structural features that make its economy extremely productive and place it on a strong footing to ride out business cycle shifts and economic shocks. Thus, despite rising concerns about the soundness of the banking sector and other macroeconomic weaknesses, the country's many other strengths continue to make it a very productive environment. The United States is ranked first for innovation, and its markets support this innovative activity through their efficient allocation of resources to their most effective use. However, the United States has built up large macroeconomic imbalances over recent years, with repeated fiscal deficits leading to rising and burgeoning levels of public indebtedness. This indicates that the country is not preparing financially for its future liabilities and is on the road to making interest payments that will increasingly restrict its fiscal policy freedom going into the future.

Even before the 2008 financial crisis, U.S. intelligence agencies had begun projecting a significant diminution of U.S. power over the next 15 years. That is a key assumption in the long-range assessment of global trends—known as the 2025 Project—that the Office of the Director of National Intelligence has been preparing for the next administration in 2009. The report notes that the post-Cold War period of overwhelming U.S. dominance was "anomalous" and that America's elevated status on the military, political, economic and possibly cultural fronts "will erode at an accelerating pace, with the partial exception of the military."

Consultant and author Harold Sirkin refers to this erosion as "globality," a world of hyper competition in which Americans and other competitive nations "compete with everyone from everywhere for everything. And not just for customers and market share: they'll compete for energy and raw materials, skilled and unskilled workers, knowledge, patents, financing, suppliers, partners, even potential acquirers." The challenge for the United States, according to Sirkin and others is that most of the world's new economic growth will take place in the developing nations, thus requiring American workers to compete for the billions of potential new customers that are starting to move from poverty to life as consumers.

In the midst of the panic of 2008, a survey conducted by Luntz, Maslansky Strategic Research asked a sample of Americans in whom they had the "most faith and confidence" when it came to guiding the economy. Only 7 percent picked "the government in Washington." "The American people" was the top choice with 25 percent, out scoring "the free market", with 14 percent. What faith and confidence do the American people have in themselves to guide the economy?

America dominated the industrial era primarily because investment and innovation was rewarded and citizens were driven by a strong work ethic. America may thrive in the knowledge-based, global economy not only by continuing to reward innovation but also by a citizenry driven by a learning and production ethic, a new work ethic. A learning and production ethic means that people expect to learn, innovate, create, produce and adapt, rather than to resist change. In some countries, India, for example learning is viewed as a sacred tradition that is woven through the culture and individual lives. America, it is said, is a country of doers, not learners, but in our ability to compete and thrive in the knowledge economy, we may be doing ourselves in. Will Americans be able to reject their sense of entitlement and have a passion for learning? Will they be able to delay gratification and invest in lifelong learning? Will there be the political leadership to explain the stakes and help Americans make the right choices? Will Americans reject appeals to their worst instincts of racism and xenophobia? Can Americans adjust to other countries becoming wealthy, relying on their own home-grown brainpower and complemented by U.S. innovation? Or will Americans turn on their neighbors and blame their leaders for selling out?

Walter Lippmann, writing in *The Good Society*, observed that Americans at the turn of the twentieth century were faced with false choices, which can be easily be restated for today: "Men are asked to choose between security and liberty. To improve their fortunes they are told that they must renounce their rights. To escape from want they must enter into a prison. To regularize their work they must be regimented. To obtain grater equality they must have less freedom."

In *Time* magazine (July 7, 2008), Peter Beinart, a senior fellow at the council on Foreign Relations wrote that in a country "where today's nativists are yesterday's immigrants and where change is practically a national religion, conservative patriotism can seem anachronistic. To be Spanish or Russian or Japanese is to imagine that you share a common ancestry and common traditions that trace back to the mists of time. But in America, where most people hail from somewhere else, that kind of blood-and-soil patriotism makes no sense. There is something vaguely farcical about conservative panic over Mexican flags in Los Angeles when Irish flags have long festooned Boston's streets on Saint Patrick's Day. Linking patriotism too closely with reverence for inherited tradition contradicts one of America's most powerful traditions: that our future shouldn't be dictated by our past."

But Americans in the first decade in the twenty first century appear afraid. According to Frank Rich writing for the *New York Times* (September 14, 2008) Americans are afraid of "a demographical revolution that will put whites in the American minority by 2042. Fear of the technological revolution and globalization . . . fear of illegal immigrants who do the low-paying jobs that Americans don't want to do and the legal immigrants who do the high-paying jobs that poorly educated Americans are not qualified to do." Americans are afraid of losing their identity, of drift and disconnection. But by and large they have freely chosen the lifestyles that have gotten them to this point.

The framers understood that the primary right to property was to exclude others. It is the nature of private property that some will have more, others less. As such, private property is capable of producing great wealth and great poverty. If the purpose of government is to protect property and to guarantee the freedom for property and labor to realize their full potential, governing elites are inevitable. What matters in a democracy are that these elites acquire their position and power through talent and experience, and that they be educated to serve the public. The framers were motivated to create a constitutional structure that protected property from rapacious oligarchs from above and mob rule from below. The Framers also understood that the more property was held in common, the more government was necessary to allocate resources fairly. Otherwise a "tragedy of the commons" would result: depletion caused by unregulated exploitation. The Framers also knew that government over time could not remain neutral and that factions would fight for control and influence.

In an information-intensive world, cognitive ability, ingenuity, determination and imagination, while intangible, are no less forms of property. As such, some will have more, others less. Inequality is an inherent quality of private property and while government's role is to ensure equal opportunity, it is not to achieve equal outcomes. As it turns out, the *new economics of knowledge* has not eradicated the law of scarcity and even a college degree does not guarantee a growing income. Since intelligence is basically another form of property, Charles Murray in his book *Real Education* has observed that far too many young people with inherent intellectual limitations are being pushed to advance academically when they are "just not smart enough" to improve much at all. It is "a triumph of hope, over experience," he says, to believe that school reform can make dramatic improvements in the academic performance of below-average students.

In a survey of the research on academic achievement, Michigan's Department of Education has summarized the findings as follows: "The most consistent predictors of children's academic achievement and social adjustment are parent expectations of the child's academic attainment and satisfaction with their child's education and school. Parents of high-achieving students set higher standards for their children's educational activities."

The lack of attention and demand for serious schooling by some parents amounts to gross negligence. Neilson Media Research reports that Americans ages two to seventeen spend an average of three hours a day watching television. A study published in *Pediatrics* in 2006 reported that weekly television and videogames were strongly correlated with poor school performance. Other studies have shown that television is correlated with slower cognitive development, as well as violence, depression and other behavioral problems. The American Academy of Pediatrics recommends parents limit children's sue of television, movies, video and computer games to no more than two hours per day.

Many American parents, regardless of income, have made a mess of child rearing. In 2007, one in three children were born to a single mother. These single mother births cut across race and income levels as the percentage of women who are married has declined steadily for fifty years: 57 percent for white women and 62 percent for black women. Most of these single parent households are poor and lack health insurance, costing nearly $43 billion to cover their health claims in 2007. When changes in the economy have required good judgment by parents and other adults, millions of Americans have acted with an astounding lack of common sense with little or no thought for the consequences. The illusory quest for happiness has led, in many cases, to a substantial portion of an entire generation facing economic insecurity.

In the global economy, millions of Americans face the prospect of lower standards of living and underemployment, many through no fault of their own, but many because of incredibly poor choices. For them, the information intensive, global economy has become hard and unforgiving. The prospects for the children that they have freely brought into the world are no less dire. Should this segment of the population continue to rely on the welfare state to survive, their well being may well depend on the money borrowed from foreigners. To support that borrowing, America will be required to export more of its wealth. The wealth that remains will continue to concentrate in fewer hands at home. As such, the nature of American sovereignty will emerge at a crossroad, stuck between the rock of exporting jobs, intellectual property and revenue producing assets, and the hard place of potential default bankruptcy, and upheaval. If foreigners begin to leverage U.S. borrowing to pursue their own nation-sate interests, America will be faced with the hard choices of retaliation or accommodation. The global economy is transforming America in unintended and unpredictable ways, challenging the basic notions of national identity and wealth, as the developing countries of the world build their own natural and human resources and pursue equal status.

Robert Solow, the Nobel laureate economist concedes that growing inequality is the result of "fundamental forces" of the global economy. "It's hard to know what to do about it, other than to accept it and repair it, rather than try to prevent it," he says. As the nature of the global economy creates more economic disparity, the risks of autocratic, non-democratic institutions increase. In a Zogby poll taken in 2008, as many as 44 percent of those Americans polled agreed that "the United States' system is broken and cannot be fixed by traditional two-party polices and elections." From the Left, property confiscation and wealth redistribution represent alternative ways to bridge the wealth and knowledge gaps; from the Right, a massive security and prison apparatus would be necessary to ensure domestic tranquility.

What faith and confidence do Americans have in themselves?

Twentieth century America has come to a close. It exists only in myth and collective memory and in the endless electronic loops of sounds and images long gone. The long dominant forces of the industrial revolution are also reaching their endpoint. For the elite of the world, notions of nationality and patriotism exist only as convenient nostalgia. The average American feels disconnected from social context at work and increasingly isolated in a multi-cultural world. This vague sense of victimhood and grievance can still be reliably stoked by government to legitimize its power, particularly in America where fear has taken hold; fear that natural selection will leave millions behind. In response, walls are built, telephones are tapped, and the national discourse degenerates into trivia and political celebrity. "Character issues" have replaced policy differences. While it is true that America's political leadership lacks the capacity for being truthful and has therefore failed the public, it is equally true that Americans deserve the leadership that they have freely chosen, aided and abetted.

Time examined American voting habits over a twenty-year period and concluded that most people do not vote for issues but rather for the perceived personality traits of the candidates. Specifically, they vote for people who are perceived as most like themselves. This impulse does not necessarily mean that Americans are ignorant of the issues. It does mean, however, that Americans are emotional and superficial and on occasion will vote, to the extent that they vote at all, against their own economic interests. Now perhaps this infatuation with personality has something to do with the value of equality in America; indeed, one of the nation's core values. DeTocqueille observed repeatedly that Americans placed equality at the center of their democracy. He observed that the United States maintained a more ardent and enduring love of equality than for liberty, particularly during periods of upheaval or struggle when "men pounce upon equality as their booty, and they cling to it as to some precious treasure which they fear to lose . . . their passion is ardent, insatiable, incessant, invincible . . . They will endure poverty, servitude, barbarism: but they will not endure aristocracy."

So perhaps Americans' emotionalism and superficiality in politics is, in reality, an impulsive reaction to the perception of elitism and so they support the leader that is perceived as the most like them, even if it means a vote against their interests, in much the same way that organized labor and African Americans fervently supported Bill Clinton, who pushed NAFTA through Congress, cut social programs, and signed welfare reform. "The era of big government is over," he declared. His supporters may have detected a wink and a nod, but downsizings accelerated and the stage was set for a widening wealth gap.

Daniel Patrick Moynihan, the late Democratic senator from New York, once set the difference between American capitalism and the older

European version by observing that America was the party of liberty, whereas Europe was the party of equality. Indeed, DeTocqueville also warned about the "depraved taste of equality, which impels the weak to attempt to lower the powerful to their own level, and reduces men to prefer equality in slavery to inequality with freedom." DeTocqueville was not speaking of Communism, which he would have recognized as a form of aristocracy. Rather, he was speaking about the excesses of American democratic populism, where the obsession with equality driven by class envy and the fear produced by economic insecurity would result in the type of command and control authoritarianism that would decree equality; in modern parlance, a corporate welfare state with just a "regular guy" as the elected figurehead.

Nevertheless, post-industrial America teems with fluid identities, disconnected meanings and blurred boundaries. A case can be made that social and technological changes have brought civilization once again to the brink of an explosion in innovation and creativity that will result in the exponential growth necessary to scale the rule of scarcity. Hierarchies are collapsing in the face of hyper-linked networks of disaggregated units. These social arrangements could make possible a process of decentralized innovation to solve common problems and produce public goods. It is probable, however, that the trend to inequality will grow even stronger well into the twenty first century, particularly if new genetic techniques offer those with sufficient resources the possibility of enhancing the intelligence, health, beauty and strength of their children. Yet, to the extent that success in the global economy depends on personal character, discipline, and perseverance, Americans should not be afraid to let freedom take its course.

During the one hundred years from the end of the Civil War to the mid-twentieth century America changed dramatically. Among other things, population swelled with millions of immigrants, factories grew in size employing thousands of workers, population shifted from the farms to the cities, and the nation became connected with mass transportation and communication systems. At the center of this enormous economic and social transformation was the progress to secure civil rights for all Americans. The war ended with the abolition of slavery and the nation's first federal civil rights legislation. After one hundred years of violence, intimidation, segregation, protest, struggle and litigation the period ended with the Civil Rights Act of 1964.

The Civil Rights Act of 1866 declared all persons born in the United States citizens and guaranteed civil rights, including the rights of property and contract, and the full and equal benefits of the laws. Significantly, to mid-nineteenth century Americans "race" meant more than the physical characteristics that distinguish groups from one another, but also meant ancestry, the decent from a common stock. In short, Congress intended to protect identifiable classes of persons who were subject to discrimination solely because of their ancestry or ethnic characteristics, which obviously included former slaves but also encompassed immigrants of all nationalities. Such legislation faced fierce resistance in the defeated Confederacy and among others who opposed the newly ratified power of the federal government to govern internal state matters and private affairs.

Six hundred thousand Americans perished in five years of horrific warfare but race discrimination lived on. Such was the epochal contradiction of a nation founded on the creed that "all men were created equal." Indeed, at the time the Declaration of Independence was written, 50,000 slaves resided in the colonies and while seven of the thirteen states had outlawed slavery at the time that the Constitution was ratified, 30 of the delegates to, the Convention owned slaves. Slavery was constitutionally preserved but two opposing systems, one slave and one free, generally speaking, were on a collision course from day one.

Western expansion and economic development exacerbated the conflict. The battle raged over whether each new territory would be slave or free and reached fever pitch when vast new lands were wrested from Mexico by war. Many Southerners insisted that Northern industrialism treated labor brutally and by comparison slaves were at least cared for by their masters. However, taken to its logical conclusion, this view led to slavery as the best condition of labor. In contrast, many Northerners viewed slavery as abhorrent and its very existence debased human dignity and self worth. Compromise worked for a time but the industrial, free labor North and the agrarian, slave South could not co-exist.

As noted previously, post-war amendments to the Constitution shifted power away from the states to the federal government, the result of which was the passage of the Civil Rights Act. But in addition to ending 244 years of legalized slavery in America, the war also vindicated free labor and enterprise and the U.S. Supreme Court was not reluctant to invalidate state laws that interfered with the free market/ regardless of the inherent inequalities between owners and workers. The Civil Rights Act was not a state economic law. Rather, the Act was federal legislation with the purpose of ensuring "the full and equal benefit of all laws for the security of persons and property as is enjoyed by white citizens." However, this law too was struck down as unconstitutional, the U.S. Supreme Court holding that Congress had no power to interfere with "private" discrimination.

In these consolidated cases under the Act several people were indicted for denying African Americans access to a theater in California, an opera house in New York, and a railroad car in Tennessee. The Court observed that post-war constitutional amendments established universal civil and political freedom throughout the United States by abolishing slavery and vesting power in the federal government to overrule state laws that discriminate because of race or color. In these cases, however, there was no state law involved. Instead, private individuals refused access to public places. According to the Court, their refusal had nothing to do with slavery or any state law, their refusals were merely personal acts. "When a man has emerged from slavery, and by the aid of beneficent legislation has shaken off the inseparable concomitants of that state/ there must be some state in the process of his elevation when he takes the rank of mere citizen, and ceases to be the special favor of the laws . . . Mere discriminations on accord of race or color [are] not regarded as badges of slavery." In short, federal law could guarantee political equality and due process of the law, but could not end discrimination by individuals, which included not only access to public places but presumably job discrimination as well. Having had the protection of the federal government after the war/ but no longer enjoying protected status, African Americans were left to state law to vindicate their rights.

Shortly after the Civil Rights cases were decided, several states enacted civil rights laws which provided that all persons were entitled to the full enjoyment of places of public accommodation, "applicable alike to citizens of every race and color." Other states, however, enacted civil rights laws that turned the idea of equality on its head and when the U.S. Supreme Court had the opportunity to evaluate the constitutionality of a Louisiana law that segregated passengers on a railroad based on their race, the court found that "separate but equal" accommodations were not constitutionally offensive. "A statute which implies merely a legal distinction between the white and colored races—a distinction which is founded in the color of the two races and which must always exist . . . has no tendency to destroy the legal equality of the two races or reestablish a state of involuntary servitude," the Court held.

Plessy v. Ferguson was decided by the U.S. Supreme Court at the same time as it was declaring state wage and hour laws unconstitutional. On the one hand, states were not permitted to enact economic legislation because employers and employees stood as equals and their equality was enshrined by the Constitution and reaffirmed by the Civil War amendments. On the other hand, states were left with their inherent power to enact social legislation permitting, even requiring, racial segregation because individuals were free to affiliate with whomever they pleased and the sovereign states had the power to express this public will. No doubt the Court believed that extremism in the defense of liberty was no vice. On the other hand, this decision led to more than fifty years of legal segregation, relegating millions of American citizens to inferior schools and jobs and disenfranchising them from any meaningful political participation. "Legislation is powerless to eradicate racial instincts or to abolish distinctions based upon physical differences, and the attempt to do so can only result in accentuating the difficulties of the present situation/' the Court said. "If one race be inferior to the other socially, the Constitution cannot put them upon the same plane."

No court can be separate from the dominate social and political views of its time. In the late nineteenth and into the first three decades of the twentieth century, American and European philanthropy combined with prestigious academic support to advance a pseudoscience that institutionalized racial policies in most industrial countries. As previously discussed, These policies focused on ending immigration of inferior (non-white) races, creating health programs to increase the strength of the Anglo-Saxon race, and the elimination of "unfit" persons, primarily through sterilization. In short, all non-white persons were viewed as naturally inferior and many policies, from immigration to health care to territorial expansion, were influenced by this view.

This view also led to vicious stereotyping and obvious prejudice in employment. Many fretted about immigrants taking away jobs. For example, rather than seeking to organize immigrants, unions blamed them for job loss and low wages. Labor unions often represented immigrants as "a menace to the American standard of living." Immigrants were systematically threatened and harassed on the job by other workers that resented their willingness to work for lower wages.

Further, as noted, racial characteristics encompassed more than skin color, but also included ancestry and ethnicity. As such, many immigrants, particularly from southern and eastern Europe were considered non-White, and therefore inferior. For example, in 1890, Popular Science Magazine carried an article entitled "What Should We Do with the Dago?" As for Eastern Europeans, a prominent turn-of-the-century physician argued that Slavs were "immune to certain kinds of dirt. They could stand what would kill a white man." Of Polish Jews, the bestselling book *The Passing of the Great Race*, argued that Jews diminished "the stock of the nation" with their "dwarf stature, peculiar mentality and ruthless concentration of self-interest." A popular cartoon of the time called The Last Yankee drawn by Thomas Nast (who also popularized the image Santa Claus) was published widely. It portrayed a straight, tall, virtuous American (which was later used as Uncle Sam during the First World War) being crowded out by foreigners with exaggerated racial and ethnic characteristics. The message was clear: while immigration was necessary to fuel economic expansion, too much immigration, particular "non-white" immigration was an economic, social and biological threat to the nation.

It is clear that much of the constitutional law during the fifty years from the end of the Civil War to the Great Depression was deeply reactionary and was influenced by the racial policies of the time. The courts impeded the political progress needed to cope with dramatic social and economic change, both domestically and globally. But even as New Deal economic legislation was eventually upheld, it would take many more years to overrule "separate but equal" with the landmark *Brown v. Board of Education* decided in 1954, midway through the American Century. By then a proactive federal government explained that "it is in the context of the present world struggle between freedom and tyranny that the problem of racial discrimination must be viewed ... Racial discrimination furnishes grist for the Communist propaganda mills, and it raises doubts even among friendly nations as to the intensity of our devotion to the democratic faith." The whole world was watching and the Supreme Court was prepared to accommodate a new meaning of equality, no less absolute, but much more inclusive. Building on the federal government's power to regulate the national economy, it was willing to expand that power further to uphold civil rights legislation. In 1964 in *Heart of Atlanta Motel v. United States*, the Court held that the same constitutional authority which enabled the federal government to enact and enforce wage and hour laws permitted it to mandate equal access to places of public accommodation. Four years later, in *Jones v. Mayer Co.* the Court upheld the Fair Housing Act which prohibited racial discrimination in private housing transactions. By then, no one doubted the validity of a federal law that prohibited employment discrimination but in 1975 the Court confirmed its constitutionality in *Johnson v. Railway Express Agency*.

The purpose of Title VII of the Civil Rights Act of 1964 is to ensure that employers are not motivated by prejudice when making employment decisions. It also requires the elimination of artificial, arbitrary and unnecessary barriers to employment that discriminate because of race, color, religion, sex and national origin. It empowers individuals to file a charge to the Equal Employment Opportunity Commission (EEOC) and when that remedy is exhausted, to file a civil complaint in the United States District Court.

About 825,000 charges of job discrimination are filed with the EEOC a year, the majority of which allege racial discrimination. According to a research group at George Mason University, Title VII cost employers $6.6 billion a year in compliance and litigation risks. What is it about Title VII that makes compliance and risks so costly? For one thing, as of 2000 about 62 percent of the current workforce is comprised of woman, minorities or both. In addition to the emergence of many women in the workforce, the number of foreign born workers living in the United Sates increased 57 percent from 1990-2000. As a result, Title VII is probably more relevant now than it was when it was enacted in 1964. Given this heightened relevance, how then does an employer comply with Title VII? Does the law require "equal opportunity or does it require "preferential treatment?

Consider the change in substance in Lyndon Johnson's public remarks at the time the Civil Rights Act was enacted. When initially describing the intent of the law he stated that "it does not give special treatment to any citizen." However, within a year of this statement violence against civil rights activists did not abate and a wave of terrorist acts and murder shocked the world. At that moment, the gradual civil rights policy gave way to a more active, outcome-oriented policy. Responding to mounting political pressure, the president concluded: "To this end, equal opportunity is essential but not enough, not enough ... We must go beyond opportunity to achievement [of outcomes]." The social tension between opportunity and outcome may account for the $66 billion annual price tag associated with Title VII compliance by employers.

This cognitive dissonance was fully expressed in 1989, when the Piscataway school board was faced with declining enrollment and was forced to layoff a high school business teacher. Sharon Taxman, who is white, was one of two teachers with the least seniority. The other, Debra Williams, was the only African-American high school business teacher in the school's history. After deciding that the teachers were equally well qualified in all respects, the school board discharged Taxman, saying that students tend to receive a more well-rounded education when they are exposed to teachers from different races.

Taxman sued in federal court alleging that she had been discriminated against because of her race in violation of Title VII. Both the U.S. District Court and the Third Circuit Court of Appeals ruled that race could not be used as a deciding factor in an employment decision and ordered Taxman's reinstatement. While Taxman's case was limited only to her job, her cause generated enormous public debate. The case eventually settled in her favor.

The courts' rulings in the Taxman case was based on the leading case in a private employment setting, *United Steelworkers of America v. Weber*, which involved a racial preference plan set up in 1974 under a collective bargaining agreement between Kaiser Aluminum & Chemical Corp and the United Steelworkers. Craft jobs were almost exclusively held by whites, and the plan reserved half of the openings in a newly created on-the-job training program for African American employees until the percentage in the plant equaled the percentage of blacks in the local labor force.

A majority of the U.S. Supreme Court held that Title VII allowed for a voluntary, private, race-conscious plan aimed at eliminating a racial imbalance in a traditionally segregated job category, provided that the plan was temporary and did not absolutely bar job opportunities for whites. In short, although Title VII does not require an employer to adopt an affirmative action-type plan, it does not prohibit temporary plans to give preferences on the basis of race. However, according to the court, qualifications must remain a controlling factor in making employment decisions.

It is clear from this case that the focus of Title VII is to guarantee equal employment opportunities by requiring an employer to be guided by qualifications and not race. However, employers may adopt race-conscious policies to remediate past discrimination. But taking proactive steps to expand job opportunities has been a difficult process in corporate America, where the perception held by many corporate employees is that expanding job opportunities for one group means shrinking opportunities for another.

In *Griggs v. Duke Power Co.*, a 1971 decision, African American employees at a generating plant filed suit challenging the company's requirement of a high school diploma or passing of standardized intelligence tests as a condition of employment in or transfer to other jobs in the plant. The company had a history of segregating jobs on the basis of race before Title VII was enacted. The court of appeals held that in the absence of a discriminatory purpose, use of such requirements was permitted by Title VII. In so doing, the court of appeals rejected the claim that because these two requirements operated to render ineligible a disproportionate number of African American employees, they were unlawful under Title VII unless shown to be job related. The US Supreme Court reversed, noting that the purpose of Title VII was "to achieve equality of employment opportunities and remove barriers that have operated in the past to favor an identifiable group of white employees over other employees." On the other hand, the Court stated that Title VII "does not command that any person be hired simply because he was formerly the subject of discrimination, or because he is a member of a minority group." According to the court, "[the] touchstone is business necessity. If an employer's practice which operates to exclude [African Americans] cannot be shown to be related to job performance, the practice is prohibited."

Evidence showed that 34% of white males had completed high school, as compared to 12% of African Americans. Fifty-eight percent of whites passed the test, but only 6% of blacks did. However, neither the high school completion requirements nor the general intelligence test had any demonstrable relationship to successful performance of the job for which it was used. Both were adopted without any meaningful study of their relationship to job performance. Rather, the company simply contended that the requirements were instituted on the judgment that they would generally improve overall quality of the workforce.

This decision affirmed the "disparate impact" theory of discrimination where the employer's intentions are irrelevant. Rather, it is the outcome of the test or other selection criteria that matter. If such a test or other selection criteria has a disparate impact on minorities, the employee has the burden of demonstrating conclusively that the test or other selection criteria is predictive of or significantly correlated with successful performance of essential job functions. According to EEOC guidance, a selection rate for any race, sex or ethnic group which is less than 80 percent of the rate for the group with the highest rate is generally regarded as evidence of adverse impact.

In 1995, after a generation of litigation, the President's Glass Ceiling Commission examined the impediments to greater equality in the workplace and concluded that many white males perceived that they are losing—"losing the corporate game, losing control and losing opportunity. Many middle and upper middle white male managers view inclusion of minorities and women in management as a direct threat to their own chances of advancement." Evidence of this conclusion could have been seen at Texaco Corporation, the petrochemical giant. Two years after the Glass Ceiling Report was issued, the company paid $176.1 million to settle a race discrimination lawsuit, at the time the biggest such settlement in history. While the media portrayed the company's culture as poisoned by bias, prejudice and stereotyping, a more careful examination reveals a company in crisis, where anger, fear and resentment pervaded the organization.

As a big corporation, Texaco's culture was fairly typical. A command-and-control organizational structure required conformity throughout the corporate hierarchy. Individual autonomy was suppressed in favor of a safe place in the bureaucracy and as was typical of the post-war deal between employer and employee, job security was exchanged for loyalty and discipline. Also typical of this culture, was the absence of objective criteria for promotion and widespread subjective decision making when it came to personnel. Many managers, mostly middle-aged white men, had spent their entire careers playing by the rules of "the club."

As with most corporations, Texaco was not immune from global competition and deregulation of its industry and its eventual restructuring called for major consolidation and layoffs. The layoffs in particular were viewed as an act of betrayal by the men who had devoted the better part of their working lives to the corporation. At the same time, the company was under an obligation to fulfill an affirmative action goal of increasing the percentage of minorities in management jobs. Anger and resentment spilled into meetings and corporate functions, including a holiday party. Well-meaning but poorly executed "diversity training" backfired and left the rank-and-file deeply divided along racial lines. The division and conflict were secretly captured on an audio tape, a transcript of which was widely published. The result was a disaster for the company, its employees and shareholders. For Texaco to survive, the corporate culture needed to change. The change was driven by pressure which was applied from both within and without the organization. But how much change is enough for Texaco to regain its credibility and meet the imperatives of equal opportunity and equal treatment? Time will tell but the same year as Texaco's settlement, a survey asked whether African Americans were subject to "flagrant or obviously discriminatory practices." Fifty-five percent of blacks agreed with the statement, only four percent of whites agreed. This wide gap in perception can only be bridged by outcomes. Accordingly, Texaco increased its efforts to promote African Americans in management jobs through mentoring and training programs in order to be consistent with Title VII's mandate to stay focused on qualifications.

However, it appears that most diversity training efforts at U.S. companies are ineffective and even counterproductive in increasing the number of women and minorities in managerial positions, according to an analysis that turned decades of conventional wisdom, government policy and court rulings on their head. A comprehensive review of 31 years of data from 830 mid-size to large U.S. workplaces found that the kind of diversity training exercises offered at most firms were followed by a 7.5 percent drop in the number of women in management. The number of African Americans and female managers fell by 10 percent, and the number of black men in top positions fell by 12 percent. Similar effects were seen for Latinos and Asians.

The analysis did not find that all diversity training is useless. Rather, it showed that mandatory programs, often undertaken to avoid liability in discrimination lawsuits, were the problem. When diversity training is voluntary and undertaken to advance a company's business goals, it was associated with increased diversity in management.

Today, U.S. businesses spend from $200 million to $300 million a year on diversity training, but the new study is one of the first attempts to systematically analyze its impact. What the report found is that programs work best when they are voluntary and focus on specific organizational skills, such as establishing mentoring relationships and giving women and minorities a chance to prove their worth in high-profile roles.

When attendance is voluntary, diversity training might lead to an increase in managerial diversity. Most employers, however, force their managers and workers to go through training, and this is the least effective option in terms of increasing diversity. It appears that forcing people to go through training creates a backlash against diversity.

Much of the time, diversity training is mischaracterized by most employers as a legal issue. And if they are doing it for legal protection, most employers really don't care whether the training works. It was hardly surprising that when such training is not meant to be transformative it could have counterproductive effects, leaving employees feeling cynical and distrustful of the company and in the worse case sowing the seeds for conflict.

Like corporate ethics training, the main reason for ineffective diversity training is that employers and lawyers have misunderstood U.S. Supreme Court rulings holding that companies with mandatory training are in a stronger position if they face a discrimination lawsuit. But training supervisors on the law and how to avoid job discrimination liability has nothing to do with diversity training. Diversity is about interpersonal communication, cultural competency and business success. Such training is social and voluntary; in short, the same social dynamic that supports the free flow of information to advance innovation.

And what of the remaining vestiges of racial and gender inequality and other forms of discrimination in the wider society? When the conflict is over how scarce resources such as jobs and promotions are allocated, can a case be made for "reverse discrimination" against the majority group to remedy systematic discrimination? The U.S. Supreme Court has split on whether the economic benefits of a diverse work force can ever legally justify decisions based on race, gender or ethnicity. The legal and social issues arising out of affirmative action remain contentious.

In 1965 President Johnson issued Executive Order 11246, which expanded a previous Executive Order issued by President Roosevelt in 1941. The purpose of the order was to prohibit racial, religious, gender and national origin discrimination by employers that provide goods and services under a contract with the federal government. The Order also required *affirmative action* to ensure that employment decisions are made without regard to race, religion, sex or national origin.

In 1965 African American unemployment was 11 percent, while for whites the figure was 5 percent. Whereas a white family earned on average about $6,500 a year, a black family earned $3,500. Affirmative action was one of the federal government's attempts to narrow the employment and income gaps between races. By 1972, little progress had been made. Unemployment stood at 9.4 percent for African Americans and 4.6 percent for whites. By 1995, after 30 years of affirmative action, unemployment among African-Americans stood at 11.3 percent, for whites 4.8 percent. Family income for blacks was $19,533, for whites $32,960. In 2004, median family income of African Americans ages 30 to 39 was only 58 percent that of white families.

Critics claim that affirmative action has failed because black unemployment has remained consistently twice that of whites and black family income has remained consistently half that of whites. Adapting the Social Darwinist framework, some controversial studies have even concluded that affirmative action has no purpose because minorities have inferior mental capacities. But the apparent reason that affirmative action has not substantially narrowed the employment and income gaps is because it does not address the root problem: unequal educational opportunity. Even opponents of affirmative action concede that the economic gap between blacks and whites has nothing to do with pseudo-scientific theories or any other half-baked explanation based on inferior mental capacities of minorities. The economic gap is the direct result of the persistent problem of inferior schooling. In short, the debate over affirmative action will become increasingly more heated but arguably less relevant if the U.S. educational system cannot be reformed to compete with global standards. That means a national priority must be achieving a world-class educational system that is open to every child, a monumental challenge presently obscured by racial politics.

Grutter v. Bollinger, involved a university's law school. Barbara Grutter, who is white, applied for admission there in 1996. She was rejected. She investigated and found out that African Americans and ethnic minorities who had lower overall admissions scores were admitted. Grutter sued, saying she was a victim of illegal discrimination.

Grutter's lawyers argued that the admissions program at the university's law school was unconstitutional. They based the argument on a 1978 case, *Regents of the University of California v. Bakke*, where the court ruled that a school could take race and ethnicity into account—but couldn't use quotas. Instead, admissions programs must be "narrowly tailored" to harm as few people as possible.

In *Grutter*, Justice Sandra Day O'Connor was the eventual deciding vote for the majority of the U.S. Supreme Court, saying that affirmative action is still needed in America—but hoped that its days were numbered. "We expect that 25 years from now, the use of racial preferences will no longer be necessary to further the interest approved today," she said.

In her article *The Knowledge Economy and Diversity: New Opportunity for Black Americans*, Angela Larson has opined that "many black Americans believe that Capitalism is evil" and that this historic suspicion of free markets has posed profound obstacles to economic progress for blacks. She has observed that the percentages of black men and women employed in managerial and professional occupations are far below that of whites and that "blacks account for precious few" knowledge workers. She suggests that when diversity translates into dollars, blacks will have more opportunity. Therefore she has urged African Americans to "relinquish the tunnel vision that has dominated the past half century, and refocus energies upon increasing opportunity through job training and education."

As I have previously discussed, capitalism was founded on the Western belief of private property, which included slavery. After slavery and involuntary servitude were abolished after the Civil War, free capitalism thrived but so did segregation. The U.S. Supreme Court finally invalidated the legal principle of separate but equal and the Civil Rights Act of 1964 reaffirmed and reestablished equal opportunity. But Ms. Larson suggests that many African Americans equate the free market with racial oppression. I would extend that argument somewhat and also postulate that many Americans, black and white, have equated civil rights with a posture that rejects the Western values of free markets and wage labor. Somehow in the post civil rights era, employment has become a type of post-colonial servitude. For many, black and white, liberation from state sponsored racial segregation has morphed into a kind of license to reject the conventions of work and family as forms of oppression. But their "freedom" has only perpetuated a cycle of poverty and alienation, thus proving that only more unconventional lifestyles are the answer.

Moreover, for the more affluent, consumption has become a type of post-civil rights entitlement. Consumer products from sneakers to iPods, from alcohol to junk food, cater to this vague notion of freedom and liberation. Thus, consumption itself is experienced as a form of personal freedom, autonomy and expression. Since consumption lies at the core of experience, work and learning, which require delayed gratification, are viewed as alien and uncool. As work is viewed as a means to consume, the wage slave of the nineteenth century has been replaced by the debt slave of the twenty first.

In *Empowerment Ethics for a Liberated People*, Cheryl Sanders discusses an approach to achieving African American social transformation but I believe that her thoughtful exposition concerning the spiritual and economic well being of American blacks in the face of incarceration, alienation and self-destruction transcends race. Arguing that the experience of oppression has been the catalyst for black moral life and thought, Ms. Sanders traces several paths that African Americans have taken in moving from victimization to moral agency, including cooperation and achievement. The challenges facing many Americans in the so-called "new" economy (alienation and self-destruction) are just as profound as the challenges imposed by a legacy of slavery and segregation. These challenges transcend race. According to Sanders, what's necessary for the "remoralization" of African Americans (but I am suggesting that the process of remoralization could apply to *most* Americans, regardless of race) is a "tough-minded Puritanism, sobriety, an ascetic spirit of the abolition movement and the social gospel, which has served so well in the past as the basis of civil religion, civil rights, and progressive movements in church and state."

Sander's "tough-minded Puritanism" means, in part, a return to the Judeo-Christian work ethic that trained people to defer gratification in order to meet long term goals. I have discussed the basis of property and free markets that sprung from this ethic and so have many others. In Civilization, Niall Ferguson recounts a meeting with a member of the Chinese Academy of Social Sciences who was researching the factors that gave rise to Western development. The official says: "At first we thought it was your guns. Then we thought it was you democracy. Then we thought was capitalism. But for the last twenty years we have known that it was your religion." The prescription to return to a work ethic that advances innovation, production and investment may treat many ills. But in a free society, there is no government policy that can change a person's will. If there is one thing that recent history has demonstrated it is that tyranny can temporarily break or destroy the will, but it cannot really change it. People are capable of enduring change only through the free exercise of their own will. Free will lies at the heart of personhood and societal transformation. In the end, it is the American people who will freely choose their fate and create their destiny in the twenty first century. For those who cannot rise above their deep sense of entitlement or feelings of helplessness, victimization, chronic unemployment, underemployment or crime, life at the margins will no doubt always be an option. In other words, survival could either be ennobling or degrading.

Nevertheless, the question remains whether government should actively promote policies that seek to expand opportunities for those at the margins. Ms. Larson suggests that if diversity has a bottom line payoff, market forces will promote diversity. A 1994 study by Covenant Investment Management, which rated the performance of the Standard and Poor's 500 on a series of factors relating to the hiring and advancement of women and nonwhites, found the annualized return for the companies that rated lowest in equal employment opportunities issues, average 7.9 percent, compared to 18.3 percent for the 100 companies that rated highest in their equal employment opportunities. According to the report, "the stock market performance of the firms that were high performers on the glass ceiling-related goals was 2.5 times higher than that of the firms that invested little in glass ceiling-related issues." However, there is no clear correlation between diversity and profits and therefore for most firms diversity is viewed as simply being "politically correct."

But, in reality, a firm's brand matters—to its employees, customers, suppliers and shareholders. In the global economy, businesses simply cannot afford to ignore diversity. Given the racial and ethnic mix of both domestic and global markets, ignoring entire segments of the consumer base makes no business sense. By employing a natural mix of men, women, and employees form diverse backgrounds, a business is more likely to develop and market products that will sell in today's pluralistic environment. In the *Grutter* case, a group of brand name corporations filed a brief in support of the university's diversity efforts, writing that cross-cultural experiences helped them succeed both domestically and internationally. In their experience, they argued:

> Individuals who have been educated in a diverse setting are more likely to succeed, because they can make valuable contributions to the workforce in several important and concrete ways. First, a diverse group of individuals educated in a cross-cultural environment has the ability to facilitate unique and creative approaches to problem solving arising from the integration of different perspectives. Second, such individuals are better able to develop products and services that appeal to a variety of consumers and to market offerings in ways that appeal to those consumers. Third, a racially diverse group of managers with cross-cultural experience is better able to work with business partners, employees, and clientele in the United States and around the world. Fourth, individuals who have been educated in a diverse setting are likely to contribute to a positive work environment, by decreasing incidents of discrimination and stereotyping. Overall, an educational environment that ensures participation by diverse people, viewpoints and ideas will help produce the most talented workforce.

By and large, the racial wedge issues of the nineteen seventies and eighties, such as busing, crime, welfare and affirmative action have subsided and been replaced by the anxiety caused by globalization—free trade and immigration. In recent decades the face of America has changed. At one end of the economic ladder, low wage workers have streamed in from Latin America and elsewhere. At the other end, America's elite knowledge workers have become more multicultural. Affluent foreigners have flooded into America, transforming housing patterns, schools, and whole communities. There were 3 million mixed-race couples in the U.S. in 2005, ten times as many as in 1970.

Generally, Americans should not fear this diversity, either at home or in the world. All myths and pretense aside, Americans do not represent a superior race and they do not worship the only God. If Americans turn

14. We the People

inward and become more fearful that the rest of the world is catching up economically; if they become resentful of their dependence on foreign economies; if they deny the changing character and color of America, the values of liberty and property will become seriously compromised, and perhaps damaged permanently. The concentration of government power required to unilaterally stem the tides of globalization and integration does not exit, and never has, at least completely and for long. But history has shown repeatedly that attempts to create and maintain that kind of government would be ruinous to economic freedom and civil liberties.

Besides, why turn inward when the values of liberty and property are shared, in varying degrees, by most of the world? Indeed, they are pillars of globalization. In the process, the whole global middle class is becoming "Americanized," speaking English and consuming roughly the same media, goods and services. The developing economies will ensure a steady flow of talent people to the United States, further enhancing its technical and intellectual prowess. America has won the great battles of the nineteenth and twentieth centuries, but for many it doesn't feel like it.

In Silicon Valley, where it is rumored that some start-up executives take amphetamines so they can work twenty-hour days, the drive for power and profit follows freedom's course. For others, the trade off of higher salaries for more flexibility and control over one's life follows freedom's course. Still others will seek to avoid the "human capital management" systems of employers who de-skill and degrade work and follow freedom's course to find and secure more meaningful work, paid or unpaid. And for those who insist on making choices that flagrantly undermine their well being, whether through over consumption or under achieving, freedom's natural course will end in their failure and undoing.

In the end, it could be that dignity and self-respect may be the only truly inexhaustible resources on the planet.

Epilogue

In 1932, Franklin Delano Roosevelt was elected president as the nation was already into a severe economic recession. The stock market had crashed in 1929, the world's economy was slowing down, and all economic indicators in the U.S. showed signs of serious trouble. FDR's response was to gain congressional approval to regulate the economy with an expansion of government regulation unimaginable until that time. While the New Deal was built on prior reforms and was essentially conservative in nature, there is still no consensus whether it prolonged or helped to end the Great Depression.

Today, President Obama faces similar economic circumstances. Polls on Election Day 2008 found that three out of four Americans believed that the country was in poor economic shape and two-thirds were frightened. The relatively high voter turnout—about six and ten registered voters cast a ballot—was no doubt driven by this fear but also, paradoxically, by an enormous amount of hope for the future.

According to the Bureau of Economic Analysis, government spending at all levels—federal, state and local—had risen to 37 percent in 2011 from 27 percent in 1960. It may reach 50 percent with the next twenty five years. At the same time, the Tax Foundation reports that between 1986 to 2009, the percentage of Americans who pay zero or negative federal income taxes has increased to 51 percent from 18.5 percent. Reaching a point where so few people actually pay for their share of government spending, America has relied, in large part, on borrowing from foreign banks and sovereign wealth funds. In 1945 when the U.S. was still a production based economy, foreigners owned just one percent of U.S. Treasury notes. By 2010 foreigners owned 46 percent of U.S. Treasuries. Thus, the long-term health of the U.S. economy is dependent on foreigner's willingness to buy U.S. assets, which may be tested as government spending grows

For the last quarter century, the stability of the U.S. economy and the preeminence of its financial system have made it easier to run up big budget deficits, as foreign national banks bought U.S. Treasury bonds. If foreigner's stopped buying these bonds or started selling them, the dollar would plummet and interest rates would soar. Such an scenario would result in a permanent state of austerity leading to a long painful restructuring of the debt. Living standards would decline over many generations.

The demand for U.S. assets from foreign banks and corporations should remain high, particularly in uncertain and unpredictable times, permitting the federal government to continue borrowing to increase investments in schools, roads, transportation, research and development. Moreover, a margin call by foreign creditors would create losses all around, as American consumers stopped supporting the export economies of the world. In short, the status quo prevails and there is still plenty of deficit spending that can be done well into the mid-twenty first century. But the annualized national debt reached 100 percent of GNP in 2011 up from 42 percent in 1980. Even though this debt can be carried more or less indefinitely, the politics of debt has created widespread feelings of anxiety.

As of late 2008, three-quarters of Americans thought that the country was "on the wrong track". The number of people who were hostile to trade and immigration rose sharply, as had the numbers who thought that America should engage less in world affairs. Trust in government was half what it was in 2001. In the first post-election poll taken by the *Wall Street Journal*, six of ten respondents stated that globalization of trade was bad for the U.S. economy. And people were increasingly pessimistic about the future. Ninety percent stated that the economy was worse than the year before. Barely a third thought that their children would be better off than they themselves were. Articulating why it is in the national interest for American consumers to become investors in future generations, without any short-term gain in sight, will require transformational leadership.

Investment, of course, means public investment, which means tax hikes. During the campaign, President Obama promised a tax increase limited to top earners. In 2005, the richest one percent of Americans had 18 percent of total income, a hefty figure, but they also paid 28 percent of all federal taxes, according to the Congressional Budget Office. This group also owned 34 percent of stocks and mutual funds, accounting for $100 billion dollars in capital gains taxes. While the average American feels little sympathy for the laid off investment banker or portfolio manager, New York City, which is heavily dependent on Wall Street for taxes, faces a huge deficit and may therefore cut city services accordingly. In other words, the government cannot distribute wealth that does not exist.

Articulating how a more equitable distribution of rivalrous resources, such as health care, will require enormous leadership as well. In the 2008 national election is any guide, explaining why health care should be allocated more rationally and equitably will most likely unleash a torrent of rage and fear about socialism, rationing, even euthanasia.

Already commentators such as Daniel Henninger of the *Wall Street Journal* have argued that "federalizing" medical insurance will lead to a "social market economy." He continues: "Obama's federalized medical insurance system starts the transition away from private medical care and toward Obama's endlessly promised 'universal health care.' This has always been the *sine qua non* of achieving a U.S. social-market economy." But a few days before the 2008 election, Peggy Noonan observed: "Something new is happening in America. It is the imminent arrival of a new liberal moment. History happens, it makes its turns, you hold on for dear life. Life moves."

But can President Obama move the American people. In so doing he will need to explain why isolationism, protectionism and xenophobia will be disastrous for the United States and the world.

For example, as of 2008, there were sixteen foreign-owned auto assembly plants in the U.S. and many more that built engines, transmissions and other components. As the U.S. auto industry seeks a government bailout, foreign auto makers from Japan and India are rushing in to be closer to U.S. consumers. Similarly, Japans' Mitsubishi bank bought a stake in Morgan Stanley, rescuing it from bankruptcy and Spain's Banco Santunder purchased Sovereign Bancorp. In short, foreign investors are not only buying U.S. Treasury debt, they are insisting on taking equity positions and buying hard assets. Maintaining a climate that is conducive to foreign investment will require astute leadership. If China's $2 trillion foreign exchange surplus is going to be tapped by U.S. and other world banks, China will have more influence over world monetary policy in return. After a national campaign that whipped up the latent fear that many Americans have of foreigners and that appealed expressly to the people's worst instincts of intolerance and suspicion, it will not be easy explaining to Americans that their long term well-being is based, in part, on accommodating foreign bankers. Again, if 2008 is any guide, poisonous forms of populism are sure to escalate throughout the first decades of the twenty first century. However, accelerated globalization will create a world even more interconnected, requiring more multilateral diplomacy and international collaboration.

Nearly half of those who responded to the post-election poll said that 2008 will go down as one of the worst years in U.S. history. Confidence in the federal government to correct a sinking economy was at an all time low. Nevertheless, many Americans, some grudgingly, are invested in President Obama's success.

Business leaders too will need to step up. In the near term there is probably no new information technology innovation on horizon that will carry productivity to new heights, as the computer has done over the last thirty years. The easy efficiencies have been achieved. But even as they are forced to layoff workers, the best companies will need to do more than simply survive during long business slumps. The best companies will continue to find ways to invest in those employees who create long-term value. While some employers believe that workers should be content to just have a job, making investments in value-adding employees during down business cycles, when it is most needed, will create big payoffs in the future when business picks up. Any firm, even if mismanaged, can succeed during the good times. Only the best succeed when the going gets tough. Management requires more than counting time, pointing out mistakes, and disciplining employees. Employers that succeed have managers and supervisors that lead from core values, have superior communication skills, and who can tap the reservoir of ingenuity and know-how that exist within the organization. Trust and commitment must be instilled within the organization to avoid hoarding ideas and feet dragging. Since knowledge workers, much like volunteers, are intrinsically motivated by core values, the hard work of leadership will be to nurture an open environment where information is freely shared and expectations for performance are transparent. The measure of the leader's success is not only how well they inspire employees to perform their best, but also to perform at the highest level of trust, sharing and cooperation. Exceptional leadership at all levels, public and private, is needed.

Oddly, it was DeTocqueville, a Frenchman, who enshrined American exceptionalism in the public consciousness. As he wrote in 1831:

> The position of the Americans is therefore quite exceptional, and it may be believed that no democratic people will ever be placed in a similar one. Their strictly Puritanical origin, their exclusively commercial habits, even the country they inhabit, which seems to divert their minds from the pursuit of science, literature, and the arts, the proximity of Europe, which allows them to neglect these pursuits without relapsing into barbarism, a thousand special causes, of which I have only been able to point out the most important, have singularly concurred to fix the mind of the American upon purely practical objects. His passions, his wants, his education, and everything about him seem to unite in drawing the native of the United States earthward; his religion alone bids him turn, from time to time, a transient and distracted glance to heaven. Let us cease, then, to view all democratic nations under the example of the American people.

However, like the ending of the frontier, globalization has created a new social, political and economic reality for the United States. When the frontier closed and industrialization accelerated, great wealth amassed at the top, straining the social fabric and creating political and economic upheaval. But as manifest destiny was projected out into the world, the United States found itself the dominate world power. The end of the Cold War validated American exceptionalism. But as globalization accelerates into the twenty first century, wealth is becoming much more diffused around the globe. For example, Microsoft sees sub-Saharan Africa, among the poorest places on earth, as one of the last great computing frontiers. It wants to make its Windows software a fixture there. To that end, it has established a presence in thirteen countries, donated Windows for thousands of school computers, and funded programs for entrepreneurs and the young. The company describes its efforts in Africa as a way to bridge the "digital divide"—the gap between computer use in rich and poor countries. Microsoft estimates that in the nearly fifty countries of sub-Saharan Africa, roughly 750 million people have access to about 10 million computers. In many of those countries, less than one percent of the population uses the Internet at all. This will change over time as private and public entities invest heavily in community projects across the continent.

In short, economic growth is not the sole province of the developed economies of the world, but increasingly will advance in the developing economies as well. Much of this is growth will create new wealth, meaning that it should not be at the expense of the developed world. But as the U.S. borrows to consume the world's products, it also exports its national wealth. This redistribution of wealth is creating a more equalitarian world. Ending world poverty can actually be envisioned as a reality. Ending the tyranny of poverty and despotism was the U.S. justification for the Cold War. The United Nations expects that by the end of the century the average person in the world will be some 1,400 percent richer. The world's food production will double by 2080 and by 2100 the number of malnourished people in the world will drop by 100 million. If enabling the developing world to become wealthy is such a laudable goal, why are Americans so afraid?

Nearly a decade after September 11th, the earnest vows made by many Americans during the emotional aftermath to live more meaningful, purpose-driven lives has all but been forgotten. What followed was a consumption binge. The run up to the financial panic was a testament to the false hope of perpetual affluence, or perhaps more likely, profound hopelessness. What remains after the crash is an unmitigated fear of the world; a world where being an "American" carries less weight, even as the world becomes more westernized. At the end of the first decade of twenty first century, Americans feel like strangers in the world; a world that many believed was their birthright to dominate. But globalization is unleashing the forces of a revolution, and having been on top for so long, or at least having the illusion of being on top, Americans are afraid of losing their birthright. It was this fear that was stoked and exploited during the 2008 presidential campaign and which remains like a poison in the system.

The culture itself is submerged in the muck of nostalgia—a particular character flaw of aging Baby Boomers made worse by the instant access to America's cultural archives via the Web. President Obama was directly attacked for his heritage and multicultural background. He was smeared mercilessly as a foreigner, even as a member of a terrorist sleeper cell. He was called a Nazi and portrayed as Hitler. As a new globalizing era emerges rapidly leaders that espouse the type of internationalization that will be indispensable for America's success will no doubt be attacked as selling out America and branded as traitors.

At present, there is no systematic political program that promotes both diversity and the free exchange of information and voluntary cooperation—what might be called a politics of innovation. Traditionally, U.S. politics are based either on identity or property. Identity politics imbeds a socio-political status upon the individual, which is usually based on race, sex, gender or some other immutable or socially constructed characteristic defined in relation to outsider or minority status. Such a political agenda is based on securing an entitlement based on the imbedded status and ensuring that the entitlement is not diluted in the competition for resources. Identity politics tends to use the language of equality and social justice and individuals will often disregard their best advantage in favor of some vague sense of solidarity or pride. However, a plank of an innovation platform that embraces diversity would state that race, gender and other characteristics are obstacles because the politics of entitlement and victimization are anathema to innovation.

The politics of property is also based on a type of entitlement in the context or market power and concentrated wealth and resources. Like the advocates of identity politics that use the language of "justice" to justify the vice of envy, property advocates use the language of "freedom" to justify the vice of greed. The politics of property are dominated by capital and promote the deregulation and privatization of public resources as a way of tapping new pools of wealth. In contrast, an innovation politics would advocate the decentralized allocation of public resources based on invention, information exchange and collaborative social structures that reward outcomes based on both profit and social utility.

As such, an innovation politics would be ironically and inevitably vulnerable to the perceived undemocratic impulses of innovation, meritocracy and elitism. Indeed, value added knowledge workers do comprise an elite cadre of the workforce and policies that foster even greater innovation and productivity will in the short run inure to the benefit of an educated and skilled minority. Thus, policies that promote innovation could very well be viewed as a pretext for greater inequality. On the other hand, policies that codify Supreme Court precedents that make it easier to challenge patents, promoting the decentralization and wide diffusion of intellectual property, broadly defined, potent antitrust enforcement and regulation of the telecommunications industry to ensure open access could be viewed a pretext for wealth redistribution.

While defining and articulating a viable politics of innovation remains a fertile area for future dialogue and engagement, suffice to say, at a minimum a political agenda promoting an "innovation ethic" would include supporting present and future "knowledge workers" with the proper incentives to ensure lifelong learning, mobility and advancement. For the many other workers that are needed to support systemic innovation, reliable access to health care and wage insurance are important policy considerations. An education system that meets the needs of the twenty first century is also imperative.

Marc Andreessen, co-founder of Netscape and later a venture capital firm, has made a persuasive case that software powered Internet firms are building "real, high-growth, high-market, highly defensible businesses," the intrinsic value of which are being overlooked. The U.S. is "in the middle of a dramatic and broad technological shift in which software companies are poised to take over wide swaths of the economy." Much of the discussion and analysis here has been about the perils of this transformation. "There are challenges," Mr. Andreessen notes, as "many people in the U.S. and the world lack the education and skills required to participate in the great new companies coming out of the software revolution."

Recent research indicates that an individual's genetic makeup accounts for about half of the difference in IQ between any two people in a developed society, meaning that education has the potential to make a substantial difference in the ability of individuals to compete despite their background and circumstances. The U.S. has more than doubled speeding in real dollars on K through 12 education since 1970. The number of teachers has increased by more than a third and salaries and benefits have increased. Yet fewer than 40 percent of the students that graduate from high school are ready for college. Unless an innovation strategy is applied to the educational system, the U.S. will end up as a country with a small, educated upper class and a vast, uneducated underclass which will require ever more public resources to maintain order. An innovation agenda for education would promote at least two policies: holding principals and teachers accountable for measurable student performance outcomes and more school choice, which would include privately operated and publicly funded charter schools that are nonunion.

Ultimately, however, success in the knowledge-intensive global economy will depend on Americans' willingness to confront their fears and to adapt to a changing world order; to defer gratification, perhaps for a generation, maybe more; to relinquish their sense of entitlement; to accept diversity; to consume less, including health care; to accept the economic burdens of cleaner energy stoically and with dignity; to invest in future generations; and to let go of the dogma of American exceptionalism—that is, the belief that Americans are superior to the rest of the world by virtue of some biblical decree, the manifestation of the ultimate entitlement mentality. Both the politics of identity and property—envy and greed—feed this sense of entitlement and have appropriated the words "innovation," "freedom" and "equality" to continue the zero-sum struggle over resources. Both engage in the type of triangulation and disassembly that permits blue collar workers to give up their jobs and accept constant economic security so long as they are convinced that "minorities" are thrown off the gravy train or to accept a "national health care reform" that is a giveaway to the pharmaceutical, health insurance and medical device industries.

Letting go of the entitlement mentality will be difficult, and no doubt letting go to redefine the founding mythology of the "pursuit of happiness" will be deeply disturbing. Moreover, as a practical matter the transformation from an economy based primarily on consumption to one geared more toward production will be enormously disruptive. Already as of 2010 more Americans are unemployed in absolute numbers than at the peak of the Great Depression in 1933. The wealth and income gaps in real terms are also at 1933 levels. As the economy transforms, the long-term unemployed—greater than 99-weeks—will likely never work again during their lifetimes. In 1996 *The New York Times* published a series of articles on the corporate downsizing and summarized research showing that long-term unemployment doesn't just affect the jobless in the short term but also has deep implications for the lifelong health and well-being of long term unemployed individuals, as well as their children and families. One study by sociologist Kate Strully, found that people who lose their jobs were 83 percent more likely to develop stress-induced conditions, such as diabetes, arthritis and depression. Till von Wachter, an economist at Columbia University, looked at mortality and income records of workers in Pennsylvania during the recession of the early 1980s. Wachter found that death rates increased substantially for the unemployed in the year that they lose their jobs. Mortality rates remained significantly higher for those who lost their jobs than for comparable workers who didn't. Some research suggests that the life expectancy of the unemployed is lowered by as much as a year to a year-and-a-half.

For many Americans it will feel like each day is a struggle for survival, a joyless, lost world without direction but as the developing economies grow their own middle class consumers and implement social welfare programs, a less disruptive transformation is feasible. As their middle classes expand and they spend more on social programs, they will increase consumption exponentially. When that happens, America's competitive advantage will slowing trend back to production and exporting. But to compete with low wage labor, U.S. workers must be prepared to perform at the high end of the value chain. Unless high-end goods can be exported, unemployment will remain high and wages low. The wealth and income gaps will also grow worse and more perilous. It is clear therefore that at least two things are certain: the wellbeing of each American is co-dependent on the wellbeing of much of the rest of the world and America's standard of living will rise or fall on the skills and ingenuity of its workforce and the quality of its leadership.

Molly Funia, a specialist in grief and mourning has observed that to be joyful in such a fearful world is a "brave and reckless act." It is likely that America is on the verge of developing new tools that will affect all aspects of life but it may take a generation before a better balance between consumption and production can be achieved. Economic growth and national purpose are likely not over but the country is hurtling full speed into unchartered territory. As America lurches forward into the second decade of the twenty first century a consensus appears out of sight. It takes courage in a cynical world to be "happily surprised," Ms. Funia adds.

Epilogue to Revised Edition

In this second edition, I have revised, reordered and distilled primarily as a result of the insightful and dynamic discussions I have had with students. *Perils of Prosperity* was never meant to be a text book; rather its purpose was to provide a framework for dialogue and a context for class assignments. As my thinking has evolved thus warranting a revision, the progress of events since the book's publication in early 2009 has provided evidence of my basic hypothesis: that economic and social development in the U.S. has reached an existential moment, a tipping point, which requires a breakthrough not only in technical expertise but ethical leadership on all levels.

New and complex problems have emerged with the end of the Cold War more often than not related to the drive toward global integration on the one hand and the assertion of national identify on the other.

As the economies of the world grow more interdependent, global corporations have basically shed their national identities. U.S. multinational firms created 2.4 million jobs abroad in the last decade of the twentieth century and by 2010 over 10 million people worked for a U.S. company outside the United States. Reciprocally, millions of Americans worked for foreign firms in the U.S. and more are expected to do so. The U.S., the world's biggest economy is the top recipient of foreign investment, more than double the foreign investment in the second biggest economy, China. It is inevitable that in both East and West the commingling of cultures, perspectives, talents and information will create new thinking about social structures governance models.

Moreover, in 2010 the demographic composition of California became "majority-minority," and as California goes the rest of the country follows. While many immigrants are qualified for low skilled, lower paying jobs today, their children will presumably be moving up the economic ladder in the future. In the meantime, major U.S. corporations are clamoring for an increase in the visa quota to import individuals with special skills. It is clear that the workplace will become more diverse.

While managing this multicultural diversity poses real challenges, scientific advancement has challenged long established prejudices about race, national origin and sex. In deciphering human DNA, researchers have uncovered a rich diversity of early humans and have traced their evolution to a single dominant species, which is comprised of individuals that share 99.8 percent of the same genetic ingredients regardless their race or national origin. In short, humans are basically the same. It is inevitable that the commingling of cultures, perspectives, talents and information will create new thinking about social structures governance models.

Moreover, the view that markets share the same characteristics as biological organisms and therefore are predetermined and immutable is belied by genetic engineering. Markets were not created by natural law. Markets are social networks created and maintained by human agency. They are supported by ideologies, which are also the result of choice. National ideologies in China and throughout Asia and the Middle East have been laid bare by globalization and the spread of ideas. Rigid ideologies that support inherited power structures and authoritarian political regimes are now seen for what they are—social inventions that are malleable and subject to change as conditions warrant. Today, no social structure or political system is immutable; all are subject to experimentation and revision.

Conflicts over fundamental governing principles remain unresolved in the U.S. The general post war consensus about the role of government has broken down and for many the divided government established by the Founders has become a suicide pact. Intransience over something as fundamental as raising the debt ceiling in 2011 risked the default of U.S. sovereign debt exacerbating systemic economic problems. Disagreement over basic principles, such as the role of government in a liberal democracy, should serve the purpose of achieving a governing consensus not precipitating a crisis. Indeed, one of the central governing features of the U.S. Constitution is to propel compromise through divided government. But for many along the U.S. political spectrum, constitutional conflict is fast approaching the point of diminishing returns as the Chinese model of a "harmonious society" gains adherents among global corporate elites even as many Chinese ridicule the term as code for political oppression. Indeed, while Milton Friedman preferred democratic social and political systems, and was a strong advocate of them, he did not hesitate to make the point that markets and authoritarian regimes were not incompatible. Ordered liberty was a choice among other choices made in 1783. Certainly the great monopolists of the Gilded Age understood that their interests could be well served with authoritarian government, if for no other reason than the efficiency of ordered graft. During his trip to China, Robert Herbold the retired chief operating officer of Microsoft Corporation was greatly impressed with the Chinese leadership's ability to achieve consensus over competing national policies. To a person, they all seemed to be working from the same plan he observed. Upon his return to the U.S. he wondered: "Which is the developing country and which is the developed country?"

In any event, it is quite clear that the cultural, economic and financial interconnectedness of the world are causing great apprehension and anxiety in the U.S. The survival instinct in an industrial zero sum economy is to consolidate corporate and political power, as was the case when New Deal legislation promoted industrial and labor monopolies and centralized regulatory power to deal with economic depression. That same instinct propelled the Recovery Act of 2009. Clearly it would be counterintuitive to decentralize power during a time of increasing complexity, particularly since technology has created ever more power to direct human knowledge and exploit natural resources and the laws of nature—But as risk increases, human factors such as greed, arrogance, hoarding, laziness and indifference increase the likelihood of catastrophe.

As knowledge is the critical element of problem solving its diffusion is a priority. But bureaucracies tend to impair communications because of the information has to pass through layers. Days before the massive storm hit the city of New Orleans in 2006 government meteorologists informed the Department of Homeland Security that Hurricane Katrina was going to be "the big one." Six months after the disaster, Congressional and White House inquiries into the government's response faulted every level of response, especially the Federal Emergency Management Agency (FEMA). Some of what the Congressional report found: during preparations, FEMA denied local official's request for rubber rafts; turned away trucks filled with water and refused to accept generators; turned away food delivered to the city by the Red Cross; left 20,000 trailers sitting in Atlanta; and told first responders in neighboring states to wait until they received formal orders to dispatch.

Key decision makers remained in Washington, far removed from eyewitness accounts. When the storm hit, critical information was slow to reach these decision makers. The single most important piece of information—that the levees had been breached—took 24-hours to reach the White House. As the storm took hold, communications between agencies was impaired. Because of red tape, bottlenecks were not promptly dealt with. Homeland Security officials were slow to resolve conflicts between jurisdictions.

How could so many people exercise such poor judgment? Some blamed racism or other conspiracies. But the incompetent response presents familiar problems faced by most big bureaucratic organizations: lack of responsibility, fear of making a decision, hoarding of information between departments and jurisdictional jealousy. Since bureaucratic organizations tend to reward managers by allowing them to easily take credit for organizational success but to just as easily blame others when things go badly, there's no incentive to change.

The sheer amount of information that is available has also created dilemmas. Keeping track of the amount of information to predict certain risks has led to information overload and has weakened the role of public watchdogs so that big corporations and government institutions basically regulate themselves. Therefore, it can be argued that high technology and high risk require a higher level of ethical reasoning and decision making than in the past.

The British Petroleum Gulf of Mexico explosion is an illustration of a corporation pushing the envelope of risk taking within the context of profit maximization and executive compensation discontented from ethical considerations. Consumers demand cheap gas and shareholders demand profit. The company's executives apparently pushed the boundaries of human intelligence and technology to meet these demands, thus actually pushing up the level of risk. The ensuing catastrophe may be a preview of the unfolding global disaster of climate change, as consumers craving cheap prices, shareholders craving returns, and executives craving bonuses conspire to deplete global resources and wreak political havoc.

The impulse to confront insecurity and uncertainly is to get big, to control as much as possible. But bureaucracies are ill suited to deal with the sheer volume and complexity of information; they are ill suited to innovate. Globalization and technological advancement have already unleashed a decentralizing counterforce. Therefore the need to engage the full potential of the world's talent through flexible, decentralized networks rather than to harmonize social structures from the top down is the greater moral imperative.

Sources

Books

1. Allen, F. *The Big Change* (Harper & Row, 1952).
2. Ambrose, S. & Brinkley, D. *Rise to Globalism* (8th ed.)(Penguin Books, 1997).
3. Anderson, F. & Clayton, A. *The Dominion of War* (Viking, 2005).
4. Beard, C. *An Economic Interpretation of the Constitution of the United States* (The Free Press, 1946).
5. Bobbitt, P. *The Shield of Achilles: War, Peace and the Course of History* (Alfred A. Knopf, 2002).
6. Bookchin, M. *Our Synthetic Environment* (Harper & Row, 1962).
7. Bloom, A. *The Closing of the American Mind* (Simon & Schuster, 1987).
8. Boorstin, D. *The Americans: The Democratic Experience* (Random House, 1973).
9. Bremmer, I. *The End of the Free Market* (Portfolio, 2010).
10. Brill, S. *Class Warfare* (Simon & Schuster, 2011).
11. Chang, L. *Factory Girls* (Spiegal & Grace, 2008).
12. Chua, A. *Day of Empire* (Anchor Books, 2007).
13. Commager, H. *The American Mind* (Yale University Press, 1950).
14. Cox, M. & Alm, R. *Myths of Rich and Poor* (Basic Books, 1999).

15. DeTocqueville, *Democracy in America* (ed. R. Heffner, Penguin Books, 1956).
16. Diamond, J. *Collapse* (Penguin Books, 2005).
17. Easterly, W. *The Elusive Quest for Growth* (MIT Press, 2001).
18. Eidsome, J. *Christianity and the Constitution* (Baker Books, 1987).
19. Eisler, R. *The Real Wealth of Nations* (Berrett-Koehler, 2007).
20. Epstein, R. *How Progressives Rewrote the Constitution* (Cato Institute, 2006).
21. Epstein, R. *Forbidden Grounds* (Harvard Univ. Press, 1992).
22. Fannin, R. *Silicon Dragon* (McGraw Hill, 2008).
23. *Federalist Papers* (Signet Books, 1961).
24. Ferguson, N. *Civilization* (Penguin Group, 2011).
25. Ferris, T. *The Science of Liberty* (HarperCollins, 2010).
26. Florida, R. *The Rise of the Creative Class* (Basic Books, 2002).
27. Foner, E. *Reconstruction* (Harper & Row, 1988).
28. Fraser, J. *White Collar Sweatshop* (W.W. Norton Co., 2001).
29. Friedman, M. *Capitalism & Freedom* (University of Chicago Press, 1962).
30. Friedman, L. *A History of American Law* (Simon & Schuster, 1973).
31. Galbraith, J.K. *The Great Crash 1929* (Houghton & Co. 1954).
32. Galbraith, J.K. *The Affluent Society* (Houghton & Co. 1958).
33. Galbraith, J.K. *The New Industrial State* (Houghton & Co. 1967).
34. Gillman, H. *The Constitution Besieged* (Duke University Press, 2005).
35. Goldstein, P. *Intellectual Property* (Penguin Group, 2007).
36. Hammer, M. & Champy, J. *Reengineering the Corporation* Harper Collins, 1993).
37. Haradon, A. *How Breakthroughs Happen* (Harvard University Business School Press, 2003).
38. Hartman, T. *Unequal Protection* (Berrett-Koehler, 2010).
39. Hayek, F.A. *The Road to Serfdom* (University of Chicago Press, 1944).
40. Hayek, F.A. *Constitution of Liberty* (University of Chicago Press, 1960).

41. Hayek, F.A. *The Fatal Deceit* (University of Chicago Press, 1988).
42. Hobsbaum, E. *The Age of Capital* (Vintage Books, 1975).
43. Hobsbaum, E. *The Age of Empire* (Vintage Books, 1987).
44. Hobsbaum, E. *The Age of Extremes* (Vintage Books, 1994).
45. Hobsbaum, E. *On Empire* (Vintage Books, 2007).
46. Hofstadter, R. *The Age of Reform* (Vintage Books, 1955).
47. Hofstadter, R. *The Paranoid Style in American Politics* (Vintage Books, 1952).
48. Hofstadter, R. *The American Political Tradition* (Alfred A. Knopf, 1948).
49. Hofstadter, R. *Social Darwinism in American Thought* (Beacon Press, 1944).
50. Hofstadter, R. *Anti-Intellectualism in American Life* (Vintage Books, 1962).
51. Holmes, O.W. *The Common Law* (Little, Brown & Co., 1923).
52. Homer-Dixon, T. *The Ingenuity Gap* (Vintage Books, 2000).
53. Horsman, R. *Race and Manifest Destiny* (Harvard University Press, 1981).
54. Huntington, S. *Who Are We?* (Simon & Schuster, 2004).
55. Innes, S. *Creating the Commonwealth* (W.W. Norton Co., 1995).
56. Jaffer, J. & Lerner J. *Innovation and its Discontents* (Princeton University Press, 2004).
57. Jay, A. *Corporation Man* (Random House, 1971).
58. Kennedy, P. *The Rise and Fall of the Great Powers* Random House, 1987).
59. Kessner, *Capital City* (Simon & Schuster, 2003).
60. Kolko, G. *The Triumph of Conservatism* (The Free Press, 1963).
61. Kolko, J. *Restructuring the World Economy* (Pantheon Books, 1988).
62. Korten, D. *When Corporations Rule the World* (Kumarian Press, 1995).
63. LeBon, G. *The Crowd* (Viking Press, 1960).
64. Landers, D. *The Wealth and Poverty of Nations* (W.W. Norton & Co., 1999).
65. Leisinger, K. & Schmitt, K. *Corporate Ethics in the Time of Globalization* (Vishva Lekha, 2003).
66. Lessig, L. *The Future of Ideas* (Vintage Books, 2001).

67. Lindsey, B. *The Age of Abundance* (Vintage Books, 2007).
68. Little, D. *Religion, Order and Law* (Harper & Row, 1969).
69. Lippman, W. *Drift and Mastery* (University of Wisconsin Press, 1985).
70. Lippman, W. *The Good Society* (Transaction Publishers, 2005).
71. Locke, J. *The Second Treatise on Government* (Liberal Arts Press, 1952).
72. Luttwak, E. *Turbo Capitalism* (Harper Collins, 1999).
73. Malthus, T. *An Essay on the Principle on Population* (W.W. Norton & Co., 1976).
74. Mann, J. *The China Fantasy* (Penguin Books, 2007).
75. Marx, K. *Das Kapital* (Gateway Publishers, 1965).
76. McGary, H. & Lawson, B. *Between Slavery and Freedom* (Indiana University Press, 1992).
77. McDonald, F. *Novus Ordo Seclorum* (University Press of Kansas, 1985).
78. Mills, C.W. *White Collar* (Oxford University Press, 1951).
79. Moe, T. *Special Interest* (Brookings, 2011).
80. Murray, C. *Real Education* (Crown Forum, 2008).
81. Neff, W. *Work and Human Behavior* (Aldine Publishing Co., 1968).
82. Nelson, W. *The Fourteenth Amendment* (Harvard University Press, 1988).
83. Patterson, J. *Restless Giant* (Oxford University Press, 2005).
84. Peden, J. & Glahe, F. (eds.) *The American Family and the State* (Pacific Research Institute, 1986).
85. Peters, T. & Waterman, R. *In Search for Excellence* (Warner Books, 1982).
86. Perelman, M. *Steal This Idea* (Saint Martin's Press, 2002).
87. Petzinger, T. *The New Pioneers* (Simon & Schuster, 1999).
88. Pink, D. *Free Agent Nation* (Warner Books, 2001).
89. Posner, R. *The Economics of Justice* (Harvard University Press, 1981).
90. Rand, A. *Capitalism* (Signet Books, 1966).
91. Reich, R. *The Work of Nations* (Vintage Books, 1991).
92. Rifkin, J. *The End of Work* (Putnam Books, 1995).
93. Sanders, C. *Empowerment Ethics for a Liberated People* (Fortress Press, 1995).

94. Schlesinger, A., Jr. *The Coming of the New Deal* (Houghton Mifflin Co. 1959).
95. Schlesinger, A., Jr. *The Disuniting of America* (W.W. Norton & Co., 1998).
96. Sennet, R. *The Corrosion of Character* (W.W. Norton & Co. 1998).
97. Sennet, R. *The Culture of the New Capitalism* (W.W. Norton & Co. 1998).
98. Smith, A. *The Wealth of Nations* (ed. A. Skinner, Penguin Books, 1976).
99. Smith, P. *The Rise of Industrial America* (McGraw-Hill, 1984).
100. Sowell, T. *Ethnic America* (Basic Books, 1989).
101. Stephanson, A. *Manifest Destiny* (Hill & Wang, 1995).
102. Stewart, T. *Intellectual Capital* (Doubleday, 1997).
103. Stewart, M. *The Management Myth* (W.W. Norton & Co., 2009).
104. The *Downsizing of America* (N.Y. Times Books, 1996).
105. Thurow, L. *The Future of Capitalism* (William Morrow & Co., 1996).
106. Trachtenburg, A. *The Incorporation of America* (Hill & Wang, 1982).
107. Turner, F. *The Frontier in American History* (University of Arizona Press, 1986).
108. Whyte, W. *The Organization Man* (University of Pennsylvania Press, 1956).
109. Wilcox, R. *Whatever Happened to Thrift?* (Yale University Press, 2008).
110. Wilson, J. *When Work Disappears* (Vintage Books, 1996).
111. Woodward, C. *The Strange Career of Jim Crow* (Oxford University Press, 1955).
112. Zakaria, F. *The Post-American World* (W.W. Norton & Co., 2008).

Articles

1. Andreeseen, M. "Why Software is Eating the World," Wall Street Journal (Aug. 20, 2011).
2. Bailey, R. "The Pursuit of Happiness," *Reason* (December, 2000).

3. Ball, Jeffrey, "Green Goal of Carbon Neutrality Hits Limit," *Wall Street Journal* (December 30, 2008).
4. Batson, A. & Dean, J. "China's Economic Gains Give Way to Hazy Future," *Wall Street Journal* (August 25, 2008).
5. Beinart, P. "Patriot Games," *Time* (July 7, 2008).
6. Ben-Atar, D. "A U.S. Technology Double Standard?" *The Globalist* (October 20, 2004).
7. Buruma, I. "Victim or Victor? China's Olympic Odyssey," *Wall Street Journal* (June 7-8, 2008).
8. Carfagna, A. & Adams, J. "Students in a World of Trouble," *The Star Ledger* (June 13, 2006).
9. Carr, N. "Tracking is an Assault on Liberty, with Real Dangers," *Wall Street Journal* (Aug. 6, 2010).
10. Dougherty, C. "High-Degree Professionals Show Power," *Wall Street Journal* (September 10, 2008).
11. Eizenstat, S. & Mailbach, M. "Protect Our Heritage," *Wall Street Journal* (March 30, 2006).
12. Golub, H. "We Are the World," *Wall Street Journal* (January 7, 2004).
13. Hahn, R. & Passell, P. "Microsoft: Preditor or Prey?," *The Berkeley Electronic Press* (April, 2008).
14. Henkel, J. & Reitzig, M. "Patent Sharks," *Harvard Business Review* (June, 2008).
15. Hitt, G. "Foreign Investment in U.S. Rises, Current-Account Deficit Widens," *Wall Street Journal* (March 15, 2006).
16. Holtz, R. "The Really Smart phone," *Wall Street Journal* (April 23, 2011).
17. Ip, G. "Wages Fail to keep Pace with Productivity Increases," *Wall Street Journal* (March 27, 2006).
18. Karmin, C. "Foreigners Seem To Be Souring On U.S. Assets," *Wall Street Journal* (July 26, 2004).
19. Letzing, J. "Yahoo Says it Followed Chinese Laws in Handing Over Dissidents' Information," *Wall Street Journal* (Sept. 28, 2007).
20. Lemonick, M. "How We Grew So Big," *Time* (June 7, 2004).
21. Jenkins, H. "Google and the Search for the Future," *Wall Street Journal* (Aug. 14, 2010).

22. Kucera, D. & Nazareth, R. "Patents Part of Kodak's Big Picture," *Bloomberg News* (August 21, 2011).
23. Kumar, v. & Rhodes, C. "Google Wants Its Own Fast Track," *Wall Street Journal* (December 15, 2008).
24. Malone, M. "Taking On the World," *Wall Street Journal* (April 5, 2008).
25. Meckler, Laura, "Poll Shows Obama Gains Support," *Wall Street Journal* (December 5, 2008).
26. Mitchell, J. & Boles, C. "Auto Chiefs Willing to Accept Oversight Board as Condition for Aid," *Wall Street Journal* (December 4, 2008).
27. *National Alliance of Business*, "Globalization: Friend or Foe?" (June 2007).
28. Perry, J. "Nobel Laureates Say Globalization's Winners Should Aid Poor," *Wall Street Journal* (August 1, 2008).
29. Quittner, J. "Who Will Rule the Internet," *Time* (June 16, 2008).
30. Ridley, M. "A Truce in the War Over Smarts and Genes," *Wall Street Journal* (Aug. 20, 2011).
31. Rosen, J. "Google's gatekeepers," *New York Times* (Nov. 30, 2008).
32. Rubin, P. "Get Ready for the New New Deal," *Wall Street Journal* (October 21, 2008).
33. Salerno, Steve. "Happy Talk," *Wall Street Journal* (October 3, 2008).
34. Solomon, D. "Seeking to Soften the Blows of Globalization," *Wall Street Journal* (June 26, 2007).
35. Surowiecki, J. "Exporting I.P.," *The New Yorker* (May 14, 2007).
36. *The Economist*, "Who's Afraid of Google?" (August, 2007).
37. Vascellaro, J. & Morrison, S. "Google Gears for Tougher Times," *Wall Street Journal* (December 4, 2008).
38. Vascellaro, J. "Brin Drove Google to Pull Back in China," *Wall Street Journal* (March 24, 2010).
39. Von Drehle, D. "A New Line in the Sand," *Time* (June 30, 2008).
40. Walker, M. "Just How Good Is Globalization?" *Wall Street Journal* (January 25, 2007).
41. Wessel, D. "Looking Out for Globalization's Tweeners," *Wall Street Journal* (July 28, 2005).

42. Wessel, D. "Globalization Study Moves Past Rhetoric," *Wall Street Journal* (July 26, 2008).

Other

1. The Report of the Task Force on the Future of American Innovation (2005).
2. Economic Mobility Project (2004).
3. The Financial Services Forum, "Succeeding in the Global Economy," (2007).
4. Public Policy for a Knowledge Economy, speech delivered by Joseph E. Stiglitz (1999).
5. *Centesimus Annus*, Encyclical Letter by John Paul II (1998).
6. World Economic Forum Competitiveness Report (2008-2009).

Index

Symbols

401 (k) accounts 52

A

Actra Corp. 51
Adobe 232
Affirmative Action 255, 289, 291, 293-295, 298
Afghanistan 47
Africa xii, xxx, 6, 24, 40, 306
African Americans 18, 281, 284, 289-96
Agency model 110-11
Alexy, Oliver 62
Alliance for Excellent Education 21
America's Promise Alliance 18
American Dream 44
American families 8-9, 11, 187
American Heart Association 38
American International Group (AIG) 256
American Solar Energy Society 211
American work ethic 39, 74

Aon Consulting 106
Apache 61
Apple, Inc. 147
Arendt, Hannah 18
Asia xii, 6, 9, 14, 24, 40-1, 179, 205, 314
Association of American Publishers 169
AT&T 50, 64, 145, 196, 242-3
Authors Guild 169
Autocratic governments 10
Autonomy xix-xxii, xxx, xxxii, 4, 14, 17, 71, 77-9, 81-3, 91-3, 101-3, 111-13, 117-19, 132, 238, 251

B

Baby boomers 23, 32, 39, 307
Ballmer, Steve 148
Bankruptcy 99, 203, 206, 249-50, 273, 280, 304
BEA Associates 146
Bell Labs 77
Berle, Adolph 188
Berlin Wall 242
BlackBerry 231

BMW 58-9
Bobbitt, Phillip 240
Bonds xiii, xv, 2, 7, 22, 50, 99, 182, 190, 203, 302
Bonito Boats, Inc. v. Thunder Craft Boats, Inc. 198
Book of Genesis xxviii, 149
Bork, Robert 74
Borrowing xiii, 31, 47, 56, 249
Bristol-Meyers Squibb 27
Budget deficit 12, 50, 217, 223-4, 230, 251
Built to Last xxxi, 257, 259
Bureaucracy 132, 148, 225, 291

C

Calhoun, John C. 119
Cap-and-trade 83, 248-9
Capital City 134, 321
Capital investments xiv, xxxi, 11, 31, 41, 48-9, 53-4, 56, 65, 141, 160, 180
Capitalism xxix, xxxi, 4, 39, 76, 95, 98, 108, 128, 133, 152, 156-7, 239-41, 256, 295-6, 322-3
Carbon dioxide 213
Carbon value tax 213
Carnegie Mellon University 151
Cato Institute 320
Cell phone 55, 64-5, 179, 271
Center on Budget and Policy Priorities 126
Centers for Disease Control 38, 198
CEO Project 16
Chandler, Alfred 40
Child labor xxx

China xii-xv, xvii-xix, xxvi, xxix-xxx, 27-9, 32-3, 40, 47-8, 58-9, 126-7, 138-40, 155-7, 177-9, 205-6, 239-41, 269-71
Cigarette smoking 40
Cincinnati Bell Foundry v. Dodds 89
Civil War 2, 82-5, 90, 149, 217, 282, 285-6, 295
Clean Air Act 259
Clean Tech Sector 211
Cleveland, Grover 253
Clinton, Bill 243, 317
Cold War xv, xxix, 6, 36, 50, 239, 258, 276, 306, 313
Collapse xv, xxxvi-1, 6, 30, 34, 43, 46, 100, 187, 189, 229, 231, 242, 320
College education 126, 215
Commanger, Henry 121
Commerce Clause 200
Communications technology xxviii, 5, 53-4, 69
Communism 6, 30, 37, 138, 205, 282
Compensation xvii, xxxv, 9, 12-13, 17, 60, 100, 106, 114, 169, 228, 252, 254, 266, 272, 317
CompuServe 50
Computers 44, 49, 51, 54, 59, 68, 202, 212, 219, 256, 304, 306
Conflicts of interest 35, 283, 303
Congressional Budget Office 339
Congressional Research service 12
Consumption xii, xiv, xviii, xxxiv, 17, 34-9, 41, 44-8, 50, 62,

68-9, 187-90, 193-4, 215-16, 296, 310-11
Contingent work 228
Coppage v. Kansas 87
Copyright Act 163-4, 167, 170, 174
Core values xxx, 17, 98, 117, 259, 281, 305
Cornell University 36, 70
Corporations xii-xiii, xviii-xx, xxxi-xxxii, 25, 79, 129-32, 140-4, 193-4, 207, 221-2, 225-6, 247-52, 254-6, 258, 265-6, 272-3
Council on Foreign Relations 7, 277
Creative destruction 30, 76
Credit card debt 33
Cuno Engineering v. Automatic Devices 230

D

Darcy v. Allen 150
Darwin, Charles 36, 122
Declaration of Independence 153, 283
Deng Xiaoping 240
Department of Homeland Security 5, 316
Depression xxxi, 1, 43, 134-5, 181, 187, 190, 203, 207, 279, 286, 301, 310, 315
Deregulation 50, 99, 101, 128, 177, 239-43, 245, 258, 262, 291, 308
DeTocqueville, Alexis 117, 169
Diamond, Jared 82

Digital Millennium Copyright Act (DMCA) 167-8, 170
Digital Style Corp. 51
Dimension X. Inc. 87
Dot-Com Bubble 56, 108
Dow Chemical 212
Dred Scott v. Sanford 85
Drift or Mastery 1, 3, 5, 7, 9, 11, 13, 15, 17, 19, 21, 23, 25, 27, 29, 47-8
Drucker, Peter 97, 140, 164, 168
DuPont 196, 212

E

Earning potential 68
Easterly, William 209
EBay v. MercExchange 232
Economic Policy Institute 17
Eldred case 165
Electronic Data Systems 29
Employee commitment 107
Employee Free Choice Act 185-6
Employment Act 34
Empowerment Ethics for a Liberated People 296, 322
Engineers xxvi, xxx, 32-3, 59, 122, 128, 144-7, 178-9, 211, 225-6, 268
English common law 149, 161, 223
Entrepreneurship 24, 96-7, 181, 240
Ethics xvi, xxxi, xxxv, 115-16, 201, 237, 249, 251, 253, 255, 265, 267, 269, 273, 296, 321-2
Eugenics 86-7, 93
Euro Zone 213

Europe xxxi, 1, 14, 27, 34, 58, 80, 82, 85, 93, 115, 131, 187, 191, 206, 220
European Union 212, 219, 239
Exports 6, 40, 50, 139, 188, 204-7, 280, 306

F

Facebook 23, 221-2
Factory Girls 206, 319
Factory system 80-2
Farmer, John, Jr. 74
Federal Communications Commission (FCC) 64
Federal Reserve Bank 31, 34, 92, 182, 240
Financial Services Forum 208, 326
Finland 127, 140
Flex-Time Act 185
Florida, Richard 154, 164, 177
Foreign bankers 304
Foreign companies 29, 48
Foreign investment xvi, 7, 304, 313, 324
Fortune 500 142
Fourteenth Amendment 84, 200, 322
France xxix, 46, 56
Free agent 87, 102, 107-9, 322
Free the Mouse 164
Free trade xxxii, 14-15, 25-6, 40, 53, 55, 59, 80, 97, 131, 163, 195, 204, 207-8, 242, 298
Friedman Thomas 133, 250

G

Galbraith, John Kenneth 71
Gandhi, Rajiv 277
Gates, Bill 88, 269
GDP 6, 9-10, 21, 45, 53, 74, 159, 183, 197, 204, 215
General Agreement on Tariffs and trade (GATT) 174
General Electric xxvi, 77, 212
General Motors (GM) 167, 220, 248, 258, 291
General Public License 59
Genetic engineering xix, 314
Geography and Trade 58
George, Henry 119, 125
Germany xxxiii, 21, 35, 46, 56, 62, 93, 140, 187, 202, 216
Global trade 7
Global water consumption 73
GNP 11, 34-5, 45, 50, 69, 90, 123, 127, 140, 193, 215, 254, 302
Goldilocks economy 53, 183
Goldman Sachs 37, 101
Google xxvi, 26, 59, 64-5, 113, 122, 144-5, 151-2, 155, 157, 167-9, 221-8, 232, 260, 268-73, 324-5
Google Book search 169
Gorbachev, Mikhail 275, 309
Gore, Al 74
Great Britain xxv, 3, 80
Great Depression 31, 79, 170, 217, 223, 226, 239, 243, 322, 339, 346
Green collar jobs 211
Greenspan, Alan 85, 88
Grisswold V. Connecticut 93-94

Gross Domestic Product 6
Gross National Happiness 45
Gross National Product xiii, 188
Grove, Andrew 86, 214
Grutter v. Bollinger 294
GTE 196

H

H-1B visas 108, 192
Harvard Business Review 103, 324
Harvard Business School 60
Hauser, Kurt 51
Hayek, Friedrich 60, 216
Health care insurance 125, 197, 199
Health care reform 32, 310
Hewitt Associates 117
Hidden paycheck 11
Hidden paycheck 47
Higher Education Research Institute 32
High-school dropouts 242
Hispanics 20
Hobsbawn, Eric 134
Holmes, Justice 122, 128
Home equity debt 41
Homer-Dixon, Thomas 44, 91, 145, 159, 195, 245
Hotmail 51
Household income 11, 21, 70
How Breakthroughs Happen 160, 320
Human capital management 144, 299
Huntington, Samuel 229

I

Iceland 127
IDEO 140
Illiteracy 21
Immigration 1, 8, 20, 108, 192, 285-6, 298, 302
In re Quinlan 94
Incarceration 18-19, 296
Income gains 8
Independent contracting 107, 128
India xii, xvii, xxx, 9, 21, 27-9, 32, 47, 50, 59, 66, 68, 107, 126-7, 177-8, 241
Indonesia 213
Industrial Revolution 4, 20, 28, 56, 68, 80, 103, 121, 280
Inflation 16, 43-4, 50, 55, 57, 67, 70, 82, 85, 89, 106, 137, 169, 218, 223, 276-7
Ingenuity Gap 8, 55, 109, 159, 321
Ingersoll-Rand v. Ciavatta 171
Innovation xviii, xxi-xxiii, xxvi-xxviii, xxxi-xxxiii, 13-14, 16-17, 109-12, 139-40, 146-8, 159-60, 178-9, 220-3, 225-8, 230-7, 261-2, 307-9
In-sourcing 225
Intel Corporation 7, 24, 126, 178
Intellectual property 26, 46, 49-50, 95-6, 100-3, 114-15, 125-6, 150, 173-8, 191-2, 197-9, 201-11, 218, 243, 254-5, 264-5
Intellectual Property xxvi, 10, 13-14, 59-60, 64-7, 78-9,

89-90, 114, 137-42, 155-6, 161-3, 165-75, 182, 207, 218-19, 228-9
Interconnected networks 30
Interest rates 31, 92, 181, 187, 205, 240, 302
International Alert 37
International Business Machines (IBM) 114
International Energy Agency 213
Internet xxxi-xxxiii, 7-8, 24-6, 50-2, 55-6, 59-60, 64, 66, 96, 144-5, 147, 169-70, 179, 221-3, 225-7, 268-70
Internet Explorer 51-2, 221, 235
Internet Service Providers 86
Interse Corp. 51
iPhone 31, 63
Iraq xxxi, 47
Irrational exuberance 52
Israel xxx, 127, 140, 160
Italy 46, 140

J

Jails 18-19
James, William 37
Japan xiii, 29, 34-5, 40, 46, 53, 127, 131, 140, 304
Java 51
Jefferson, Thomas 40, 169, 189, 197
Jobs, Steve 269
Johnson & Johnson 196
Johnson, Lyndon 324
Jump Point 55
Junk debt 99

K

KIVA Software Corp. 51
Knowledge assets 10, 13, 51, 79, 139, 150, 174
Knowledge commons 61-2, 67, 165, 168, 228
Knowledge economy iii, xxii, xxvii, xxxv, 12, 17, 20, 25, 53, 55-7, 102-3, 124, 156-7, 228-9, 231, 245
Knowledge intensive work 22, 146
Knowledge workers xxi-xxii, 7, 14, 17, 32, 60-1, 70, 77, 104-9, 111-14, 116-19, 121, 126-8, 146-7, 244-5, 308
Kolko, Joyce 90
Krugman, Paul 94, 292
KSR International v. Teleflex 269-70
Kyoto Protocol 213

L

Labor law 186
Labor theory of property 82, 85, 88, 149-50, 153, 189
Layoffs 65, 68, 143, 160, 162, 195, 218, 222, 224, 240, 324, 327
Leadership xxi, xxxiii-xxxv, 41, 43, 48, 99, 117, 147, 214-16, 247, 249-51, 253, 255-9, 261, 281, 303-5
Lee, Kai-Fu 187, 263
Lessig, Lawrence 113, 200-1
LG Electronics 65

Liberty iv, xxiii, xxviii, 83-5, 87-91, 94-5, 97, 134-5, 149-50, 153-7, 196-7, 199-200, 228-9, 281-2, 299, 320
Life expectancy 39, 197-8, 310
Lincoln, Abraham 118, 120, 250
Lindsey, Brink 48, 72, 74, 157
Linux 59, 61, 221
Lippmann, Walter 39, 313
Lobbying 64, 221, 227, 235, 258, 262
Lochner v. New York 85
Locke, John 185
Lucent Technologies 196

M

Machinery xxvii, 13, 34, 53-4, 57, 69, 79-80, 139, 159, 175
Madison, James 190
Malthus, Robert 92
Manifest Destiny 2, 306, 321, 323
Manufacturing xiv, 9-10, 15, 29, 33-5, 45, 81-2, 123-4, 126, 133-4, 137, 139, 162, 178-9, 183-5, 212
Master-servant relationship 110, 154
MBA graduates 32, 193
Means, Gardiner 283
Medicaid 197-8
Medicare xxix, 9, 14, 197-8, 201, 215
Mercer, LLC 12
Merrill Lynch 257, 262
Metro-Goldwyn-Mayer Studios v. Grokster 165

Microsoft Corp. 51
Middle class xii, xxx, 12, 17, 21, 23, 40, 43, 178, 187, 195, 218, 299, 310
Middle East 14, 24, 41, 205, 314
Minimum wage 101
Mitsubishi Bank 304
Moynihan, Daniel Patrick 317
MP3-player 212

N

NASDAQ 56
National Assessment of Educational Progress 19
National Institute of Health 38, 211
National Labor Relations Act xxxiii
National Science Foundation 21, 140
National Science Foundation 57, 176
Nationalism xiii, xvii, 99, 205
NCR Corporation 196
Neff, Walter 110, 147
Netcenter 52
Netherlands 140
Netscape Communications Corp. 51
Netscape Navigator 52
New Deal 183, 190-1, 229, 233, 243, 286, 301, 315, 322, 325
New economy 3, 5, 53-4, 68-9, 97-8, 109, 118, 121-2, 126-7, 139, 141, 145-7, 159, 168-9, 178, 183
New York City 2, 68, 212, 303

New York City 38, 104, 248, 339
New York city Council 212
NTP, Inc. 231

O

Obama, Barack 11, 137
Obesity 20, 38-9, 198
Oil consumption 82-3
Oil prices 46
Open source 7, 59-67, 191, 221-2, 237
Oracle 146-7, 235
Outsourcing xvii, xxviii, 13, 15, 20, 26-9, 32, 40, 106-7, 124, 126-7, 138-9, 143, 177-80, 195, 241

P

Pakistan xxx, 47
Panic of 2008 97, 99-100, 102, 203, 249, 256, 260, 276
Parenting 101
Patent Act 162, 170, 172, 230
Patent sharks 237, 324
Patent trolls 230, 232
Patents 54, 56, 59, 66-7, 90, 105-6, 138, 140-1, 150, 156, 160-2, 170-1, 175, 219, 228, 230-7
Patriotism 5, 205, 216, 277, 280
Peer-to-peer 23, 30, 78, 125, 165-6, 262
PeopleSoft 146-7
Performance improvement 253
Petzinger, Thomas 178
Pew Research Center 22, 43
Philippines 107, 145

Pink, Daniel 138, 143
Pope John Paul II 120
Portola Communications, Inc. 51
Portugal 57
Posner, Richard 208
Poverty xii, xxix, xxxii, 1, 7, 9, 14, 21, 23, 56, 84, 89, 122, 180, 217, 306
Principles of Scientific Management 178
Private property xxviii, 61, 82, 85, 87, 89-90, 149, 151, 153-5, 157, 182, 189, 197, 218, 228-9, 278
Procter & Gamble 222
Prodigy 50
Productivity xiv, 8-11, 13, 17-18, 31, 48-9, 53-5, 57, 69, 80, 88, 90-1, 110-11, 133, 159, 182
Proprietary information 140, 151, 174
Proprietary technology 16
Prosperity iii, xi, xxii-xxiii, 2, 4-6, 34-6, 40, 42-4, 56-8, 98-100, 122, 144, 154-6, 206-10, 214-16, 242-4
Protestant Work Ethic 36, 121, 152
Public schools 18, 28, 209

R

Real estate 50, 175, 194, 219
Recycling 212
Reengineering the Corporation 125, 320
Regents of the University of California v. Bakke 330

Reich, Robert   64, 140, 174, 245
Remoralization   296
Research in Motion   231
Restructuring   xxviii, 27, 41, 54, 124-5, 144, 204, 239, 242-3, 291, 302, 321
Restructuring the World Economy   321
Ricardo, David   44, 92-3
Rifkind, Jeremy   227
Rivalrous resources   303
Robotics   53
Rockefeller Foundation   18
Roe v. Wade   94
Roosevelt, Franklin   79, 166, 225, 250
Russia   99-100, 270

S

Samsung Electronics   65
Sanders, Cheryl   332
Sarnoff Corporation   250
Schumpeter, Joseph   112
Sears, Roebuck and Co.   27
Second World War, World War II   15, 67, 70, 72, 77, 165-6, 226
Sennett, Richard   139, 144, 155
September   xxiii, 5, 50, 68, 269, 277, 306, 324
Sherman Antitrust Act   xxxiii, 217
Siebal Systems   146
Silicon Valley   xvii, 29, 160, 179, 209, 212, 228, 299
Singer, Peter   65, 128
Singhal, Amit   180

Skilled labor   xiv, 43, 106, 138, 159
Slavery   xvi, 75, 77, 82-5, 122, 149, 153, 282-4, 295-6, 322
Smith, Adam   47, 60, 66, 92, 146, 168, 189, 254, 283
Social Darwinian   29, 144
Social Security Act   189
Software acquisitions   67
Software applications   7, 30, 64, 178, 218, 229, 236
Solow, Robert   93, 316
Source code   59, 61-4
Soviet Union   xv, 34, 239-42, 273
Spain   304
Spence, Michael   45
Spencer, Herbert   122
Sprint-Nextel   64
State Street Bank v. Signature Financial Group   234
Statute of Anne   161
Stocks   3, 7, 41, 50-2, 56, 141, 188, 203, 243, 249, 252, 303
Stress   xxx, 44-5, 70, 134-5, 144, 206, 310
Sun Microsystems   24, 59, 269
SUV, sports utility vehicles   73, 82
Sweden   58, 127, 140
Switzerland   140
Symbolic analysts   104

T

Taft, William Howard   125
Taiwan   65
Talent Alliance   196
Tax Code   15

335

Tax Policy Center 8
Taylor, Frederick 178
Teamwork xxv, 24, 112, 117, 131, 185, 262
Television 38, 44, 167, 212, 216, 279, 339
The Age of Abundance 12, 36, 121, 321
The Age of Capital 134, 321
The Churchman 37
The Craftsman 39, 155
The Creative Class 128, 320
The End of Work 13, 322
The frontier 2, 4, 83-5, 305, 323
The Future of Ideas 77, 164, 321
The Ingenuity Gap 8, 55, 109, 159, 321
The New Pioneers 142, 322
The Post-American World 7, 323
The Rise and Fall of the Great Powers 2, 80, 321
The Third Side 54
The Wealth of Nations 10-11, 56, 323
The Work of Nations 28, 104, 322
Time Warner 55
T-Mobile USA 65
Total direct compensation 48
Totalitarianism 38, 270
Trade imbalance 7, 139
Trade secrets xxvi, 89, 127, 140-1, 151, 155-6, 172-5, 228
Trademarks 169, 174
Transistor 68
Turbo-Capitalism 39
Turner, Frederick Jackson 38, 121
Two income families 70

U

U.S. Census Bureau 8
U.S. Chamber of Commerce 140
U.S. Constitution 81, 88, 154, 157, 161, 164, 199, 272, 315
U.S. Department of Justice 219, 221, 223, 249, 269
U.S. Department of Labor 21, 113
U.S. Department of Labor 57, 149
U.S. Energy Department 47
U.S. Financial industry 290
U.S. Human Genome project 66
U.S. Patent Office 115, 126, 273
U.S. Superintendent of the Census 2
U.S. Supreme Court xviii, 85, 89, 92-4, 162, 164-6, 189, 199-201, 229-32, 234, 237, 268, 272, 284-5, 293, 295
U.S. Surgeon General 39
U.S. taxpayers 8
U.S. Treasury debt 304
Underemployment 122, 279, 297
Unemployment xiii-xiv, xvii, xxix, 9, 15, 31, 34-5, 53, 84, 91, 107, 126, 128, 134, 293-4, 310
Unions xviii, 25, 76, 84, 87, 101, 130-1, 153, 183-6, 209, 261, 272, 286
United Auto Workers (UAW) 184
United Kingdom 46, 192
United Nations, UN 73, 248, 342
United Parcel Service of America (UPS) 184

United States v. Addyston Pipe & Steel Co.   90
United States v. Microsoft   218, 229
United States' trade imbalance   43
Urbanization   1-2
Ury, William   90

V

Value added knowledge   xxxii, 16-17, 109, 112, 118, 147, 308
Venezuela   46
Venture capital   179, 212-13, 308
Verizon   64-5
Viacom   167-70, 222
Viet Nam   145, 216
Volunteers   xxxvi, 60-3, 66, 195, 244, 305

W

Wage gap   21, 123
Wage labor   80, 82-3, 132-3, 142, 152, 295, 310
Wages   xii-xiv, xvi, 8-9, 11-15, 17, 27, 70, 80-4, 88, 126, 133-4, 183-4, 187, 189-92, 194-5, 286-7
Wagner Act   183-5, 209
Wall Street   xxvi, xxx, xxxv, 5, 14-15, 27, 29, 52, 70, 99-100, 108, 148, 157, 249-50, 302-3, 323-5
Wall Street Journal   xxvi, xxx, 14-15, 27, 70, 99, 108, 148, 157, 244, 249, 259, 268, 302-3, 323-5
Wealth gap   11, 44, 70, 101, 206, 218, 240, 281
Weber, Max   72
WebTV Networks Inc.   87
West Coast Hotel v. Parrish   229
White-collar production   125-6
Whyte, William   113, 167
Wilson, William Julius   226
Windows   44, 51, 218-21, 229, 306
World Economic Forum   66, 71, 190, 261, 275, 326
World Trade Organization   138, 241
World Wide Web   25, 51
WorldCom   xx-xxi, 50, 242, 247, 249-52, 257, 261-2

Y

Yahoo   xxix, 145, 147-8, 221-2, 227, 232, 260, 269-70, 324
Yale University   39, 319, 323

YouTube   146, 167, 226

About the Author

John Sarno is president of the Employers Association of New Jersey. He teaches frequently and is the author of numerous articles, some of which have been cited as legal authority by federal and state courts. He is also the content writer for *www.eanj.org*. Mr. Sarno has extensive experience in all areas of business and employment law and has successfully argued landmark cases before the Supreme Court of New Jersey and the Third Circuit Court of Appeals. He teaches regularly on business and law and holds a Bachelors degree in Psychology, a Masters degree in Counseling, and a Law degree. Mr. Sarno is also the creator and host of *Issues in the Workplace* on Cable Television Network and of *Competing to Win*, a weekly business column.

CPSIA information can be obtained at www.ICGtesting.com
Printed in the USA
LVOW080616290212

270922LV00002B/33/P